GUNSMITHING AT HOME

Lock, Stock & Barrel

Second Edition

GUNSMITHING AT HOME

Lock, Stock & Barrel

Second Edition

JOHN E. TRAISTER

STOEGER PUBLISHING COMPANY

COVER DESIGN: Ray Wells

Published by Stoeger Publishing Company,
17603 Indian Head Highway
Accokeek, MD 20607

ISBN: 0-88317-190-2
Library of Congress Catalog Card No.: 95-069190

Manufactured in the United States of America.

Distributed in the U.S. by Stoeger Industries, 17603 Indian Head Highway,
Suite 200, Accokeek, MD 20607
Phone: 301-283-6300   Fax: 301-283-6986
E-mail: info@stoegerindustries.com
Web Address: www.stoegerindustries.com

PREFACE

Sooner or later, almost every shooter becomes intrigued by the mechanics of firearms and the methods of repairing, improving, customizing, and altering them. A few of these gun buffs eventually become professional gunsmiths, but most simply improve their personal firearms — and their shooting. Whatever your goal may be, this book will be a valuable addition to your workshop library.

Gunsmithing At Home starts with some do's and don'ts of home gunsmithing, and immediately jumps into setting up and equipping your shop.

Cleaning and caring for firearms is one of the most important aspects of firearm maintenance. A complete chapter is devoted to this subject.

Mounting and adjusting sights and making trigger adjustments come next. Both of these subjects can mean a hit or miss with any weapon.

To repair firearms efficiently and keep them in good condition, a person must have a thorough knowledge of "troubleshooting" — the technique of determining the cause of any problem and correcting it without wasting time or using unnecessary new parts. Troubleshooting covers an enormous range of problems, from replacing a mainspring in a revolver to diagnosing why a repeating shotgun jams or a rifle fails to shoot accurately. A systematic and methodical approach is necessary for troubleshooting, and this technique should be mastered by every gunsmith. The author covers some of the common problems encountered with many types of sporting firearms.

Few gun repair operations are more rewarding than seeing a rusted and badly worn firearm turn into a thing of beauty by using the chemical processes of either bluing, browning or plating. Metal coloring is also an excellent way to learn about the operating characteristics of firearms because all must be completely disassembled prior to applying the chemicals. Chapters are included in this book to aid professionals and hobbyists in obtaining perfect gun-metal finishes.

The remaining chapters are devoted to stock work — from gunstock furniture installations to completely refinishing and checkering gunstocks. Repairing damaged stocks is also covered.

Although this book is intended primarily for home gunsmiths, it will be an extremely helpful desk reference for professionals as well. Apprentice gunsmiths will especially find the material valuable when used with other textbooks or vocational school lessons. In fact, it will be a useful manual for anyone who is interested in guns and shooting.

ABOUT THE AUTHOR

John Traister has authored more than 100 different books, and continues to write at the rate of about three or four per year. In 1978, he launched a gun-trading/gunsmithing business in his present hometown of Bentonville, Virginia — and continued to write about the arms as well. Traister first found the need for gunsmithing at home when he had to wait thirteen months to get a simple trigger spring replaced in his Iver Johnson shotgun. He finally retrieved the unrepaired gun, ordered the part from a dealer and did the job himself in a matter of minutes.

Actually, this was not Traister's first encounter with gunsmithing. He finished the stock on an old beat-up Remington Model 12 before he was 10 years old; began bluing guns for neighbors using the hot-water bluing method when he was 13; and served as an apprentice gunsmith for a professional in Manassas, Virginia, while stationed at the Marine Corps base in nearby Quantico.

"In those early days," says Traister, "I was not allowed to use power tools. Everything had to be done by hand. It took nearly two weeks of my spare time to hand polish an old Marlin lever-action rifle with octagonal barrel, using umpteen different grits of abrasive paper until an even, bright polish was obtained. It then took another four or five hours to obtain the desired finish using Stoeger's Old Connecticut Gun Bluer (no longer available). As I recall, I received a total of $5 for that

first bluing job, and the same fee for several others to follow."

While operating his part-time gunsmithing business from 1978 to 1994, Traister performed and supervised all types of gunsmithing operations from mounting both telescopic and iron sights to completely restoring antique firearms. Most of his work, however, dealt with firearm repairs — from inexpensive .22-caliber single-shots to elaborate English and European double guns.

He continues to work on his own firearms from time-to-time (at home), mainly because finding a capable professional who can do the work in a reasonable length of time is becoming harder and harder to find.

CONTENTS

Chapter 1
Introduction To Gunsmithing

Scene: A gunsmith's shop.

Place: Anywhere in the United States and Canada.

Time: The present. (The owner is frantically thumbing through a card index file trying to locate a customer's gun.)

GUNSMITH: When did you say you brought the gun in?

CUSTOMER: The end of January, or about the first of February. (The search continues without success.)

CUSTOMER (impatiently): It had to be January because I bought a new car that same day and it's just six months old.

GUNSMITH: Oh, you mean January of this year. Heck, we haven't even gotten around to the guns that were brought in last year. That's how busy we are! (Customer exits muttering, holding his retrieved, still rough-looking shotgun, a bottle of Belgian blue and a book on firearm refinishing.)

So it goes. There are a lot of sick guns out there and not enough qualified repairmen to fix them, at least not in time to keep their owners happy. For this and other reasons, more and more gun owners are setting up shop in basements, attics or garages and performing a lot of gunsmithing work themselves. Most usually start by cleaning their firearms, then progress to perhaps refinishing a gunstock or fixing some worn places on the metal with instant cold-bluing solution. The projects advance in complexity until, eventually, a gun ends up in a professional shop where the amateur's mistakes are corrected — frequently at many times the cost of repairing the initial problem, because of the damage caused by attempting a project beyond the amateur's capabilities.

There is really nothing wrong with a knowledgeable person performing gun repairs and refinishing projects. In fact, the practice should be encouraged, provided you know your capabilities, and when and where to stop. Then, home gunsmithing is not only fun, but can save money and enable your firearms to have features not obtainable from most manufacturers.

If you are just beginning the fascinating field of gunsmithing, you should always remember not to attempt any project beyond your capabilities. If you are not certain, stop immediately and seek advice. Not only can you ruin an otherwise valuable firearm, but your work may cause it to be unsafe to fire, resulting in serious harm to the shooter and persons close by.

There are certain safety rules that apply to everyone who handles firearms. The first rule is never point a firearm at anyone or anything unless you intend to kill or shoot it. This applies to loaded and unloaded guns. Second, make sure the gun you intend to shoot is in good operating condition, with the proper ammunition being used, and that no obstructions — such as a cleaning brush — are in the chamber or bore. Before firing any firearm, make sure you have a safe backstop so that a stray bullet or load of shot will not do any unintentional damage. When firing a rifle in the air, remember that the bullet has to land some place.

Beyond these, anyone who performs work on firearms should observe the following:

- Never apply heat to any part of a firearm unless you know exactly what you are doing; even then, proceed with caution.

- Never remove excessive amounts of metal from any firearm action at points of stress; that is, receiver rings, locking lugs, etc.

- When installing new parts, make sure that these parts are functioning properly before firing the gun.

- Be careful with trigger pulls; avoid "hair" triggers.

- When inspecting a new gun, make sure it is unloaded, but always treat it as if it were loaded.

- Wear safety goggles when grinding, chipping, sanding or working with springs or caustic solutions.

- Always make sure that you are competent and understand the principles of a job before attempting it. If in doubt, seek further advice.

The Art of Gunsmithing

Gunsmithing is the art of repairing, refinishing, modifying, customizing, or building a firearm of any type. A gunsmithing job may be as simple as cleaning a firearm or as complex as building a complete rifle or shotgun from raw materials and other pre-manufactured components. In most cases, however, the professional gunsmith's work will consist mostly of repairing malfunctioning firearms; that is, replacing broken or worn parts. Next in line to repairing firearms is the refinishing of rifles, shotguns, and handguns. This consists of rebluing or browning the metal, as well as refinishing the wood. It is estimated that repairing and refinishing firearms make up about 75 percent of the gunsmith's work nationwide.

The remaining 25 percent of gunsmithing jobs in the United States consists of customizing existing firearms. Many serious shooters prefer to have their firearms customized, for it is seldom that standard factory-made products carry the individual features some shooters want or need. Perhaps a factory stock does not fit perfectly, or the trigger pull needs adjusting. Maybe the owner wants an extremely fancy firearm with elaborate metal engraving, stock carvings and inlays — one that fits the shooter's physique exactly.

Although there is a wide variety of guns available from the major manufacturers for almost any conceivable type of hunting or shooting imaginable, some gun buffs still want something different, such as a "wildcat" cartridge for which no factory ammo is available. These cartridges are usually modifications of the existing factory ammunition, designed to perform better than their factory counterparts. Here again, the gunsmith must be consulted for chambering and rebarreling a rifle receiver for the new wildcat cartridge, and make the entire conversions.

While most professional gunsmiths do mostly what may be classified as general gun repair, some experts specialize. For example, dozens of "stockers" throughout the country do nothing but make custom stocks. Prices usually start at $1,000 or more per stock, and some stockmakers are able to turn out a stock every week or two. The better stockers, however, report that about 15 or 20 per year is their limit.

Another specialist may do only metal engraving on firearms — charging anywhere from $2,000 and upward per gun. Still another concerns himself only with accurizing target rifles for serious competitive shooters. Many years ago, Harry Pope, for example, was noted for his highly accurate rifle barrels; although he also did other gunsmithing jobs, most of his time was spent making fine rifle barrels for a few select customers.

A specialist in any line of work isn't made overnight; it takes much study, practice, and a desire to be the "best" in the field. A gunsmith is no exception.

You no doubt have a strong interest in firearms already or you wouldn't be reading this book. Perhaps you have been a hunter or shooter since you can remember; you probably like to discuss guns with your friends, and have read everything you can get your hands on about shooting and firearms in general. If so, you're well on your way to becoming a good home gunsmith.

You are also probably handy with your hands; that is, you have taken care of many repairs around the home. Perhaps you do minor repairs on your auto, and maybe have even refinished a gunstock or two during the past few years.

On the other hand, you may already have worked for years under another gunsmith and now you want to break out on your own. Or you could have served in the Armed Forces as an armorer and are now retiring and wish to pursue a gunsmithing career in civilian life.

Regardless of whether you plan to work only on your own guns, do part-time gunsmithing work for others, or pursue a full-time career, this book has much to offer.

Do's and Don'ts of Home Gunsmithing

A growing number of people want to keep their firearms in first-class condition and have the pleasure of doing the work themselves. In doing so, these gun enthusiasts not only economize on the cost of repairs and alterations, but obtain a better knowledge of firearms in general. Some gunsmithing jobs — either because of the lack of proper tools or the absence of mechanical ability — should be attempted only by a seasoned professional. But for the beginner, the information that follows details what jobs you can attempt to perform at home (with the proper knowledge and instructions) and, more importantly, what jobs not to try. Do not, however, attempt any of these projects until you have become familiar with the related subjects contained in this book.

Nothing is more frustrating than to begin a repair or alteration on your favorite firearm and find — about halfway through — you don't have the proper tools or materials to complete it, or the knowledge to make the most of those you do have.

When you begin home gunsmithing, you will need some sound fundamentals before you loosen even one screw. Jumping into the task of taking your pride-and-joy apart without first considering some of the rudimentary techniques can be discouraging, if not downright disastrous. For example, if you use the wrong kind of screwdriver on a tightly seated screw, you will certainly damage the screw slot and perhaps the surrounding metal finish. Before you disassemble a firearm, what steps will you take to put it back together again? Some owners might apply heat to a firearm, say, to anneal the receiver of a bolt-action rifle to enable drilling and tapping for a sight. If the job is done precisely, okay; if not, the practice can lead to a forehead full of brass particles or a couple of missing fingers!

The charts that follow give a small sampling of some do's and don'ts of home gunsmithing. They should be used only as a guide, and certainly not as gospel.

HANDGUNS				
Type of Project	**Do**	**Don't**	**Comments**	**Special Tools or Items**
COLT LIGHTNING REVOLVER				
Replacement of trigger-spring arm		✔	Replacement parts are available, but these require careful fitting by a gunsmith.	
COLT MODEL 1911				
Replacing spring	✔		Long blade-type spring that powers sear, trigger and other parts can be replaced by home gunsmiths provided disassembly instructions are used.	Brownells Colt wrench
Tightening loose spring housing		✔	Housing is attached to the grip by means of two rivets and should be sent to the factory or a competent gunsmith for tightening.	
IVER JOHNSON REVOLVER				
Tightening barrel latch by welding		✔	Requires detailed stripping of the frame, adding a spot of steel weld to the back of each latching lug, and recutting them to fit.	
Tightening barrel latch by peening	✔		Place small steel block tightly between lugs to prevent bending and peen an impression on the side of each lug. A slight bump on the back of each lug will tighten latch.	Hammer, blunt punch and anvil
LLAMA REVOLVERS				
Tightening ejector rod	✔		Sometimes becomes loose from heavy loads or insufficient torque during assembly. Be sure to tighten in proper direction.	

HANDGUNS (*Cont.*)				
Type of Project	**Do**	**Don't**	**Comments**	**Special Tools or Items**
LLAMA REVOLVERS				
Removing sideplate for cleaning	✔		If you must remove sideplate for cleaning, never pry plate out. Tap it gently with a wooden screwdriver handle and it will pop out.	
MAUSER HSC				
Replacement of firing pin	✔		The WWII models frequently have firing-pin breakage, but replacements are available.	Conventional disassembly tools
MAUSER MODEL 1896				
Replacing extractor	✔		The extractor is tempered to be its own spring, and when a replacement part can be found, it's a relatively simple operation.	
Replacing rear-sight spring	✔		This is a blade-type spring that is easy to reproduce.	
Replacing safety extension		✔	The tempered safety extension snaps into two notches in the sub-frame, but if this should break, it's a job for the pro.	
RAVEN P-25 PISTOL				
Complete disassembly	✔		Design of this pistol makes it extremely easy to completely disassemble it for cleaning or repairs.	Assembly/disassembly instructions
Replacing broken parts	✔		Parts are readily available and are easily replaced. Make sure the firing-pin protrusion is correct or you may get fully automatic firing or an inadvertent discharge.	

HANDGUNS (*Cont.*)				
Type of Project	Do	Don't	Comments	Special Tools or Items
SAUER MODEL 1913 PISTOL				
Replacing rear sight and extractor		✔	Both of these parts are tempered to be their own springs and will probably have to be made by a professional.	
Replacing trigger bar and magazine-catch spring	✔		If this spring breaks, it is not difficult to make.	
SAUER MODEL 38H				
Replacement of cocking-lever spring		✔	Can be cold-formed from round-wire stock, but not a job for the amateur.	
STOEGER .22 LUGER				
Complete disassembly		✔	It is possible to turn the safety beyond its normal arc, causing the spring to fly out like a buzz bomb. Because of its small size, you'll probably never find it. Reassembly is tricky and therefore disassembly should be left to a professional.	
Replacing plastic screw	✔		Screw closing access hole is plastic and should be replaced with a steel one from the manufacturer, or you might try ordering one from Navy Arms or the Gun Parts Corp.	
WEBLEY REVOLVER				
Replacing mainspring	✔		Remove grips for the repair.	Screwdriver and pliers

HANDGUNS (*Cont.*)				
Type of Project	**Do**	**Don't**	**Comments**	**Special Tools or Items**
WEBLEY SEMIAUTOMATIC PISTOL				
Partial disassembly for cleaning	✔		The Model 1909 strips down to four basic groups for cleaning.	
Complete disassembly		✔	Not recommended for the amateur.	
Replacement of V-spring	✔		Remove grips to reveal V-spring and lever, which act as the recoil system.	

RIMFIRE RIFLES				
Type of Project	**Do**	**Don't**	**Comments**	**Special Tools or Items**
BROWNING .22 AUTO				
Barrel adjustment		✔	Should be attempted only by a competent gunsmith.	
Extractor repairs		✔	The four separate parts of the extractor assembly fit together unconventionally and should be left to professionals.	
H&R MODEL 760				
Replacing fiber buffer	✔		If replacement parts cannot be found, use 16-gauge shotshell wad.	
ITHACA MODEL 49				
Disassembly		✔	Disassembly of this rifle is sufficiently complicated that it should not be attempted by the amateur until sufficient experience is gained.	
Removal of breechbolt		✔	For same reasons as above.	
ITHACA MODEL 72				
Removal of receiver sideplate for cleaning	✔		Remove stock and then remove the four side screws holding the plate.	Screwdriver to fit screw slot
Removal of remaining receiver parts		✔	Disassembly of these parts is not for beginners.	
MARLIN MODEL 49				
Replacement of bolt buffer	✔		Easily replaced by home gunsmith.	

RIMFIRE RIFLES (*Cont.*)				
Type of Project	**Do**	**Don't**	**Comments**	**Special Tools or Items**
MARLIN MODEL 49 (*Cont.*)				
Replacement of cartridge guide		✔	Installation by professional.	
Adjustment of cartridge-lifter spring		✔	Becomes deformed if handled incorrectly. Can usually be reshaped by competent gunsmith.	
Adjustment of trigger pull		✔	Sear and disconnector engagement is of unusual design; amateur should not attempt to adjust trigger pull.	
Disassembly of firing-pin mechanism		✔	Stress direction is critical to proper operation.	
MARLIN MODEL 57M				
Tightening main sideplate screw	✔		Check occasionally for tightness.	
Removal of main sideplate screw		✔	Removal should only be done by professional as sideplate will come off, exposing internal parts.	
Installing cartridge guide		✔	Best done by competent gunsmith.	
Installing firing pin		✔	Involved; requires dealing with several small pinned parts.	
MARLIN MODEL 783				
Installing new extractor	✔		Extractor subject to occasional breakage, but is not difficult to install.	

RIMFIRE RIFLES (*Cont.*)				
Type of Project	**Do**	**Don't**	**Comments**	**Special Tools or Items**
MARLIN MODEL 783 (Cont.)				
Installing firing pin		✔	The two-part firing pin should be installed only by a professional.	
Removal of bolt for cleaning	✔		Bolt can be removed while holding back on trigger.	
Adjusting trigger pull		✔	Parts are well-hardened and are difficult to alter with a file. Grinding can easily ruin trigger mechanism.	
Complete disassembly		✔	Bolt can be removed and barrel and action removed by loosening the coin-slotted takedown screw. Further disassembly is not recommended.	
MOSSBERG MODEL 151-M				
Fitting cartridge stop		✔	Should be done by gunsmith.	
NOBLE MODEL 235				
Repairs of any kind	✔		Repairs on this rifle by a professional gunsmith will often cost more than the gun is worth; it is therefore a good gun for the amateur to practice on.	
REMINGTON MODEL 66				
Replacing disconnector		✔	Common malfunction in this rifle, but repair should be left to professional.	
Partial takedown	✔		A little tricky, but within skills of the average home gunsmith.	Obtain takedown instructions from manufacturer.

RIMFIRE RIFLES (*Cont.*)				
Type of Project	**Do**	**Don't**	**Comments**	**Special Tools or Items**
REMINGTON MODEL 341				
Partial disassembly	✔		Remove bolt from action, and then action stock.	
Takedown of bolt		✔	Improper reassembly could cause damage.	
REMINGTON MODEL 512				
Replacement of extractor	✔		Most parts in this rifle are easy to replace and replacements are usually available.	
Replacement of firing pin	✔			
Replacement of cartridge lifter	✔			
Replacement of most parts	✔			
Replacement of barrel		✔	Not for the amateur.	
REMINGTON MODEL 550				
Complete disassembly		✔	Complete takedown should be left to a gunsmith.	
RUGER 10/22				
Repairing magazine	✔		Keep large magazine screw tight.	
Disassembly of magazine		✔	A little complicated for the amateur.	
SEARS MODEL 31				
Replacement of extractor	✔		Easy to replace.	

RIMFIRE RIFLES (*Cont.*)				
Type of Project	**Do**	**Don't**	**Comments**	**Special Tools or Items**
SEARS MODEL 31				
Replacement of cartridge lifter		✔	Should be left to a gunsmith.	
STEVENS "CRACK SHOT"				
Replacement of breechbolt pivot screw	✔		Any of these parts can cause looseness of the action.	
Replacement of lever-link pin	✔			
Replacement of locking-roller screw	✔			
STEVENS MODEL 87-A				
Replacement of cartridge lifter	✔		One of the most common malfunctions.	
WINCHESTER MODEL 75				
Bolt disassembly		✔	Takedown of bolt should not be attempted by nonprofessionals.	
WINCHESTER MODEL 190				
Replacement of sear/disconnector unit	✔			Common disassembly tools
Replacement of cartridge guide	✔			Common disassembly tools
Adjusting trigger pull		✔	A tricky operation that should be left to the professional.	

CENTERFIRE RIFLES				
Type of Project	**Do**	**Don't**	**Comments**	**Special Tools or Items**
BROWNING LEVER-ACTION RIFLE				
Adjusting trigger pull		✔	Improper adjustment can cause the hammer to chew into the gear teeth on the bolt.	
Cleaning	✔		Lugs and recesses must be kept clean and lightly oiled for proper operation.	General cleaning gear
Complete disassembly		✔	Precise mating of parts requires that only a professional gunsmith should completely disassemble this rifle.	
MARLIN MODEL 336				
Replacing extractor	✔		Easy operation for the amateur.	
Replacing spring above rear firing pin	✔		Another easy operation.	
Replacing ejector		✔	Curved ejector spring is clinch-mounted on ejector and should be installed by a gunsmith.	
SAKO RIFLES				
Tightening screws	✔		Two screws securing the safety and other external screws may work loose periodically and should be checked and tightened if required.	Gunsmith's screwdrivers
Adjusting firing pin		✔	Miscalculation in adjustment can cause either misfiring or pierced primers.	

CENTERFIRE RIFLES (*Cont.*)				
Type of Project	**Do**	**Don't**	**Comments**	**Special Tools or Items**
SAKO RIFLES (*Cont.*)				
Trigger adjustment	✔		A little tricky, but within skills of the average home gunsmith.	
WINCHESTER MODEL 70 (pre '64)				
Replacing extractor	✔		If replacement part is not available, use extractor from 1917 Enfield after thinning it down.	Brownells extractor tool
WINCHESTER MODEL 94				
Replacing weak extractor	✔		Long extractor sometimes becomes weak but can easily be replaced.	Drift punch
Correcting strong safety-catch spring		✔	This should be left to the professional.	
Tightening external screws	✔		Will work loose and should be checked and tightened, if necessary.	

SHOTGUNS				
Type of Project	**Do**	**Don't**	**Comments**	**Special Tools or Items**
BROWNING A-5				
Replace ejector		✔	Ejector fits into a recess in left side of barrel extension; its replacement is best left to a qualified gunsmith.	
Replacing trigger and safety springs	✔		Replacement of flat carrier spring is a relatively simple job.	
Replacing carrier spring	✔		Another suitable operation for the home gunsmith.	
Replacing hammer spring		✔	Replacement of this heavy blade-type spring should be left to a qualified gunsmith.	
FRANCHI AUTO				
Replacing carrier latch		✔	Best left to a professional.	
Secondary shell stop		✔	Sometimes breaks or chips but welding and recutting should be left to a qualified gunsmith.	
Replacing carrier spring detent	✔		Part is frequently lost in disassembly, but is easily replaced.	
Adjusting trigger pull		✔	Engagement of sear and sear step on hammer is carefully engineered and should not be altered.	
H&R TOPPER				
Replacing broken barrel lug		✔	These lugs have been known to break and, although they may be repaired by silver soldering, the job is strictly for the pro.	

SHOTGUNS *(Cont.)*				
Type of Project	**Do**	**Don't**	**Comments**	**Special Tools or Items**
MOSSBERG MODEL 500				
Repairing broken action slide by brazing		✔	Heat required to braze will weaken and ruin hardness of metal.	
Repairing broken action by silver soldering	✔		Use silver solder of lowest melting point and take care to get a good flow.	Torch, silver solder, flux, clamps and heat-stop paste
WINCHESTER MODEL 12				
Replacing round-wire springs contacting lug on hammer		✔	These are riveted in place and replacement should be done by a qualified gunsmith.	
Replacing extractor	✔		Left extractor will break more frequently than main extractor, but installation is not difficult.	
Replacing ejector	✔		Narrow ejector mounted in a recess in the left inside wall of receiver is not difficult to replace.	
Tightening screws	✔		Numerous screws on this model come loose and should be checked and tightened periodically.	
WINCHESTER MODEL 24				
Replacement of internal action parts	✔		If replacement parts can be obtained, the operation is not difficult. Merely remove buttstock, which allows access to the inside of receiver.	
WINCHESTER MODEL 37				
Replacement of firing-pin retainer screw	✔		Make sure striker is in forward position, move top lever to right and remove screw immediately under top-lever thumb notch.	

SHOTGUNS *(Cont.)*				
Type of Project	**Do**	**Don't**	**Comments**	**Tools or Items**
WINCHESTER MODEL 42				
Replacing extractor	✔		Left extractor will break more frequently than main extractor, but installation is not difficult.	
Replacing ejector	✔		Narrow ejector mounted in a recess in left inside wall of receiver is not difficult to replace.	
Tightening screws	✔		Many screws on this shotgun come loose and should be checked and tightened periodically.	
Complete disassembly		✔	Complete disassembly is rather complicated. Home gunsmith needs practice on simpler jobs before tackling the Model 42.	

Chapter 2
Setting Up Shop

Every gunsmith, whether professional or hobbyist, needs a place to work and tinker. The professional, of course, needs the shop for his livelihood. Although the hobbyist may save a little money by doing gun repairs, the home shop is noted more for the pleasure it offers.

When planning a location for a gunshop, you must first decide what type of work you will be performing. For example, if you plan to get your Federal Firearms License and work on guns for others, one room or area in the home must be set aside exclusively for the gun business. If it's in the basement, the room cannot be used as a recreation room, nor can household chores be done in this area. The space must be devoted entirely to the gun business.

On the other hand, if you plan to work on firearms only for yourself, you can locate the "shop" any place you like — even in your own living room.

The average gunsmith will perform a variety of work on firearms covering the entire field: troubleshooting, stock finishing, rebluing, stock checkering, firearm cleaning, rebarreling, chambering, soldering, and welding, and the like. The ideal shop should be equipped so that all these jobs can be conveniently and efficiently taken care of.

This chapter is designed to show you how to equip a gunshop, even if your space is limited. We begin with the very smallest home shops and progress to shops suitable for factory-warranty stations.

SHOP LOCATION

For the aspiring gunsmith who lives in a small town house or apartment where space is at a premium, finding a place to set up a suitable workbench is somewhat of a problem. However, many guns have been repaired on foot lockers or large tool boxes. One gunsmithing student who lives in an efficiency apartment, turned his coffee table into a very functional work center. When the piece of furniture was closed, it was a very handsome coffee table — fitting in with the room's decor. However, when the top was opened, it revealed an assortment of gunsmithing tools and the folding wings gave the student a workbench that even boasted a small bench vise.

Basement Shops

Most home gunshops are located in the basement. This location has several advantages over other locations and the few drawbacks can be usually overcome. The chief advantages include:

- Easy to heat in winter.

- Cool in summer.

● It's out of the way of most family activities.

● It's quiet and it can be made relatively soundproof from the living area.

● If you have to, you can leave it messed up overnight without worrying about guests seeing it.

The basement area also has several disadvantages, most of which can be corrected. Most basement areas (as finished by the builder) are usually poorly illuminated, giving a dark, dingy appearance. So, if the basement is the area chosen for the shop location, one of the first projects should be the installation of adequate lighting. Fluorescent fixtures are ideal. However, if an acoustical T-bar ceiling is used, you may want to go with recessed fixtures — either incandescent or fluorescent.

One of the major disadvantages of a basement is dampness which, of course, creates rust problems. To overcome this problem, epoxy waterproofing may be applied to basement walls from the inside and then foam insulating boards can be used to insulate the walls and check dampness. A good dehumidifier is added insurance.

Flooding is another problem in some basements that can lead to a disaster. However, if all slopes are graded away from basement walls, all gutters and downspouts are kept in good repair, and an adequate sump pump is installed, the chance of basement flooding is greatly reduced.

Attic Shops

Attics are probably the worst places for a home gunshop. They are often hot in summer, cold in winter and short on head room. Add to this the difficulty of transporting materials to and from the attic, plus the noise and vibration that carry down into the living area and the disadvantages are quickly realized.

Of course, if there is no other place available, these disadvantages can be somewhat remedied. First of all, insulation in the walls, roof and floor will help to keep a more controlled, comfortable temperature and muffle noises. An attic ventilating fan will reduce attic temperatures considerably as will the installation of several windows if they're currently absent.

Noise and vibration produced by power tools can be overcome by mounting them on rubber mats and/or rubber washers. Tightly sealed attic doors will also help retain the shop noises in the attic and also cut down on dust escaping into the living area. Outside stairs to the attic also have their advantage.

Garage Shops

The garage is one of the best places to locate a gunshop. Although garages are often drafty and hard to heat in winter, they can be made into excellent shops having advantages that other areas in the home do not. First of all, a garage shop lets you work into the wee hours of the morning, usually without disturbing anyone in the home. If it's located far enough away from the house and other neighbors, even power tools can be operated without bothering anyone. You don't have to worry about fumes from hot bluing and other operations smelling up the home, and if you are faced with leaving a temporary mess, no one is going to care.

Even if you plan to park your cars in the garage, there are ways to use it also as a shop. The floor plan in Figure 2-1, for example, shows a two-car garage with a large workbench worked into a nook on the left side. A hinged, fold-down bench may also be used, but this, of course, requires that the bench be cleared before it can be folded out of the way.

The ideal setup is to use half of a two-car garage as a shop and the other half for parking a car. If you still want shelter for a second car, build a carport; it's much cheaper than building an enclosed shop.

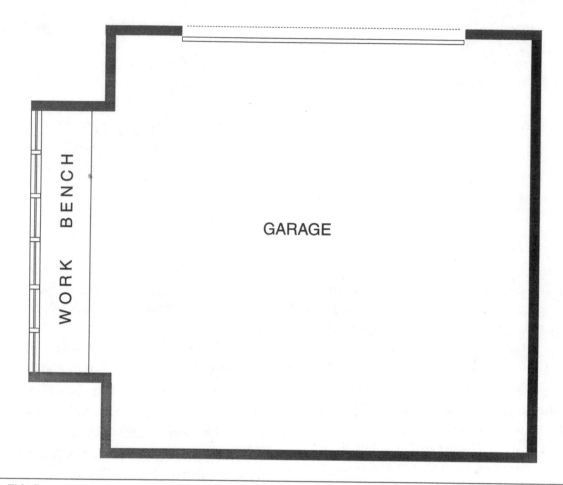

Figure 2-1: This floor plan of a two-car garage has a large workbench installed in a nook on the left side.

Even if you don't have a garage on your property, and you're an apartment dweller with no other possibilities for locating a shop where you live, look around town for the possibility of renting a garage. Then set up your shop in this rented structure and work in your spare time.

Outbuildings

If your house is small, without a basement, and there is no room in the garage, a separate building may be the answer. In it you can work late at night or early in the morning without disturbing anyone. A precut garage may be an inexpensive way to get such a shop. Or how about a trailer?

Existing barns and outbuildings may afford prime shop space for those living in rural areas.

Insulation and heating may have to be provided, possibly an electric service run out to it, but it is only a remodeling job. Most people would rather remodel than attempt to build from scratch. In some areas, zoning codes may prevent you from building an additional structure on your property, but an existing structure doesn't pose any problems in most cases. However, check with the local building inspector's office just to be sure.

Closet Shops

With a little ingenuity, an amazing amount of tool storage and work space can be fitted into a closet. Highly productive shops have been hung on the back of a closet door, with work tables that fold down to reveal an array of hand tools neatly stored on a panel of perforated hardboard. It's not the ideal solution, but it's a beginning. There may be space under a stairway or at the end of a hall that can provide comparable accommodations.

Porches

Does your home have a porch that is seldom used? If so, you can probably convert it into a very good shop at comparatively little expense. In most cases, the roof, floor, and at least one wall is already there so all you have to do is fill in the other two or three walls, add a workbench, and you're ready to start working.

Since the walls that are added will usually be exposed to the weather, be sure to insulate well. The floor and ceiling should be considered also. If you can't get to existing void spaces to install insulation, consider having insulation blown in after boring holes to reach the void spaces between studs.

Conventional framing can be used to enclose the open walls of a porch, but perhaps jalousie windows would provide a better arrangement. A jalousie window consists of a series of operable overlapping glass louvers which pivot in unison — usually by a crank-and-gear system. Such windows are best used in southern climates, where maximum ventilation and flush exterior and interior appearance is desired.

WORKBENCHES

When the beginning gunsmith starts to think of graduating from the toolbox/repair kit stage to a full-fledged workshop, his first thoughts should turn to a suitable workbench. Unfortunately, there are not very many commercial workbenches to choose from — and those that are available will make your pocketbook look like a sieve. Therefore, most gunsmiths like to build their own.

In general, a workbench should be 30″ wide and a minimum of 5′ long. Don't skimp on the length,

however, because you'll soon find that there is really no such thing as too much bench space.

The height of the workbench will vary depending on your height. Many average-built men prefer a workbench about 33½″ high. However, you may want yours anywhere from 30″ to 35″. Above all, the bench must be sturdy and firm. You cannot do your best work if the bench moves every time you take a file stroke, or tap a drift pin out of its hole. Therefore, the ideal workbench should be amply reinforced and legs and top should be made of heavy timber.

In addition to the main workbench, it is nice to have an auxiliary bench for special projects. One such bench is shown in Figure 2-2. In small shops, this bench will also suffice as a main bench, and although the legs are constructed of 2 x 4s, the plywood bracing makes it very sturdy.

Note that the frame of the bench in Figure 2-2 is made entirely of 2 x 4s, reinforced with ⅜″ plywood. The top is constructed from two layers of ¾″ plywood glued together. A piece of hardboard nailed with finishing nails to the top protect the bench top and can be changed as often as needed.

You should design your bench or benches to fit into the available space and to serve your own needs. If you are handy with woodworking tools, you will want to build a few drawers for certain tools, or you can buy the prefabricated types of steel or plastic and install them by screwing the brackets to the underside of the bench top.

To begin constructing the workbench in Figure 2-2, lay out the top pieces and shelf on a single piece of 4′ x 8′ x ¾″ plywood as shown in Figure 2-3. Use a straightedge and square for the lines, and then cut out the various pieces with a hand or power saw.

Next cut all 2 x 4s, notching the legs as shown in the exploded drawing in Figure 2-2. Mark and drill screw holes as indicated and then assemble the two end frames with glue and wood screws. You may want to countersink the screw holes for a neat

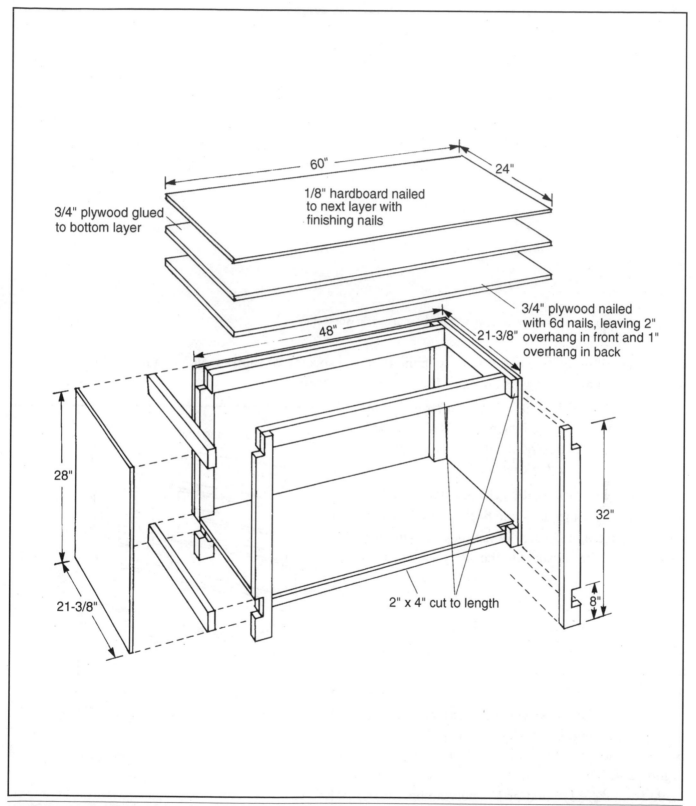

1/8" hardboard nailed
to next layer with
finishing nails

3/4" plywood glued
to bottom layer

60"

24"

3/4" plywood nailed
with 6d nails, leaving 2"
overhang in front and 1"
overhang in back

48"

21-3/8"

28"

32"

21-3/8"

8"

2" x 4" cut to length

Figure 2-2: A good basic bench for the beginning gunsmith or hobbyist. When the need for a larger bench increases, this smaller bench may still be used as an auxiliary bench.

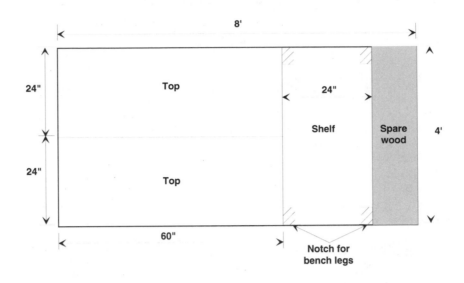

Figure 2-3: Here is the layout of the plywood pieces for the basic workbench.

appearance. Join the two end frames with the four long 2 x 4s, again using glue and wood screws.

Insert the lower shelf as indicated after notching all four corners to fit the bench legs. Nail and glue them in place. At this point, the work should be taking the form of a workbench.

Continue by marking the cutting diagram on the $3/8''$ plywood for the sides and back — again using a straightedge and square. When they are cut out, nail and glue these panels to the sides and back as shown.

Now nail and glue the lower $3/4''$ top panel to the top rails of the frame, followed by the next panel and the sheet of $1/8''$ hardboard (nailed only). Keep all of these panels under pressure (using C-clamps) until the glue dries.

If you prefer shelves over your bench, a shelving unit may be hung on a wall directly in back of the bench or mounted to the bench top as shown in Figure 2-4. The top, sides, and shelves may be made from $3/4''$ plywood or 1'' shelving boards of a width to suit your needs. A pegboard area is also handy for tool hanging. The overall size of the unit,

spacing of shelves, etc., can be varied to suit your needs.

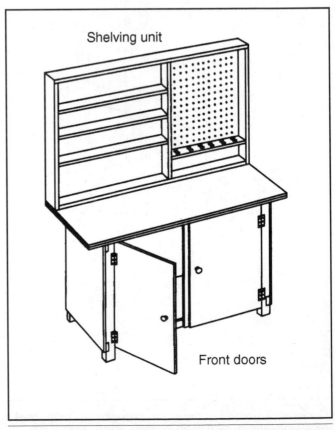

Figure 2-4: Shelving is often a handy addition to any bench.

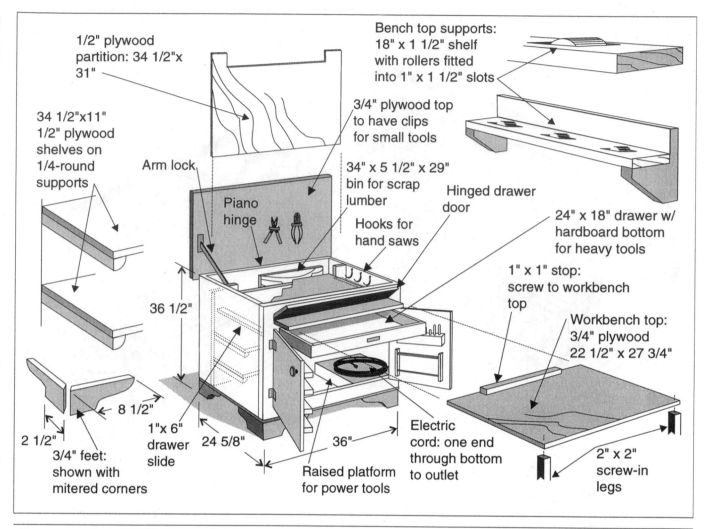

1/2" plywood partition: 34 1/2"x 31"

34 1/2"x11" 1/2" plywood shelves on 1/4-round supports

Arm lock

Piano hinge

Bench top supports: 18" x 1 1/2" shelf with rollers fitted into 1" x 1 1/2" slots

3/4" plywood top to have clips for small tools

34" x 5 1/2" x 29" bin for scrap lumber

Hooks for hand saws

Hinged drawer door

24" x 18" drawer w/ hardboard bottom for heavy tools

1" x 1" stop: screw to workbench top

Workbench top: 3/4" plywood 22 1/2" x 27 3/4"

36 1/2"

8 1/2"

2 1/2"

3/4" feet: shown with mitered corners

1"x 6" drawer slide

24 5/8"

36"

Raised platform for power tools

Electric cord: one end through bottom to outlet

2" x 2" screw-in legs

Figure 2-5: Construction details of an apartment workbench.

Apartment Workbench

Apartment dwellers in cities are usually handicapped by not having sufficient space in which to do gun repairs. However, it is possible to have a complete workshop in a handsome cabinet that looks like a respectable piece of furniture. The details of one such cabinet is shown in Figure 2-5.

The hinged top opens to display an ample assortment of gunsmithing tools which are held securely in place by hold clips fastened to the bottom of the ¾" plywood top. The narrow panel on the front of

the cabinet hinges outward and up to provide access to the 24″ × 27¾″ workbench top, which is supported by rollers fitted into slots as shown in the drawing. Stops cut from 1″ × 2″ wood blocks keep the workbench top from coming all the way out from the cabinet while 2″ × 2″ screw-in legs are used to support the work surface.

A raised platform on the bottom shelf of the cabinet can be used to house power tools, such as a Dremel Moto-Tool or even a small metal-turning lathe. Note also that an electric power cord runs through a hole cut through the bottom to a power

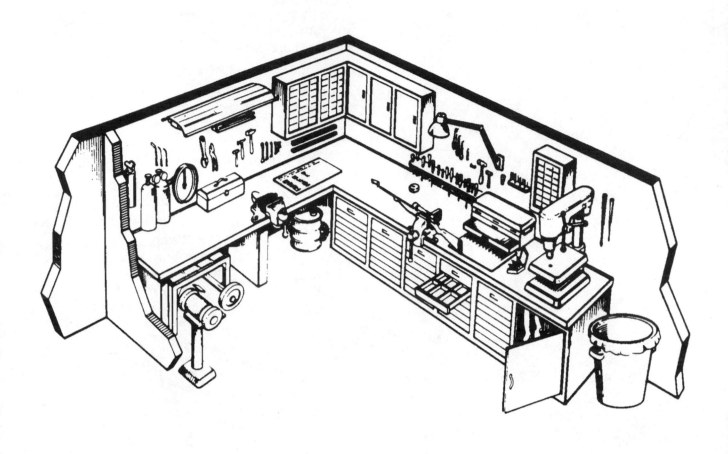

Figure 2-6: One possible shop layout for gunsmithing work. The bare necessities may be installed initially and elaborated as economy permits and the need arises.

outlet. A 24″ x 18″ drawer may be used for other heavy tools while the inner sides of the cabinet doors hold bits, blades, sandpaper, and other gunsmithing supplies.

PLANNING AHEAD

The beginning gunsmith or hobbyist will probably start out with minimal tools, but should start out with a solid workbench and bench vise; then more tools can be added as economy permits or the need arises. For example, the workshop shown in Figure 2-6 is a good shop for the beginning gun-

smith or hobbyist, and is about the minimum one can get by with to perform even basic work on guns. Still, you are looking at a sizable investment. But if you concentrated only on the bench tops themselves (without drawers), or just one "wing" of the bench first, and added the bench vise along with your basic hand tools and tool box, you could probably get by for less than $500, especially if you are handy with woodworking tools and you can scrape up some scrap lumber here and there. At the first opportunity, you would probably want to purchase a drill press and a bench or pedestal grinder that can also be used as a buffer. This basic setup is shown in the floor plan in Figure 2-7. Sure, your

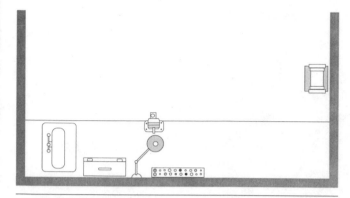

Figure 2-7: Floor plan showing how the layout in Figure 2-6 can be started.

shop is relatively bare at the moment, but you have high hopes of expanding it into the shop shown in Figure 2-6. Later on, a metal-turning lathe could be placed in back of the operator, opposite the bench containing the drill press, bench vise, etc., and you will have one excellent setup for performing nearly all phases of gunsmithing on a small scale.

If you are planning to eventually expand into a part-time or full-time business, your planning should extend even further.

Chapter 3
Tools To Get You Started

Because of the critical nature of gun repair and the value of the guns being worked on, you must be very selective when choosing gunsmithing tools; only the best will do! The holding power of a screwdriver, for example, depends upon the quality of steel in its blade, the design of the blade and the external force that may be applied to the screwhead. For best results, the blade should also be selected to fit the width and depth of the screw slot.

If you are starting from scratch, with few or no gunsmithing tools, you will save considerable time and confusion by buying one of Brownells gunsmithing tool kits. Its Assembly/Disassembly Tool Kit, for example, contains 30 tools and pieces that will enable you to disassemble and assemble practically any gun. Here are some of the tools you'll find in the kit:

- Pin punches
- Cleaning brush
- Mainspring vise
- Gunsmith's bench knife
- Parallel pliers
- India stone
- Nylon/brass drift punch set
- Eight-inch narrow hand file
- Screw Check'R
- Speed hex wrench ($^7\!/_{64}''$)
- Sight base file
- Brass/nylon hammer
- Hollow-ground screwdrivers
- Specialty tools

A brief description of each follows:

Pin Punches

Assembly pins are used in most firearms and pin punches are used to remove them. Two starter punches are included in the Brownells set: a $^1\!/_{16}''$ and a $^3\!/_{32}''$. It is important that you learn always to use a starter punch when removing a drift pin, rather than try to break loose a stuck pin with a long drift or pin punch; this usually ends up with the punch getting bent or broken. Avoid this by getting the pin started with a starter punch, and then "drifting it

Figure 3-1: Brownells Assembly/Disassembly Tool Kit.

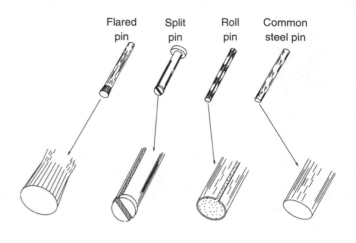

Figure 3-2: The four types of pins commonly used in both current and obsolete firearms.

out" with a pin or drift punch. Several sizes of drift punches are included in the kit.

Brownells also offers a special gunsmith's replaceable punch set that allows the tips to be replaced should they bend or break. The handles are made of steel with removable knurled-chuck to hold the pins. The pins may be ground down to the exact length required for each job — giving the user a set of custom punches with a minimum investment.

In general, there are four types of pins used in firearm assembly (Figure 3-2):

- Common steel pins
- Split pins
- Roll (spring) pins
- Flared-tip or serrated pins

Before attempting to remove any pin, examine it carefully to determine just what type it is. Then use the appropriate drift-pin punch to remove it. The object is to remove the pin without damaging it, the surrounding surface or finish, or any internal parts.

When removing drift pins, you must first position the gun so the pin will have clearance to be driven out. A padded vise works most of the time,

but sometimes this is going to a lot of trouble just to remove one pin. A hardwood block with a hole drilled through it (about 1-inch in diameter) keeps the gun high enough off the bench for driving out pins. A starter punch is used to get the pin started. This is the short, tapered, flat-nose punch found in most gunsmith's pin-punch sets. Hold the punch squarely on the pin and then give it a short, medium-heavy tap. If it resists, give it a harder blow. Once the pin moves, a pin punch just a bit smaller than the pin is used to drive or push it the rest of the way out.

If you suspect that the pin is serrated, you obviously must hit the pin on the opposite end from the tiny serrations to avoid damaging the pin or the gun parts. A close examination will reveal which is the serrated end; use a magnifying glass if necessary.

The increasing use of roll or spring pins in modern firearms makes it necessary to use special roll pin punches for removal. They permit the removal and reuse of the same pin without glaring damage to the pins. A kit of punches in sizes from $1/16''$ to $3/16''$ will take care of most of your needs in the gunshop. *See* Figure 3-3.

Select the proper size punch for the pin and then insert the pilot into the hollow pin until the driving

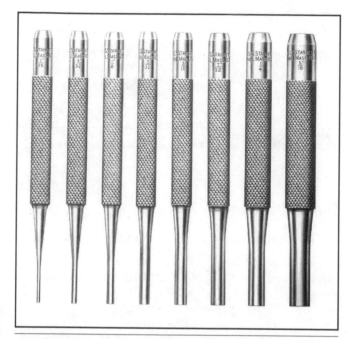

Figure 3-3: Pin punches are necessary to disassemble practically any gun that has ever been manufactured.

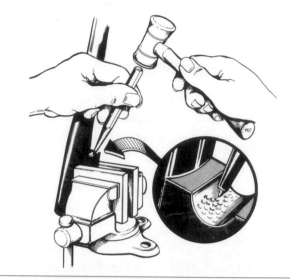

Figure 3-4: Peening barrel lug to tighten barrel/receiver fit on single-shot shotgun.

shoulders rest on the end of the pin. Then drive out the pin as discussed previously. Be sure to clean and oil the pin before replacing it.

Besides removing pins and using center punches for drilling, punches, in general, have many other uses around the gunshop. For example, a stuck screw can sometimes be loosened by tapping it with a pin punch to get it moving. Secure the firearm in a padded vise, then place the tip of the punch inside the outer edge of the screw slot and tap it with a hammer. This will usually start the screw turning when other methods have failed. The principle is the same as tapping a tight jar lid with a table knife to loosen it. Use care not to let the punch slip and mar the adjacent metal or wood finish.

A center punch may also be used to temporarily correct minor headspace problems of inexpensive single-shot, break-open shotguns. The inside curvature of the barrel lug is peened with a center punch as shown in Figure 3-4. The raised metal craters will cause the barrel to close tighter with the standing breech. In a similar manner, a center punch can be used to raise metal in the bottom of

dovetail slots in barrels when they are too loose to hold dovetail sights properly. To correct, rest the barrel on a solid object with some type of protection so as not to damage the barrel's finish, then give several hits with the center punch directly in the dovetail slot. Try the dovetail sight and, if it's still not tight enough, raise more metal with the center punch until the correct fit is obtained. *See* Figure 3-5.

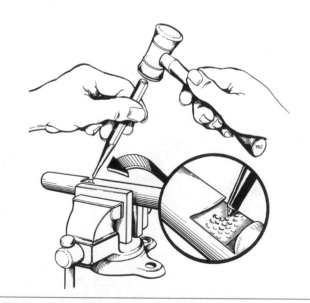

Figure 3-5: The raised metal from peening will tighten against the bottom of the sight base.

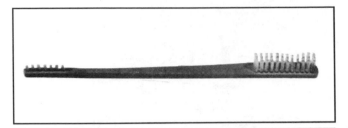

Figure 3-6: A small cleaning brush will have many uses on a gunsmith's bench.

Figure 3-8: A good bench knife always comes in handy.

Cleaning Brush

You will find many uses for this special gunsmithing brush, such as cleaning the action, brushing off parts, dipping it in solvent, working in tight places, cleaning out checkering and grains of gunstocks after sanding and prior to finishing. *See* Figure 3-6.

Mainspring Vise

One of the most difficult gun parts to control without breaking, or without it slipping out of your holding device, is the V-type mainspring found in many different types of firearms. The little mainspring vise (Figure 3-7) will save you many problems.

Figure 3-7: This mainspring vise can be a real time-saver when working on blackpowder arms and sidelock shotgun actions.

Gunsmith's Bench Knife

This knife will come in handy for gunstock inletting, cutting leather rifle slings, incising, relieving and a host of other cutting uses around the shop.

India Stone

A necessary item for honing trigger sears for smoother trigger pull and operation.

Parallel Pliers

These are not intended for twisting/turning jobs, but for precision holding of gun parts. Because the jaws are parallel, when you grab something, such as a spring or a rounded object, there is no tendency for it to slip out from between the jaws when pressure is applied. Because of the compound nature of the leverage, tremendous pressure can be exerted. This is particularly valuable when inserting drift pins, holding springs or other small parts. By taking a heavy rubber band, and wrapping it twice around the grips, you have a practical and useful small pin vise, not only for shop use but for emergency use in the field. As your gun repair work progresses, you will probably need other types of pliers for intricate jobs; these may be obtained at your local hardware store and include those shown in Figure 3-9.

While not in the basic Assembly/Disassembly kit, the assortment of pliers shown in Figure 3-9 will fit nearly all gunshop requirements — from

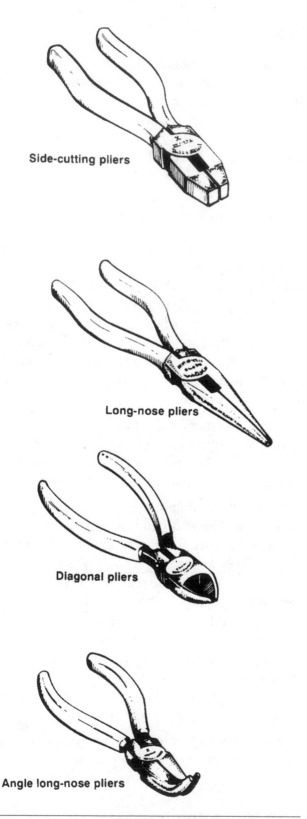

Figure 3-9: Assortment of pliers that has proved useful around the gunshop.

reaching inside a small action and inserting a small part to holding red-hot screws or drift pins that are being blued by the oil-heat method. Insist on the steel varieties and not the cast-iron models found in some discount houses.

Adjustable combination pliers (not shown) have been around for a long time. They are a common household tool and have been used for everything from driving tacks to pulling teeth, but they have a definite place in the gunshop. In general, a slip joint holds the two parts of the pliers together so that the jaws can be opened or closed to hold large or small objects. Most adjustable combination pliers have two cutting edges at the back of the jaws for wire cutting, but their main purpose is for gripping – holding a small part against a grinding wheel.

Long-nose pliers, often called "needle-nose pliers," are used with small objects in hard-to-get-at locations, such as starting the replacement of a pin or spring inside an action. The tips of these pliers are easily bent if they are misused and they should never be used for loosening or tightening a screw or nut. Starting them, yes; but tightening them, no!

Other types of pliers similar to long-nose pliers include round-nose, half-round-nose, and flat-nose pliers. All three types are used for similar situations as the long-nose version.

Side-cutting pliers are used in the gunshop for cutting wire — like black iron stovepipe wire used to hold barreled actions and parts while being blued. Their use, however, on hardened steel or heavy material will quickly nick or dull the cutting edge.

Pump pliers (often called Channel-Locks) have a quick adjustment for widening or narrowing the jaws to hold various materials, especially round objects. The interlocking tongues and grooves on the two parts of the pliers enable the jaws to be moved closer together or farther apart.

Self-adjustable locking pliers act as a small portable vise. These pliers have a toggle and floating-wedge arrangement that automatically adjusts the jaws of the pliers to the size of the object being gripped. Pressure on the handle then enables the jaws to lock around the object very tightly and remain in this position until reverse pressure is applied to release the vise grip.

The various cutting and gripping pliers are available in a number of sizes and each has a specific purpose. Any of them can be ruined if used for the wrong job.

Nylon/Brass Drift Punch Set

The dual tips provide a punch suitable for a variety of jobs. The brass tip, for example, is excellent for such jobs as knocking out a dovetail sight base. It should not be used on blued surfaces, as it may leave brass marks on the metal. With the nylon top, you can drive out a sight or a pin without marking or transferring brass coloration to the finish.

Eight-Inch Narrow Hand File

This file is similar to a conventional pillar file, but has the advantage of having one cutting edge and one safe edge. You will find many uses for this file, including draw filing described later on in this book.

Screw Check'R

Since few beginners have a screw gauge and a micrometer, this simple little tool is included to take their place. This gauge will also give drill sizes.

Speed Hex Wrench

This tool is included in the Brownells kit mainly for use on Redfield scope rings, a job that can be a real knuckle-buster if you don't have the right tool at hand.

Sight-Base File

Only one side of this file cuts to form a dovetail in the metal for fitting iron sights to rifles and handguns. This file can also serve many other purposes, in which the user must come right up to a side wall, or slightly undercut without damaging the sides of the cut itself.

Brass/Nylon Hammer

A brass hammer is standard equipment on all gunsmithing benches. Because of the soft nature of brass (compared with steel), it is ideal for driving or tapping parts where marring or nicking is to be avoided. A nylon surface available on the opposite face makes the hammer more versatile, offering the user a second choice in cases where even more care must be taken to avoid marring or deforming delicate or softer parts.

Other hammers will find a variety of uses in benchwork: driving pins; installing or removing sights; seating inlays; peening dovetail sight bases to tighten sights; and a host of other jobs.

One of the first hammers purchased by the gunsmith should be a no-mar type. These nylon, rubber or leather-headed hammers may be used for a multitude of jobs around the shop in which you have to pound but don't want to mar the metal or wood you are working on. Of the several sizes available, you'll probably want to get the 1" diameter tip size first. You can also purchase a brass hammer tip that will screw into the 1" no-mar hammer. When this is used in combination with a no-mar plastic, nylon or phenolic tip, it makes an excellent all-purpose gunsmith hammer.

Metal working hammers (*see* Figure 3-10) may be classified with respect to peen as:

- Ball peen
- Straight peen
- Cross peen

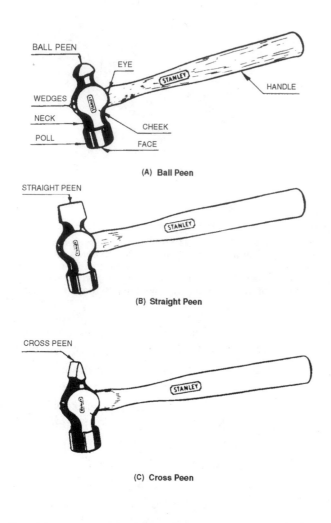

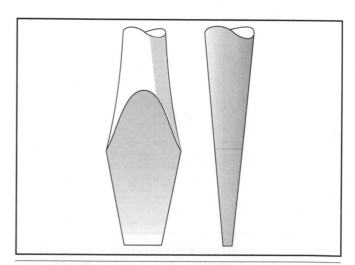

Gunsmith Screwdrivers

The selection of gunsmith screwdrivers should be given careful consideration, since a marred or otherwise damaged screwhead is a sure indication that an amateur has tackled the job. The efficient holding power of a screwdriver depends upon the quality of steel in its blade, the design of the blade, and the external force that may be applied to the screwhead. The blade should also be fitted to the width of the slot for best results.

For instance, if a common double-wedge type screwdriver, shown in Figure 3-11, was used in a deep screw slot, the blade would transmit its torque to the top of the screw slot, as shown in Figure 3-12 on the next page. With such a small slot area coming in contact with the blade, there is a good chance that the screw will be scored or worse yet, cause one section of the screwhead to break off. Wedge-shaped tips also tend to back the driver out of the screw slot — again causing damage to the screwhead.

A screwdriver tip, properly ground to fill a screw slot, as shown in Figure 3-13 (next page), is ideal for gun repair work, since the torque is applied at the bottom of the slot where the screw is the strongest; also, that blade will fill the slot completely (and should be the same width as the shank). *See* Figure

Figure 3-10: Description of the different types of peening hammers frequently used by gunsmiths.

They are used mainly to hammer metal; that is, to indent or compress it or to expand or stretch that portion of the metal adjacent to the indentation. One use of peening hammers is to tighten dovetail sights. Remove the sight base and lightly peen the top of the dovetail slot — forcing the overhand downwards to grip the sight base tighter. Marred metal areas can sometimes be peened back into their original condition if care is taken; and, of course, a gun part — such as a bar or shaft — may be straightened by peening with the convex portion of the hammer.

Figure 3-11: The common double-wedge screwdriver is not the best choice for gun work.

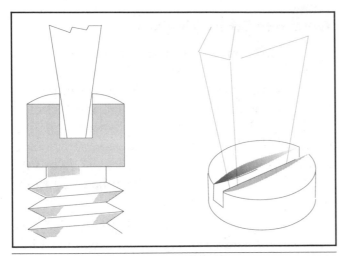

Figure 3-12: Here's the double-wedge screwdriver in use. Note the lack of close fitting — the blade transmits its torque only to the top of the screw slot. As can be seen, this screw slot (right) was damaged by improper blade fit.

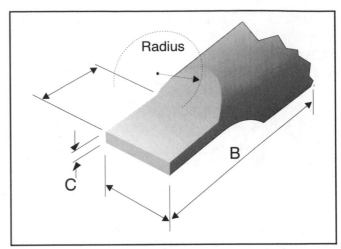

Figure 3-14: Gunsmithing screwdrivers are measured as follows: (A) blade width, (B) shank length, (C) blade thickness, (D) blade length, (E) radius of the curve from the flat portion of the blade to the outside of the shank. To fit a gun screw properly, all of these dimensions must match the screwhead.

3-14 for an explanataion of gunsmithing screwdriver measurements and terminology. This is how gunsmith screwdrivers should be ground.

The hollow-ground Magno-Tip handle (Figure 3-15) and interchangeable bits that are included in Brownells Assembly/Disassembly kit, have proven to be very popular with gunsmiths. The two smaller instrument screwdrivers in the kit are for working on very small screws, like on sight mounts.

Grace gunsmith screwdrivers made by Grace Metal Products have long been favorites with knowledgeable gunsmiths. They are made with a standard taper, but the tip of each bit is ground parallel for a short distance to fit screwheads better. They have a high-quality feel and will handle 95 percent of your needs around the gunshop. If you select this set, you will also need a stock bolt screwdriver with a $\frac{1}{2}$" blade, about 15" long. A set of jeweler's screwdrivers will also come in handy.

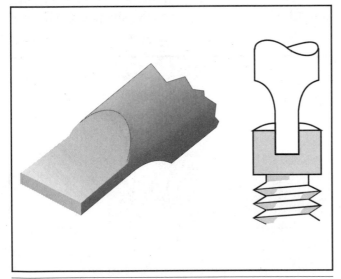

Figure 3-13: This type of blade is ideal for gun work. It has been ground to conform perfectly to a screw of specific dimensions. Notice that this screwdriver blade fits the screw slot perfectly.

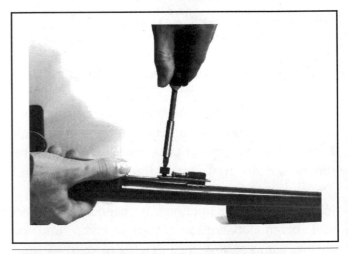

Figure 3-15: Brownells Magno-Tip screwdriver, with interchangeable blades, is popular among amateur and professional gunsmiths alike.

Another good set of screwdrivers is made by Chapman Manufacturing Company. This set contains one screwdriver handle, an extension, 12 slotted head adapters, two Phillips head adapters, a midget ratchet and one Allen hex-type adapter. This kit will handle nearly all of your gun repair needs, except for a long-shank bolt screwdriver.

The adapters for the Chapman screwdriver blades are relatively inexpensive and should be reshaped (if necessary) to conform to a specialized job such as an extra thin screw slot. When grinding adapters, however, be careful not to let the temperature get too hot (above 400°F) or they will lose their hardness.

Reshape the adapter so that it fits the screw slot exactly. Then inspect each adapter under a magnifying glass before use. Also carefully dress off any burrs that may be present before attempting to remove any screw. Use great care at all times, as one slip can damage the finish on an expensive firearm.

Strength of the individual adapter relates closely to its size, diameter, width of blade, thickness and the like. In general, the smaller the adapter, the weaker it is, and, therefore, the less torque that can be applied.

Even with a fine set of gunsmith screwdrivers, you must understand that some screws cannot be removed with a screwdriver. All screws are not made, fitted or installed in exactly the same manner. Neither are all screws manufactured with a proper "thread-to-thread" tolerance. Few of them are ever visually inspected before use and, therefore, they can carry a burr or chip that may jam them in position. Some screws — especially those used to secure gun sights — have a holding compound applied to them so they will not back out under recoil. It also makes them difficult, or impossible, to remove with a screwdriver.

Tapping the screwdriver in the screw slot will sometimes help to loosen the screw. This tends to drive the screw forward in the thread slot affording movement — in most cases. Liquid Wrench or WD-40 (commercial products used for loosening rusted metal screws and bolts) may also be tried. Heat applied to the surrounding area (not the screw itself) should be tried only as a last resort, because intense heat will draw the hardness from most metals.

Remember, once a screw is broken, it is too late for common sense or judgement. The broken screw must then be drilled out and replaced the best way possible — often taking much time and effort.

Making Your Own Screwdrivers: Even though commercial gunsmithing screwdriver sets come with many different sizes of bits, you might still have to grind a screwdriver tip to fit a particular screw slot. In fact, most professionals make their own screwdrivers out of drill rods and then install either a wooden or plastic handle on them for gripping. A circular grinding stone attached to a drill press will do the trick, but you will have to eyeball the radius and width of the bit. It is easier to purchase an MMC Hollow Grinding Fixture set from Brownells Inc. This set will enable you to grind screwdriver blades accurately or make your own. This device can be clamped to any bench grinder or drill press to hold screwdriver blades, and the design assures parallel blade faces and blade tips.

To grind screwdriver tips from a tool steel drill rod, use a steel consisting of 50 percent carbon, 40 percent manganese, 1 percent silicon, and 0.5 percent molybdenum, the finest steel available for screwdriver blades. Once the tips have been ground to size, wrap them in stainless steel foil to prevent scale from forming during the hardening. Using a propane torch, heat the rod to bright cherry red, and just before it changes to red-yellow, quench the part in oil. To draw, preheat the kitchen oven to 300 degrees Fahrenheit, put the part in the oven for an hour, and then allow it to air cool. This will make one of the toughest screwdriver blades available. Just be careful with the torch while heating the parts. Do not burn yourself or use an open flame around any combustibles.

When making your own screwdrivers, you will eventually want at least one screwdriver for each type of gun screw that you encounter in your work. The size and depth of screw slots can be measured with the measuring tools described later in this chapter, or their dimensions may be obtained from gun-screw dimension tables.

Bench Vise

A bench vise mounted on a sturdy workbench is the first non-portable tool the gunsmith should buy. The Versa-Vise (Figure 3-16) is one of the most useful items a gunsmith can have. It turns a full 360° in either the upright or laid-flat position. The vise automatically locks in the desired position when the jaws are clamped tight. Serrated pipe jaws for round objects up to $1\frac{1}{2}$" diameter are provided as well as a builtin anvil. Later on, you might need a much heavier vise for certain jobs for which no others will do. *See* Figure 3-17.

Files

Files are available in many shapes and sizes, with teeth of varying coarseness. Files and rasps have three distinguishing features:

Figure 3-16: The Versa-Vise is an ideal "first" vise for the home gunsmith.

Figure 3-17: This bench vise is sturdy and heavy enough for the amateur and professional alike.

- Length
- Type
- Cut

The length of the file is the distance between its heel (that part of a file where the tang begins) and the point (or opposite end). The tang (that portion of a file designed to hold the handle) is never included in the length. In general, the length of files bears no fixed proportion to either their width or their thickness, even though the files can be of the same type.

By "type" we mean the various shapes or styles of files, as distinguished by such technical names as flat, mill and half-round. Files are divided, from the form of their cross-section, into three general geometrical classes:

- Quadrangular
- Circular
- Triangular

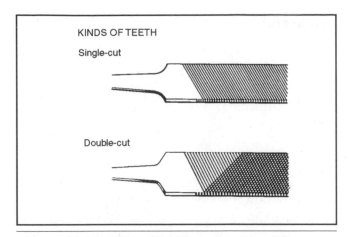

Figure 3-18: Comparison of single- and double-cut files.

From the above shapes are derived other odd and irregular forms or cross-sections, which are classified as miscellaneous.

The cut of a file is divided, with reference to the character of the teeth, into single, double, rasp and curved (see Figure 3-18); and, with reference to coarseness of the teeth, into coarse, bastard, second, and smooth cuts.

Single-cut files are usually used with a light pressure to produce a smooth surface finish, or a keen edge on a knife, shears, saw-tooth or other cutting implement.

Double-cut files are usually used under heavier pressure for fast metal removal and where the rougher finish is permissible.

The rasp cut is a series of individual teeth produced by a sharp, narrow, punch-like cutting chisel. It is extremely rough cut, and is used principally on wood, leather, bone, aluminum, lead, and similar soft substances for fast removal of metal.

For unusual types of files, such as those used on the flat surface of aluminum and steel sheets, a special curved tooth type is used.

Regarding coarseness, it should be obvious that coarse and bastard cuts are used on the heavier classes of work; the second and smooth cuts are used for finishing or more exacting work.

The 8-inch narrow hand file and the sight-base file have already been discussed. After purchasing these two files, you may want to start adding others to your inventory of tools. An 8-inch and a 10-inch mill file (both in fine cut) will see plenty of work around a gun shop, and a 12-inch flat bastard cut can take off a lot of metal in a hurry. Next in line will be a set of gunsmith needle files in both medium and fine cuts.

Eventually, you will also want several 6-inch round files for adjusting screw and pin holes, scope mount holes, fine cuts on tightly curved parts, and all types of parallel round cuts. Four diameters—$3/32$ inch, $1/8$ inch, $5/32$ inch, $3/16$ inch—will handle most gunsmithing needs. Cuts are normally 00 (very coarse), 0, No. 2, and No. 4 (very fine).

If you do much gunsmithing work, you will frequently have to deepen old screw slots, make slots in new screws, and touch up botched screw slots. Screwhead files are just the thing for these jobs. Such files cut only on the edge; the wide flat sides are smooth and will not damage the screwhead while filing.

Files are very simple tools, yet a person who knows how to use them can do remarkable things with them. For example, gunsmiths in Afghanistan frequently make their own gun parts using only files. Sure, hand filing is slower and more difficult than machine filing, but with patience, quite a lot can be accomplished.

Files are meant to cut in one direction only and unless the right amount of pressure is applied, the piece will be damaged. In addition, the teeth of the file get clogged up with metal filings. If this condition is allowed to go unchecked, the file will no longer cut effectively and will also score the work. So when buying your first file, buy a file card — a wire brush made especially for cleaning the teeth of files. Common chalk rubbed across the teeth will minimize clogging (often called *pinning*), but still use the file card to ensure proper cutting.

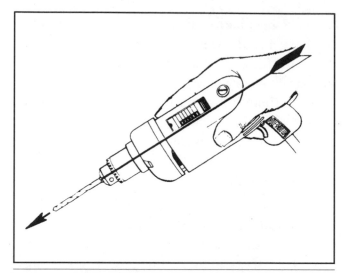

Figure 3-19: The little electric hand drill can accomplish many gunsmithing tasks, provided a few attachments are obtained.

Each file should be provided with either a plastic or wooden handle to protect the user's hands. It will give you a firmer grip on the file tang, but, even more important, if the file binds or catches on the work, the sharp tang will not cut a hand or wrist.

Drills

A hand drill (Figure 3-19) is relatively inexpensive and can suffice for most of the hobbyist's drilling. However, you will eventually need a drill press. With this, you can drill holes for mounting telescopic sights, drum-sand irregular wood shapes, grind screwdriver tips, and polish trigger guards and other small parts when a polishing bob is chucked into the drill.

Drill bits are another consideration, along with taps to thread screw holes. These can be purchased as needed, but it might be better if you buy Brownells Sight and Scope Mounting Drill and Tap Kit No. 2. If you anticipate doing much scope mounting on rifles that have not been predrilled at the factory, this kit will pay for itself many times over.

Disassembly Tools

Brownells Assembly/Disassembly Took Kit contains three specialty tools for disassembly of certain guns: Colt Pistol Wrench, Winchester Model 12/Ithaca 37 Wrench, and Extractor Spring Pliers.

Power Tools

Buying power tools can quickly get expensive, but to save time and elbow grease, it is advisable to purchase a few. Make your first power tool a $\frac{1}{4}$-inch or $\frac{3}{8}$-inch portable, electric drill. You will be able to use it and its many accessories as a drill press; as a disc sander for shaping stocks and recoil pads; as a buffer for polishing gun metal prior to bluing; as a carding wheel to remove rust during the hot water method of gun bluing; and as a bench grinder.

SPECIALTY TOOLS

About the time you think that you are equipped to tackle any project, you will have a gun that requires additional tools — either to disassemble it or repair it. Do not let this bother you. More than likely, an additional tool can be purchased locally, and you will have it when the situation arises again. One of the exceptions is the purchase of a tool to remove the stock bolt from some two-piece stocks. In most cases, a standard screwdriver with a ½-inch blade and 15-inch shank will work. Recently, however, manufacturers have strayed from the conventional screw-slot bolt. Some have hexhead bolts, some screw slot, and others are a combination of both. All are difficult to remove and often require special tool setups to handle the force required to remove them correctly and to retighten solidly. Also, many stock bolt holes are only slightly over-sized, requiring special thin-walled sockets.

Brownells Stock Take-Down Tool Kit is designed to handle all stock takedown problems. The

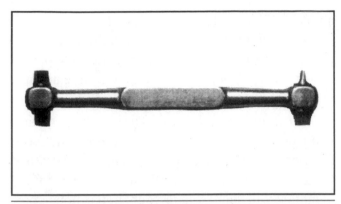

Figure 3-20: A midget offset screwdriver is unbeatable for removing screws in small spaces.

socket heads are correct to prevent slipping and burring. The drag-link bit-and-socket screwdriver is round at the socket end, which automatically centers the blade in the stock bolt hole and makes fitting it into the slot much easier than when using a conventional screwdriver. This set is expensive, but when you need it, nothing else will do. There are also other uses for it in gun work, so it will provide multiple service for the investment.

Another hair-pulling problem is trying to loosen or tighten a screw in close quarters, such as the trigger spring screw in some break-open, single-barrel shotguns. The receiver tangs prevent a direct approach using conventional screwdrivers, and you usually wind up bruising knuckles and botching screwheads. A midget offset ratchet, such as the one in Figure 3-20, will help tremendously. The short 18-degree working arc is unbeatable for removing screws in close quarters. The ratchet direction reverses instantly by turning the tool over. It can be used with several types of screwdriver bits, but it is recommended for use with the Chapman screwdriver set.

Bench Block

When trying to remove drift pins from various gun parts, you will discover that it is difficult to position the part solidly to take the blow, and still provide an escape area for the drift pin to come through. A bench block affords a means to remove

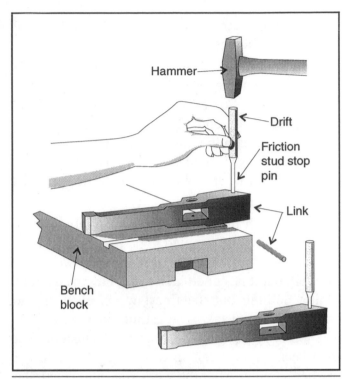

Figure 3-21: The gunsmith finds all sorts of uses for a simple bench block.

the drift pins easily from practically any weapon without any damage to the gun or the pin itself. *See Figure 3-21.*

To make a bench block, cut a scrap of 2" x 4" lumber to a 6" length; sand all edges smooth. Lay out and mark the groove and retrieval pocket. Make several saw cuts within the margin of the groove layout lines, then finish cutting to size with a wood chisel. Use a tight-fitting sanding block with sandpaper, and smooth all edges of the groove. Make diagonal saw cuts for the retrieval pocket and remove the remaining wood with a wood chisel. A ½-inch drilled hole will complete the project.

You may want to fill the pores of this wooden bench block and then varnish it to prevent the wood from soaking up the oil that drops off the various gun parts. To do so, sand smooth, apply wood filler, and resand to bare wood after the filler is completely dry. Apply another coat, and when dry apply a coat of spar varnish. When the varnish is dry, rub the block lightly with fine sandpaper. Apply another coat of varnish very evenly. When this final coat is dry, the bench block is ready for use.

The dimensions given for this bench block are flexible. If another size would serve you better, change them. For example, a piece of 4" x 4" lumber may be better. In this case, other dimensions will remain the same, except that the ½-inch hole from the groove to the retrieval pocket will be longer, enabling the block to handle longer drift pins.

This bench-block project is relatively simple, and many may be tempted to do the work without taking too many pains. It will probably work just as well, but it is a good idea to get into the habit of doing nothing but the finest work, even on the simplest of projects. A gunsmith once was given the job of refinishing an entire gun collection that had been slightly damaged by a small fire in the owner's home. After the work was completed, the owner admitted that he had been reluctant to entrust the entire collection to just anyone. But after he happened to notice the fine work that the gunsmith had put into a simple block of wood on his bench, any doubts he had vanished. If the gunsmith took that much trouble with a block of wood that made little difference, he reasoned, he must really do fine work when it counts.

Time-Saving Devices

A skilled gunsmith can turn out a large amount of work with only a few hand tools. However, few professionals rely solely on hand tools; most have shops equipped with loads of special tools to make the work proceed easier and faster.

Power tools can help the hobbyist turn out certain gun repair jobs faster, but few part-time gunsmiths can afford to invest in a large array of power tools. A good lathe, for example, could cost $3,500 or more, and a milling machine about the same

amount. If you add accessories, the amount can quickly double. But face it, eventually every serious hobbyist is going to wind up with some power tools. The main objective is to be selective and not waste money.

Plan Before Purchasing: The purchase of any good power tool is going to require a relatively large cash outlay, so careful planning is necessary to stretch your dollar the farthest. A piece of equipment that will stand idle in your shop is not a good investment. Don't, for example, buy a drill press just because another gunsmith has one. The majority of that gunsmith's work may consist of mounting telescope sights on rifles, in which case, the drill press is almost indispensable. On the other hand, if your work consists mostly of bluing firearms, a power buffer to polish the metal parts prior to bluing would be a better investment. By the same token, if you specialize in making small replacement parts for obsolete firearms, a milling machine and a small, inexpensive lathe would be a good investment. Before purchasing any expensive power tool, be sure you have a need for it.

Once you decide that a certain power tool would be beneficial to you, begin gathering all the information available about the various types on the market. Look through tool catalogs, compare capabilities and prices, and then decide which model suits your needs the best. Compare the specifications of different models. Then ask people who have been using the tool how it performs for them, what they like about it, and what they do not like.

Also keep in mind that the most expensive piece of equipment is not necessarily the best; or it might not be the best one for you. Carefully investigate each piece of equipment, and then decide which one is best on the merits of how it will suit your own needs. To quote John Ruskin of yesteryear, as described in Brownells tool catalog:

TOOLS TO GET YOU STARTED   53

It's unwise to pay too much. . .but it's worse to pay too little. When you pay too much, you lose a little money. . .that is all. When you pay too little, you sometimes lose everything, because the thing you bought was incapable of doing the thing it was bought to do. The common law of business balance prohibits paying a little and getting a lot. It can't be done. If you deal with the lowest bidder, it is well to add something for the risk you run. And if you do that, you will have enough to pay for something better.

It would be difficult, if not impossible, to recommend an assortment of power tools to fit everyone's needs. But for hobbyists who will be doing average gun work and for those who eventually want to branch out into full-time careers, the following section lists power tools that might be needed in the recommended order of purchase.

Drill Press

The first large power tool purchase for your shop should be a drill press and stand, as it will pay for itself time and time again. Besides its obvious uses — drilling holes in metal for mounting sights and such—the press enables you to do precision jeweling on gun bolts and other parts, makes sling swivel installations a snap, and aids in inletting stocks when a Forster wood bit is used in the chuck. In fact, after using the press for a while and learning to use the various accessories, you will wonder how you ever got by without it.

If a good drill press is too expensive at this time, do not bother buying an inexpensive one that will not bore true holes or handle the work. Instead, purchase a press that will attach to a hand drill motor and make this do until you can afford a better drill press.

The accessories for drill presses are numerous and permit all sorts of jobs to be done on the press. If the press tilts for angle drilling, you can chuck an arbor into the press, and attach buffing wheels for polishing gun parts prior to bluing, or wire wheels for carding during the hot water method of bluing. Swing the table away from the spindle, tilt the spindle out for accessibility, and you are in business.

Lathe

Many experts would recommend a bench grinder as the second power tool for the gunshop. It is a very handy tool to have around. But since an inexpensive grinding wheel can be purchased for use in either the drill press or a small lathe that will accommodate most of the grinding operations encountered, a small bench lathe is recommended here instead.

Once you learn to use the lathe, you will be able to make many other tools and accessories with it, including headspace gauges, and chamber-ironing tools. You will be able to mill an occasional trigger guard or hammer, but be prepared to spend several hours on each.

When selecting a lathe for gunsmithing work, the most important consideration is the size and amount of work that it will be used for. The lathe should be large enough to accommodate the various classes of work that will be handled. This is determined by the greatest diameter and length of work that will be machined in the lathe.

If you anticipate many conversion jobs that require barrel turning, bolt facing, and chambering and threading of barrels, then you will need a lathe like the one in Figure 3-22 on the next page. Each lathe, however, has advantages and disadvantages, and the final decision to purchase one should be made only after you have thoroughly and candidly analyzed your abilities and your anticipated specialty, and your probable future desires.

Milling attachments are also available for most lathes that will do a great deal of milling in the gunshop. The milling cut is controlled by the hand wheel of the lathe carriage, with the cross-feed

Figure 3-22: A good lathe and a working knowledge of its use will enable the gunsmith to handle almost any metal-working job conceivable.

screw of the lathe and the vertical adjusting screw at the top of the milling attachment.

Bench Grinder

A bench grinder (Figure 3-23) will mainly be used to sharpen tools and drill bits and maintain the other tools used in gunsmithing work. It will also grind down metal surfaces rapidly and is excellent for such purposes prior to final finishing with a file or polishing wheel. With one or both grinding wheels removed, buffing wheels can be attached to the arbors to polish metal surfaces for gun bluing. Or, when wire wheels are used, it is possible to card metal surfaces when using the hot-water method or slow-rusting process of gun bluing.

Welding Outfit

Although it is not really a power tool, an oxya-cetylene welding kit to use for welding, silver

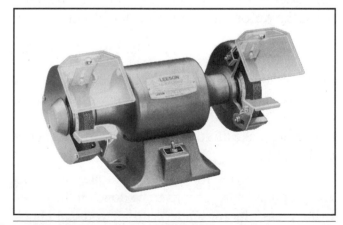

Figure 3-23: Heavy-duty bench grinder.

soldering, brazing, and heat-treating parts should be the next purchase. Heating and bending or welding bolt handles is just one job the welding outfit will perform. There are countless broken parts for which replacements are not readily available that can be mended with a welding outfit and silver solder.

Milling Machine

A milling machine can be a worthwhile investment if the shop is engaged in making a lot of gun parts from patterns or duplicates. By today's standards, a milling machine is really not too expensive, but the machine itself is only part of the story. When several milling cutters are required (and they usually are), the investment is quite large.

In general, a milling machine is designed to cut metal by means of a multitooth rotating cutter. The machine is constructed in such a manner that the workpiece is fed to a rotary cutter instead of a fixed cutter being applied to a rotating workpiece, as on a lathe.

Figure 3-24: Typical milling machine.

The milling machine is ideal for the gunshop because it is also a complete drill press. Almost any small gun part, including a receiver, can be machined on this tool. In fact, the milling machine was developed for use in gun factories. A seasoned operator can use the machine to make all sorts of replacement parts for firearms or to make complete firearms.

Heat-Treating Furnace

Another tool that deserves mention is the heat-treating furnace. Several types are available in a wide price range. The Hupert Electric Heat-Treating Furnace, available from suppliers of gunsmithing tools, is designed specifically for precision heat-treating in gunshops. It is simple to operate and service.

The gunsmith who makes tools and parts, such as firing pins, drift pins, sears, reamers, and springs, will have to harden them correctly. Many use the color method of hardening in a gas flame, but the process cannot be controlled this way. The odds against obtaining the correct hardness every time are high. Therefore, for the shop that turns out a lot of this work, an electric furnace is a good investment.

For removing parts from the hot furnaces, one or more sets of tongs are necessary. Special tongs, available from Frank Mittermeier, Inc., are specially designed for handling small parts in heat-treating furnaces and are highly recommended. They are made from $\frac{1}{4}$-inch stock and are about 16 inches long. Insuring a positive grip on various objects, they permit the operator to handle parts easily from a distance.

Miscellaneous Power Tools

With the addition of a barrel vise and wrench, the experienced craftsman who has the tools mentioned will be able to handle almost any type of work encountered in the operation of a gunshop.

A look through any gunsmith supplier's catalog reveals a large array of gunsmithing tools that have time-saving capabilities. For example, electric checkering tools will speed up the process of checkering once you have practiced enough to use the tools correctly. Power buffers by Baldor or B-Square speed up the polishing process prior to bluing firearms. As a gunsmith, you might get into reloading ammunition, developing new wildcat cartridges or new loads for factory cartridges — in which case you may want an electronic chronograph and maybe even a pressure gun to check the chamber pressure of your reloads. The variety of gunsmithing tools is almost endless!

Chapter 4
Cleaning and Caring for Firearms

Part of the *pleasure* of handling a gun is the proper maintenance of it. Part of the *responsibility* of owning a gun is its proper maintenance and care.

Maintenance and care are necessary to keep a gun in a reliable, safe, operating condition. A gun that is rusty and dirty won't look good, may not operate properly, and may actually be unsafe.

The cleaning of a firearm at regular intervals takes only a few minutes and insures accuracy, good working order, and a long-lasting gun finish. On the other hand, a neglected firearm will be difficult to clean and will often be badly pitted — sometimes beyond repair. Therefore, if shooters keep their guns in first-class condition at all times, they can expect them to function properly and last several lifetimes.

Weapons firing cartridges with smokeless powder and noncorrosive primers need not be cleaned immediately after firing. But don't put the job off any longer than necessary because the chances of rust forming increase with time. A pitted bore can render a shotgun or rifle useless.

All that is required to clean a firearm is one of the basic cleaning kits available on the market. These kits contain a cleaning rod, rod tips, oil, powder solvent, and gun patches. Some include a wire brush. These kits are compact and easily transported to the field for cleaning weapons immediately after a hunt or while on the range.

This chapter is designed to show you how to properly clean rifles, shotguns, and handguns.

BASIC GUN MAINTENANCE AND CLEANING

A gun is a beautiful thing — when it leaves the factory. It has many metal parts that have been very carefully machined, inspected, tested, polished, and given some sort of attractive finish. The wooden parts have been made from a piece of carefully selected wood, turned precisely to shape, carefully sanded and smoothed, and given a handsome protective finish. A new gun is a delight to see and a delight to handle. It not only looks good but it feels good.

It takes only minimal care to prevent the gun from becoming marred, dented, and scratched. Guns should be carried in a case when possible. They should never be thrown down carelessly or placed in a position where junk gets piled on them in, say, a car trunk. Just a little care will work wonders and marks the person using this care as a knowledgeable, expert gun handler.

Most of the parts of a gun are made of steel, and many of them are blued. But, whether they are blued or not, all the metal parts need a light protective coat of oil to prevent rust from atmospheric conditions. When a gun is used on the range or carried in the field, the oil should be wiped off so it won't gather dust and dirt. But the oil should again be applied to the gun when it is returned to the gun rack. It is also a good idea to have a silicone cloth or a very lightly oiled wiping rag stored in a metal container near the gun so that finger marks can be wiped off after the gun has been handled. The salty perspiration from fingers and hands is very likely to cause rust.

Like any other piece of machinery, the gun's mechanism should occasionally be cleaned and lubricated. A gun that is used in the field will get dusty, and some of this dust will get into the working parts. During shooting, bits of unburned powder or carbon may work their way into the action. Previous lubrication will dry up and get gummy or sticky. If a gun is used much, the mechanism should be cleaned rather often. But if it is not used a lot, a cleaning once or twice a year should be enough unless the gun is used and stored in a humid climate.

Basic Gun Gleaning

Before you start to work on a gun or clean it, be sure that it is unloaded and there is no ammunition in the magazine. Open the gun's action, inspect the chamber and magazine, and remove any ammunition from the gun. Leave the action open during the cleaning operation. For break-open single-shot rifles and shotguns, you depress a lever or button to open the action. The same is true for double-barrel shotguns — either side-by-side or over/under types. When cleaning bolt-action rifles and shotguns, remove the bolt from the receiver prior to starting the cleaning operation. All of the above

firearms can be cleaned from the breech (chamber) end without further disassembly.

Most lever-actions, semiautomatics, and slide-action firearms will have to be disassembled further or else the tip must be inserted into the muzzle end of the barrel. One possible way to avoid disassembling the gun and still be able to insert the cleaning tip from the chamber end is to use a flexible cleaning rod. This is nothing more than a long, heavy coil spring that allows bending. In either case, the action must be opened before the cleaning operation begins.

Be very careful to follow the maker's directions in taking the gun apart and putting it back together again. It is not necessary to take it down to the last pin and part, but only far enough so that it can be cleaned properly. The less you take apart, the better off you are.

Barrels are usually easy to remove from semiautomatic pistols for cleaning; just follow the manufacturer's field-stripping (basic disassembly) instructions exactly. If you are cleaning a revolver, it will take a little more time since you should clean all cylinder chambers in addition to the bore. Remove the cylinder from the frame, if possible, because it is easier to handle and the barrel will then be readily accessible. *See* Figure 4-1 for an overview of firearm maintenance.

If at all possible, always insert the cleaning-rod tip into the breech end of the barrel. This is primarily to prevent wear on the rifling at the muzzle from the cleaning rod. This last fraction of an inch of a rifle's barrel is very important, as any wear at all will reduce the rifle's accuracy. Another reason for cleaning any gun from the chamber end toward the muzzle is to keep debris out of the receiver. If you clean from the muzzle to the chamber, the cleaning patch will push all the gunk out of the bore and right into the action, making additional cleaning necessary.

To use a gun-cleaning kit, soak a gun patch in powder solvent (bore cleaner) and push the patch through the slotted tip attached to the end of the

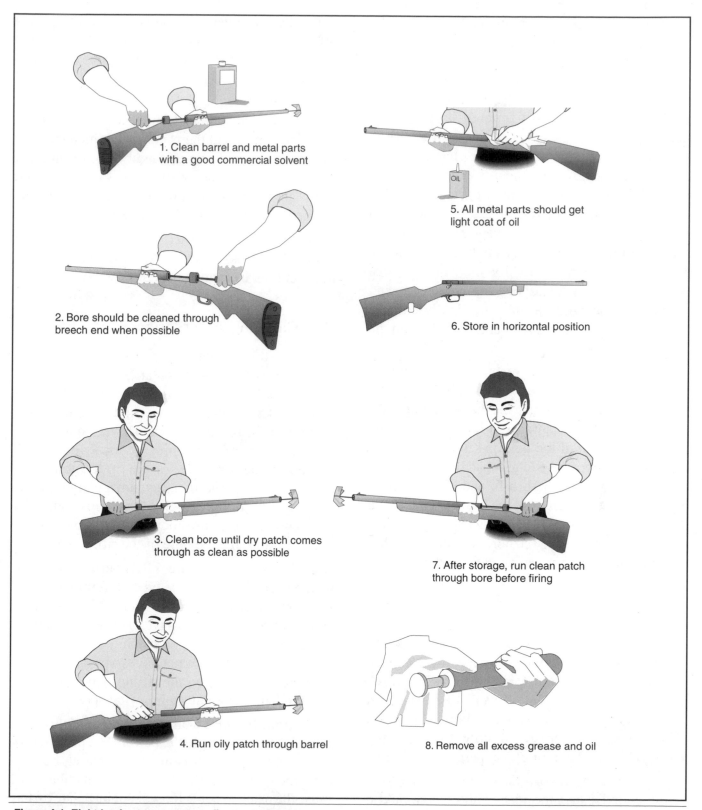

1. Clean barrel and metal parts with a good commercial solvent

2. Bore should be cleaned through breech end when possible

3. Clean bore until dry patch comes through as clean as possible

4. Run oily patch through barrel

5. All metal parts should get light coat of oil

6. Store in horizontal position

7. After storage, run clean patch through bore before firing

8. Remove all excess grease and oil

Figure 4-1: Eight basic steps to proper firearm maintenance.

cleaning rod. Insert the tip into the barrel from the breech end, if possible, and run the patch the full length of the barrel. This first patch usually contains the bulk of the loose residue in the bore, and if you pull it back through the barrel on the return stroke, you will redeposit some of it back in the bore. Therefore, always discard the first patch when it comes out the muzzle (the chamber if you have to insert the tip into the muzzle end). Insert a new patch through the slotted tip, saturate it with bore cleaner, and again run the patch the full length of the bore, and back again. Repeat this operation as many times as necessary, usually 15 or 20 times. Then use a dry patch to dry the bore. Change patches often until the last one comes out clean and dry. Finish the bore cleaning by lightly oiling a clean patch and running it up and back through the bore.

Extra-dirty bores require the use of a bronze bristle brush. Soak a clean patch with powder solvent (bore cleaner). Push the patch through the slotted tip of the cleaning rod and run it up and down the bore until the bore is saturated with the cleaner. Remove the slotted patch tip from the cleaning rod, insert the brush, and dip it into the powder solvent. Then push the brush up and down the bore about a dozen times to loosen the dirt and grime. Finish by drying the bore with clean patches until the last patch comes out clean and dry.

The receivers of semiautomatic, slide-action, and lever-action firearms collect all sorts of debris and foreign matter and must be cleaned periodically to insure proper functioning. An old toothbrush or Brownells M-16 cleaning brush can be used to get into actions and other hard-to-reach places. A squirt or two of WD-40 (a standard cleaner) sprayed into the action, followed by a good scrubbing with the brush will do wonders to keep actions clean and in first-class operating condition.

When cleaning revolvers, always give the front of the cylinder and the rear of the barrel careful attention. A lot of powder residue builds up in these areas and should be cleaned frequently.

Finally, the outside of the gun should be wiped off with a silicone cloth to prevent rust and corrosion and it will also remove finger prints and eliminate salt spray damage. This cloth may also be used on the gunstock.

The frequency of the cleaning will vary with the use of the guns and the weather to which they are subjected. A good rule-of-thumb is to clean them after each firing. Also, when a gun is used or stored near salt water or in humid areas, it should be cleaned, or at least wiped off, every few days.

When cared for as described, guns will rarely be injured from rust, fouling, or corrosion from routine handling by human hands.

Gun Cleaning Accessories

Of the various types of cleaning tips, the single-slotted tip is the most popular (*see* Figure 4-2 on the next page). Its advantage is that it holds onto a patch under all conditions. On the minus side, sometimes the patch jams when reversed inside the bore, and often the cleaning action is one-sided, permitting the bare sides of the tip to rub against the rifling and perhaps cause damage after a time. The patch used with single-slotted tips should be large enough to require about 4 pounds of pressure to force it through the bore of the rifle.

The roll-jag tip (Figure 4-2B) permits rolled or wrapped patches and is the type preferred by many shooters for cleaning rifles, such as lever-actions and semiautomatics, that have to be wiped out from the muzzle end. The rolled patch bears against the rifling equally and does not have to be dragged into the bore. Accordingly, the rifling is preserved instead of being worn away in a vital spot.

Plain-jag tips give a uniform cleaning action and reverse perfectly inside the barrel. The patch sticks to the tip as long as it is inside the barrel, but any movement beyond the muzzle or chamber will cause the patch to come loose. A pointed-jag tip has the advantage of centering the patch before being inserted into the bore.

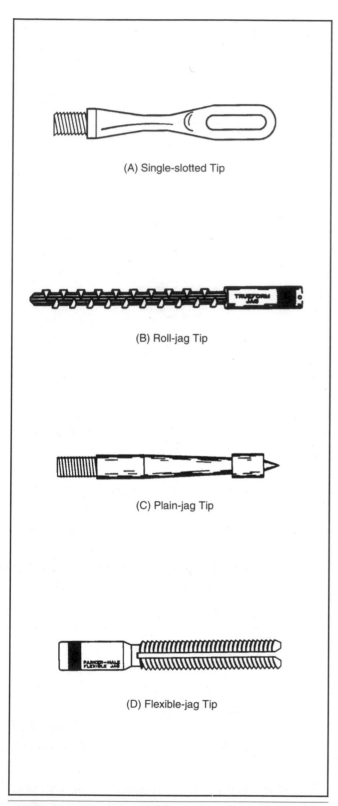

Figure 4-2: Types of cleaning tips: (A) a single-slotted tip, (B) a roll-jag tip, (C) a plain-jag tip, and (D) a flexible-jag tip.

(A) Single-slotted Tip

(B) Roll-jag Tip

(C) Plain-jag Tip

(D) Flexible-jag Tip

Many shooters prefer to use flexible-jag tips, especially for cleaning shotgun barrels. A patch is slipped into the slot of the jag and wrapped around it. The slot, which imparts a measure of flexibility, causes the patch to press evenly on the bore, thereby squeezing the oil into the pores of the steel. The slot also permits the cleaning patch to be compressed by the choke, insuring a thorough cleaning of the bore throughout its entire length. This jag is also good for holding steel wool and crocus cloth for polishing shotgun bores.

Wool and cotton mop tips are fine for oiling the bores of shotguns but must be kept clean. Damage may result by the fouling of the wool, which will neutralize the preserving powers of the oil.

The leather shotgun bore polisher is made up of several buff leather discs that absorb polishing material, such as Clover abrasive compound, and aid in repolishing the bores of shotguns that have been neglected. Since no metal touches the bore, they can be used without fear of damage, even on the more expensive weapons. Just be careful not to polish too much around the muzzle end of the shotgun because a change in choke pattern could result.

No attempt should be made to polish rifle barrels as the rifling will surely be damaged, causing the barrel to be inaccurate and worthless. Rifle barrels can sometimes be restored by lapping, but this is a job for the experienced gunsmith and is not recommended until some experience has been gained.

Cleaning Rods

Most of the cleaning rods on the market today are made of aluminum. This soft metal picks up bits of dirt, which may have an abrasive effect on the bore. If possible, try to find a brass, fiberglass or wooden cleaning rod to fit your rifle or shotgun.

The cleaning rods used on rifled barrels should have a swivel joint so that the patch will rotate inside the bore as the patch is being run back and forth, following the twist of the rifling. Without this rotation, the patch will drag at right angles across the lands and will destroy the sharp edges of the rifling, impairing accuracy.

A shotgun cleaning rod does not require a swivel joint because there is no rifling in a shotgun bore. Many experienced shooters prefer to use high-quality, all-wood cleaning rods on shotguns. In most cases, these are made from prime, well-seasoned hickory wood. All woods do not make suitable shotgun cleaning rods, nor is kiln-dry wood satisfactory, as it tends to be too brittle. For this reason, the hickory used for better rods is air dried to prevent warpage and insure the finish quality.

Metal Fouling and Leading

Metal fouling is not too common, except in the small-caliber, high-velocity rifles, but when it does occur, you should know how to handle it. When the fouling of metal is caused by jacketed bullets, the term *metal fouling* is used. However, when caused by lead bullets, it is called *leading*.

A rifle barrel that is smooth and well cared for will seldom have any problems with metal fouling. On the other hand, a neglected barrel will always develop metal fouling to some extent.

Regardless of the cause, metal fouling can disrupt accuracy. Examine the bore with a bore light. Any fouling will be visible as long streaks, flaky deposits, or lumps of metal particles sticking to the lands and grooves of the barrel.

To remove metal fouling, many shooters use a solution of ammonium persulfate, ammonium carbonate, stronger ammonia, and distilled water. However, this solution will damage the gun's finish if allowed to come in contact with it (which is easy to do since the solution is poured into the bore and allowed to soak for a period of time). Consequently, it is not a recommended procedure for the beginner. Instead, purchase a quantity of J-B Non-Imbedding Bore Cleaning Compound. Besides removing lead, metal, and powder fouling from rifles, pistols, and shotguns, it is guaranteed to im-

Figure 4-3: Corbin Bore Cleaner is one commercial cleaner available for cleaning rifle and handgun bores.

prove the accuracy of your present firearm. It will not injure the finest bore and will also help guard against rust. Another commercial solution that is highly recommended for removing all traces of lead, copper, powder, and plastic fouling is Corbin Bore Cleaner, shown in Figure 4-3, and Hoppe's Benchrest-9 Copper solvent.

Even the best match ammunition will cause leading in the finest target handguns and this leading can affect accuracy to a disastrous degree. However, a perfect cleaning job on handguns can be accomplished in a few minutes with a Lewis Lead Remover, available from Brownells. This tool will remove lead from the forcing cone, chamber(s) and bore with ease.

In revolvers, the forcing cone (or bullet seat) may be cleaned by first swinging the cylinder out of the firing position and then inserting the handle (with the tip and cloth patch removed) through the barrel

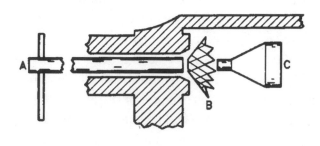

Figure 4-4: To assemble the Lewis Lead Remover rod, pass the rod body through the barrel and screw the cone tip (C) through the brass cloth patch (B) into the rod body (A). Then bend the patch back over the taper of the screw-cone tip, and you're ready to remove lead from a revolver's forcing cone using the tip shown.

from the muzzle end. Screw the cone tip with attached cloth patch into the handle hand-tight (Figure 4-4). Hold the revolver with the fingers around the handle and the thumb through the frame, and with the right hand, pull the cone tip and patch snug into the forcing cone. It won't go very far; just a fraction of an inch. Holding this pressure, turn the handle in a clockwise direction four or five turns; then push the cone back and examine the brass cloth patch. If the forcing cone is badly leaded, repeat this operation after flipping the lead off the patch with a thumb nail, pocket knife or similar object.

Clean the revolver barrel with the rubber tip unit by first removing all grease and solvent from the barrel. Then insert the handle through the barrel from the muzzle end as before. Screw the rubber tip with the formed brass cloth patch into the handle hand-tight and examine the knurled nut to see that it is backed one-half turn away from the rubber

portion of the tip. This allows the assembly to turn with the rifling. Hold the revolver as described before and pull the tip through the barrel, allowing the handle and tip assembly to turn with the rifling. Repeat this operation until all lead is removed.

Revolver cylinders may be cleaned in a similar way to the barrel; that is, insert the handle from the forward end of the cylinder and screw the rubber tip with formed brass cloth patch into the handle. Hold the cylinder with the left hand and pull the rubber tip with the formed patch into the cylinder. When the tip engages the front end (reduced diameter) of the cylinder, begin turning it in a clockwise direction.

The brass cloth patch should be good for several cleanings. Should it become clogged with grease and lead, it may be cleaned with lighter fluid and a toothbrush. If any of the above operations tighten either tip too tightly to be released with the fingers, a key is provided to loosen them.

Holding Guns For Cleaning

Firearms can be held for cleaning in a conventional bench vise as long as padded vise jaws are used to protect the finish. Furthermore, guard against tightening the vise jaws too much as you can bend receivers and damage other parts, especially thin shotgun barrels. When using a bench vise, clamp the firearm into the vise in a horizontal position with the butt resting on the bench top. You will then have access to the bore for pushing a cleaning rod through it. Some shooters prefer to clamp the rifle or shotgun in a vertical position with the butt resting on the floor directly under the vise.

For very little expense, you can build a suitable gun-cleaning rack similar to the wooden cleaning

Figure 4-5: The Decker Vise is a solid vise used to hold rifles and shotguns for scope mounting, cleaning, etc. The padded rests and clamp jaw protect the gun's finish.

racks made available at one time to all military recruits. These were merely notched, wooden frames that held rifles securely while they were being cleaned. A commercial shooting vise, such as the Decker Shooting Vise (Figure 4-5), is reasonably priced and greatly simplifies the operation of gun cleaning. When used properly, all scratching and marring are eliminated because the Naugahyde covering over the sponge padding is all that comes in contact with the gun. The base can be permanently mounted to a workbench or secured with C-clamps. This vise can also be used when boresighting, mounting scopes, and zeroing or adjusting sights for rifles.

Chapter 5
Installing and Adjusting Rifle Sights

Most rifles with iron sights are carefully sighted at the factory by teams of expert target shooters as part of the final inspection. These sharpshooters fire several series of shots at targets, then make any necessary sight adjustments to ensure that the sights are in proper alignment.

However, no two shooters have identical eyesight, and everyone has a different method of sighting a rifle. Even if a rifle fresh from the factory is sighted satisfactorily, the new owner must find his or her proper rear sight setting to ensure correct high and low shooting at various ranges.

Rifle sights are manufactured in what appears to the beginner as a bewildering variety. To understand the simplest of sights, you need to know the basic principles of sighting. The two most common sights are the *bead front sight* and the *notched, open rear sight.*

In aiming with these sights for target shooting, the top of the bead on the front sight should be held directly at the bottom of the target's bull's-eye, as shown in Figure 5-1. The rifle should be held so that the notch in the rear sight is in line with the

Figure 5-1: Open rear sight and bead front sight correctly aligned on target.

front-sight bead, with the front bead centered in the notch and the top of the bead level with the top of the notch. Experience will enable the shooter to vary elevation, but at the start it is best to adopt a regular way of sighting.

Figure 5-2: Peep rear sight and bead front sight on game.

Figure 5-3: Hooded, or aperture, front sight.

Hunting requires a different sight alignment: either the top of the front sight or the entire bead should be held on the exact spot the bullet is to strike. See Figure 5-2. As long as the shooter is not holding the rifle high to make allowance for range differences (holding high), this method of sight alignment will prove satisfactory.

A peep rear sight, instead of an open sight, gives the shooter a better combination when used with the bead front sight. An open rear sight, when used at long range and in combination with the bead front sight, may hide too much of the target. In any case, a shooter's method of sighting with both types of sights should be uniform.

By knowing the simple details of sighting, a shooter will be able to concentrate more on his or her target or game and increase shooting accuracy.

Sight Styles

If the shooter is using a simple blade front sight in combination with either the peep or open rear sight, the sights should be aligned as described in

the instructions previously given, following either the hunting procedure or the target-shooting procedure. If the shooter is using an *aperture front sight,* also called a *hooded front sight* (shown in Figure 5-3), with a peep rear sight (shown in Figure 5-4), the aperture should "ring" the bull's-eye in such a way that a thin, white ring shows around the bull'seye as shown in Figure 5-5.

When using a peep rear sight with a blade or post front sight, the front sight should be held on the target as described previously, with one exception: now only the front sight is seen, and there is not a notch in the rear sight to align the sight to the target. Because the shooter's eye is so close to the peep

Figure 5-4: Micrometer receiver target sight, a form of peep rear sight.

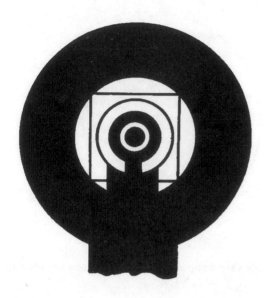

Figure 5-5: Micrometer peep rear target and aperture front sight on target.

sight, he or she will tend to look through the center of the hole. *See* Figure 5-6. Here again, it is important to firmly establish a regular habit of sighting through the rear sight. The eye should always center the top of the front sight in the center opening of the rear sight.

Figure 5-6: Peep rear sight and blade front sight aligned on target.

To prevent injury from recoil when shooting a high-powered rifle, do not hold a peep sight too close to your eye. The same precaution applies when using a telescopic sight.

Adjusting Sights

Most sights have some means of adjustment for both windage, or sideways movement, and elevation. Most adjustments are made at the rear sight. On some rifle and handgun sights, windage adjustment can be made by moving the rear sight to the right or left in its slot. Use a brass drift punch and a hammer. If your gun is shooting to the right, move the rear sight to the left. Always move the rear sight in the direction you want the shot to go. In rare cases, it may be necessary to move the front sight, too. Always move the front sight in the opposite direction you want the shot to go. To make this adjustment is to "zero" your rifle for windage. When shooting in the field, you must allow for wind drift by pointing the rifle right or left of the target.

On the ordinary open rear sight, elevation adjustments are made by means of a notched slide, or elevator, moving forward or backward in line with the barrel. Remember that raising the rear sight raises the point of impact of the bullet on the target. The notches on the elevator provide the simplest form of indicator scale for elevation. For example, if the shooter finds that for correct elevation in shooting at 100 yards, the rear sight must be set in the second notch of the sight's elevator, that notch becomes the 100-yard notch.

Peep sights are equipped with an elevator scale and are raised or lowered by means of either a screw or a slide and clamp. After zeroing, or sighting, at the desired range, the shooter notes the reading on the elevator scale. This becomes the rifle's zero for that range.

Micrometer Adjustment

Most aperture or peep rear sights and all telescopic sights have a micrometer caliper graduated in $\frac{1}{4}$-, $\frac{1}{2}$-, or full-minute divisions. A change in elevation or windage of 1 minute, or $\frac{1}{60}''$, will move the point of impact of the bullet $1''$ at 100 yards, $2''$ at 200 yards, $3''$ at 300 yards, and so on. For a $\frac{1}{4}$-minute change, one click will move the bullet $\frac{1}{4}''$ for each 100 yards of range. With this precise method of changing sights, it is easy to get an exact adjustment.

First, fire a group of at least three shots. Determine the center of this group and measure the distance in inches from this center to the center of your target (for example, $6''$). Divide each distance in inches by the range in hundreds of yards (for example, 200) to get the number of minutes change in sight needed ($\frac{6}{2} = 3$). Move the rear sight the proper number of divisions in the direction you want the shot to go. Figure 5-7 illustrates lateral movement, or windage; Figure 5-8 illustrates elevation. If your sight is graduated in $\frac{1}{4}$ minutes, you'll need four times as many clicks as you have minutes. (3 x 4 = 12 clicks).

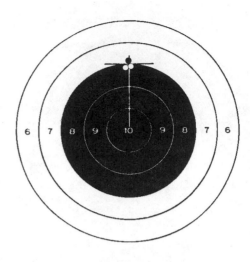

Figure 5-8: Target showing need for elevation adjustment.

In many cases, both windage and elevation will be off. When this is the case, measure the vertical distance from the center of the group to the vertical center line of the target to determine the elevation change. Measure the horizontal distance from the center of the group to the horizontal center line of the target to determine the change in windage. This is shown in Figure 5-9.

After changing the calibration, it is a good idea to fire another group of three to five shots to verify your settings.

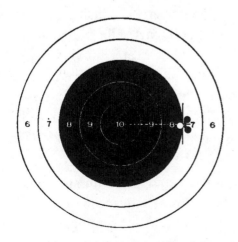

Figure 5-7: Target showing need for windage adjustment.

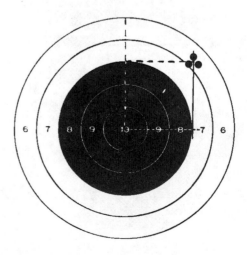

Figure 5-9: Target showing need for both elevation and windage adjustments.

TELESCOPIC SIGHTS

Most hunting telescopes have interior adjustments for sighting. Knobs or screws are provided for changing adjustment and are marked *Right* or *Left*, *Up* or *Down*. Divisions are usually in minutes. Target telescopes have exterior adjustments in the mounts, with thimble and barrel calibrations similar to those on the micrometer caliper. Divisions are ¼ or sometimes ⅛ minute, with an audible click marking each division.

Installing telescopic sights on a rifle can be either easy or difficult, depending upon many factors. Most rifles manufactured after World War II were factory drilled and tapped (or grooved) to accept telescopic sights and mounts; few rifles manufactured prior to World War II had these provisions.

Rifles that have been drilled and tapped at the factory for scope sights are easy to work with, and an amateur should experience little difficulty in doing a good job — provided the project is done in the recommended sequence.

The installation of telescopic sights, or scopes, on rifles that have no factory provisions can be quite a task for both amateurs and professionals. Poor workmanship in this phase of gunsmithing is common. In most cases, poor sight work usually results from trying to align the sight mounts in their correct position by the eye alone, or from marking the location for screw holes by crude and inaccurate methods. This section is intended to supply the ground work for the proper methods and principles which, if adhered to, will always result in a correctly installed scope.

Mounting scopes on rifles that have been drilled and tapped at the factory is usually a simple job, requiring few tools. Still, certain procedures and precautions should be followed to obtain a good installation that will not fall out of line after a few shots, especially on rifles with heavy recoil.

Most .22-rimfire rifles — including the .22 Winchester Magnum — have grooved receivers to accommodate scope mounts designed especially for these rifles. Since only slight recoil is experienced with the .22 rimfires, only a firm turn of the mount screws is required to mount a scope securely. Scopes designed for .22-rimfire rifles are usually furnished with mounts at no extra cost, and the installation of these requires only the aligning of the mount clips in the receiver groove, tightening the retaining screws by hand, and exerting a final twist with a screwdriver. Before final tightening, however, secure the screw clamps so that the scope and mounts will slide in the groove. Then, test the scope for correct eye relief. Once found, tighten as previously described.

Scope mounts for .22-rimfire rifles normally use universal clamps that fit into the factory-grooved receivers; centerfire rifles are different. With only a few exceptions, receivers on centerfire rifles are drilled and tapped for specific bases and mounts. The most popular scope bases for centerfire rifles can either be a single base, or a two-piece base.

To select the proper base for a given rifle, refer to a scope-base chart, and find the make and model of the rifle. Scope-base charts are normally found in the scope manufacturer's catalogs, or else furnished in a separate brochure. Then obtain the catalog or model number of the scope base; this is the one you need for your particular rifle. You will also need scope rings to match both the scope and base mounts.

For best accuracy, a telescopic sight must be mounted solidly to the rifle so that it stays secure, shot after shot. It doesn't make sense to spend a lot of money for a scope and then secure it with a cheap mount. Precision-machined mounts that are designed for a particular scope and rifle cost more than some of the imported varieties, but the extra amount will pay off handsomely in dependability and increased accuracy.

A one-piece mount, such as the Redfield JR. system, is the most dependable scope-mounting system available. Of course, this type of mount cannot be adapted to all rifles, but it is the recommended mount when it can be used. The rotary dovetail feature acts as a cam to hold the ring into a mating dovetail in the base for a good, solid fit. This type of mount also allows you to remove the scope (but not the base), and replace it without losing the zero.

The split rings that hold the scope to the mount should be precision-bored to the exact diameter of the telescopic sight, which is usually a 1" diameter. If the rings are precision-bored so that a full radius contact with the scope is maintained, an even pressure will be provided around the tube, thereby eliminating the problem of squeezing the tube out of round, which sometimes happens with strap-type mounting rings.

The Redfield JR. base features an outside windage adjustment that overcomes scope mounting problems caused by drilling the mounting holes out of alignment with the bore, or where barrels have been threaded into the action at an angle.

Once the scope and mount have been obtained, remove the tap screws that prevent dirt and other foreign material from entering the screw holes. In most cases, there will be four. Position the mount or mounts in place, use the screws that accompany the mount, and loosely secure these screws to hold the mount or bases in place. Now, operate the action of the rifle to see if it functions smoothly. Often, in the case of bolt-action rifles, the factory-supplied screws are too deep and will jam the bolt, preventing it from sliding smoothly. In this case, the screws will have to be shortened, either by cutting or grinding. Be sure to try the action again to make sure it works smoothly.

Remove the screws and mount bases from the receiver, and then thoroughly clean the screw holes and screws with a degreaser, such as the solution that comes with instant bluing kits.

At this point, fasten the mounting screws as firmly as possible into the screw holes to prevent them from coming loose during firing with a heavy-recoil rifle. Loctite is a commercial product that is especially recommended for such applications, and

several types are available. Lock N' Seal, for example, can be applied to the screw threads to obtain a tight fit. The solution flows into and fills up to 0.015" gaps, then hardens into a tough solid with 1,700 psi (pounds per square inch) strength. Apply this solution to the threads of the screws, before tightening them. Wipe off any excess solution before it hardens. This should keep most scope-mount screws tight at all times.

For worn or extra-loose screws, and rifles with extra-heavy recoil, you might want to try Loctite Stud N'Bearing Mount solution. This sets up to 3,400 psi and usually requires heavy tools to remove the screws once they have set.

If you don't have any of the Loctite compound available, adequate results can be obtained with fingernail polish. Again, clean the threads, apply a small amount of fingernail polish to each thread, and tighten as before. It will harden quickly and lock screws in place.

With two-piece mounts, once the base is in position, the scope rings are installed on the scope, but the screws are not tightened down completely. The rifle should be secured in a padded bench vise during this operation. You want them snug, but not so tight that you can't turn the scope. Secure the rings with the scope to the base mount, and then move the scope backwards and forwards, and rotate it until it is perfectly aligned and has the correct amount of eye relief. When aligned perfectly, carefully tighten the scope ring screws (one turn or less on each screw until all are snug) to hold the scope firmly in the desired position. If you tighten one screw more than another, the scope will be pulled out of line. Therefore, the main objective is to tighten all the screws evenly. The scope should now be mounted correctly.

To align the cross hairs vertically and horizontally, use B-Square's cross-hair square, shown in Figure 5-10. It accurately sets the scope's vertical reticle, or line, in position and can also be used to align front sight ramps in a vertical position. It is not necessary to remove the action and barrel from

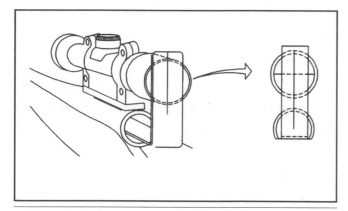

Figure 5-10: B-Square cross-hair square lets you square up a scope or front sight in seconds.

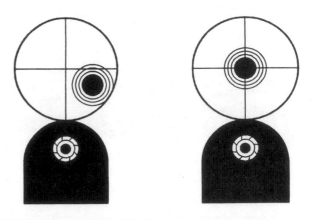

Figure 5-11: When bore-sighting a rifle, first sight through the bore of the rifle and line up your target. The target may appear as in the left-hand drawing. Then, adjust the scope until the target is centered in the cross hairs as shown in the right-hand drawing.

the gunstock when using the scope, since it fits into the receivers of most bolt-action centerfire rifles. Furthermore, it's made of optical clear plastic that will not harm the finish of the gun. The B-Square cross-hair square also squares the vertical index line with the bore.

BORE SIGHTING

Some shooters mount their scope, take the rifle to the range, and attempt to sight it in. If a large enough target is available, this will sometimes work, but usually at the expense of many rounds of ammunition. A better way is first to bore sight the rifle so the scope will be approximately lined up prior to shooting with live ammunition; the first one or two shots should be at a 12" x 12" target.

If you are sighting in a bolt-action rifle, you might want to do the bore sighting the traditional way. Place the rifle on a steady rest, such as sandbags or a Decker Shooting vise (described in Chapter 4), remove the bolt from the receiver and, looking down the bore from the receiver end, move the rifle around until the target, which should be placed at least 25 yards away, is centered in the bore. Without moving the rifle, glance through the scope, making reticle adjustments with the knobs on the scope until the reticle is centered on the target. Look through the bore again to make certain that

the rifle has not moved off target; if so, adjust it accordingly, as in Figure 5-11. If you are firing at a target beyond 25 yards, move the scope adjustments so the cross hairs appear about 1" below the center of the target. This will allow for bullet drop at the longer distance. Adjust the scope so the bore will be above the center of the target when the cross hairs are placed dead center.

Collimator

The optical bore sighter, or collimator, provides a fast, accurate way to sight in a rifle. It will give a lifetime of performance for a modest cost that is easily recovered in savings of ammunition alone.

If you use the optical bore sighter, clamp the bore sighter, or collimator, to a stud that is the correct size for the bore of the rifle being sighted in; this stud will align with the axis of the bore. *See* Figure 5-12 on the next page. The collimator is a simple optical device having an objective lens with a target grid. To the scope looking into it, the target is in focus as in Figure 5-13 on the next page. In use, this sighting grid is viewed in relation to the cross hairs of the scope, the windage and elevation adjustment of the scope mounts, and/or the internal fine adjust-

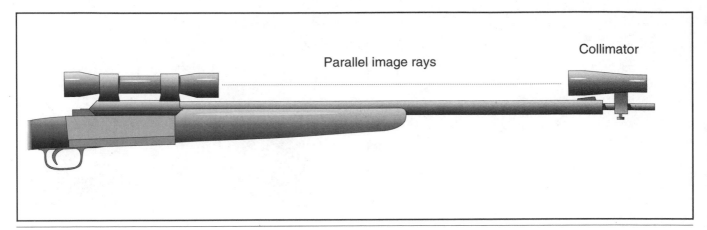

Figure 5-12: Collimator in position for presighting a telescopic sight.

ments that bring the sights into alignment with the bore of the firearm.

Once the bore sighter is in place, remove the adjustment turret caps on the scope. The elevation knob is marked UP on most scopes, with an arrow indicating the direction which will move the point of impact up on the target. The windage knob is marked R (right), with a similar arrow marking.

The increments marked on the graduated scale around the knobs indicate the amount of point-of-impact movement in minutes of angle (MOA). One MOA equals 1° of arc. Since point-of-impact change is measured in angles, the amount of actual movement on the target increases as the distance to

the target increases. For convenience, one MOA is set to equal 1" at 100 yards, although it is really 1.047 inches.

Using the scope adjustments described, align the scope reticle intersection with the center of the grid. The scope is now parallel to the axis of the bore. This adjustment will enable the first shot to be placed well within the edges of a normal-size target (for example, a 12" – 18" square). You are now ready to sight in the rifle.

SIGHTING IN

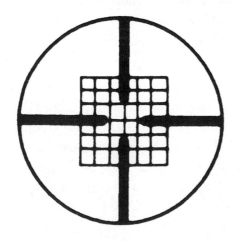

Figure 5-13: When sighting in with a bore scope, this is the image that can be seen when the collimator is in place.

When sighting in a rifle, it is best to fire on a target within your expected average range. Limited range facilities, however, may prevent you from sighting in the rifle at the desired distance. If you obtain some of the readily available ballistics charts, this handicap can easily be overcome, allowing you to sight in your rifle at a lesser range, yet having the point of impact be almost exactly as you want it for longer ranges.

For example, let's assume that you have a .270 Weatherby Magnum rifle and you are using 130-grain factory bullets. Let's further assume that you want the rifle sighted in at 200 yards, but your practice rifle range is only 100 yards. By referring to ballistics charts, you find that the midrange trajectory of the 130-grain bullet at 200 yards is 1.8 inches. Since midrange of 200 yards is 100 yards, if you sight the rifle in to shoot 1.8" high at 100 yards, you should be zeroed in exactly at 200 yards, or at least very close.

Take this example a bit further. Let's say we want the bullet to strike the target at 300 yards. Again referring to the ballistics charts ("Path of Bullet Above or Below Line of Sight"), we find that the 130-grain bullet, when zeroed in at 300 yards, will strike 2.8" high at 100 yards, so that it will be "dead on" at 300 yards.

When firing, scope adjustment knobs are moved until the rifle places the bullet where it is desired.

Sighting in should be done from a steady rest, such as a solid bench rest, tripod, or sandbags. You should also sight in your own rifle since no two people hold or fire a rifle exactly the same way.

The rifle should be zeroed in just prior to using it for target shooting or hunting.

To zero in the rifle, fire three shots from the desired range, using the center of the three-shot group as the hypothetical point of impact. Make the proper scope adjustments until the group is landing where you want it.

Humidity and other changes in the weather will change the bullet impact on the target. So, from time-to-time recheck your rifle to see if it is holding its original point of impact. If not, adjust it accordingly.

Top-Ejecting Rifles

Some rifles, like the older Winchester Model 94s, eject the fired cartridge through the top of the action, making it necessary to mount the scope in an offset position in order to allow the ejected cartridge to pass. One solution to this problem is to use a mount designed for top-ejecting rifles. Newer top-ejecting rifles require no drilling and tapping, and the mounts are installed similar to other types on which the receiver has been drilled and tapped

at the factory. When using these scopes, however, the shooter has to tilt his or her head slightly in order to view through the scope since it is offset from the line of the bore.

The offset scope mounts do have the advantage of being able to use either the scope or the open iron sights. This can be to the shooter's advantage if the scope should become fogged or if there isn't enough light to adequately use the scope.

The advantage of using either the scope or iron sights has further benefits on close shots in wooded areas. In fact, many hunters use see-through mounts on rifles that will adequately handle conventional scope mounts. These see-through mounts are designed with two sets of rings, with the scope mounted in the upper set. If the iron sights are to be used, the shooter aims through the lower set of rings, using the existing iron sights on the rifle. If the scope is to be used, the shooter aims through the scope.

Using offset or see-through scope mounts on rifles other than bolt-action rifles has been a problem for gunsmiths. Lever-action, slide-action, and semiautomatic rifles do not allow access to a clear view of the bore without a prism bore sighter. Neither could a collimator be viewed accurately with such sights until the offset spud, shown in Figure 5-14 was introduced. This collimator offset spud can be used with any bore sighter to allow bore sighting with any offset, side, see-through, or high-

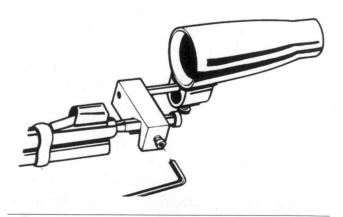

Figure 5-14: B-Square offset spud for aligning offset and similar types of scope mounts.

mounted scopes that are out of range of the conventional bore sighter. The offset spud fastens to any bore-sighter spud, and any bore sighter, or collimator, can be fastened to it.

DRILLING AND TAPPING FOR SCOPE MOUNTS

Most of the older rimfire and centerfire rifles, especially those designed for military use, were not supplied with drilled and tapped holes (or grooves) for mounting scope sights. Some of the older sporting rifles are well adapted to telescopic sights; but many of the military rifles and some sporting rifles require major alterations to enable a scope sight to be used satisfactorily. Mausers and Springfields, for example, require altering the bolts so they will miss, or pass by, the scope. The ears of the receiver sight on Enfield rifles must be milled or ground off to accommodate the scope mount. Other rifles may require that the scope be side-mounted, or offset, to allow functioning of the action and to eject the fired cartridge properly. Each problem will be dealt with separately.

Scope drilling jigs are used almost exclusively for drilling and tapping scope mounts. Many professionals make their own, although various types are available from gunsmith supply houses. By using these jigs, screw holes can be located and drilled in a fraction of the time it once took, so there is little reason for professional shops to use any other method. From time-to-time, however, a professional shop may get in a rifle for which no jig is readily available, and it would not pay to make a special jig for just one rifle.

The hobbyist might want to try mounting a scope, but doesn't want to go the expense of purchasing one of the scope jigs, which usually start out at around $100. It would be better to take it to a professional shop and have the job done for under $30. Still, there may be some who want to do the work themselves. For those who do, the following

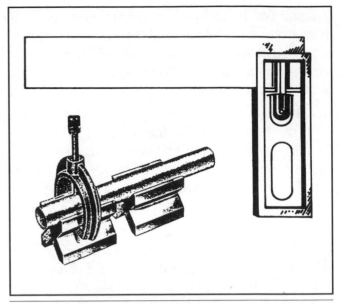

Figure 5-15: V-blocks and two tri-squares are essential for locating holes in receivers to be drilled. Sight jigs are better and quicker, but also more expensive.

describes the procedure of mounting a scope from scratch.

You will need a few tools and know how to use them before you should even begin to think about drilling and tapping a scope mount. These include an accurate level, V-blocks, and tri-squares. *See* Figure 5-15.

Obtain a scope base that is suited to the rifle you want to put it on. Manufacturers have bases for most rifles. If a factory base is not available, existing bases will have to be modified, or a new base will have to be made from scratch to fit the rifle precisely.

Clamp the sight base to the rifle in the exact mounting position. Use machinist's clamps for this operation. Be careful to ensure that this base is level, straight, and true before locating and spotting the correct position for the screw holes, which will have to be drilled and tapped.

To locate these holes accurately, some reference point must be found on the rifle to check the work as it progresses. The rifle must also be resting on a perfectly level surface, such as a piece of plate glass, or a smooth, level table or board.

Place the barrel and receiver on this level surface, resting the barrel in V-blocks, and then proceed to position the barrel and receiver absolutely vertical on this level surface. This is usually accomplished by taking some square surface on the receiver, and holding it parallel or at right angles to the surface plate by means of small steel tri-squares. This square surface on the receiver will vary with the make of rifle, but on a typical Mauser receiver, this flat surface is located on the underside of the receiver.

On most single-shot receivers the sides of the receiver are used and the squares are placed upright on the surface plate with the vertical arm brought up so the receiver can be trued against it. With some rifles and shotguns, it is best to try to align on two square surfaces, and if there is any difference divide it equally.

Once the barrel and receiver are exactly vertical with respect to the surface plate, they must be carefully kept in this position until the sight base is securely clamped in its correct position.

Now, carefully clamp the sight base in its approximate position on the rifle receiver, using a few machinist's clamps for holding. One way to accomplish this is to place a square up against either side of the barrel. With inside calipers, carefully measure from the square to the side of the base on each side to make sure that the base is in the absolute center of the barrel. *See* Figure 5-16. This should be done at both the front and rear end of the base. Then change the position of the squares to ascertain that the top surface of the base is absolutely level and parallel to the surface plate, as shown in Figure 5-17.

With the sight base absolutely correct, the clamps are then tightened so there is no danger of the base moving out of alignment. To ensure that this will not happen, it is a good idea to scribe a narrow line around the sides of the base so that any movement will be readily recognizable.

There are usually three or four screw holes in the base to hold the base to the receiver. Therefore, a

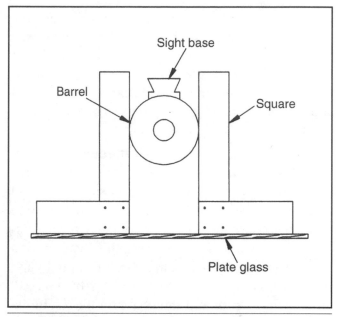

Figure 5-16: One way to align scope bases on a rifle barrel.

spot must be located exactly in the center of these screw holes to mark the drilling point.

To obtain the exact center by the method described, it is best to use the sight base itself as a guide. Use a drill that is the same size as the screw hole in the sight base. This is not the same as the

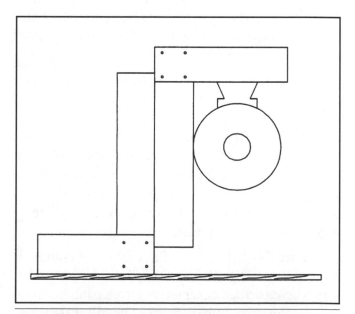

Figure 5-17: Check the sight base again by changing the position of the squares, this time trying the top of the base to make sure it is level and parallel to the surface plate.

size used for the hole that will be tapped. Since the sight base is firmly clamped to the receiver, the barrel and receiver may now be removed from the V-blocks, and the assembly clamped in a drill-press vise under the drill press, or you can leave the barrel and action where they are, and use a breast drill for the drilling.

Start the drill down straight through the hole; using the hole in the base mounts as a guide, drill a spot in the receiver that is at the exact center and correct for the receiver screw hole. At the same time, make sure the drill does not move the base(s) out of line. Mark all the holes in this manner for a two-piece mount; or just mark one front hole and one rear hole for a one-piece mount. Now you can remove the clamps and sight base for the rest of the drilling.

The most common size of a sight-base screw is a 6-48, requiring a No. 31 wire-gauge drill to drill the pilot hole prior to tapping. While a drill press is best to ensure proper straightness of the hole, a hand or breast drill will do for those who are careful. Before drilling, however, carefully examine the areas to be drilled to determine the depth of each hole. Obviously, you must not let the drill enter the bore. This mistake has been made by both professionals and amateurs, so be extremely cautious in the barrel area.

Most drilling will take place in the receiver area, and although this is not as critical as the barrel area, be careful not to drill too deeply or through areas that conflict with the functioning of the action. Go slowly and use a depth gauge to show how deep you are at any given time. You must drill deep enough to get a good bite on the screw, which is usually about three threads, or about $\frac{1}{8}$". If there is enough room, $\frac{3}{16}$" is better.

Figure 5-18 shows the three types of common taps: the taper, the plug, and the bottoming tap. For screw holes drilled completely through the receiver top, a conventional No. 2 taper tap will suffice for the entire tapping operation. For holes that go only partially through, a bottoming tap should be used,

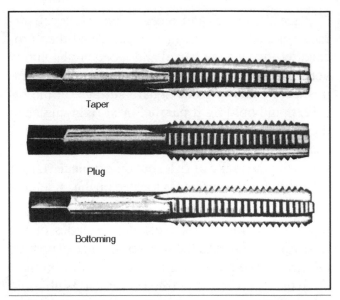

Figure 5-18: Three types of taps in common use: the taper, the plug, and the bottoming tap.

after starting the thread with the taper tap, to ensure cutting the threads squarely to the bottom of the hole. When all holes are correctly tapped, dip the screws in oil and screw the sight base onto the receiver.

CAUTION

When using the bottoming tap, it is quite easy to snap the tap off once it reaches bottom if too much force is applied. It is very difficult to get the broken tap out, so be extremely careful. When tightening the screws, use the proper screwdriver to avoid marring the screw heads.

With the base(s), in place, attach the scope rings and scope and inspect all items for correct alignment. If everything seems in order, remove the screws and bases, clean off all surplus oil, and apply Loctite solution to freeze the screws in place.

When mounting two-piece bases, they must be perfectly aligned with each other on top of the receiver. To obtain this result, many gunsmiths use a steel rule that is true and accurate. The rule is applied to the sides of the bases. Make sure it touches both bases equally for their entire length, showing them to be in line. Make any necessary adjustments to align them. Both bases should be fitted at the same time while the barrel and action are on the V-block on the surface plate. Spot the holes simultaneously.

Bore-sight and zero the rifle the same way as you would for mounting factory-tapped rifles.

Drilling Hardened Receivers

Many older military receivers have been case-hardened. With such receivers, you can dull several drill bits and not even begin to scratch the surface. Sometimes, you can take a Moto-Tool and grind the surface of the receiver exactly at the spots you intend to drill so the bit will penetrate the softer inner metal; but sometimes even this won't work. When a situation like this arises, the only solution is to spot-anneal the areas to be drilled. This is accomplished by heating the area and then letting it cool slowly. Be careful to soften only the spot where the screw holes will be drilled and not the entire receiver, otherwise the receiver might be weakened so that it will not withstand the strain of the breech pressure when fired.

To spot-anneal a receiver, first locate the screw holes and then clamp the sight base in place. Now, mark the location of each hole to be drilled. Remove the sight and use a Moto-Tool to polish the spots with an emery wheel to remove the finish and leave the spots bright and smooth. There will be small bright marks on the receiver at each location of the screw holes where they are to be drilled. The tip of a soldering iron can then be held to each of these polished spots until the bare metal turns a dark blue. Let the metal cool slowly. This will usually anneal, or soften, the receiver surface so the drill bit will enter without difficulty and not weaken the surrounding metal.

Some gunsmiths prefer to use a torch rather than a soldering iron because the heating is quicker. This will work, but extra precautions must be taken prior to heating. Drill holes through a piece of asbestos and then secure the sheet of asbestos around the receiver, aligning the holes in the asbestos with the polishing marks on the receiver. Now, wrap wet cloths all over the receiver and around the edges of the asbestos sheet so that the entire receiver is wrapped with the exception of the area to be spot-annealed. To anneal, use a torch whose flame blows into the holes of the asbestos so that the steel underneath becomes hot. Again, continue heating until the polished metal surfaces become a dark-blue color, then allow the receiver to cool slowly.

Once annealed, the holes are relocated, marked, spotted, drilled, and tapped. Just make sure that you allow sufficient time for the metal to cool slowly before starting the drilling and tapping operation.

You can skip this annealing operation by using a solid carbide drill. Brownells offers two sizes, a number 31 for 6-48 taps and a number 28 for 8-40 taps. They will drill through the hardest receivers, or can be used to "crack the skin" of casehardened receivers and a regular drill bit is used to finish the job.

There are two problems with the carbide drills, however. First, the solid carbide drills are easily broken. If kept clean they are less likely to bind and break. Second, if the inner steel is extremely hard, the taps are likely to break and getting them out can be quite difficult. But carbide drills are recommended to those who are capable of using good judgement and proper care. These drills should not be used on softer steels and should be used only after other drills have failed, or when the hardness of the steel is known.

Sight-Mounting Jigs

As mentioned previously, most professional gunsmiths use drill jigs to spot drill holes in receivers for mounting sights. The relatively high cost of these jigs is more than offset with only three or four drilling and tapping jobs.

B-Square Receiver Sight Jig: This non-marring, aluminum jig clamps to receiver bolt-lug grooves in bolt-action rifles for accurate positioning of the hardened steel drill guide-bushing. It eliminates the need for the time-consuming method of spotting holes, and is used for receiver sights and to align holes on a bore's centerline axis. The jig spaces holes to exactly match the sight. Use it on Springfields, Enfields, and Mausers.

B-Square Professional Drill Jig: This is the fastest device known for aligning, drilling, and tapping scope mount holes in the receivers of Springfields, Enfields, Mausers, Remington Model 30s, and similar bolt-action rifles.

To use, remove the bolt of the rifle and insert the drill jig. It automatically locates the holes in reference to the recoil shoulder and aligns and spaces the holes vertically on the centerline of the receiver. Holes are all drilled at one time. The hole spacing matches the mounts made by Weaver and Redfield.

Both of these jigs are recommended for professional gunsmiths who encounter a lot of scope work. The work involved is accomplished at least 10 times faster than setting up with squares and V-blocks as discussed previously.

For gunsmiths who do much sight work on firearms other than the bolt-action rifles described above, the Forster universal sight-mounting fixture, shown in Figure 5-19, is almost impossible to do without. It will handle all bolt-action, lever-action, slide-action, and semiautomatic rifles as long as the barrel can be laid in the V-blocks of the fixture.

The Forster fixture will locate the holes to a standard predetermined spacing built into the overarm, or to any spacing by sliding the overarm in either direction. "Walking" or "run out" of the drill is eliminated since the drill is guided through a hardened and ground drill bushing. Tapping is done through another bushing of the correct tap size, and eliminates cocking the tap — a major cause of tap breakage and sloppy screw holes. The sliding overarm has three holes with standard spacing of 0.500" and 0.860" between centers into which the interchangeable drill and tap guide-bushings fit. The

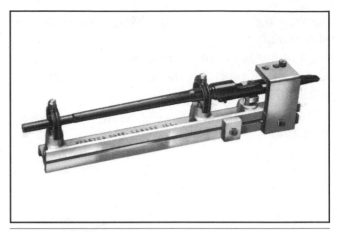

Figure 5-19: The Forster universal sight-mounting fixture is invaluable for shops that do extensive scope mounting.

overarm is keyed and slides in a T slot, keeping it in true alignment with the center of the gun barrel.

The main body of the fixture is cast aluminum. The two V-blocks are adjustable for height and are made of hardened steel accurately ground on the V as well as on the shaft. A fixture like this belongs in every professional shop.

To use, first remove the stock from the gun to be drilled and tapped. In most cases, only the forend needs to be removed on rifles with two-piece stocks, such as the Marlin 336 and Savage Model 99. The Remington 760 requires the removal of the slide and slide bolt, as well as the bolt mechanism. The trigger mechanism can usually be left in on most bolt-action rifles. Tubular magazine rifles must have the magazine removed before placing the barrel in the fixture for drilling. The barrel is then laid in the V-blocks, and the action over the end of the fixture with the clearance slot. Whenever possible, the barrel to be drilled should be positioned so that the action is close to the rear V-block, with the cylindrical or straight portion of the barrel supported by the V-block.

Slide the overarm in place over the portion of the action to be drilled and raise the rear V-block up to bring the action or receiver in contact with the correct size drill bushing. Next, measure the diameter of the barrel with a micrometer at the points of contact at the front and rear of the V-blocks. Since most barrels are tapered, it will be necessary to raise the front V-block. The amount is determined by subtracting the smaller diameter from the larger diameter, and then multiplying this value by 0.707. The resulting answer will be the height the front V-block must be raised above the rear V-block. This measuring can be done with a steel machinist's rule. If extreme accuracy is desired, use a feeler gauge between the top of the machined boss and the bottom of the V-block. Many gunsmiths use outside calipers for this operation.

Once the V-blocks are adjusted to their proper height, clamp the barrel lightly in the V-blocks, using the aluminum pads under the clamp screws to avoid marring the barrel. On bolt-action rifles, raise the flat-top support pad into firm contact with the flat bottom of the action. This squares up the action and acts as a support during the drilling operation. The clamp on top of the leveling overarm may be moved over any part of the action. Now tighten the clamps.

Some receivers will not have flat bottoms, but they still can be lined up by means of a square from the top of the overarm, or any other machined surface on the fixture. The rifle action can also be lined up by using a level; in this case, however, be sure the fixture itself is level before lining up the rifle.

One method used by many gunsmiths to locate mounts is to place the mount on the action or barrel in the desired position and mark the forward hole on the gun with a scriber or pencil. With the locator pin pointing down in the front hole of the overarm, slide it over the gun so the point lines up with the mark and lock it in place. Drill and tap this hole. Now, screw the mount onto the gun with one screw. Loosen the overarm and, with the tapered point of the locator pin, place the overarm over the second hole in the mount and lock it in place. Lock the spacer block against the overarm. The overarm then can be moved out of the way, the mount removed, and the overarm reset against the spacer block. The

second hole is then drilled and tapped. Other holes in the mount can be located and drilled in the same way. Do not drill the holes with the mount in place; this may prevent you from drilling the holes on the true center of the action.

When drilling for receiver sights, line up the barrel in the V-blocks in the usual way, but turn the action sideways and square it up using a small square laid on top of the overarm. Locate the first hole and proceed as already described. The same procedure is followed when mounting side mounts, but holds true only if all the holes are in line with the center of the rifle bore.

If the desired holes are not on the centerline of the barrel, the fixture can still be used to hold the gun squarely and steadily in the drill press. In this case, the overarm is not used.

When drilling and tapping for a front sight on a barrel, the position of the gun is reversed; that is, the muzzle end is placed at the notched end of the fixture. The V-blocks, in this case, are raised high enough so the drill bushings will contact the barrel. Allowance must be made for the taper in the barrel. It will be necessary to square up the gun with a level. Shotgun beads are mounted by following the same procedure.

When first using this fixture, go slowly and carefully, double-checking all measurements and your setup to make sure you are drilling the holes exactly where you want them. Also make sure that the V-blocks line up squarely by tightening the screws gently at first, so that the flat of the screw contacts the flat of the shaft squarely. A twisted V-block will throw you off due to the taper in the barrel, and especially so if the barrel is supported at a point where the taper is abrupt.

Extreme care must be exercised to prevent metal chips from getting between the finished surfaces of the overarm and the body of the fixture when the overarm is moved. This is equally true of the spacer block. If chips are allowed to lodge between the two finished surfaces, they will impair the inherent accuracy of the fixture. Brush away all chips with a small, dry brush before loosening the overarm and spacer block. A blast of compressed air will also do the job quickly. Do not use force when tightening the screws holding the overarm and spacer block. Doing so can damage the accuracy of the jig, and also result in inaccurate drilling.

Chapter 6
Trigger Adjustments and Repairs

Trigger pull is one of the many important factors involved in obtaining good small-arms accuracy. The adjustment of trigger pull is a job that many gunsmiths frequently encounter, and is one that the amateur can perform in the home gunshop.

Practically every rifle and handgun, as it comes from the factory, needs some adjustment of the trigger pull to meet the demands of the more serious shooters; good accuracy depends a great deal upon perfect control of the trigger. A trigger cannot be perfectly controlled if it drags, jumps, creeps, or varies in the amount of pull required.

Experience has taught us that the best trigger pull for all-around use requires a pressure on the trigger of from 2½ to 4 pounds to discharge the gun. Some shooters prefer a lighter pull, which can be dangerous except on a rifle especially designed for target and benchrest shooting. In my opinion, a clean, crisp trigger pull is more important than the amount of pressure required to pull it; that is, the trigger should not move the slightest, until it releases the firing pin or plunger. It should break suddenly, without any preliminary movement, somewhat like

the breaking of a thin glass rod. This is the type of trigger pull that the gunsmith should seek when any adjustments are made.

There are several types of triggers in use, all operating on a similar, but different principle. For example, triggers used on military rifles — such as the Krag, Springfield, Enfield, and Mauser — are always of the two-stage design, and are noted for "creep" and hard pull. Creep is the first stage of the trigger's travel, requiring a pull weight of from 1 to 3 pounds. The second stage releases the cocking piece and requires a separate 3 to 6 pounds of pull weight to do so.

The main reason for this two-stage trigger is for safety. Two-stage triggers are difficult to discharge from jolts or bumps, or from clumsy gun handling by raw recruits.

Bolt-action-rifle trigger mechanisms usually are controlled by the bearing surface smoothness of three interacting components: the cocking piece, trigger sear, and trigger. When the bolt of such a rifle is forced forward and shut, the cocking piece comes up hard against the sear, and the contact

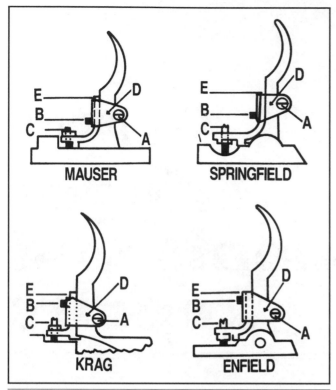

Figure 6-1: Military triggers, such as for the Mauser, Krag, Springfield, and Enfield, are of the two-stage design. All are shown here with the Miller trigger attachment to improve trigger pull.

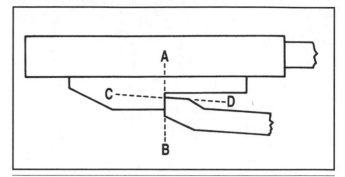

Figure 6-2: To lighten a two-stage trigger pull, first hone the surfaces on line A-B; then grind the sear to make the slide shorter on line C-D.

surfaces of the two must be large and strong enough to stand the wear, and to prevent the cocking piece from slipping and causing an accidental discharge as the breech is closed. The trigger is arranged to have two motions, each distinct from the other. During the first motion, the trigger moves to the rear quite easily on the application of about 1½ pounds of pressure. This is the "creep" mentioned previously. During this taking up of the slack or creep, the sear is lowered in its contact with the cocking piece until it rests against the nose of the cocking piece very slightly, like a conventional trigger sear resting in a hammer notch.

To lighten a two-stage trigger pull, and also to eliminate creep and drag, the first step is to polish the contact surfaces of the sear and cocking piece where they come in contact with each other. This is best done with honing stones, but do not take off too much metal at a time. Until you get several

hours of experience under your belt, this polishing should be done sparingly, trying the trigger for "feel" every few strokes of the stone. Do not attempt to change the angle too much at this stage. Simply polish the contact points so that they will slide evenly over each other without any grate.

The next step is to make this slide shorter, which is done by grinding the top of the sear. Again, go slowly and reassemble and try the parts frequently. You can always take off more metal, but it's hard to put it back on. See Figure 6-2. It is also necessary, in some cases, to lighten slightly the tension of the sear spring, which is usually a coil spring. To lighten, merely cut off one coil at a time until the right tension is felt. In some rare cases, this spring will be too light, and will have to be strengthened. To do so, use a pair of pliers and vise to stretch or lengthen the spring.

When any trigger repair is done, the entire trigger and safety mechanism must be tested several times to make certain that the rifle will not fire accidentally upon hitting the butt against the floor. Don't pound the rifle butt against a hard object; just a few light taps should do it. The gun should be unloaded. Never load a gun with live ammo while it is being repaired or tested.

Another type of military trigger utilizes two fulcrums (humps) at the top of the trigger. The forward hump is responsible for the first-stage creep, as it pivots against the underside of the receiver, creating a drag or creep. Its main purpose is to slow

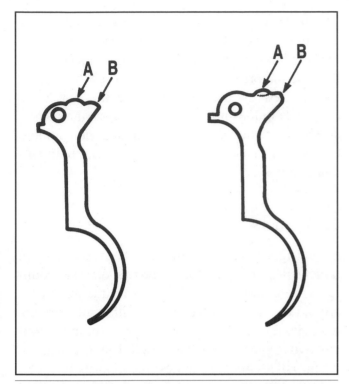

Figure 6-3: Two humps on military triggers, designated here as Hump A and Hump B, are responsible for the two-stage let-off. Creep may be eliminated by grinding off Hump A, and then slightly rounding Hump B. Use caution not to take off too much metal.

down the cocking piece letoff and let the shooter know that firing is just a hump away.

Creep on this type of trigger can be eliminated by grinding the forward hump off. In doing so, the trigger sear will rise slightly higher against the cocking piece sear, and provide a little more bearing surface. This will usually correct the problem of a rifle accidentally firing when the bolt is closed. Once the forward hump has been removed, the creep will disappear, but the trigger pull will be harder, since the bearing weight has been increased. *See* Figure 6-3.

This problem can be corrected by using a soft Arkansas stone and slightly rounding the rear hump. Again, this operation should be done gradually, with many trials, during the process. If too much metal is removed at this point, the rifle may fire on closing the bolt. With this slight alteration,

plus a final polishing of all bearing surfaces, the trigger should have a medium-light, crisp pull.

Adjusting Plain Triggers

All of us should be familiar with the plain trigger found on many shotguns and hammer rifles, such as the Winchester 94 and the Marlin 336. This type of trigger is either entirely loose in its guard, or is stationary therein. When squeezed, the trigger remains entirely stationary until it releases the hammer or firing pin. Then it gives way suddenly operating as it should — and the rifle is discharged. Many of these triggers come from the factory with a pull of up to eight pounds, which is entirely too much for any rifle. Some of these triggers also have a drag or creep, giving way slightly after a pound or two of pressure is applied. The perfect trigger squeeze is one that does not move at all until it releases the hammer or cocking piece.

To lighten and smooth up this type of trigger, you will need a set of Arkansas stones of different shapes, a sheet or two of fine emery paper and crocus cloth, and a small trigger scale to measure the weight of pull. Disassembly tools and a magnifying glass will also be needed.

A plain trigger is illustrated in Figure 6-4. It shows the trigger, the hammer, and the half-cock

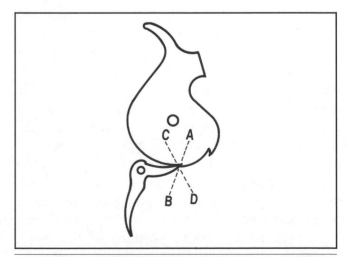

Figure 6-4: A plain trigger used on many hammer guns such as single-shot shotguns and lever-action rifles.

and full-cock notches of the latter. In this case, the trigger and sear are combined; in some guns, the trigger and sear consist of separate pieces.

First examine the surfaces of the sear and hammer notches to determine the angle at which they meet. If the pull is heavy, the mating surfaces probably will make contact, meaning that the sear, in order to release itself from the hammer notch, must act strongly against the tension of the hammer mainspring. This causes the heavy trigger pull. Also, the sear may be too deep in the notch, requiring much lifting before it disengages itself.

Remove the hammer and sear from the action and use the Arkansas stones to hone the two contact surfaces, so the angle of contact will be changed. During the honing, check the fit frequently to ensure that the mating surfaces fit exactly when reassembled. The honing must also be done straight; that is, honing no more on either side than in the middle, or vice versa.

Go very slowly and assemble the parts often to test the weight of the trigger pull on the trigger scale. Watch the scale as the pull is applied, and notice the maximum figure on the gauge just before the trigger gives way. As you get down to within a pound or so of the desired pull be extremely careful, as often only three or four more strokes of the honing stone will be all that is needed.

In most cases, this operation is all that is required to get a good trigger pull from this type of trigger mechanism, but in some cases the sear may take too deep a bite in the hammer notch. When this occurs, work only on the sear — not the hammer notch. If the hammer notches are not perfect, there is a good chance that, upon releasing the sear, the hammer will catch in the half-cock notch as it falls, preventing the gun from firing every time. One way to prevent the sear from entering into the notch too deeply is to use a small center punch to raise a small crater just in the rear of the notch. The sear will then strike against the raised portions of the metal around the crater, and will not settle down as deeply in the notch.

If the raised portions of the crater are too deep, the situation is easily corrected with a few strokes of the honing stone. This cratering will also eliminate the majority of trigger "creep," as this is usually caused by the sear entering the notch too deeply. If it does not, then it is because the mating surfaces of the sear and notch are not smooth enough; this can be corrected by honing both surfaces smooth.

Set Triggers

Set triggers have been used on both sporting and target rifles for a long time. The first ones I encountered were on the Mannlicher rifles manufactured around the turn of the century. Although there are many kinds of set triggers, the most common contain two triggers within the guard. The front trigger, when pulled alone, operates like a normal trigger; but when the rear trigger is pulled first (until it clicks) the front trigger is then set, and upon touching the front trigger with only an ounce or so of pressure, releases the hammer or cocking piece. This is truly a "hair trigger." Another type of set trigger contains only one trigger. When this is pulled rearward, ordinary pressure is required to release the hammer. However, when the trigger is first pushed forward until it clicks, this sets the rearward movement, which will release on light pressure.

Many of the muzzleloading rifles of the past century utilized a set trigger, and this practice has been carried over to the modern reproductions of these rifles.

Nearly all are adjustable by means of two adjusting screws, either in the lock or on the outside of the rifle near the triggers.

The mechanical action of all set triggers is similar, in that the action of setting compresses and locks back a strong lever or hammer; the sear of this hammer is attached to the front trigger and is very delicate. On touching the front trigger, this sear releases the hammer, or lever, which then flies up;

with a blow, it drives the true sear away from the true hammer or cocking piece, and this causes the discharge of the firearm.

Handgun Triggers

Early handgun triggers were nearly all similar to the plain trigger used on most shotguns and hammer-type rifles, and the instructions given for these also apply to the handgun triggers. This applies only to single-action revolvers, such as the Colt Peacemaker. Double-action revolvers — when used in the double-action mode — depend a great deal on the strength of the mainspring and its leverage on the hammer, as to the amount of trigger pull required.

Brownells Inc. offers several spring kits for various handguns, any one of which will greatly improve trigger pull and hammer slap. For example, its Bullseye Kit No. 2 is designed for the Colt MK III series revolvers. It consists of a new hammer and trigger spring, which are designed to lighten both the double- and single-action functions without any other work or adjustments having to be done to the revolver. Since the heavy double-action trigger pull on these revolvers is almost legendary in the industry, this modification kit will do wonders for the gun's trigger pull, by improving accuracy and eliminating those "squeeze-off" jerks.

Kits are also available for other models such as Ruger, Smith & Wesson, Browning, and Dan Wesson.

Some of the older handguns, especially double-action revolvers, had their trigger pull lightened by grinding the mainspring to make it thinner and easier to operate. However, this practice also made the mainspring weaker, and misfires were frequent. Other types of revolvers have a small screw on the front of the grip-frame near the bottom of the handle. This is a strain screw, used for applying tension to the mainspring. Some people have tried to lighten the trigger pull by loosening this screw, but trouble has almost always resulted from doing

Figure 6-5: It is good practice never to load a round in the chamber of any automatic pistol until you're ready to fire. This Beretta Model 20 is safer than the hammerless types of pistols, but it can still be accidentally discharged.

so. This screw needs to be tight to cause the mainspring to lie with the proper curve, otherwise the action of the revolver will be impaired.

Semiautomatic pistols, such as the Colt .45, Browning, Star, and Savage, can have their trigger pull improved, but care must be taken in this area when altering the trigger. If a very delicate trigger pull is obtained, a jar of the action may cause the hammer to follow the slide, resulting in an automatic-firing weapon which is both dangerous and illegal.

Trigger sears and hammers on automatic pistols are honed in a similar way as described for the firing mechanism on shotguns and exposed hammer rifles. But after the adjustment has been made, the pistol should be tested by cocking the hammer and, with the finger off the trigger and the grip safety compressed, drawing back the slide and allowing it to slam forward several times as violently as possible. If the hammer follows the slide, and fails to stay cocked, the pull is obviously too light.

A light pull can sometimes be corrected by increasing the tension on the sear spring by bending it, but in most cases, it is best to order a new hammer and sear and start over. For this reason, take great care in honing these parts of the automatic pistol to avoid making this mistake.

Automatic pistols with no hammer exposed usually have a sear which engages a shoulder or notch in the plunger, or firing pin. Most of these guns have a mean, dragging pull, which in some constructions cannot be overcome, owing to the leverage employed in the design. In other types, it can be somewhat improved by carefully honing the contact surfaces, so that they will slide evenly and smoothly.

Generally, the depth of contact or the angle of the surfaces should not be changed, because in many automatic pistols — especially those of foreign manufacture — only the safety prevents the trigger from being pulled. It will not prevent the sear from jarring out of engagement with the firing pin, in case the gun is dropped.

When these pistols are loaded they are always cocked, and to alter the sear or firing pin might render the pistol extremely dangerous to carry loaded. For this and other reasons, it is good practice *never to load a round into the chamber of an automatic pistol until the gun is ready to be fired.* Just slide the magazine into its place in the grip, but do not chamber a round. When firing is completed, unload the pistol, and make sure no round is in the chamber.

Triggers for Muzzleloaders

Those who have cleaned up and restored an old muzzleloader to firing condition can tell you that the trigger pull on these weapons leaves much to be desired. Even the modern reproduction models often have an extremely hard and rough trigger pull, so that good accuracy is virtually impossible. Nearly all of these trigger mechanisms, however, can be improved relatively easy — provided one is patient.

To smooth the trigger pull on one of these charcoal burners, disassemble the lock from the stock to gain access to the mechanism. Use only screwdrivers that the screw slots exactly; on the older models, this will probably be rusted, so use plenty of penetrating oil to help loosen the screws. Using a spring vise, such as the one discussed in Chapter 3 (*See* Figure 3-7), remove the mainspring from the lock. With the spring removed, cycle the action a number of times until you are thoroughly familiar with the interaction of each part.

You may now wish to make a sketch or take a closeup photo of the lock parts intact, to ensure that they can be reassembled correctly at a later date. At this time, carefully examine each part, trying to detect any burrs or scratch marks, indicating what areas should be honed for smoother action. Make note of your findings, and then disassemble the parts that need to be worked on. Old locks may require soaking in a penetrating oil or kerosene to allow the screws or pins to be removed without damage.

Once the lock has been disassembled, clean all debris from the back side of the lockplate, and then examine it carefully. Chances are you will find a rough surface, left just as it was when cast. First, use a No. 2 cut mill file to smooth the worst of this roughness down; then apply various grits of wet or dry abrasive paper for the final polishing. Next, polish the sides of the tumbler and sear. You will also want to check the space between the bridle and the lockplate to see if it is too wide. If it is, file the shoulder of the bridle at the point it makes contact with the lockplate, until just enough room remains for the tumbler to rotate without binding.

In many muzzleloading rifles, the sear is somewhat narrower than the tumbler, which causes excessive side play even when the bridle is snugged up tight on the tumbler. This problem can be corrected by inserting a thin washer next to the lock plate to shim the sear.

Now examine the hammer. Sometimes it will be canted and dragging against the lockplate, or there may be excessive play between the hammer and lockplate. In this case, file or peen the square hole to make the hammer stand parallel to the lockplate without too wide a gap.

Hone the sear and sear notch in the tumbler with a three-cornered Arkansas stone. In doing so, keep the sear surfaces square and parallel to retain full contact across their entire width. After establishing the correct sear angles, polish the sears as discussed previously. Be careful not to deepen the sear notch on the tumbler during the process. To remove any creep, drill a small hole in the tumbler, just below the sear notch and press-fit a small pin snugly into the drilled hole. Then file the pin back just enough to allow a safe sear engagement. Never file down the top of the sear notch on the tumbler to reduce creep. This will usually cause the sear to catch on the half-cock notch (the tumbler rotates in firing).

The strong springs in the older muzzleloaders were the chief cause of a heavy trigger pull. This was the main reason for set triggers. In most cases, it is best to replace the old spring with a new, lighter one. If the old spring is in good condition, however, it can be lightened considerably by using a small grinding wheel in one of the rotary tools, carefully grinding the spring lengthwise until the desired tension is attained. You don't want to grind the spring to the point where it might break or become so weak that misfires may result.

Once all of the surfaces have been polished, they will wear much longer if hardened by one of the

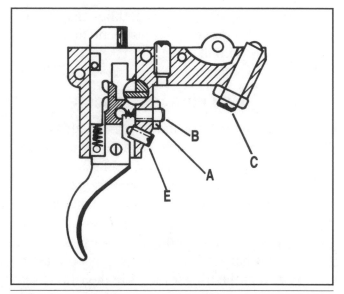

Figure 6-7: Diagram of Sako trigger assembly that is easy to adjust with only a jeweler's screwdriver.

methods described in Chapter 16. Use your notes and sketches to reassemble the lock. Test and adjust accordingly.

Adjusting Factory Rifle Triggers

Most of the better centerfire rifles manufactured today come with adjustable trigger mechanisms. The Sako trigger assembly, for example, is factory set for perfect sear engagement. The weight of pull and backlash can be adjusted simply and positively without too much trouble. Look at Figure 6-7 and then make the following adjustments:

1. To lessen weight of pull, loosen lock nut A and back off screw B until desired weight of trigger pull is reached. Then again tighten lock nut A.
2. To increase weight of pull, reverse procedure.
3. Backlash may be reduced by turning in screw E.

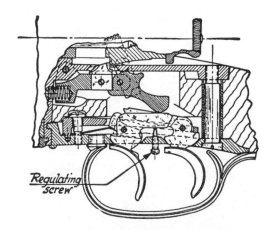

Figure 6-6: Typical double-set trigger. Some, however, have only a single trigger, the "set" being accomplished by pushing the trigger forward. In either case, the slightest rearward pressure releases the plunger, or firing pin.

In these adjustments, make sure that screw C and its lock nut are tight before going ahead.

Other makes of trigger assemblies may be adjusted in a similar way; adjustment instructions usually come with the gun.

Installing New Adjustable Triggers

Custom rifles built on military rifle actions, such as the Mauser, Springfield, and Enfield, usually have their trigger mechanisms replaced with adjustable, single-stage replacement triggers. Some of the more popular brands are those manufactured by Dayton-Traister, Timney, and N.O.C. In most cases, all require some fitting and the use of honing stones and small Swiss files. Also, wood must be removed from the trigger recess in the rifle stock.

Some rifles — especially those with set-trigger assemblies — also require modification of the trigger guard and floorplate. There are really no concrete instructions that can be given to install these trigger assemblies perfectly each time. It is simply a matter of trial and error; that is, the trigger is tried in position on the receiver, tight areas noted, these areas honed down, and then retried. Once the trigger assembly operates perfectly with the rifle's action, the barreled action and trigger assembly are lowered into the stock. If an obstacle or tight resistance is met, a portion of the wood should be removed in much the same way as when inletting a stock for a barreled action; that is, stock blackening should be used to mark the high spots.

The importance of a good, crisp trigger pull cannot be stressed too much if the best possible accuracy is desired. Trigger work is often thought of as a highly specialized field, suitable only for the professsional gunsmith. While this statement is partially true, there is no reason why a seasoned hobbyist cannot obtain good results, provided his work is done slowly, every move is carefully analyzed in advance, and care is taken to obtain the best possible workmanship.

It is suggested that the amateur's first project be done on an inexpensive military trigger mechanism, before attempting any such adjustment on a more valuable gun. When sufficient experience has been gained, the hobbyist can then progress to more complex trigger adjustments on more expensive guns, with the assurance that a good job will be the end result.

Chapter 7
Firearm Disassembly

Most firearms manufactured in the United States are designed and built to last several lifetimes, but all of them require a certain amount of maintenance, and are subject to certain common malfunctions that will occur from time to time. Worn and broken parts will need to be replaced, trigger assemblies will need adjusting, headspace will need correcting, worn finishes will be renewed, and other adjustments may be required. In every case, before a gun can be repaired, refinished, restocked, or thoroughly cleaned, the gun must first be disassembled — either partially or completely.

If you are unfamiliar with the takedown procedure, instructions and exploded views of many modern and obsolete handguns, rifles, and shotguns may be found in *Firearm Disassembly with Exploded Views*, Stoeger Publishing, 1995. Copies may be ordered directly from Stoeger Industries, 5 Mansard Court, Wayne, NJ 07470 for $19.95 each.

Some firearms may be disassembled in only one way; that is, one certain screw or pin comes out first—nothing else will do. In the case of some semiautomatic pistols, a certain lever is turned to an exact location for takedown. To do otherwise can hopelessly jam the gun, sometimes requiring the slide to be cut and discarded to correct the

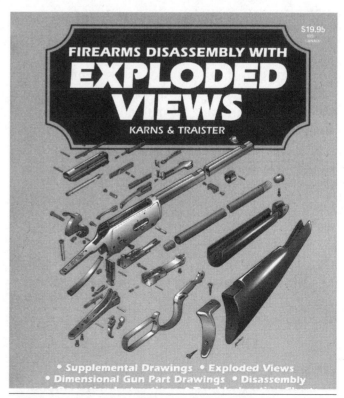

Figure 7-1: One of the latest reference manuals out that will help the home gunsmith correctly disassemble and reassemble dozens of popular firearms.

problem. Consequently, make sure you know the proper way and the correct order of disassembly of each arm before attempting the takedown.

Another common problem is not being able to reassemble a firearm correctly once it has been disassembled. Professional gunsmiths all over the country have had the experience of reassembling a customer's gun that was brought into the shop in paper bags and cigar boxes after the customer tried to "fix it up a bit" or thoroughly clean it. The customer probably had little trouble getting the gun apart, but putting it back together in the proper sequence was another matter. To compound the situation, the professional gunsmith often finds that some of the parts are missing (probably under the cushion of the owner's favorite chair); or screwheads have been badly marred, and some parts are damaged beyond repair due to use of improper tools and/or procedures during disassembly. In fact, many professional gunsmiths make a good living from correcting amateur's mistakes.

Supplemental drawings (Figure 7-2), exploded views (Figure 7-3), and extensive explanations of how guns are disassembled and assembled will help eliminate many of the problems. However, this material will not automatically make a professional gunsmith out of anyone. Some of the operations described should be done only by a professional who has the proper tools and experience. Also be aware that drawings and instructions are not available for every gun. There are so many different models that it would require many hundreds of volumes to adequately describe all of them. But the situation is not hopeless!

Visual Inspection

If you come across an unfamiliar firearm and no disassembly instructions are available, first of all examine every screw, pin, and lever very carefully. Then determine a logical sequence for removing these items.

Go slowly and make notes as you progress as to the order in which parts are removed. Supplement these notes with drawings or close-up photos. Use divided trays to keep the various groups (trigger

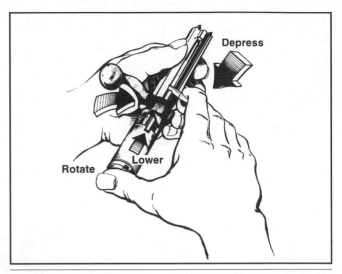

Figure 7-2: Supplemental drawing used with takedown instructions for the Winchester Model 43 bolt-action rifle. Note that a small screwdriver is used to depress the firing pin at the sear notch to releave the spring tension.

housing, breechblock, etc.) together and in the proper sequence. Following these procedures will not guarantee that you will get it right the first time, but it will go a long way towards that goal. However, if you are ever in doubt, always seek the help of a professional.

After disassembling a firearm and all parts have been given a thorough cleaning, carefully examine all internal parts for wear. This can save much disappointment later when you or a customer are using the gun in the field. Once all parts are thoroughly clean, examine the bore with a bore light. Is the barrel pitted? Should it be lapped, relined, or rebored? What is the general condition of the rifling or shotgun bore and other parts? Examine each smaller part under a magnifying glass. Look for hairline cracks, obvious breaks and excessive wear. If any are found, now is the time to replace or repair the part — not when you or your customer has lined up a big trophy animal and the gun fails.

The following is a summary of the initial inspection prior to actually performing any repair work:

- Look through the bore using a bore light to check for obstructions, bad pits,

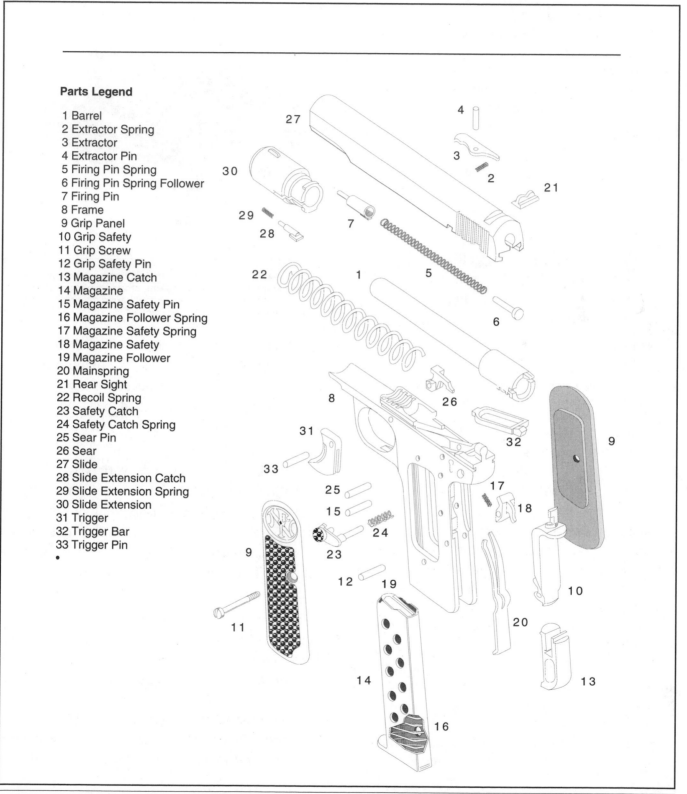

Parts Legend

1 Barrel
2 Extractor Spring
3 Extractor
4 Extractor Pin
5 Firing Pin Spring
6 Firing Pin Spring Follower
7 Firing Pin
8 Frame
9 Grip Panel
10 Grip Safety
11 Grip Screw
12 Grip Safety Pin
13 Magazine Catch
14 Magazine
15 Magazine Safety Pin
16 Magazine Follower Spring
17 Magazine Safety Spring
18 Magazine Safety
19 Magazine Follower
20 Mainspring
21 Rear Sight
22 Recoil Spring
23 Safety Catch
24 Safety Catch Spring
25 Sear Pin
26 Sear
27 Slide
28 Slide Extension Catch
29 Slide Extension Spring
30 Slide Extension
31 Trigger
32 Trigger Bar
33 Trigger Pin

Figure 7-3: Typical exploded view with parts list.

condition of rifling, excessive wear, or bulges. Examine the chamber for rough spots and for possible deformation of the extractor slots cut in the barrel. Also notice if there is any grime or debris that might prevent the gun from functioning properly.

- Check the firing-pin nose in the bolt for proper shape. If it's smooth, it may be worn, but it's not broken. A jagged or uneven surface indicates that the pin has been broken.

- Continue the visual inspection, checking all bearing surfaces for burrs and cracks, especially around the locking mechanism.

- Inspect the gunstock for cracks and loose-fitting areas where metal and wood join. While you're at it, check the swivels, sling, buttplate, etc.

- Finally, check the overall finish (wood and metal surfaces). You can then recommend touch-up work on the gun or a complete face lift.

Such an inspection of a gun will usually reveal any defects. However, if no immediate cause is determined, the weapon should be disassembled, thoroughly cleaned, then reinspected. Before disassembling, you might want to run a few dummy cartridges through the magazine and action to check the feed mechanism.

When disassembling a firearm with which you are not familiar, study the mechanism very carefully and make notes of the location of the parts. In some cases, close-up photos (Figure 7-4) of the action from several angles may be called for if a complicated mechanism is encountered and no in-

Figure 7-4: When there are no instructions or drawings available for an unfamiliar firearm, close-up photos of the action taken prior to disassembly will help ensure that the action will be reassembled correctly.

structions or exploded views are available. Then upon reassembling the gun, the photos may be referred to if there are any questions about where a certain part goes. Another good idea is to organize the parts in the order they are removed. Then, in most cases, install them in the reverse order.

If work is expected on a variety of firearms, invest in various reference books. First of all, get exploded drawings and disassembly/assembly instructions from all of the gun manufacturers. If you are a gunsmith or dealer with a Federal Firearms License (FFL), many of the manufacturers will send this information at no cost.

You'll want to purchase a copy of the *Encyclopedia of Modern Firearms,* from Brownells Inc.; *NRA Guidebook to Shoulder Arms; NRA Guidebook to Handguns;* and the *Gun Digest Book of Firearms Assembly/Disassembly* series by J.B. Wood, and as mentioned previously, *Firearms Disassembly with Exploded Views.* You will use these books daily if much gun work is encountered.

Chapter 8
Gunsmithing Handguns

The term *troubleshooting* as used in this book covers the investigation, analysis, and corrective action required to eliminate faults in the operation of firearms. Most troubles are simple and easily corrected; examples are misfeeding caused by dirty action parts, gummed up parts caused by excessive lubrication, and malfunctions caused by worn or broken parts.

Think before acting. Study the problem thoroughly, then ask yourself these questions:

- What were the warning signs preceding the trouble?

- What previous repair and maintenance work has been done?

- Has similar trouble occurred before?

- If the firearm still shoots, is it safe to continue shooting it before further testing?

The answers to these questions can usually be obtained by:

- Questioning the owner, if the firearm belongs to someone else.

- Taking time to think the problem through.

- Looking for additional symptoms.

- Consulting troubleshooting in the various publications mentioned in Chapter 7.

- Checking the simplest things first.

- Checking parts in the gun against the parts pictured in the exploded views or parts list available from manufacturers.

- Checking with gauges and calibrated instruments.

- Double-checking all conclusions before disassembling the gun or components.

The source of many problems can be traced not to one part alone but to the relationship of one part with another. For instance, improper feeding in a tubular-magazine may not be caused by a weak magazine spring but by a dented tube that prevents the spring from functioning properly. Too often, firearms are completely disassembled in the search for the cause of a complaint, destroying all evidence during disassembly. Check again to be certain an easy solution has not been overlooked.

After a mechanical failure has been corrected in any firearm, be sure to analyze what caused it so the same failure will not be repeated. Failure to extract a cartridge from the chamber may be corrected by replacing a broken extractor, but something caused it to break. Further investigation may reveal that a corroded chamber caused extremely hard extraction, which eventually broke it. A careful polishing of the chamber would prevent the extractor from breaking again in the near future.

TROUBLESHOOTING REVOLVERS

The revolver is perhaps the oldest form of repeating firearm. Wheellock ignition revolvers were in use as early as the 15th century, but the first true working revolver is generally credited to Samuel Colt.

Colt Handguns

The following information will apply directly to Colt revolvers with a design first used about 1898 and includes: Officers Model, Official Police, Police Positive Special, Police Positive, Detective Special, Bankers Special, New Service, Police Positive and Shooting Master, and the Model S. Of course, this information will also be valid, in part, to other Colt models, which should be readily apparent as you become more familiar with Colt designs.

Disassembly: Remove crane lock screw and crane lock. Press back on latch, push cylinder to the left and remove cylinder and crane assembly to the front. Remove grip stocks.

Remove sideplate screws and sideplate before removing latch and spring from sideplate. The mainspring may be removed by lifting the rear end from its seat and disengaging the long end from the hammer stirrup. Remove the hand.

Drive out the rebound lever pin to the right, and remove rebound lever. Remove trigger. Draw hammer to the rear and lift from the hammer pin. Remove safety lever and safety from its seat in frame. Remove latch bolt.

The cylinder may be further disassembled by first unscrewing the ratchet and ejector rod head from the ejector rod. Remove the crane bushing with special wrench from crane. Remove ejector rod and spring.

Function: As the hammer of these revolvers is pulled to the rear, the hammer engages the trigger, pulling it rearward at the same time; the hand attached to the trigger also rises during this operation. This hand, acting on the rebound lever, causes the rebound lever to release the "locked" cylinder. The hand further engages the ejector notches in the cylinder and causes the cylinder to rotate. The lever attached to the trigger pulls the safety from between the frame and hammer. The bolt is then released and allowed to engage the cylinder lock.

Malfunctions: The rebound lever and the cylinder bolt are subject to wear and will often have to be replaced after much use. New factory parts, when available, usually have to be hand fitted. Both new and used parts are also obtainable from gun part suppliers such the Gun Part Corp. in West Hurley, NY (see Appendix in this book for addresses). The latch and latch pin are also subject to wear.

Although rare, the crane and frame sometimes become bent. Broken mainsprings do occur occasionally.

Another common malfunction is during rapid double-action firing; the cylinder will "skip," which usually requires the installation of a new bolt spring.

Basic Tools for Colt Repairs: For more than just minor maintenance on Colt revolvers, the following tools are recommended:

- Ratchet wrench
- Crane bushing wrench mainspring clamp or long-nose pliers
- screwdriver
- Rawhide or plastic mallet
- Peening hammer
- Side-cutting pliers
- Assorted Swiss files
- Honing stone
- Bolt screw counterbore or drill
- Prick punch
- Drift punches
- $\frac{1}{8}$" brass drift punch
- Bolt spring pusher
- Fine emery cloth
- Headspace gauge
- Feeler gauge
- Firing pin protrusion gauge

Inspection and Repair: To check any of the Colt models listed previously, loosen the sideplate screws along with the crane and latch drop. Then use the headspace and feeler gauges to check the headspace. Check end-to-end cylinder play; check for loose barrel and barrel joint. Continue checking for worn or loose trigger and hammer pins; also for loose bolt or screw.

During some inspections you will find where the safety has been damaged or purposely filed; trigger sears will be worn or short; firing pin or hammer notch defective; strut out of position, or wrong shape or length; weak mainspring; worn rebound lever cam; bolt and rebound lever out of time; worn hand, or hand out of time.

DIMENSIONS & TOLERANCES	
Headspace	.060 – .065 inch
Trigger pull	3 – 4 lbs
Barrel joint	.002 – .004 inch
Firing-pin protrusion	.040 – .050 inch

Firing Pins: Measure firing-pin protrusion with a gauge by the same name (available from Brownells Inc). To use, with hammer fully forward, place the gauge over the protruding firing pin and against the revolver's recoil plate. Lock the gauge's plunger and lift from the firing pin. Use a micrometer to measure the overall length of the gauge; the difference between the original length (.5000 in.) and measured overall length of the body, plus plunger, is the amount of firing-pin protrusion. Correct protrusion should be between .040 to .050 inch.

Long firing pins may be filed shorter, but short firing pins should be replaced. In some cases, the firing pin may be built up by welding and rehardening, but this is not recommended standard practice.

Floating firing pins should not have too little or too much up-and-down travel so as not to damage the recoil plate. When the firing pin protrudes through the recoil plate, a small amount of "play" should be noted, but not too much. The back side of the firing pin may be filed to correct the up-and-down movement; file the top for higher travel, and the lower portion for lower travel as shown in Figure 8-1 on the next page.

When replacing a firing pin, the rivet hole in the hammer should be countersunk slightly and a new rivet used. Peen both ends of the rivet and then file them flush with the hammer surfaces.

Safety Levers: The safety lever should work freely at the hammer pin boss. The safety and

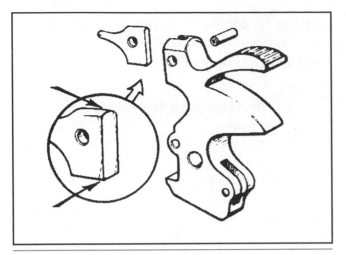

Figure 8-1: Areas to file firing pin to correct up-and-down movement.

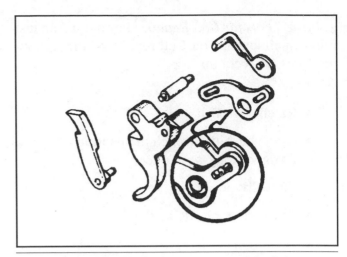

Figure 8-2: Safety and trigger pins must work freely in safety-lever slots.

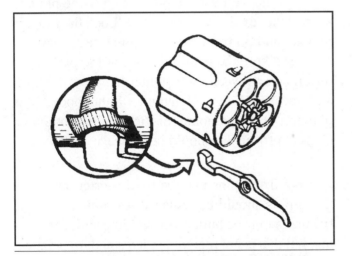

Figure 8-3: Top of bolt head should match contour of bolt leads.

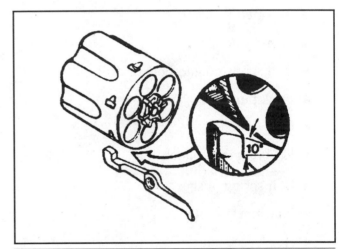

Figure 8-4: The bolt head should fit freely into the bolt cuts in the cylinder.

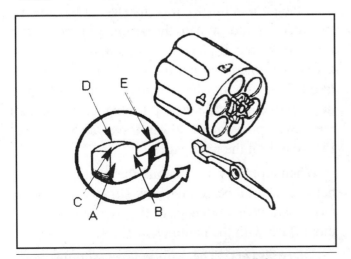

Figure 8-5: Points to file bolt head for correct fitting.

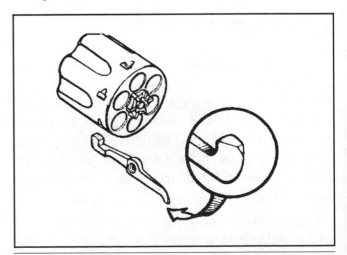

Figure 8-6: Proper shape of bolt tang when shaping.

trigger pins must work freely in the safety-lever slots as shown in Figure 8-2.

Bolt: The top of the bolt head should match the contour of the bolt leads in the cylinder as shown in Figure 8-3. The head of the bolt should be beveled approximately 10 degrees to match the contour of the cylinder with the lower side of the head contact riding point as shown in Figure 8-4. The bolt head should fit freely into the bolt cuts in the cylinder, but with as little tolerance as possible. Bolts that are worn loose should be replaced.

Figure 8-5 shows the correct places to file the bolt for correct fitting to the cuts in the cylinder. The bolt screw must be seated tightly to the frame with a slight drag noted when moving the bolt without the bolt spring in place. If the bolt is too light, file the underside of the bolt — at the screw hole — until the bolt works properly. If the bolt is too loose, the bolt screw hole in the frame should be counterbored slightly until a slight drag is noted. Either a $^3/_{16}$-inch or $^1/_4$-inch drill may be used for this operation.

When the bolt cut in the frame is worn, allowing side play in the bolt head, the cut should be peened to eliminate any excessive play. The bolt spring should be strong enough for the bolt to snap sharply into the cylinder bolt cuts, and yet allow the top of the bolt head to travel so it is at least flush with the bolt cut in the frame. The bolt head should enter the cylinder bolt cuts approximately $^1/_{32}$ inch.

If the bolt head is short, the cylinder will not lock. Correct this fit by filing the bolt at point E as shown in Figure 8-5. If the bolt head is too long, it will not allow the bolt to clear the cylinder when cocking. Correct this by filing the bolt as shown in Figures 8-3 and 8-4. Finally, polish the bolt head with fine emery cloth. *See* Figure 8-6 for the proper shape of the bolt tang.

Mainspring: A weak mainspring will cause misfires and poor rebound in any revolver action. A stiff spring increases single- and double-action

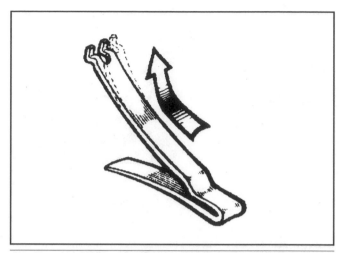

Figure 8-7: A weak or stiff mainspring can ususally be corrected by slightly bending it near the center of its arm.

pull, so a properly "tuned" mainspring has a lot to do with good accuracy.

In some cases, a weak mainspring may be corrected by bending the upper arm at its center. A stiff mainspring may be loosened up some by inserting a small drift pin between the spring arms and then cocking the revolver. See Figure 8-7.

Strut: The strut should be long, and away from the hammer as much as possible without interfering with the sear end of the trigger during its exit from the hammer notch. The strut should be sharp and smooth — never blunt. To achieve this condition, file the strut as shown in Figure 8-8.

If the strut is out too far it may be bent at the center. Set or peen holes in the hammer to prevent

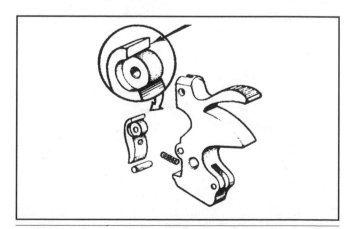

Figure 8-8: The strut should be sharp and smooth, but never blunt.

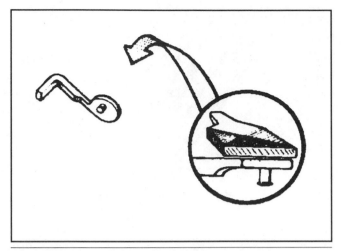

Figure 8-9: Never reduce the dimensions of the part that blocks the hammer. The remaining portion, however, can be filed for proper fit.

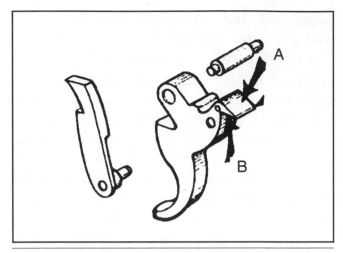

Figure 8-10: The points on the sear that will determine the weight and feel of the trigger pull.

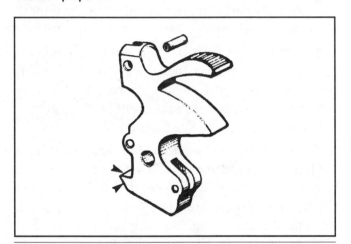

Figure 8-11: Reducing the depth of the hammer notch with a honing stone at the points indicated lightens the trigger pull.

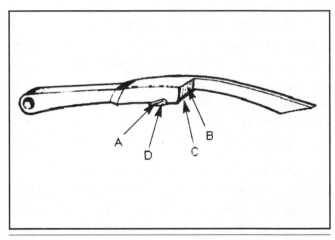

Figure 8-12: The filing or honing points on the rebound lever.

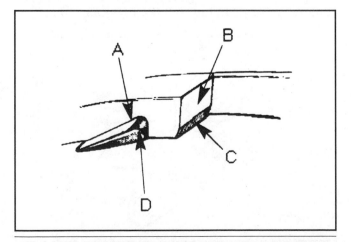

Figure 8-13: The triangular-shaped notch in the rebound lever should be smooth and slightly rounded at its outer edge.

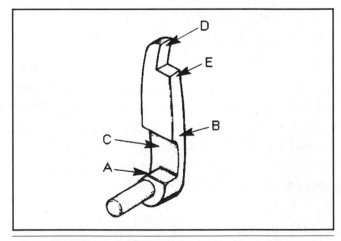

Figure 8-14: Points for filing on the hand.

the pin from coming out. Note that a short strut will cause the hammer to fall before the cylinder has indexed with the barrel when using double action; this will also cause a light hammer blow — both resulting in misfires.

Safety: The revolver's safety should work freely in its safety cut without excess play. To remove excessive play, slightly bend ball of the safety. This may also be filed somewhat when it is tight, but never reduce the dimensions of that part of the safety bar that blocks the hammer; this could be dangerous. See Figure 8-9.

Hammer and Trigger Pins: Both of these pins are drive-fit pins and should be replaced when loose. Drift out pins with a brass drift punch and hammer. In an emergency situation, temporary repairs may be made by reversing the pins.

Trigger and Hammer: The proper angle and thickness of the sear end of the trigger determines the "feel" and weight of the single-action trigger pull. See Figure 8-10.

A blunt trigger sear will cause creep, whereas too sharp an angle will cause poor cocking action and a heavy trigger pull. When the pull is too light, the sear end may be thinned by filing on the underside of the sear as shown at point "B" in Figure 8-10. When the pull is too heavy, reduce the depth of the hammer notch by honing as shown in Figure 8-11. In either case, always polish both the top and underside of the sear with fine emery to maintain a smooth cocking action.

If the hammer can be pushed off with the thumb when the revolver is in the cocked position, the trigger is obviously too light and very dangerous. The pull for most revolvers should be between 3 and 4 pounds, and the sear, along with the hammer notch, play the most important role in determining the weight of trigger pull.

An excessive amount of play between the back of the hammer and the revolver frame indicates that the sear end of the trigger is too short and needs replacing. When this condition exists, the revolver cannot be timed correctly. When any of the above operations are performed, the indexing of the cylinder must be checked to ensure proper functioning.

Rebound Lever: The cam of the rebound lever determines proper lifting and dropping action of the bolt. The lever must return to its position low enough to enable it to pick up the bolt tang. See "A" in Figure 8-12. The cam may be lowered by bending the rebound lever at the center, filing the front flat lever part of the rebound, or by filing the underside of the front angle. There should be no tolerance between the cam and bolt tang, otherwise the bolt will not clear the cylinder.

In all cases, the bolt should respond immediately when the hammer or trigger are moved. Any tolerance can be removed by bending the rebound lever up at its center, but this may cause the safety to catch under the hammer when it is rebounding. If so, replacement of the lever is in order.

The top point of the cam should be straight and slightly rounded, as shown at point "A" in Figure 8-13. The triangular-shaped notch should be smooth and rounded at the outer edge (point "D").

The bolt tang should not drop lower than $\frac{1}{3}$ the narrow part of the bolt lead in the cylinder, otherwise in rapid fire the bolt will not drop in time to lock the cylinder. To drop the bolt earlier, shorten the cam by filing the front triangular-shaped notch. If the bolt drops too early, the rebound lever should be replaced.

Sometimes the trigger will not clear the strut when rebounding. This condition may be corrected by filing the front flat of the lever ("C" in Figure 8-13) as long as the safety will clear the hammer. When the safety catches on the hammer, the front flat is too short, requiring that the rebound lever be replaced.

To test for a "bouncing hammer," bring the hammer to full cock, then push forward on the hammer with the thumb. If the hammer bounces in the frame, file the corner of the front flat at point

"C" as shown in Figure 8-13 until any bounce is relieved.

Hand: Spring tension of the hand is determined by the rebound lever fit on the cam of the hand. When no tension is noted, file the rear angle of the cam to increase the angle. *See* Figure 8-14. If, during operation, the hand misses the ratchet on the cylinder, file the front center portion of the hand (point "B") to let hand protrude farther. Furthermore, the hand must be free in the frame and as close to the frame as possible. To obtain this condition, the hand may be bent at its center.

When the cylinder does not rotate far enough to index properly, the hand is probably too short. Stretch the hand by peening with the chisel end of a cross-peen hammer at point "C." When the lower portion of the hand is too long, the cylinder will index before the trigger engages in the hammer notch. The indexing should be made uniform by filing the particular ratchet lug.

When the bolt head does not clear the cylinder, and the bolt and rebound lever are adjusted correctly, the top finger of the hand may be filed slightly to delay rotation of the cylinder. If the top finger is too short, the cylinder will bind between chambers. If this condition exists only when the gun is loaded — and you are sure that headspace is correct — the top or bottom finger lever may be interfering with the cartridge casings. Use one "dummy" or empty cartridge case to check the position of the chamber when the bind occurs. The front of the top finger may have to be filed back or the top front edges rounded; that is, point "D" in the illustration. Should the bottom finger be at fault, reduce the depth at point "E" on the bottom finger.

Latch: The latch pin should work freely in the frame. Weak latch springs should be replaced and the spring hole in the sideplate can be reamed if the spring fits too tightly. Any excess side play in the latch can be removed by peening the underside of the latch cut in the sideplate. Repair any up-and-down looseness by peening the latch guide ribs down in the direction of the latch. See "A" in Figure

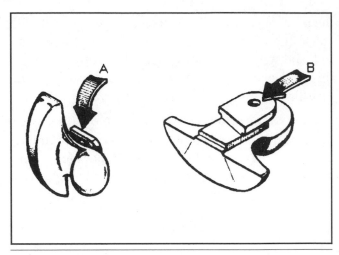

Figure 8-15: Points to correct latch problems by either (A) peening or (B) filing.

8-15. Should the latch bind, it may help to file the underside of the latch at point "B" in Figure 8-15.

Crane: A latch that works freely, but does not lock properly when the cylinder is closed, is an indication that the crane is either loose or sprung. This condition can usually be corrected by slightly bending the crane. To determine the direction to bend the crane, press in, up or down on the cylinder until the latch drops in place; bend the crane accordingly.

With the cylinder closed and the latch in place, an excessive amount of play between the front of the crane and frame is an indication that the cylinder and crane must be sprung outward. To correct this condition, open the crane fully and then tap sharply, outward from the frame, with a rawhide or plastic mallet until the play between the crane and frame is corrected, but still allows the latch to drop. *See* Figure 8-16.

When the cylinder has to be sprung inward, place an empty cartridge case between the frame and crane; then tap the cylinder inward towards the frame as shown in Figure 8-17.

If the condition dictates that the cylinder must go up, first open the crane fully; then use the wooden handle of a mallet to tap the cylinder from the right

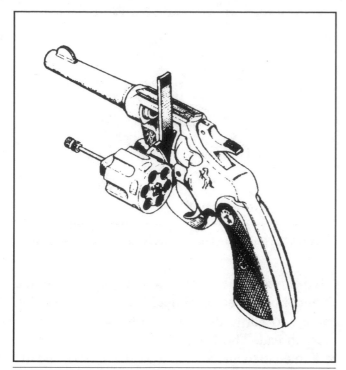

Figure 8-16: Method of correcting a crane that is sprung outward.

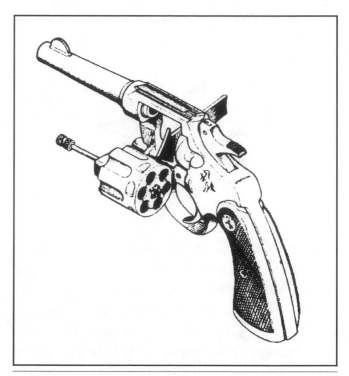

Figure 8-18: Method used to spring a cylinder upward.

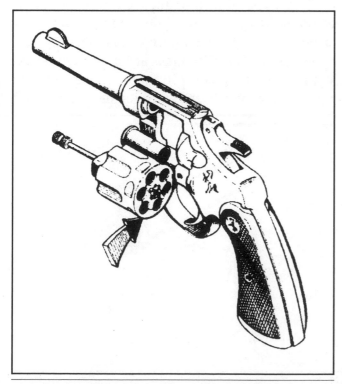

Figure 8-17: Method of springing a cylinder inward.

side (use the cylinder opening in the frame as access to the cylinder). *See* Figure 8-18.

Cylinders that must be sprung downward require the removal of the crane from the frame. Place the cylinder on a work bench, with the crane directly above the cylinder; then tap the crane downward towards the cylinder with a rawhide or plastic mallet.

Cylinder, Ratchet and Ejector Rod: Headspace for Colt Official Police revolvers should be between .060 and .065 inch. Headspace must be checked with the cylinder pressed forward. Tight headspace may be corrected by reducing the length of the cylinder collar as shown in Figure 8-19 on the next page. Conversely, excessive headspace may be corrected by stretching the cylinder collar. However, many times on the older models, after this headspace correction has been made, there will be excessive end-to-end play in the cylinder. If this condition occurs, the ratchet must be replaced. Because of this, the headspace should always be corrected before fitting a new ratchet. If the new

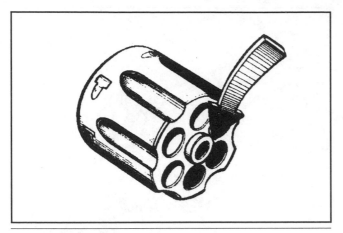

Figure 8-19: Headspace can be corrected by changing the length of the collar.

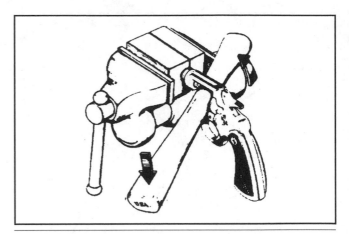

Figure 8-20: Equipment needed for removing revolver barrels.

ratchet offers problems, such as difficulty in closing the cylinder, file the ratchet evenly until the cylinder closes freely with no end play. It is sometimes recommended to peen-punch the ratchet and end of the ejector rod slightly to keep them from coming loose.

The end of the ejector spring should be crimped so as not to jump the collar of the ejector rod. The ejector rod sometimes becomes bent during operation and also during repair jobs; if so, merely remove it and straighten.

Barrel: The barrel joint between the breech and front of the cylinder should be spaced between .002 to .008 inch. The barrel should have a moderate throat at the breech. If the throat is too small the revolver may "spit lead," shaving off a portion of each bullet as it is fired. On the other hand, if the throat is too large, the bullets may "keyhole" upon firing.

Most revolver barrels can be removed by making a set of wooden blocks as shown in Figure 8-20, which are used to secure the barrel tightly in a vise. Powdered rosin is used on the barrel to keep it from turning when pressure is applied to the frame. With the barrel tightly secured, and the crane and cylinder removed, insert a wooden member through the cylinder opening in the frame and twist frame counterclockwise to remove; clockwise to tighten.

To correct a loose barrel or open barrel joint, the shoulder of the barrel should be turned on a lathe, enough to allow the barrel to be screwed in one more thread. The barrel, of course, must then be re-jointed to form the proper gap between it and the cylinder.

During an emergency situation, a loose barrel may be corrected by removing the barrel from the frame; then peening down the shoulder of the barrel before refitting as shown in Figure 8-21. If care is taken, a relatively even peen can be obtained just by using a ballpeen hammer and a wooden block. With the barrel removed from the frame, hold the barrel by the muzzle end and with the threaded end

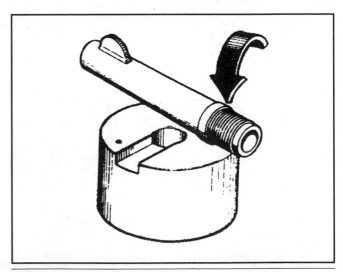

Figure 8-21: Loose barrels can be temporarily corrected by peening down the barrel shoulder.

resting on the wood block, lightly peen the shoulder of the barrel as you slowly revolve it on the block.

An even simpler method is to use a tubing cutter with the round cutting blade replaced by a roller bearing. With the barrel secured in a padded vise, rotate the tool on the barrel shoulders, tightening down the pressure screw on the tool after each complete revolution. Apply only slight pressure with each revolution, otherwise the tool may be damaged.

Smith & Wesson Revolvers

Smith & Wesson revolvers that were manufactured within the last 50 years or so all function approximately in the same way. As the hammer is pulled to the rear it cams the trigger back against the compressed rebound lever spring, and at the same time the cylinder bolt is disengaged from the cylinder notch. The hand attached to the trigger is pushed upward, rotating the cylinder. When the hammer is approximately halfway back, the cylinder bolt is disengaged by the trigger; the force of the cylinder bolt spring then forces the cylinder bolt against the cylinder. When the cylinder chamber is in line with the barrel, the cylinder bolt engages in the cylinder notch, locking the cylinder in place for firing. The sear on the trigger engages the hammer, holding it in its cocked position — ready for firing.

When the trigger is released by being pulled or squeezed, the hammer and trigger are disengaged, allowing the hammer to fall upon the firing pin. As the trigger is released, force of the compressed rebound lever spring forces the rebound lever forward. A lug on the rebound lever engages the hammer, camming the hammer back enough to withdraw the firing pin, and at the same time, forces the trigger to return to its normal position.

Ejector Rod: One of the most common problems found in some of the older Smith & Wesson revolvers is loosening of the ejector rod head during firing. When this head is loose, the ejector rod is lengthened, which causes the cylinder to bind,

sometimes to the extent that the cylinder cannot be rotated or opened.

To correct this problem, use a pair of soft-jawed pliers to screw in the ejector rod (right-hand thread on early models; left-hand thread on later models) until it is short enough to swing out the cylinder; then tighten further to prevent it from working loose again.

All later model S&W revolvers (with a dash number after the model number) are supposed to have a left-hand thread that will prevent this malfunction.

Stop Catches: When the stop catches, the hammer cannot be pulled back in either single- or double-action operation. When this malfunction occurs, many times the point and bevel of the stop have been filed too much — causing the stop to come back into the notch it just came out of, before the hand has a chance to move it to the next cylinder notch. If this happens, install a new stop. The problem can also be caused by an oversize ball which will stick in the cylinder notches. *See* Figure 8-22.

Overhaul: If there is no overhaul, the handgun cannot be cocked in single-action operation. A bent

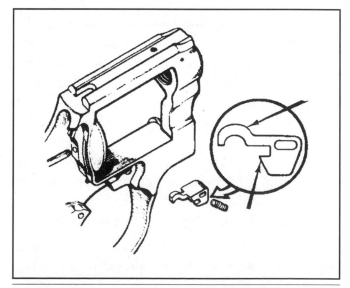

Figure 8-22: Points on S&W revolver cylinder stop that can cause it to catch.

spur is one possibility that will cause this problem, especially if the gun has been dropped. Also, look for tape or other foreign matter on the spur; perhaps the trigger stop may not be in its correct position.

Push-off: To check for push-off, cock the gun in the single-action position, making certain that the sideplate is in place. Place thumb in back of hammer and then with a normal amount of pressure, push the hammer forward. If the hammer disengages from its cocking notch, you have what is called *push off*.

Push-off may be caused by a chipped or broken cocking notch on the hammer, a broken bevel on the trigger, or a point of the bevel not being sharp enough.

It is recommended that no work be done on the hammer. In repairing, all adjustments should be made to the trigger.

Creep: Creep is checked only in the single-action position. This condition will not give a crisp fall-off when the trigger is pulled. There will be a little jump off the bevel in the cocking notch, which is sometimes caused by a rough cocking notch or a rough bevel. To repair, try stoning the bevel the same as for a push-off.

Hammer Block: The hammer block of S&W revolvers is a safety feature in addition to the rebound and hammer seat. If the revolver operates better without the hammer block in place, check to see if the hammer block is damaged. It may be bent or burred. Rough edges will also cause problems. Also check to see if the top of the rebound or hammer seat is too low. This will cause the hammer to move too far forward and close the opening for the flag or the hammer block. If the hammer seat is too low on rebound, replace with a new rebound.

Rough Cylinder Opening: When the cylinder opens or closes hard, one or more of the following may be the reason:

- Loose rod.
- Short or longer center pin on knurled end of rod.
- Yoke out of line.
- Sticky center pin.
- Tight yoke screw.
- Bent or crooked rod.
- Locking bolt may be too big and sticking in rod.
- Short bolt — dirt may be behind bolt in front of the front leg or on the frame.
- Check for long hand.
- Cylinder hits on closing.
- Leaded breech.
- Check for end shake on cylinder and yoke.

Stubs: This is a sear problem. Stubs are only found during double-action operation. This situation is generally caused by too much play between the sear and bevel of the trigger, causing the cam of the trigger to hit the bottom of the cocking notch. This problem can be repaired by installing a new sear, either regular or long. A long sear may have to be cut so the trigger bevel will return in and under the sear. Letting the sear out too much may cause stubs.

Rough Double-Action Operation: Items to look for when this malfunction occurs are:

- Check for cylinder cramp.
- Loose or bent rod.
- Locking bolt top fitted too tightly.
- Yoke out of line.
- Not enough space between barrel and cylinder.
- Leading around breech.

- Check to see if all pins are down and in place.

- Make sure hand is free.

- Make sure there is no sticky hammer nose.

- Check hammer boss along with trigger boss.

Sear click: Sear click involves the sear and only happens during double-action operation. If the sear has a click or jump in it, this may be caused by an improper angle at the end of the sear. This can be caused also by the sear not being let out enough.

During repair, try to change the angle at the sear bevel or let the sear out by filing the seat as shown in Figure 8-23.

Stop Problems: When a revolver stop sticks, look for the following:

- Stop sticks in notch of cylinder.

- Stop sticks inside frame.

- Stop travels too far below frame.

- Point of stop is too long which causes it to travel below the frame.

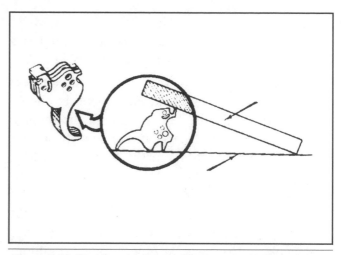

Figure 8-24: Stop bevel points to file to correct stop recovery.

When the stop doesn't recover, the hook of the trigger is not getting back into the slot of the stop. It will feel like a "stubber" or stop catch problem.

To repair a long stop, file the bevel and point of the stop as shown in Figure 8-24.

Loose Rod: This will always cause the cylinder to open hard. First try tightening the rod with the fingers. If this does not help, push the thumbpiece forward to push the locking bolt out. Then take pliers and grasp the locking bolt and pull it toward the muzzle. Now tap the cylinder lightly on the bench. If this also fails to open the cylinder, try pulling back on the hammer until the stop is out of the cylinder notch. At this point, take a piece of paper and slip it between the cylinder and stop. This will allow the cylinder to be turned while holding onto the rod. After the rod has been tightened, always check it for rod "run-out."

Rod run-out is a bent rod and can cause rough extraction. This problem will also cause rough opening and closing of the cylinder. After the rod has been straightened, always check the yoke alignment with the yoke liner.

Rough Extractor: Check to see if the extractor pins are missing. If lost, replace by fitting through top of the extractor. Also check internal parts of the cylinder.

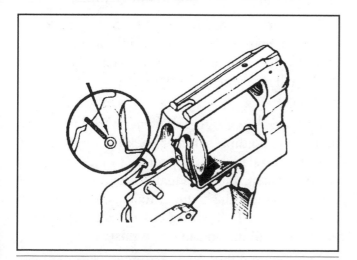

Figure 8-23: Filing the sear bevel to correct sear click.

Rough Center Pin: This condition could be caused by rod run-out, the rod or its knurled end crushed, or a weak or missing center pin spring.

Cylinder Hits on Closing: This condition pertains to the cylinder and yoke end-shake. To check, hold the barrel in the left hand with the muzzle facing down. Take the rod in the right hand and close the cylinder until it hits the "ear" of the frame with the center pin. Turn the cylinder and look to see if there is an opening or a space between the barrel and the cylinder. At this point, the gun should be checked out for end-shake on the cylinder and on the yoke. Also check the breech for lead buildup.

Rough Hammer: Check for sticky hammer nose. Also make sure that the sear pins are flush in position. Check for old or new hammer stud.

Hammer Hits Bolt: This condition may cause the cylinder not to open. It is usually caused by the tail of the hammer hitting the rear leg of the bolt. Check by pushing the thumbpiece forward to see if it clears the hammer tail.

To correct a rough hammer, file the top of the hammer seat as shown in Figure 8-25. Too much filing, however, can cause too little space for the hammer block. If too much is filed, a new rebound will have to be installed.

Loose or Binding Hammer: If the hammer is found to be very loose, the cause could be over-

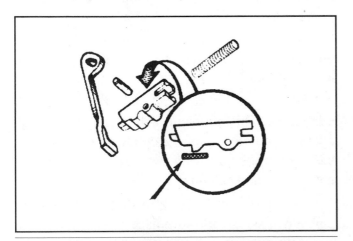

Figure 8-25: Filing the top of the hammer seat can often correct a rough hammer problem.

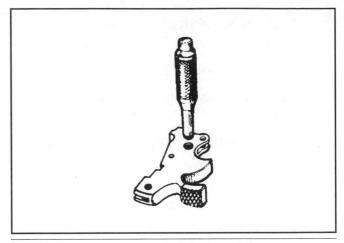

Figure 8-26: Swaging tool used to correct a binding hammer in S&W revolvers.

grinding on the hammer. In this case, a new hammer must be installed. If the stud hole is too big from wear, swage the hammer stud hole with a swaging tool (Figure 8-26), but never over-swage. This could make the hammer bind. Use a tapered reamer to open the hole to correct size.

Hammer Hits Rebound: This problem may cause misfires. To check this condition, pull trigger back while holding hammer forward; there should be a little play or wink between the front of the rebound and the back of the hammer. If no wink is found, the hammer could hit the front of the rebound, which in turn would hinder the hammer nose from coming through the frame to hit the primer.

To repair, file the front of the hammer seat as shown in Figure 8-27. After filing, always brake corner with a file and Arkansas stone. Too much wink will prevent the safety feature to operate correctly.

Hammer Hits Trigger: To check for this condition, while holding hammer back (in single-action operation), release the trigger from the hammer's cocking notch, then gradually move the hammer forward to see if the hammer foot is hitting the cam of the trigger. If this happens, it can impede the trigger return, which can cause misfires.

The hammer hitting the trigger is sometimes caused by the trigger stop on combat S&W models.

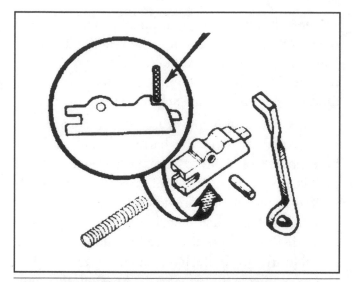

Figure 8-27: File the front part of the hammer seat to correct a hammer hitting the rebound slide.

The same two parts involved in a stubber are involved in the hammer hitting trigger malfunction. Light stoning on the trigger cam will help (see Figure 8-28), but never stone the hammer. This condition can also be caused by the hammer not cocking fully.

Hammer Nose Hits: If the hammer nose is bent, this can cause the hammer to hit off center of the firing pin hole — causing damage to the frame. Bend nose back to its normal position.

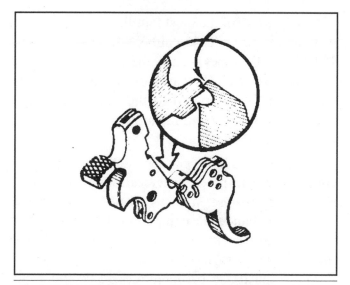

Figure 8-28: Light stoning on the cam of the trigger usually helps prevent the hammer from hitting the trigger.

Knuckles (end of spring hits under hammer): This condition is caused when the strain screw has been loosened or filed too much; alternating the mainspring will also cause this condition, and is first noticed in double-action firing when misfires occur.

Check by holding trigger back, and then move hammer all the way back; notice if hammer has a rough feeling.

To repair, replace the strain screw or mainspring. Tightening of the strain screw may help.

Poor Recovery: After a revolver has been fired, it may have a poor trigger recovery. This could be caused by the rebound spring being cut off too much. Also, check to see if the hammer block has room to return in front of the hammer and frame. This problem could be caused by too much filing of the hammer seat, located on the rebound. If so, replace with a new rebound. Also check for recover points on the stop, trigger hook, rebound friction points, and the sear. Polishing any recover points will help. However, never cut more than two coils off of any rebound spring.

For better double action operation, hone the cylinder hook located on the trigger.

Bolt Locks Hammer: Check this condition with the gun closed. Push thumbpiece forward, and observe whether it returns to its original position upon releasing thumb pressure. Repeat this check on all chambers. If it does not return on all six, check to see if the rod is running out. Perhaps a sticky locking bolt is the cause, or the yoke may be out of line.

Stop Doesn't Hold: Using normal pressure, try to lift cylinder off the ball of the stop; it should not lift off for correct functioning. Sometimes this condition exists only on one cylinder notch. To correct, file the top of the stop as shown in Figure 8-29 on the next page.

Hand Sticks: Spin cylinder and see if gun "sings." The hand could be sticking in the hand slot, or the hand may be disengaged from the torsion

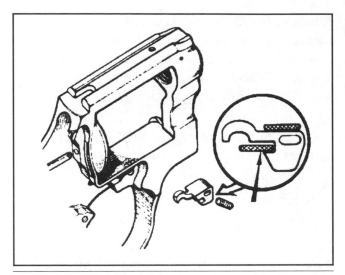

Figure 8-29: Filing the top of the revolver stop can correct a nonholding stop.

spring. Also check for buildup of lead, carbon, or other foreign material in the hand slot in the frame.

Long Hand: This condition will cause the cylinder to close hard. Check to see if throat of hand is up above the face of the frame. If so, file the hand throat until it is flush with the frame. However, be careful not to file the hand too much; a short hand will not pick up the cylinder to turn it.

Shaving Lead: When the revolver shaves lead, check for a loose cylinder stop, a loose locking bolt, the space between the barrel and cylinder, and for any lead buildup in the cone. Also make sure the yoke is aligned.

SEMIAUTOMATIC PISTOLS

Semiautomatic pistols are divided into two types based on the method used to operate the action. The types that use low-powered rimfire and centerfire cartridges usually utilize a blowback system; that is, the pistol does not use a locking mechanism to hold the breechblock in place. Instead, the weight of the breechblock and the power of the recoil spring keep the breech in place while the pistol is being fired.

The slide on an automatic pistol can extend over the barrel, as in the case of the .45- and .32-caliber Colt, or the slide can extend toward the rear of the receiver with the barrel remaining stationary, as in the Colt Woodsman and similar rimfire pistols.

Other semiautomatic pistols that incorporate a slide extending over the barrel operate off of a breechblock or delayed blowback system. These pistols are the more powerful ones, such as the .45 Colt that uses centerfire ammunition. With this system, the barrel and breech travel rearward for a short distance while they are attached; then they separate after the bullet has cleared the muzzle. The slide completes its trip to the rear of the gun, allowing the spent casing to be ejected and, as the slide returns, it picks up a new cartridge. When the breech contacts the barrel, they lock together and the pistol is ready to fire again.

Other types of semiautomatic pistols include the short recoil design, or a combination of short recoil and blowback systems. These pistols operate and complete all functions of firing in the same way as automatic rifles. After chambering the first round manually, all that is required of the shooter from then on is trigger pressure. The gun completes all the other functions automatically.

Possibly two of the most familiar semiautomatic pistols are the Colt .45-caliber Models 1911 and 1911A1 — the types used by the U.S. armed forces for over 50 years. It was only recently that our Government decided to drop the Colt for a design introduced by a foreign manufacturer, chambered for the 9mm Parabellum!

The Model 1911 is very dependable in operation and almost jam-proof in its various refined versions. Furthermore, it bows to no other for the accuracy demanded by competitive target shooters. The secret of accuracy in the Colt .45 semiautomatic pistol is in the bushing, or barrel sleeve, through which the barrel moves back and forth when firing, returning the barrel to the same position after each shot.

The Colt Model 1911 is a short-recoil design and, after firing, the barrel and receiver travel to the rear together for about $\frac{3}{8}$ inch, then the barrel unlocks from the rest of the recoiling mechanism and the action is opened. The barrel, which is attached to the receiver by means of a small, oval-shaped pivoting link, is arrested in its rearward travel down and away from the slide as the slide proceeds to the rear. Once the barrel stops, the slide — in its rearward movement — extracts the fired case from the chamber and then the case is expelled from the gun by an ejector mounted at the top left rear of the frame.

When the slide is in its most rearward position, the hammer is cocked and the disconnector is depressed. This slide position also allows the magazine spring to force a new cartridge up in line with the breech so that the slide — on its forward movement — strips this cartridge from the magazine and feeds it into the chamber. In its forward movement, the slide also engages the barrel and moves it forward and upward, pivoting on the oval link attached to the frame. The barrel is then cammed so that two ribs, cut at right angles to the axis of the barrel, engage recesses milled in the top of the slide, locking the action. The gun is again ready for firing.

Troubleshooting Pistols

Malfunctions such as jams and failure to feed, extract or eject are some of the problems that will be encountered in semiautomatic pistols. Use the same tools mentioned earlier in this chapter.

In many cases, a good cleaning is all that will be required to put an ailing semiautomatic pistol back into shooting condition, although other problems — requiring more time — may also be encountered.

Failure to Feed: When a semiautomatic pistol fails to feed, the first step is to clean and polish the chamber with a brass brush, as a dirty or badly fouled chamber is the primary cause of jams and hang-ups in semiautomatic pistols.

If feeding problems persist after the chamber is polished, check the magazine for dents, weak springs, etc. Should the magazine be found defective, replace it with a new one if at all possible. Straightening a magazine or removing dents can be very time-consuming, and may cost more than a new magazine. However, you might want to try honing the inside of the feed lips. Oftentimes, these lips become burred and cause jamming; smoothing them will often solve the problem. Of course, a broken spring should be obvious and should be replaced. If the spring is bent or rusted, it also should be replaced.

Still no luck? Then examine the feed ramp; a badly fouled or burred feed ramp may be causing the trouble. Use a wire brush saturated with bore cleaner to scrub the ramp and free it from all fouling. Then use a piece of crocus cloth wrapped around a small wooden dowel to polish the ramp bright. A moto-tool with a polishing head is ideal for this, but do not change the contour of the ramp when polishing with power tools. If the ramp is badly burred, an Arkansas stone (round) or a half-round file should be used to remove the burrs before polishing. Burrs in the chamber will also cause problems, but these should have been removed during chamber polishing.

Failure to Extract: The most common reason for extraction problems in a smallbore pistol (.22 rimfire) of blowback design is a dirty chamber. Cleaning it will solve the problem. However, in centerfire pistols — like the Model 1911 Colt — a weak extractor is almost always the reason for poor extraction. To test an extractor, place an empty case under the extractor claw so that the case is flush against the bolt face. Move the slide back and forth along the frame — not closed, but just an inch or so each way. If the shell case falls out or if it can be easily jiggled out, the gun has a weak extractor and should be replaced.

Failure to Eject: An ejector for Browning-type pistols has sharp edges to function properly. Grip the head on the cartridge case securely. Anything less will result in poor ejection, with hang-ups an almost certainty. If, upon examination, the shoulders or edges of the ejector look rounded or contain burrs, use a small flat file and restore the ejector to its proper shape.

Failure to Fire: Headspace problems and grime on the face of the pistol bolts are two sure ways to cause a semiautomatic pistol to misfire. A broken or burred firing pin, or a broken, bent, rusted or dirty firing-pin spring, can also cause misfires. Disassemble the firing-pin mechanism and thoroughly clean all parts prior to inspecting them for wear or damage. The firing pin and firing-pin spring may then be examined under a magnifying glass if necessary. Worn or damaged parts should be replaced if possible.

On .22-caliber blowback actions, dirt may prevent the bolt from closing completely on the cartridge. Then when the hammer falls, the cartridge is pushed forward and away from the pin, resulting in a misfire. Most problems can be solved by field stripping the pistol, and then giving it a thorough cleaning. If field stripping fails to solve the problem, look for burrs on the slide rails.

Chapter 9
Gunsmithing Rifles

The most common problems with faulty rifles are:

- Failure to fire
- Failure to extract
- Failure to eject
- Failure to feed

On rare occasions, the gun may fire upon closing the bolt. All rifles are also subject to leading, and most inexpensive .22 rimfire rifles have creepy, heavy triggers that sometimes need work.

Failure to Fire: When a gun won't fire, examine the cartridge that was chambered when the trigger was pulled. If the cartridge shows no mark on the rim or primer, then the cause is most likely a broken firing pin — especially if you hear a distinct snap of the striker when the trigger is pulled. On the other hand, if the cartridge has a slight indentation or you don't hear a definite snap when the trigger is pulled, the problem is caused by a broken or weak firing-pin spring, or dirt or other foreign matter in the firing-pin channel.

In either case, the bolt should be disassembled and the mechanism inspected. This procedure is best approached with an exploded view of the bolt and detailed disassembly instructions.

Once the bolt is disassembled and you find that the firing pin is broken, a factory replacement is always best. However, if the gun is obsolete and parts are not readily available, you may have to repair the old one. A new pin can be made from flat stock and welded on, but it must be heat hardened or it will wear and break quickly.

If you have the time, entire firing pins can be made in the shop from drill rod and/or flat stock. Use the old pin as a guide and check the dimensions frequently. A firing pin that is too long may fire the gun upon closing the bolt, and one that is too short will result in misfires.

If the firing pin is not broken, the second most common cause of misfires is a weak or broken firing-pin spring. Sometimes part of a spring may have been broken and the owner may have stretched it enough to make it function. However, this stretched tension won't last. The only sure solution is to replace the spring. When you get a new spring from the factory, it's going to be longer than the replaced one because it takes a while to set. Before long, though, the new spring will feel like the old one except that it will work.

If neither the firing pin nor the firing-pin spring is damaged or weak, the most logical remaining cause is debris inside of the bolt. Of course, in sub-freezing temperatures a small amount of grease inside the bolt can congeal and gum up the entire works. Only a light coat of thin gun oil should be used in moderately cold climes, and in sub-zero temperatures the gun should be completely free of any oil or grease; remove it with AWA 1,1,1, or a similar degreaser.

To clean grease and debris from the bolt assembly under normal conditions, obtain a container large enough to hold the parts and a good cleaning/degreaser solution. The ratio should be about four parts water to one part cleaning solution. The dirtiest parts, if left to soak in this solution for 15 or 20 minutes, will come out clean and ready to dry, oil, and assemble. You can help the process by scrubbing the parts with a toothbrush after they have soaked for about 10 minutes.

Remember that a thorough cleaning of a firearm will often correct many malfunctions without any further work. Grease, and the assorted debris it attracts, can gum up any action to the point that it functions poorly. This is especially true of semi-automatic guns. Make it a habit to clean every firearm thoroughly before troubleshooting malfunctions or making repairs. Even if the trouble is due to worn, broken or damaged parts, their cleanliness will help you spot the trouble more quickly.

Failure to Extract: An extractor withdraws fired cases from the chamber and, in the case of magazine rifles, guides each live round of ammunition into the chamber as it is stripped from the magazine. Worn, broken, and missing extractors are common problems with older rifles. When one of these problems is encountered, however, installing a new extractor may not always solve the problem — for long. For example, .22 rifle chambers may become extensively corroded by frequently firing .22 Shorts in a gun chambered for the .22 Long Rifle cartridge. *See* Figure 9-1. Then when .22 Long Rifle cartridges are fired, the longer cases swell into the eroded area, making extraction difficult. Extractors are under a great deal of strain in normal circumstances. When this additional strain is encountered, the extractor wears quickly, slipping over the case rim when the bolt is withdrawn. A new extractor will help for a while, but the problem will reoccur in due time.

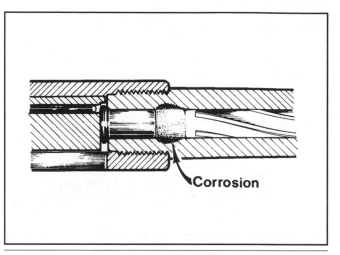

Figure 9-1: Twenty-two caliber rifle chambers may become extensively corroded by the frequent firing of .22 Shorts in a rifle chambered for the .22 Long Rifle.

The worn extractor can be due to a dirty bore, and a thorough cleaning along with a new extractor will normally solve the problem. If the extractor isn't worn too badly, the angle of the hook can sometimes be corrected by light honing.

When extraction is a problem, first check the chamber of the weapon (after cleaning) and look for tool marks and pits. If either are present, smooth the chamber as best as possible using a very fine emery cloth, and then polish with crocus cloth. A hardwood dowel turned to the approximate shape of the chamber, and of a diameter so that one thickness of abrasive paper wrapped around the rod will fit snugly into the chamber, should be used for the polishing. Just be sure not to enlarge the chamber so much that it will be oversized for the cartridges.

Now try some new cases for extraction. If the problem has not been corrected with the polishing, a new extractor will have to be installed or the old one honed to the proper angle to make it serviceable. Also check the extractor spring; this obviously can cause problems, too. Replace the spring if worn or broken.

Failure To Eject: The ejector flips the cartridge from the extractor's grip at the proper instant. Therefore, both the extractor and the ejector work as a team, and a problem with one could cause a problem with the other. For example, the extractor could be worn or damaged, preventing the ejector from working. A loose extractor can prevent the ejector from throwing the spent cartridge away from the gun.

When an ejection problem is encountered, first check for dirt and foreign matter, which could be blocking it and preventing it from functioning properly. A broken or worn ejector should be easily recognized and must be replaced. If you can't find anything wrong with either the extractor or the ejector, and the gun still doesn't eject properly, check the pin holding the ejector in the bolt. It may be bent or burred, thus preventing the ejector from moving freely.

Inoperative Safeties: Safeties on .22-caliber single-shot bolt-action rifles vary considerably. The Winchester Model 69, for example, uses the cocking piece as a safety. In other words, the bolt does not cock on opening or closing, but must be cocked by pulling back on the cocking piece until the trigger sear engages and holds in a cocked position until the trigger is pulled. Other rifles must be cocked in a similar manner, but also have a rotary safety screw. Some cock upon closing the bolt and have either a safety screw on the bolt or a button safety along the side of the action.

The Mossberg Model 320K has a safety that goes on automatically when the action is opened and won't fire until the action is locked and the safety is in the OFF position. Some of the early .22s utilized a simple slide-type safety that, when on, blocked the trigger with a thin piece of flat metal as shown in Figure 9-2. However, some of these models fired with the safety on if enough pressure was exerted to the trigger. Some of them would go off quite easily and were certainly not safe in that condition.

In most cases, it's best to order a new safety assembly from the manufacturer. When this is impossible (obsolete weapons), new safeties can be made or available safeties can be modified. Once

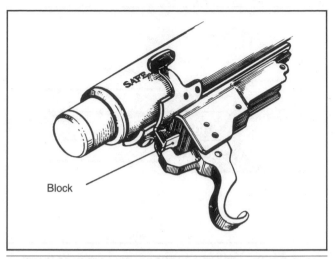

Figure 9-2: Typical .22 rifle safety mechanism.

the principle of a safety is understood for a particular weapon, repairing it should not be difficult. In all cases, the safety either prevents the trigger from being pulled or prevents the firing pin from moving forward. The former method is used the most on .22s.

Trigger Repairs: Since many single-shot bolt-action .22-caliber rifles are designed to be built as inexpensively as possible (except for a few high-grade target rifles), most have creepy, heavy triggers powered by a spring arrangement that more properly belongs in a toy cap gun. These trigger assemblies use an inverted L-shaped protrusion on the trigger, which acts as a sear. This protrusion bears against a notch or sear in the firing pin or striker. When the trigger is squeezed back against the spring pressure, the L-shaped extension disengages from the firing-pin notch, permitting the mainspring to drive the firing pin forward to discharge the gun.

All types of springs are found in trigger mechanisms for the various .22 rifles, and all can break after much use. Most can be replaced from packaged spring assortments sold by gunsmiths' supply houses. Helical and similar springs can be made from music wire spring stock. Common sizes run from .020 to .045 inch. Flat springs can be made from flat spring stock, but they will have to be

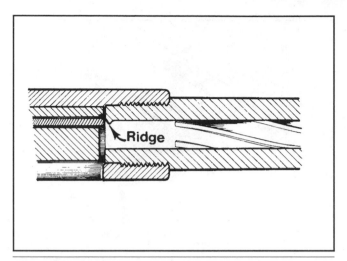

Figure 9-3: Dry-firing any .22 rifle can cause damage to the chamber.

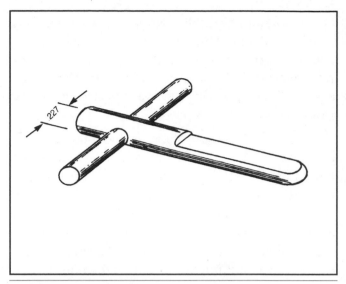

Figure 9-4: Ironing tool for .22 rimfire chambers.

annealed and retempered. However, when only one or two springs are necessary, order a replacement from the manufacturer.

It is difficult to lighten the trigger pulls on many .22 rifles because of the stiff springs that must be used to provide positive cocking. Improvements can be made, however, by honing all contact points smooth, then polishing. The springs on some of these guns can be lightened slightly, which in turn will lighten the trigger pull. Proceed in this direction with caution and have a replacement spring on hand in case you err.

Burred Chambers: Dry-firing any .22 rifle can break the firing pin or also force a ridge of metal into the chamber as shown in Figure 9-3. This ridge can cause feeding and extraction problems. Since the bolt may not close completely, headspace may be a problem leading to non-ignition or a ruptured case.

If care is used, a small bastard file may be used to remove the burr, but file only the ridge and don't touch any other portion of the chamber.

A safer way to remove the burr is to make a .22-caliber ironing tool (Figure 9-4). To use it, slide the tool into the chamber, using only moderate force, and rotate it. The flat blade side pushes the

extruded metal back into position without any loss of chamber surface or change in dimensions.

Damaged Muzzles: Occasionally you will run across a rifle that doesn't shoot accurately even though the rifling appears to be in excellent condition and the action and related mechanism are tight and functioning properly. Chances are, rifling at the crown of the muzzle has become burred due to some sharp object striking it. Use a magnifying glass when inspecting.

The best solution to burred muzzles is to recrown the barrel, cutting the barrel back about $\frac{1}{8}$ inch. If a lathe is available, this is your best bet. Chuck the barrel in the lathe headstock and use a dial indicator or other gauge to make sure the barrel runs "true." Then, using a barrel-crowning lathe bit, take careful cuts until the proper degree of crown is cut.

The crowning problem may also be solved by using a muzzle-crowning ball in either a hand or electric drill. For badly damaged muzzles, a rotary file may be used first to start the crown cut, and then a brass ball for lapping and finishing. Coarse and fine muzzle crowning rotary files are available in diameters of $\frac{3}{8}$, $\frac{1}{2}$ and $\frac{5}{8}$ inch. The muzzle crowning brass balls are available in $\frac{7}{16}$ inch, $\frac{9}{16}$ inch and $\frac{11}{16}$ inch.

REPEATING RIFLES

Common Malfunctions

Many problems associated with repeating rifles can be solved by a thorough cleaning and degreasing, so make this operation your first before you begin any diagnosis or repair work. Strip the gun down to its basic action components and clean and degrease them thoroughly. Once the parts are clean, those requiring replacement or touching up are fairly easy to detect.

Burred or scratched chambers and peened muzzles are quite common. Repeating rifles are especially prone to hang-up because of hardened grease and foreign matter in the receiver and extractor recesses. Here, the problem is compounded by the lubed ammunition used by most shooters and by the comparatively small size of the various action recesses.

Faulty extraction and ejection are most often related to badly fouled or burred chambers (usually caused by dry firing) or by jammed extractor springs.

Failure to Feed: Most repeating rifles have either a tubular or box magazine. Both are subject to denting which can cause misfeeding. Therefore, first check over the magazine for dents, rust, or corrosion.

A weak, rusted, or badly bent magazine spring can also cause feeding problems. A weak spring can usually be diagnosed and temporarily corrected by stretching or by inserting a small wooden dowel in the spring compartment to compress the spring more. If either of these techniques corrects the feeding problem, a new spring needs to be installed.

Extraction and Ejection Problems: The most probable cause of faulty extraction is either a faulty dull extractor claw or a weak extractor spring. The former problem can be corrected in most instances by sharpening the claw. The latter problem is corrected by replacing the weak or broken spring.

If the extractor has too much space between the claw and the face of the breechblock, the spent cartridge may not eject. The extractor lug can sometimes be bent to shorten the space at the claw.

Another cause of ejection failures is an improperly fitted or worn firing pin. The fitting of a new firing pin will normally cure the ailment.

Action Failures: When the action fails to release when fired, the carrier probably does not rise high enough at the front end to clear the carrier dog. To remedy, adjust the mainspring rod by bending its middle slightly down where it engages with the rear of the carrier.

Action Fails to Lock Forward when Arm is Cocked: This problem is just the opposite of the previous one and is caused by the carrier not going down far enough at the front end to engage properly with the carrier dog. Remove the carrier and cut away some metal from the carrier where it rests at the front end of the guard.

Also check for rounded corners on the carrier where it engages the carrier dog. If this is causing the problem, a new carrier will have to be fitted. By the same token, check for rounded corners on the carrier dog. If this is causing the problem, a new carrier will have to be fitted. Finally, inspect the carrier dog spring and replace it if it is weak or broken.

Breechblock Starts Forward Hard: Inspect the gun to see if the recoil lug of the breechblock is catching into the well hole in the rear top of the receiver (on some rifles), which is slightly rounded at the corner. If so, peen the metal of the receiver to make the front corner of the well hole reach farther toward the rear, or fit a new breechbolt.

Carrier Fails to Lift Cartridges when Action is Moved Forward: The most probable cause is a weak or broken carrier dog spring, which should be replaced if found defective. The carrier dog itself may be the culprit. If it is badly worn or broken, refit a new one.

Cartridge Strikes Edge of Chamber: If this problem occurs, first thoroughly clean the rifle; dirt under the extractor is probably preventing the extractor to swing far enough toward the cartridge. Once cleaned, check the space between the extractor claw and the face of the breechblock. If excessive, bend the lug of the extractor forward to shorten the distance. A dirty or gummed-up extractor spring could be causing the problem, but the initial cleaning should solve this problem. If not, check for a weak or broken spring and replace if necessary.

Failure to Fire: On activating the action, sometimes the hammer will not stay cocked. This is more than likely caused by a broken hammer notch. Disassemble, check the hammer, and replace it if necessary.

Continue the inspection by looking for a broken or worn firing pin, mainspring, etc. Replace all broken or worn parts.

The cartridge-supporting surface at the end of the barrel where the firing pin strikes can become upset. When this problem occurs, the shell rim is allowed to bend as the firing pin hits and, in many cases, will not puncture the primer. The barrel must either be set back a thread or two and rechambered, or a new barrel should be installed.

Check for dirt and debris in the receiver grooves which could prevent the action from locking completely. This, of course, will prevent the cartridge from firing, or if it should fire, escaping gases may endanger the shooter.

Firing-pin length and condition are also important to ignition and in preventing damage to the action or the chamber.

If a worn or broken firing pin is suspected, disassemble the bolt and inspect the firing-pin tip or striker. If it is broken, it is best to install a factory replacement. If time is critical or a new pin isn't readily available, a new tip can be welded on, dressed to size, and heat-treated to harden. By

doing so, however, the customer's expense will increase dramatically.

Semiautomatic Rimfire Rifles

Most .22-caliber semiautomatic rifles use the blowback design in which the barrel remains stationary while the bolt or breechblock moves to the rear under the force of push from the exploding cartridge; that is, blowback systems function through manipulation of the laws of inertia.

Some .22-caliber semiautomatics with badly worn parts can fire fully automatic, creating dangerous and highly illegal firearms. Most, however, incorporate a disconnector that holds the hammer back and prevents it from following the barrel to the firing position, making a separate trigger pull necessary for each shot.

If one were to list all of the potential trouble sources and adjustment-repair sequences for all semiautomatic rifles, he or she would wind up with a sizable volume. However, the similarity in function (and malfunction) of the various semiautomatics is more pronounced than the design differences. While such guns generally fail more often than guns of other designs (bolt-actions, pumps, etc.), the reasons for the malfunctions can be weeded out and usually are not difficult to correct.

Common Malfunctions

Failure to Feed: The most common malfunction found with semiautomatic rifles is misfeeding. At least nine out ten of these rifles come into repair shops with feeding problems, usually due to a weak magazine spring or a worn or broken cartridge lifter. A dirty action is another cause of misfeeding.

In tubular-magazine .22 semiautomatic rifles, such as the Stevens Model 87-A rifle, the cartridges are cammed up for feeding by a lifter or carrier actuated by the bolt. As the bolt rebounds forward under spring pressure after being blown back by the fired cartridge, it cams the carrier up in its track to

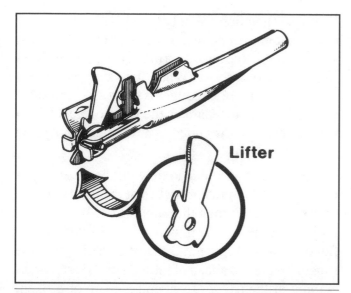

Figure 9-5: Typical lifter on .22-caliber semiautomatic rifles.

position a new cartridge so the bolt can pick it up and push it into the chamber. *See* Figure 9-5. These grooves often become worn, binding the carrier and resulting in the action jamming. A replacement operating slide is the answer.

The cartridge lifter or carrier is another frequent source of trouble. This is the device that lifts the cartridge from the magazine tube up to the feed lips so the cartridge can be picked up by the bolt on its return or forward movement. Its movement on Savage .22 semiautomatics is controlled by two lobes on top of its pivot end, and any wear on these can cause trouble with the feeding. A worn lifter will either fail to depress far enough for a cartridge to enter the magazine guide or fail to move far enough for a cartridge to enter the feed lips.

A lifter spring is another potential source of trouble that can cause misfeeding and jams. When the spring is weak, it does not depress the carrier far enough to permit cartridges to feed from the tube into the action. A replacement is the only answer.

Broken or bent cartridge or feed guides also cause feeding problems. On the Savage rifles, the cartridge guide is made of formed sheet steel, and the ejector is an integral part of the guide. Should

the ejector become worn or break, the entire guide must be replaced. If the guide is only bent, needle-nose pliers may sometimes be used to correct the situation, except when the part is cast.

The disconnector system on the Savage .22s can be somewhat tricky, as the spring tension in this system is critical — resulting in feeding problems, fully automatic firing, etc.

Failure to Fire: When a semiautomatic rifle fails to fire, the cause is most often due to debris and foreign matter in the bolt, which prevents the firing pin from moving forward the proper distance and/or at the proper speed. Complete disassembly and degreasing is the solution for this problem.

The firing pin may be rusted at the front end or broken off completely. In either case, a new firing pin should be installed. Also check the mainspring and replace it if it's weak or broken. Here are some other things to check in case of misfires:

- Check the protrusion of firing pin. It should be at least $1/16$-inch.

- Check the extractor to be sure it isn't binding.

- Check the face or hook of extractor for burrs.

- Check the extractor cut in the barrel for burrs, and also be sure the extractor lines up and isn't hitting the edges of the cut due to a slight rotation of barrel.

- Check the striker for burrs.

- Check the firing-pin assembly to be sure the ejector and its spring can move rearward in the assembly.

Action Fails to Close: The most probable causes of this malfunction in .22-caliber semiautomatic rifles lie in the breechblock, the bullet incline in cartridge guide, or a fouled magazine tube. The solution to all of these is simple — clean and degrease all affected parts. Also polish the bullet incline and oil it to prevent rust.

When an action fails to close and a thorough cleaning does not solve the problem, look for a cartridge guide spring that is out of adjustment. If found defective, adjust or fit a new one. Here are some other items to check when an action fails to close:

- Check for rub marks in the stock caused by the moving parts of the action.

- Check for alignment of operating slide guide to receiver.

- Check the end coil of mainspring.

- Check for bolt interfering on the feed lips of the magazine.

- Check the extractor to be sure it isn't binding.

- Check the face or hook of the extractor for burrs.

- Check the extractor cut in the barrel to be sure the extractor lines up and isn't hitting the edges of the cut due to a slight rotation of barrel.

If any of the above faults are found, replace any worn or broken parts; hone and polish any surfaces that contain burrs or rough edges.

Loose Barrel or Stock: Check for a loose barrel adjusting ring or for a broken barrel locating pin. Adjust the ring or replace the pin. In Winchester Model 77 rifles, check the inletting and bedding of the barrel to stock; the pressure point should be at the forend tip only.

Loose stocks in some rifles may be caused by the stock bolt nut being loose or by bolt holes enlarged due to wear. Cracks in the wood can also loosen the stock.

Faulty Safeties: Nearly all rimfire semiautomatic rifles use trigger block safeties (Refer to Figure 9-2), which are not as positive as the striker block systems found in many centerfire rifles. Most safeties of this type use a spring-loaded plunger that works in two notches. When the safety is pushed from safe to fire, the plunger is depressed and rides over a "hill" that separates the two notches. When this hill becomes rounded, a new safety should be installed.

The problem could also lie with the trigger. If it is cut away too much or broken at the front end, the trigger will pull when the safety is on. If this is the problem, a new trigger will probably need to be fitted. Note in Figure 9-2 that the safety is in the trigger guard just ahead of the trigger. If just a small amount of the trigger front end is worn or broken, the safety will fail.

Remember, most problems with .22-caliber rimfire semiautomatic rifles can be corrected by cleaning the rifle thoroughly. This procedure usually requires the metal parts to be removed from the wooden stock, and then the metal parts soaked in a commercial cleaning solution to remove all oil, grease, and grime. A plastic tank large enough to hold the barreled action is ideal for soaking. You will also need a selection of brushes to get to the hard-to-reach places. Toothbrushes, baby-bottle brushes, etc., can be purchased locally and are excellent for cleaning firearms. Use enough cleaning solution in the plastic tank to completely cover the firearm. Use the brushes to get any stubborn grime off of the parts and in the action. This is a good time to inspect all parts for damage or wear. Once clean, dry the parts with either compressed air or a conventional hair dryer and then coat all parts with a light coat of gun oil.

CENTERFIRE RIFLES

Much of the work performed by gunsmiths involves the repair and maintenance of centerfire rifles. To keep these firearms in good shooting condition, the gunsmith must have a thorough knowledge of troubleshooting, the ability to determine the cause of a gun problem and correct it without wasting time or using unnecessary new parts. Troubleshooting centerfire rifles covers a wide range of problems, from replacing an ejector spring to diagnosing why a rifle is not shooting accurately. In any case, troubleshooting usually requires a good knowledge of basic firearm design and the use of tools, and a systematic and methodical approach to the problem.

Single-Shot Rifles

Single-shot, centerfire rifles vary widely in design and quality, the simplest designs malfunctioning least. Single-shot actions have been made in regular falling-block, rolling-block, and drop-block versions. Among the best of the single-shot actions is the famous Winchester high and low sidewall and the relatively new Ruger Model 1 (Figure 9-6), which is based on the excellent falling-block action and is quite complex in design.

Falling Block Design: This type of single-shot action was designed so that the breechblock travels vertically in a mortise in the receiver. It is exceptionally strong and provides a perfect gas seal.

The direct ancestor of most modern single-shot rifles was the Sharps rifle, employing a falling block design. The original Sharps had an exposed hammer, but a number of hammerless variations followed including the Ballards and Farquharsons, while the Winchester Model 1885 single-shot rifle retained the exposed hammer. This latter model, designed by John M. Browning, is known in its many versions as high wall, low wall, thick wall and thin wall, which refer to the receiver dimensions.

In general, falling-block actions operate by a pivoting trigger guard (or lever behind the guard), which drops the breechblock when the lever is moved forward, exposing the chamber for loading. The lever is then pulled back to close the block for firing. After firing, extraction (and ejection in some cases) is accomplished by opening and/or snapping the lever.

Rolling-block Design: The rolling-block system is the simplest of all single-shot designs and consists basically of two pivoting breech-locking mechanisms, one mounted directly behind the other, attached to the frame by large axis pins.

The primary mechanism is the breechblock, which also contains the firing pin. It can be rolled up and down from the chamber (when the hammer is cocked) by means of a thumb spur or extension. When flush against the chamber, the breechblock is spring supported but not locked into place. The locking occurs a split second before the hammer

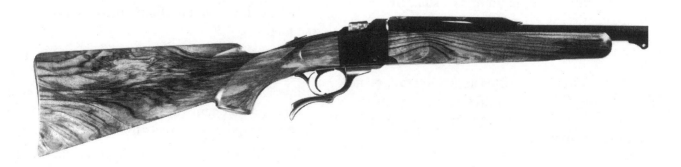

Figure 9-6: Ruger No. 1 Single-Shot rifle, custom stocked by Bob Emmons of Grafton, Ohio.

hits the firing pin by means of a projection under the surface of the hammer assembly, which slides into place behind and under the breechblock.

The Remington Rolling Block rifle was used for military purposes by several countries in such calibers as 7 x 57 mm, .45-70, .43 Egyptian, and several others.

Tipping-Block System: The tipping-block system is used in the famous Martini-Henry action and employs a block hinged at the rear which, when activated by a lever, lowers the front edge and exposes the chamber. A lever arrangement in the Martini action also cocks a concealed hammer when the action is opened.

In modern hammerless single-shot actions, the gun is usually cocked as the striker mechanism is pushed back against the spring tension of the mainspring until the striker is caught and held by the sear. This motion also unlocks and drops the breechblock, exposing the chamber for feeding and loading. When the lever is brought back up, the block rises behind the cartridge, locks the action, and is ready for firing. Once fired, the downward and forward motion of the lever lowers the breechblock, extracts and ejects the fired cartridge case from the gun, and is again ready for reloading by hand.

Hammer models work essentially the same way, except that the hammer must be cocked manually after the cartridge is chambered and the action is locked. Actually, the hammer is usually cocked before the action is opened, and then the hammer is lowered to half-cock until the gun is ready for firing.

The many single-shot rifles manufactured by the Stevens Arms Company utilize a variety of designs, but all of them are based on the actions described here to some extent.

Common Malfunctions

Unlike .22-caliber rimfire single-shot rifles (of the bolt-action design), single-shot centerfire rifles are sometimes very complex in design, often more than their repeating counterparts. Of the half dozen or so models currently in production, the Browning '78, Hyper-Single Rifle, Ruger No. 1, and the Wickliffe all use the falling-block design. The Riedl single-shot rifle utilizes a rack-and-pinion action, while Harrington & Richardson uses the break-open action almost exactly like its single-barrel (single-shot) shotguns. There are also replicas of rolling blocks and Springfield rifles currently available.

Since Harrington & Richardson uses the break-open single-shot shotgun design in their single-shot rifles, the same troubleshooting methods as described under single-shot shotguns in Chapter 10 may be used. The remaining models, however, are unique.

Ruger Single-Shots: The Ruger No. 1 single-shot rifle and the Ruger No. 3 single-shot carbine have essentially the same type action, except that the carbine has a different lever. Loading and ejection on both models are accomplished by lowering the lever (which opens the breech) and inserting a cartridge fully into the chamber. The lever is then raised until the lever latch engages; this action closes and locks the breech. The operation of the lever opens and closes the breech, automatically ejects the fired cartridge, and cocks the hammer, which is concealed within the mechanism. On this model, the breech is fully in position and locked before the lever latch engages, but firing the rifle with the lever latch unengaged is not recommended.

The safety on the Ruger Models 1 and 3 can be engaged only when the hammer is cocked. These rifles can be loaded and unloaded while the safety is on. The mechanism not only blocks movement of the sear but also retracts the hammer.

When the hammer is cocked, it protrudes slightly from the lever, serving as a cocking indicator that can be felt and seen.

When engaging the safety (by sliding it to the rear), be sure that it is moved all the way to its

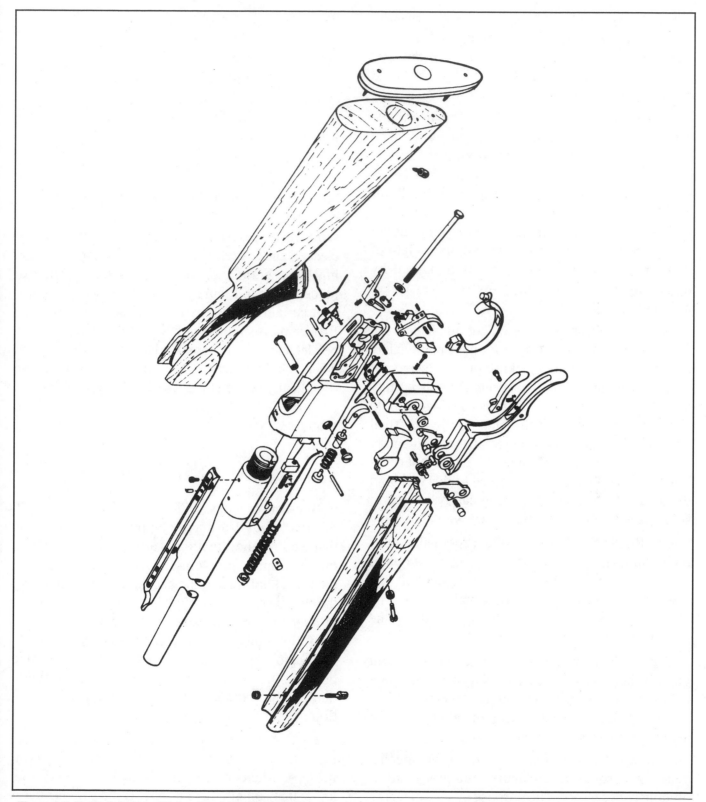

Figure 9-7: Exploded view of Ruger No. 1 Single-Shot rifle.

extreme rear position. There is an extra resistance to the safety movement about halfway back, and some may confuse this resistance with the true safety position. The word *SAFE* or *SAFETY* should be clearly visible when the safety is on.

The trigger sear is preset at the factory to provide a recommended minimum sear engagement with the hammer. The safety is fitted after the sear is adjusted. Accordingly, the sear should not be altered by untrained persons, as this is a job only for professionals. The minimum weight of pull is established by the sear spring and this spring should not be modified. On the other hand, the weight of pull can be increased beyond this minimum by tightening the adjustment screw on the trigger mechanism.

In the event that snap-action automatic ejection is not desired, the ejector spring can be removed by taking the forearm and backing off on the ejector strut adjustment screw. The ejector will then function as an extractor only, and the cartridge will be partially removed from the chamber by the final downward motion of the lever. If the snap-action mechanism is replaced at a later date, do not overtighten the adjustment screw because this will bind the action. The force of ejection can be altered to some extent by the adjustment screw.

The Ruger No. 1 rifle is an exceptionally well-built gun with many hand-fitted parts. If the owner of such a rifle does his part, such a gun will last several lifetimes without a single malfunction. The following maintenance is recommended by the manufacturer:

The mechanism should be lubricated with light gun oil, but not too heavily. As a rust-prevention measure, all surfaces, including the bore of the barrel, should be wiped with oil after use. But again, do not flood the bore with oil.

A comprehensive field cleaning of the mechanism is not required more than once a season unless obviously necessary. The purpose of such cleaning is only to remove powder residue from internal components and as a rust prevention procedure in the event that the gun has been soaked or submerged in water. The barrel should always be cleaned after each use.

If sand or other foreign matter in any appreciable quantity enter the mechanism, the reliability of functioning will probably be impaired until the gun is dismantled and thoroughly cleaned.

Malfunctions in the Ruger No. 1 can usually be traced to a dirty and gummed-up action, worn or broken parts, or parts assembled incorrectly. Unless the problem is obvious, the rifle should be disassembled as described previously and thoroughly cleaned and degreased. Inspect every part for wear, breakage, burrs, etc. Note your findings. The exploded view in Figure 9-7 should serve as a guide to ascertain that the rifle is assembled correctly. Broken parts should be obvious and worn parts can be detected by rounded edges and bright spots where mating surfaces were rubbing. Replace or rebuild any broken or cracked parts, assemble, and test fire. Remove any burrs and polish the surface smooth.

Bolt-action Centerfire Rifles

Bolt-action rifles seldom give trouble even if misused, but occasionally a problem will develop that requires the attention of an expert. Some of the more common problems include: poor accuracy, the breechbolt binds, the cartridge won't feed into the chamber, the breechbolt pulls out of the receiver or overrides the cartridges in magazine, the firing pin follows down, gun misfires, safety is defective, the magazine cover fails to open, gun fails to extract or eject. These categories cover just about every malfunction possible in the conventional bolt-action rifle.

Poor Accuracy: The bolt-action rifle has the reputation of being the most accurate rifle ever made, so when one does not group as it should, you know that something is wrong. If the rifle is old or shows signs of hard use, you can assume that the rifling is shot out or pitted so badly that accuracy has been affected. Of course, the only way to be sure is to check the rifling carefully with a bore light.

At the first sign of poor accuracy, the stock should be the first area to check thoroughly. If the stock is warped and the barrel does not line up properly in the barrel channel, coat the bottom of the barrel with Prussian blue — applied in a thin, even coat — and insert the barrel into the barrel channel of the stock. Any high spots or interference in the barrel channel will be clearly marked so that they can be scraped away. Of course, if the stock is too badly warped, it should be replaced.

In most cases, the barrel of bolt-action rifles should bear on the bottom of the barrel channel in the stock only at the forend tip. This bearing point can be from a point contact up to about $\frac{1}{2}$ inch. Glazed spots in the channel indicate barrel contact with the wood. Again, Prussian blue coated on the barrel should show these spots readily. Any such interference points found should be scraped away using conventional inletting tools. Note particularly the area around the point where the barrel joins the receiver.

If these checks turn up okay and the accuracy still isn't up to what it should be, continue checking the rifle to see if any of the screws holding the stock to the action are loose. Then inspect the crowning on the muzzle for eccentricity of crowning to bore and for any upsetting of the rifling at the muzzle. If the latter problem is discovered, place the barrel in a lathe and turn back the barrel and recrown.

Metal fouling is not too common in the larger centerfire calibers, but just the opposite is true for the small-caliber, ultra-high velocity cartridges. When metal fouling does occur, accuracy is badly affected. A metal fouling solution that has been around for a long time consists of the following:

- 1 oz. ammonium persulphate

- 200 gr. ammonium carbonate

- 6 oz. stronger ammonia

- 4 oz. water

Mix these ingredients in a large glass bottle and let stand. Then plug the chamber end of the barrel with a rubber plug or cork. Secure the barrel and action in a position so that the muzzle is pointed upward. Carefully pour the solution into the barrel until it is full, but be careful not to get any of the solution on the outside of the barrel as it might injure the bluing. If the solution is allowed to remain in the bore about 30 minutes, all metal fouling should be removed. Then pour all of the solution out and rinse the barrel thoroughly with hot water — the hotter the better. The barrel should dry almost instantly due to the heat generated by the hot water. When dry, lightly oil the bore to protect it from rust.

After removing the metal fouling, bore sight the rifle and check accuracy with ammunition from different lots.

Breechbolt Binds: A tight bolt can indicate burrs on the action mating surfaces, or the bolt may be fitted too tightly in the receiver. A small amount of filing, followed up with honing and polishing with crocus cloth, will relieve tightness where interference is confined to one or two small areas, but not enough to loosen a snug fit in a receiver.

The extractor ring may be high, causing the bolt to ride tight. To correct, remove the ring and remove any high spot on the ring channel. Refit the ring and try for smoothness. If this doesn't solve the problem, a new ring will have to be fitted.

Failure to Feed: The most probable cause of this malfunction is a tight extractor. In altering the extractor, extreme care should be used and any adjustments made should be done on a trial-and-error basis; that is, take only one or two file strokes at a time, then try the extractor for fit. With some experience, you'll be able to look at the degrees of tightness and then know almost exactly how much metal to remove. Too much filing may cause further malfunctions.

If the extractor is correctly fitted, check the magazine follower spring, as it may be too weak. To correct, remove the spring and open it up slightly (stretch it) but carefully to avoid over-spreading and injury to the spring. Again, use the trial-and-error method until it functions properly.

The follower could be binding in the magazine due to the spring leaves canting sideways. This will cause the follower to bind on the inner wall of the magazine. Straighten it with care and watch for this point when opening up the spring.

Breechbolt Pulls Out of Receiver: The bolt stop is not functioning properly when this malfunction occurs. Check to be sure it is free in the slot in the receiver and that the trigger pin, on which the stop pivots on some bolt-action rifles, is not loose in the receiver. Make sure the spring functions freely in its seat and does not bind or is too weak. If necessary, replace either or both spring and stop.

Breechbolt Overrides Cartridges in Magazine: A weak follower spring is probably the culprit, but can be remedied by removing the spring and spreading the three angles slightly to increase the tension on the follower. This should be done on a trial-and-error basis as explained before. Make sure the spring is not twisted, causing the follower to bind on the side of the magazine.

Firing Pin Follows Down: This problem is caused by an over adjustment on the trigger adjusting nuts or no follow-through on the trigger. Readjust the trigger according to the type of trigger mechanism installed in the rifle. Make sure the trigger has follow-through after the adjustments are made.

Another possible cause is that the sear may not be engaging the firing pin enough to retain it. Make sure the sear and sear spring are not binding in the receiver.

Headspace Problems: Insufficient headspace is seldom encountered in modern American firearms but is found on some of the older military weapons. Many bolt-action rifles were used for military pur-

poses in foreign countries. These were imported to the United States, distributed through gun dealers, and have since fallen into the hands of many shooters. The majority of these guns were checked by the distributor, and the bad ones were rejected and dismantled for parts. The better ones were sold for shooting. However, some of these weapons have dangerously excessive headspace and many of them have let go, to the dismay of the shooter. Therefore, before firing any of the older military weapons, check the headspace. If it is excessive and the gun is a common inexpensive piece, you are better off not using it.

If, however, you're working with a basically good and/or desirable firearm, you may wish to set the barrel back to correct the headspace problem. Sometimes, you may be able to correct a headspace problem, especially on the Springfield and Mauser bolt-action rifles, by finding a slightly over-long bolt and substituting this for the original. Otherwise, the problem will have to be solved by setting the barrel back.

To set the barrel back, you'll need access to a heavy barrel vise. If you don't have one, don't attempt the job. Once the barrel is removed, it is inserted into a lathe and metal is removed from the shoulder equal to one full turn of the threads. This is to make sure the sights, extractor slots, etc., will line up perfectly as before.

When a barrel is set back, the chamber is usually shortened and must be lengthened to the proper tolerance with a finishing chamber reamer. The reaming operation is sometimes done on a lathe, but more often it is done by hand. Once completed, the action is threaded forward on the barrel until the bolt can be easily closed on the GO headspace gauge with a slight feeling of resistance.

Excessive headspace, even if not to the point of being dangerous, can affect accuracy considerably. So check the headspace on all guns owned by shooters who complain of poor accuracy.

Failure to Fire: Here is another problem that can be caused by excessive headspace — so excessive

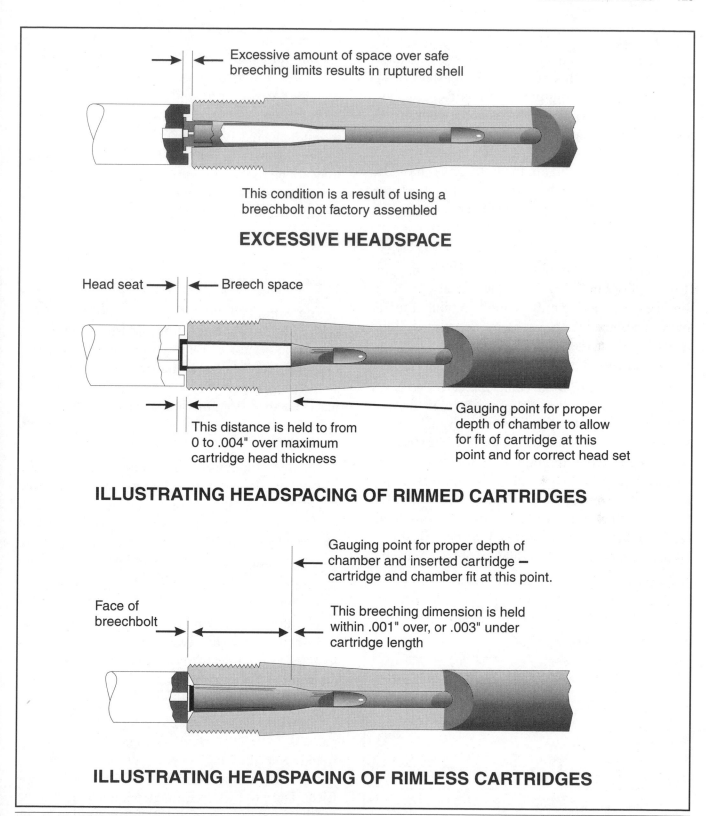

Excessive amount of space over safe
breeching limits results in ruptured shell

This condition is a result of using a
breechbolt not factory assembled

EXCESSIVE HEADSPACE

Head seat → | ← Breech space

This distance is held to from
0 to .004" over maximum
cartridge head thickness

Gauging point for proper
depth of chamber to allow
for fit of cartridge at this
point and for correct head set

ILLUSTRATING HEADSPACING OF RIMMED CARTRIDGES

Gauging point for proper depth of
chamber and inserted cartridge —
cartridge and chamber fit at this point.

This breeching dimension is held
within .001" over, or .003" under
cartridge length

Face of
breechbolt

ILLUSTRATING HEADSPACING OF RIMLESS CARTRIDGES

Figure 9-8: Headspacing for rimmed and rimless centerfire cartridges.

that the firing pin cannot reach the primer with sufficient force to puncture it. However, the most probable cause of this malfunction is a short firing pin. Remove the firing-pin assembly from the bolt and examine it closely for breaks or a worn firing-pin tip. At the same time, check for a broken or weak firing-pin spring. Replace all broken or worn parts. Of course, debris in the bolt can cushion the firing pin as it moves forward, restricting the force of the plunger. So always give the bolt assembly a good cleaning and degreasing when it's torn down.

Defective Safety: In most cases, this problem can be traced to a worn or altered cam on the firing pin. If the safety binds, try filing the bearing point on the firing pin, taking only a small amount of metal away at a time until the problem is corrected. If the safety is tight in the bolt sleeve, it may be fitted, but usually a new safety is suggested.

Fails to Extract: Most centerfire cartridge cases swell when fired, and if the chamber is dirty or pitted, the case will have a tendency to stick. When an extractor hook is somewhat worn, it can slip over the case rim when the bolt is withdrawn, leaving the fired case in the chamber. Sometimes, if the wear is not too bad, the problem may be corrected by honing the extractor hook angle (Figure 9-9). Do not remove too much metal, as described previously. Proceed on a trial-and-error basis until the

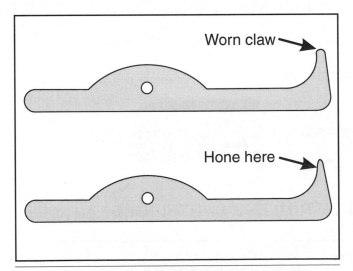

Figure 9-9: Worn or dull extractors may sometimes be corrected by honing the extractor hook angle.

extractor functions properly. Also check the extractor ring for tension and adjust it to acquire bite. In rare cases, it may be necessary to replace either or both the extractor ring and extractor.

Fails to Eject: The ejector is probably not free in its cut in the receiver; the cut may be too narrow or the ejector may be bent. A binding ejector spring may not be functioning properly, or the slot for the ejector in the bolt may not be in line with the ejector. See that the parts are free and functioning properly or replace as needed.

Lever-action Centerfire rifles

The worst and most common problem that occurs with old Winchester and Marlin lever-action rifles is looseness caused by wear of moving parts. Original round holes in parts have become egg-shaped, mortises in the receiver are worn, and metal has been shed from mating surfaces. Any of these defects can lead to malfunctions making the gun unsafe to fire.

Feeding problems are often encountered that are caused by dented, dirty, or corroded magazine tubes and/or weak magazine springs. Recesses in the receivers of lever-action rifles are prone to collect all sorts of debris and foreign matter which, when combined with gun oil and grease, cake and gum up the action, causing feeding, extraction, and ejection problems.

The third most common problem in the older lever-actions is excessive headspace. These rifles lock up at the rear of the sliding breechbolt and, after much firing, stretching occurs which causes excessive headspace.

Worn Parts: The easiest solution to worn parts is to replace them — if new parts can be found. Many of the recently produced lever-actions, such as the Winchester Model 94 Angle Eject, late-production Savage Model 99s, and the Marlin Models 336 and 1895, are similar to the same models produced nearly 100 years ago, but not quite! While some parts are interchangeable, certain modifications to ease manufacturing have taken place, and all parts are not interchangeable.

Replacement parts for the older lever-action guns are becoming more difficult to obtain each year. They are out there, but their cost is a pretty penny. A hammer, for example, for a pre-World War II Winchester Model 94 rifle or carbine is currently selling for over $50. A pistol-grip lever for a Winchester Model 1886 will run from $60 to $90. A 22-inch carbine barrel for a Winchester Model 1886, in excellent condition, will run as high as $1000 . . . maybe more.

Many worn or broken parts can be made service-able by welding, brazing, and honing. For example, worn contact surfaces on trigger sear and hammer notches can sometimes be put back into service by judicious notching with a file, then honing smooth. The surface metal removed will often expose the soft interior metal and the part will have to be rehardened.

Many cracked or broken gun parts can be re-paired by silver soldering. The worn surfaces also can be built up by welding, filing to shape, polishing, and heat-treating.

Oversized holes caused by excessive wear can also be repaired by welding the hole closed. Grind off any irregularities on each side; then drill a new hole. Or, if practical, merely drill a slightly larger diameter hole through the worn one to true it up, and use a larger-diameter pin or screw.

Misfeeds: Feeding problems in lever-action rifles can often be cured by giving the action and magazine a thorough cleaning, removing any dents and replacing the magazine spring if weak or broken. Also look for burrs in all areas that the cartridge will contact. Remove any burrs with an Arkansas stone, using plenty of honing oil. Kerosine will work fine.

Another common problem — dirt — can be remedied easily by giving the entire gun a thorough cleaning. Completely disassemble the gun and then submerge all parts in a cleaning solution mixed with five parts water. Leave the parts in the solution for about 15 minutes before removing them from the tank, drying and finally oiling them. This cleaning will also help you detect worn surfaces.

Slide-action Centerfire Rifles

The *pump*, *slide-*, and *trombone*-actions are simply different names for the same type of rifle. This was the fastest-shooting rifle until the introduction of the semiautomatic. It did not, however, enjoy the same popularity as the bolt- and lever-action rifles.

The slide-action rifle has existed since the late 1800s, but the early models were adapted for use only with relatively low-pressure cartridges. It was not until Remington introduced the popular Model 14 in 1912 that the pump-action became a big-game rifle. The newer Remington Model 760 and its predecessors can handle many of the modern high-powered cartridges, such as the .30-06, .270, and .243 calibers.

Malfunctions in the pump rifles are second in frequency only to semiautomatics. The biggest cause of problems with both of these action types is the presence of dirt, dust, and assorted debris that, when combined with gun oil and grease, prevent proper operation. Therefore, at the sign of any malfunction, first strip the gun down to its basic action components and degrease — unless, of course, obvious symptoms dictate otherwise.

Other problems found in pump rifles are:

- Failure to feed properly
- Double-feeding
- Failure to retain cartridges in the magazine
- Action bars sticking
- Action failing to lock
- Failure to extract and eject
- Failure to fire

- Failure to cock

- Gun fires on closing of the action

- Safety malfunctions.

Feeding Problems: The most common cause of improper feeding is rust or corrosion within the magazine tube. The solution is simple. Merely clean out the tube with a cleaning rod and brush of the proper size saturated with bore cleaner. The job can be hurried by inserting the handle end of the cleaning rod in a drill motor, which will rotate the brush rapidly and remove the rust and polish the metal surfaces quickly.

Next check for a weak, rusted, or badly bent magazine spring. Try stretching the spring, then try the rifle for proper feeding. If this works, it's only a temporary solution, and a new spring should be installed.

In box-magazine pump-action rifles — like the Remington Model 760 — check for deformation of the lug on the front end of the magazine box, which would prevent holding the magazine firmly in place; that is, into its recess in the front section of the receiver. Also check for deformation of the lug on the rear end of the box to prevent it from locking up securely with the magazine latch.

Check lips on both sides of the top rim of the magazine for deformation. The magazine latch must rotate freely on its spring and be located properly on the right end of the hammer pin. It must also engage the notch in the rear of the magazine firmly and locate the magazine securely into its proper operating position. Any deformation or breakage of the locating lug of the magazine latch will hinder its function. Replace if necessary.

The movements of the magazine follower must be free to maintain a level pressure against the feeding shells. Check for breakage or deformation of the two rear ears on the top surface (Figure 9-10) and the magazine spring locating lugs on the under surface.

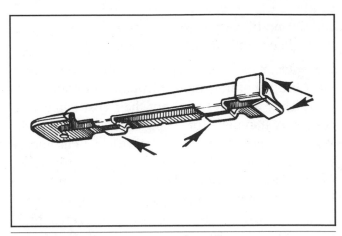

Figure 9-10: When feeding problems develop in the Remington Model 760 slide-action rifle, check for breakage or deformation of the two rear ears on the top surface, and the magazine-spring locating lugs on the under surface.

Check the magazine spring for free passage in the magazine and to insure that it is securely located to the under surface of the follower. If the spring is weak or broken, it must be replaced.

The magazine filler piece (Figure 9-11) must be properly assembled to prevent the free passage of the follower or spring. If this part must be replaced, disassemble from the front end of the magazine.

A defective magazine can also prevent the gun from being loaded. The lips on both sides of the top

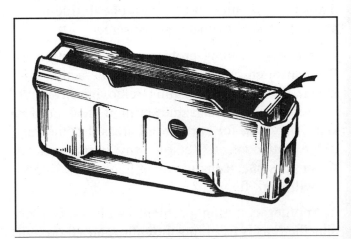

Figure 9-11: The magazine filler piece must be properly assembled to prevent free passage of the follower and spring.

Figure 9-12: There must be no deformation or breakage of the lips on the top rim of the magazine to prevent the free forward-sliding motion of the feeding cartridges.

rim of the magazine must be free of deformation or breakage. They must hold the cartridges securely in a level position. Also the sides and ends of the magazine must be free of deformation, burrs, etc., for free passage of the magazine follower. Deformed lips can sometimes be bent and burrs can be removed by honing, but in most cases it's best to invest a few dollars and replace the magazine.

If the gun fails to load and the above possible causes have been checked, look for breakage or deformation of the magazine follower ears on the rear top face. Also check for deformation or breakage of the locating lugs on the under surface of the follower.

Gun Fails to Lock: In box-magazine pump rifles the magazine latch may be locating the magazine too high, causing the action to bind. There must be no deformation or breakage of the lips on the top rim of the magazine to prevent the free, forward-sliding motion of the feeding cartridges. *See* Figure 9-12.

Gun Fails to Open and Eject: Check the ejector to insure that it has free movement and is secure on its retaining pin with no breakage or deformation. The extractor must also be free of movement, secure on its rivet or pivot pin, and tight over the rim of the shell. The breechbolt must have free travel and proper heading with no deformation on the face, the lugs, the cam ways, or the shell rim. Both

cam pins must be firmly in position. Also check the ejector spring.

A pitted or rusted chamber or deformed extension lugs can hinder the ejector on pump rifles. The action bar assembly is another possible source of trouble. The action bars must have free travel with no deformation of the bars on the receiver slots. The bolt carrier must be securely brazed to the action bars and cam pins properly staked; that is, not protruding.

Check to see that the magazine assembly is secure in its proper location and is not hindering the passage of the action bars. It must retain the oncoming cartridges firmly and in a level position.

Pump-action rifles, like all repeating firearms, have a tendency to collect dirt and debris in the action. When this mingles with oil or grease, a variety of malfunctions can occur. Therefore, all components should be thoroughly cleaned and degreased before attempting to diagnose any problems. In addition, pump-action rifles should be completely disassembled at least once a year and given a thorough cleaning, whether the gun is malfunctioning or not.

In disassembling any gun for cleaning or repair, have a good assortment of gunsmith's screwdrivers, drift punches, and a padded vise. Never use the wrong-sized driver when working on a gun, as unsightly burred or scratched screw heads are sure to be the result. Always mark screws so they will be returned to the proper holes. Screws may look alike and even be identical, but they should always be returned to the same hole for a proper set.

Any surface rust found can usually be removed with fine steel wool (000 or 0000 size) without damaging the bluing. First, however, spray the affected area with solvent, let stand for a few minutes, and go to work with the terry cloth towel. If this doesn't work, then use the steel wool very gently.

Semiautomatic Rifles

Besides feeding problems, you'll find autoloaders that fail to extract fired cases; some that won't eject; some that won't fire; and others that won't lock up properly. The problems are quite similar to slide-action rifles, with the exception of the following:

- Action is binding.
- Gas orifice is defective.
- Gas nozzle or tube is defective.
- Barrel chamber is rough or defective.
- Gas nozzle hole in action sleeve has broken through into spring hole in receiver.
- Gas orifice ball and screw need to be replaced.

These problems may be corrected by checking the gas orifice for the proper size according to the manufacturer's specifications. The barrel may have to be replaced. Also check the gas tube opening for damage and adjust or replace the barrel. Replacing worn components may solve the problem; action sleeves and action springs are two parts that sometimes need replacing.

- Replace ejection port cover.
- Replace magazine latch with one that assembles lower in the gun.
- Replace action spring.
- Replace ejector spring or clean ejector hole.
- Replace action bar assembly or clean up rivet head.
- Replace receiver, barrel, or bolt carrier, whichever is at fault.

Gun Fails to Lock: The breechblock is improperly rotated forward, usually caused by a cartridge that is too long or a misalignment of the receiver, barrel, or bolt carrier. Try another cartridge of proper length; replace any of the faulty parts.

Look for a disconnector that binds the action bar and adjust it to hug the receiver wall if defective. If the extractor closes hard over the chambering cartridge, smooth the extractor with an Arkansas stone or adjust the tension on the cartridge. Replace the extractor if necessary.

If the fault still persists, smooth the ejector. Also disassemble and clean the ejector hole. Replace the ejector or spring if necessary.

If the breech jams in the receiver rails, try smoothing up the rails. If this doesn't work, the receiver will need to be replaced. A cartridge primer could have been pierced on a previous round. This primer or pieces of brass must be removed from the firing-pin hole. Fouling in the barrel chamber is another possible cause. Clean the chamber, removing all grease and foreign deposits.

Chapter 10

Gunsmithing Shotguns

The modern scattergun is versatile. In the hands of an expert hunter, and with the proper loads, it can account for all species of game throughout North American — from fowl to bear.

Shotguns probably are used for hunting more than any other firearm in the United States and are available in several types — from the inexpensive single-shot models, up through the repeaters and semiautomatics to the doubles — some of which are extremely expensive. Troubleshooting techniques will vary with each type.

Since shotguns are widely used throughout the world, it stands to reason that this type of firearm will frequently find its way to the bench for repairs or modifications.

SINGLE-SHOT SHOTGUNS

Figure 10-1 shows a cross-sectional view of an Iver Johnson single-barrel ejector shotgun. Many

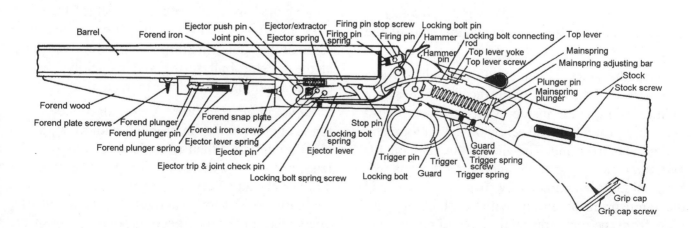

Figure 10-1: Cross-sectional drawing of an Iver Johnson single-barrel ejector shotgun.

of the hammer single-shot shotguns of this century are similar to this model in design and operation.

Although most single-shot shotguns are relatively simple in design, all will have their share of problems — due mainly to worn-out parts and misuse. Many repairs take only a few minutes — like replacing a broken trigger spring — but some can be very time consuming and costly. Therefore, many of these old-timers are retired to the gun rack or scrap pile. A person with the knowledge, however, can repair one of these shotguns in his spare time and have a good utility gun to knock around the farm or camp.

Common Problems

Besides loose actions, the two most frequent problems occurring with this type of gun are a broken trigger spring and a broken or weak locking-bolt spring. The former is easily detected by the action of the trigger. If the trigger does not spring back after it is pulled, the problem is usually caused by a broken trigger spring. Of course, if a gun looks dirty, clean it before starting your diagnosis.

Replacing Trigger Springs: The exact method of replacing the trigger spring might vary slightly with different guns, but using the Iver Johnson in Figure 10-1, first remove the buttplate, then with a long heavy-duty screwdriver ($\frac{1}{2}$-inch shaft) remove the stock bolt. Be careful, since a wrong size screwdriver could slip, splintering out the side of the stock while you are exerting force.

Once the stock is removed, you will have a partial view of the inside of the receiver. Use a bore light to examine the inside of the receiver. You'll be looking for a flathead screw on the bottom tang under the mainspring. The view is not good on this particular model, since the receiver sidewalls will be blocking your direct view from the sides, and the mainspring assembly will be blocking your view from the top. You might have to remove the mainspring assembly to get at the screw head, but try to avoid this if at all possible.

You may be able to get enough working room by sliding the mainspring adjusting bar in its notch slightly to the right or left. Then use a ratchet screwdriver to loosen the trigger-spring screw. Insert a new spring, with the curvature of the saddle positioned as shown in Figure 10-1 and retighten the screw. Replace the mainspring adjusting bar in its original position and then replace the stock and buttplate. The job should take about 15 minutes if you have a replacement spring on hand and if you don't have to remove the mainspring.

If the inside of the receiver is rusted — and it probably will be — use a good penetrating oil on the screw before extracting it. You don't need a frozen screw — resulting in wrenching its head off — to add to the original problem.

Replacing Locking-bolt Springs: The symptoms of a loose or broken locking-bolt spring include a very loose top lever movement (one which does not align with the rear tang); play in the up-and-down barrel movement when the action is supposedly locked; and the barrel opening automatically upon firing without touching the top lever. A factory replacement spring here is best, but if the parts are not available, one can be made by conventional methods.

The locking-bolt spring in most single-shot shotguns can be reached through the front of the receiver. Remove the forend, break the gun open, remove the barrel, and you may be able to reach it. On some guns, however, you will have to remove some of the "guts" in this part of the receiver to get at the locking-bolt spring and its screw; that is, ejector lever and the ejector/extractor.

Replacing Firing Pins: A worn or broken firing pin is another common problem with many of the older shotguns. When a single-shot shotgun misfires, it is usually due to the firing pin being either worn or broken. These coil springs in single-barrel shotguns are very tough and seldom break, but after years of use they may become weak. Most of the time, more tension can be added to the spring (enough to enable the hammer and firing pin to do their jobs) by moving the mainspring adjusting bar another notch or two closer to the hammer. If this doesn't do the trick, then a new spring must be installed.

The pin is easily replaced (if a replacement is available) by removing the firing-pin stop screw — being careful not to let the remaining firing pin and spring fly out and become lost — then slipping the firing pin and spring out of its channel. Replace with a new one in the reverse order.

The only other springs normally found in this type of gun are the ejector-lever spring and the ejector spring. Both seldom break but, when they do, replacement springs are easily made from coil-spring stock.

Any of the above repairs can be performed at very little expense. However, the description of the problems to follow may be a different story. You will have to weigh each repair and then decide if an inexpensive single-barrel shotgun is worth the time and expense.

More Challenging Problems

One of the main and more complicated problems that occurs with the older single-barrel shotguns is a loose action. To check for looseness, hold the gun with one hand on the forend and the other on the buttstock at the grip (Figure 10-2). By twisting your hands in opposite directions, you should be able to detect any play that might be present. Try this check to the sides and up and down.

Headspace problems are another common fault with older single-shot guns. Hold the gun up to a light source so you can see where the barrel meets the standing receiver or breech. If you can see light through this gap with the action closed, the gun is probably dangerous to fire. A feeler gauge may also be used to measure the exact dimension of the gap as shown in Figure 10-3.

Another problem is short chambers. Over the years, there have been a variety of standard chamber lengths for the shells that were manufactured

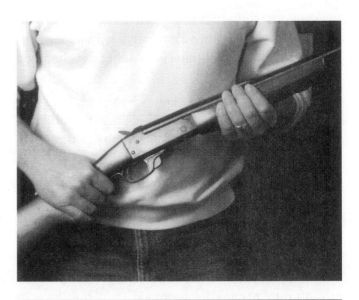

Figure 10-2: To check for loose action, hold the gun as shown and twist your hands in opposite directions.

when the gun was built. Most of them were less than 2.760 inch overall length — the minimum dimension to handle the overall length of today's plastic shells. Because of these obsolete chambers, the already-weak action takes an extra beating due to the higher pressures caused by these short chambers. The shell's crimp must have room to unfold completely flat when the shot and wads go from the case to the bore. Any little bit of case forced into their path because of a short chamber will deform

Figure 10-3: Feeler gauge being used to measure the gap between the barrel and standing breech.

the shot, tear hulls, cause excessive recoil, and raise chamber pressures above normal. Chamber lengths may be lengthened by hand with a shotgun chamber reamer.

The final problem is choke. Many of these old single-shots had long 32- to 36-inch barrels that were tightly choked. This is why many of these old guns — like the Winchester Model 37 — are still coveted by persons in certain types of shooting matches. Some of these guns, however, in an effort to "modernize" them, had their barrels cut off to, say, 26 inches, leaving the barrel with no choke at all. They work fine on rabbits and quail at close range, but beyond about 30 yards their shot pattern is so thin that few kills are made.

Remedies

Short Shotgun Chambers: Short shotgun chambers can be reamed out by using a special reamer. This chambering reamer cuts short chambers to modern length and reams a new, long forcing cone at the same time without lengthening the chamber. They are currently available from Brownells Inc. for 12, 16, 20 and .410 gauges. Complete instructions accompany the reamers when they are requested with the order.

In general, the shotgun barrel is tightly secured in a vise with the muzzle pointing toward the floor and the chamber end up, just slightly above the vise jaws. A good cutting oil is used in the chamber for the lubrication, and the chamber reamer is inserted lightly into the chamber. A T-handle wrench is used to turn the reamer one complete revolution in the chamber. The reamer is then removed while still turning it clockwise (never back a reamer out by turning it counterclockwise), the chamber is cleaned of all oil and metal shavings, then a measurement is taken. Continue this procedure — cleaning the chamber and reamer each time before continuing — until the desired chamber length and/or forcing cone is cut.

Chokes: A choke may be put back into shotguns, but it takes some time, skill, and effort to do so. Many gunsmiths will charge $45 to $100 to choke a shotgun barrel, and once the job is done, if all you have is a $75 shotgun, is it worth it?

Shotgun chokes are normally cut to the desired measurements with an angle-blade expanding choke reamer checked with barrel calipers, then honed smooth with a shotgun barrel hone. Barrels on inexpensive single-shot shotguns are frequently choked with a barrel swager which reduces the inside muzzle diameter. A swage offered by B-Square is constructed of heavy-duty steel to transmit power to the adjustable rollers which can swage any degree of choke desired. More recently, integral choke tubes have become quite popular and can often be installed for about the same price as other chokes.

Loose Actions: The best remedy to correct a loose action is to replace the worn pivot pin. Since the strength and functioning of the action depend a great deal on this pin, care must be exercised during the job. Even then, it is a difficult and time-consuming operation on many brands of single-shot guns.

With the pin already in the action, it would be difficult to heat the outside of the hole and cool the pin at the same time. More than likely, the old pin will have to be drilled out using a bit slightly smaller than the pin. The remaining metal in the hole can be reamed out, but be careful not to enlarge the original hole.

The new pin should be made of hard chrome-alloy steel, turned on a lathe to a diameter of about .001 inch larger than the finished hole, and slightly tapered for a start at one end. The frame should be stripped of all parts that will be affected by the heat, then heated just to the point of changing color — about 400 degrees F. While reaching this temperature, the pin should be immersed in ice water to contract it, and when the correct temperature is reached, the new pin should be removed from the ice water and quickly driven into the hole in the heated frame.

When both parts have cooled, the result should be a very tight fit. If any metal protrudes on either side of the frame, it should be ground off, filed, and polished smooth on the buffing wheel. This operation will no doubt damage the original finish and will probably require refinishing (casehardened or reblued) once the pin has been installed.

If the above operations were done by a professional gunsmith, the costs would probably exceed $200. Therefore, such restoration work can only be justified on a single-shot shotgun with sentimental value; the gun's actual value would come no where near this amount.

On the other hand, an old single-shot shotgun might be a good candidate for the advanced hobbyist to practice on. Just the above operation will give the worker experience in lathe operations, metallurgy, and bluing and/or case-coloring.

If the looseness is not too bad, it can often be corrected by peening lightly around the semicircular cut-out on the barrel lug as shown in Figures 10-4 and 10-5. If done correctly, the metal will be displaced and moved slightly forward to close the gap. Peen both sides with a block of steel under the lug. When the pivot-pin junction is tight, smooth the sides of the lug, where the peening took place. This operation may be done with a fine pillar file, honing stones, or even several grades of abrasive paper.

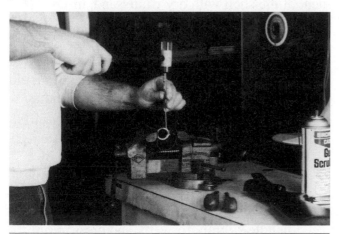

Figure 10-4: Peening lightly around the semicircular cutoff.

Figure 10-5: A temporary remedy for a loose single-shot shotgun action is to peen lightly around the semicircular cutoff.

DOUBLE-BARREL SHOTGUNS

Before the advent of repeating shotguns, the double-barrel, side-by-side shotguns was the only way available to get off a second shot at a covey of quail or a flock of low-flying ducks over decoys. Thus, the double side-by-side was the most popular hunting firearm around the turn of the century until repeating shotguns came into production. Then repeating shotguns and semiautomatics started to boom. Today, more hunters use semiautomatic shotguns for hunting than any other type.

Still, for upland game shooting many hunters consider a light double in either 12 or 20 gauge the ideal shotgun. Double-barrel shotguns usually handle and point nicely, aren't bulky, and most weigh quite a bit less than their semiautomatic or pump counterparts.

Double-barrel shotguns include both the side-by-side and over/under guns. Drillings or three-barrel guns are essentially a double-barrel shotgun with the addition of a single rifled barrel centered under the shotgun barrels. Troubleshooting techniques applying to double-barrel shotguns would certainly apply to drillings and similar types of firearms.

Malfunctions

Most of the malfunctions described for the single-shot, break-open shotgun also apply to double-barrel shotguns; that is, action looseness, broken mainsprings, firing pins, etc. The remedies are essentially the same as discussed previously.

One type of malfunction that is sometimes encountered is the inadvertent firing of both barrels. This problem especially prevails in older European double-barrel guns in which hammers and sears are made of soft steel. With age and wear, the trigger/sear contact becomes poor, and when one barrel is fired, the second barrel is jarred off at the same time.

The problem of both barrels inadvertently firing can sometimes be corrected by inspecting the sears with a magnifying glass and truing up any rounded surfaces by light honing. Since shotgun sears ride in extremely shallow grooves, usually only minor polishing is required to smooth, lighten, or heavy-up the trigger pull. However, if the contact points are badly worn, they may have to be recut, polished, and heat-treated. If this still does not solve the problem, the sear may have to be cut off, a new piece of heat-treated steel silver-soldered in its place, reshaped and polished. The problem may also be corrected by welding.

Rough Trigger Pulls: These may also be corrected by lightly honing the sear/hammer contact points, but go easy. Never allow a shotgun to have a "hair trigger." Many have discharged from merely bumping the butt against the ground. Remember, too, that any time much metal is removed from a sear's surface, it's likely that the casehardening has been removed. In this case, the part must be heat-treated.

Troubleshooting charts in Stoeger's book, *Firearms Disassembly with Exploded Views* list malfunctions common to many shotguns. The probable cause of these malfunctions along with their corrective action are also listed.

SLIDE-ACTION SHOTGUNS

The biggest single cause of a malfunction in other repeating firearms holds true for pump or slide-action shotguns: dirt, dust, and assorted debris when combined with gun oil and grease prevent the proper operation of the many different components. Other common malfunctions include: failure to feed properly, double-feeding, magazine failure to retain shells, headspace problems, action jams, action failing to lock, failure to extract or eject, gun failing to fire, hammer failing to cock, gun firing on closing the action, safety sticking, and cracks or seams on the bolt face. Also, badly pitted chambers and barrels are relatively commonplace on some of the older models that were used before the invention of noncorrosive primers.

Initial Inspection: When a pump shotgun is cleaned or in the shop for repairs, the mechanism should be tested for proper functioning. However, during this initial test, live ammunition should not be used. When dummy rounds are not available, fired shells may often be used for testing by turning in the uncrimped end so that the length of the shell will be approximately that of a live shell. If handloading equipment is available, dummy rounds may be produced by taking fired cases and leaving the fired primer intact. Fill the powder compartment of the shell with dry white sand, insert a wad over the sand, then load the remaining portion of the shell with shot in the normal way — including proper crimping. This will make an excellent dummy round for testing shotguns. You should have five rounds each of the various gauges.

To test pump shotguns, operate the gun in the following manner:

- With the sliding breech locked and the hammer cocked, push the operating handle slightly forward, and press in on the slide lock release. On the Winchester Model 12, Stevens Model 620, and others, this slide lock is on the left rear of the trigger guard. On Ithaca Model 37 shotguns, this slide-lock release latch is at the right side of the forward end of the trigger plate guard bow. Other models may have the latch located in other positions — on the side of the action, at the rear of the action near an exposed hammer, etc. — but in all cases the release will be a spring-operated button that depresses inward. With the slide-lock release button depressed, pull the operating handle fully and smartly to the rear and then push it fully and smartly forward. Reciprocate operating the handle several times in the same manner to test for the smoothness of the action.

- Retract the operating handle again, release the slide-lock release, and push the operating handle smartly forward to lock the sliding breech. Then attempt to retract the operating handle. The operating handle should not retract.

- Pull the trigger, allowing the hammer to move forward to the fired position, and attempt to retract the operating handle. The operating handle should retract.

- Retract the operating handle fully and then push it forward until the sliding breech is fully forward, but not locked, and the locking block not fully engaged. Then pull the trigger to release the hammer. The hammer should not be released until the sliding breech is fully locked and the locking block is fully seated in its aperture.

- Place two or three dummy rounds in the magazine and work them through the action to test the gun for feeding, loading, extraction, and ejection of

shells. The second shell should not leave the magazine until the first shell has been loaded into the chamber and the sliding breech is locked behind it.

- With the sliding breech locked and the hammer in the cocked position, slide the safety all the way to the right or ON position and attempt to pull the trigger. The trigger should not pull, nor should the hammer release. Try bumping the butt stock on a solid surface to see if the hammer will release or if the safety will be bumped to the OFF (firing) position.

- Slide the trigger safety to the OFF position and pull the trigger. The trigger should pull and the hammer be released to fire the gun.

If everything checks out during the preliminary inspection and the gun looks tight and in safe working condition, you may wish to test fire the gun with three rounds of live ammunition to insure that the gun will fire during actual operation.

Common Malfunctions

When the gun does not operate and function as it should during the preliminary inspection, damaged or improperly assembled parts are the most probable causes. Here are a few of the more common problems, causes, and solutions.

Operating Handle Sticks: When the forend cannot be easily moved forward or backward, the cause is often foreign matter in the receiver recesses. A bent or battered slide handle (the rear extension of the action slide) may be the culprit. Also check for burrs in the bar slot in the receiver or barrel head. A magazine may sometimes be dented enough to jam the action by binding the slide.

Clean and degrease the operating mechanism thoroughly, then check the action bar for bends or marring. If the action bar is damaged, the judicious

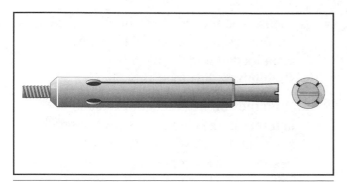

Figure 10-6: Expanding dent plug.

use of a hammer and file will often correct it. Burrs in the bar slot in the receiver or barrel head may be removed with a file or Arkansas stone, but proceed with caution, as the stoning process must be exact with no change in the angle of the faces and the volume of metal must not be materially reduced.

Dents: Dents in the magazine tube can cause a feeding problem and if much work is encountered in raising dents in shotgun barrels and magazine tubes, you may want to consider purchasing a simple expanding dent plug (Figure 10-6) and brass hammer. They should be made of bronze to prevent jamming or marring the surfaces. Expand the dent plug until it fits tightly under the dent, and then use a brass hammer to tap around the edge of the dent to force the dented metal up (Figure 10-7). Keep hammering until the dent is up or the plug comes loose. If the plug comes loose before the dent is up,

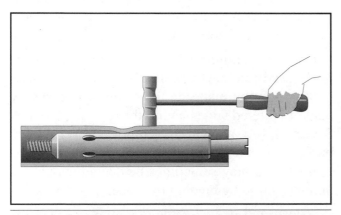

Figure 10-7: Expand the dent plug until it fits tightly under the dent, and then use a brass hammer to tap around the edge of the dent to raise the metal.

repeat the process of expanding the dent plug, pushing it under the dent and hammering around the edge until the dent is completely up. This same procedure may also be used to remove dents from shotgun barrels.

Sliding Breech Does Not Lock: This problem may be due to foreign matter on the face of the sliding breech, in the extractor grooves in the barrel head, or in the locking block aperture in the sliding breech. If cleaning and degreasing doesn't correct the problem, look for a broken firing pin or burrs on the edges of the locking block or locking aperture in the receiver.

A broken firing pin should, of course, be replaced. If burrs are present, carefully hone these away with an Arkansas stone and plenty of honing oil.

Hammer Does Not Cock Properly, or Slips: This condition may be due to burrs or foreign matter on the sear hooks of the hammer or sear, worn or broken hooks, missing or improperly assembled parts in the trigger mechanism, or a broken mainspring.

If cleaning does not solve the problem, deepening the notches with a file may help; otherwise the parts will have to be replaced. Check the assembly drawings to see if all trigger mechanism parts are assembled correctly. Replace any broken parts.

Firing Pin Does Not Retract into Sliding Breech: Check for a broken firing pin and burrs on the firing pin or locking block. Replace a broken firing pin. Remove burrs with emery cloth and honing stones.

Slide Does Not Go Fully Forward: Check for debris in the slide apertures. The problem may also be caused by a jammed locking block or slide plunger. Less frequently, you will find that a broken firing pin may be causing the trouble.

Thoroughly clean and degrease the gun, then check to see that all parts of the mechanism are assembled properly. Look for worn or broken parts and replace any that are defective.

Slide Lock Does Not Function: The most probable cause of this malfunction is a bent slide-lock release spring. However, if this is not the cause, look for burrs on the rear of the slide and also on the slide lock. The slide lock may also be bent.

Replace the slide-lock release spring if this is the instigator of the trouble. Burrs may be removed, as before, with a file and Arkansas stone. Straighten the slide lock with a hammer and file it if it is bent.

Slide Does Not Retract Fully: This malfunction may be due to a broken hammer, an improperly assembled mainspring, an improperly assembled stock tank, and, in some cases, a broken firing pin.

Disassemble the gun and check for improperly assembled parts as well as worn and broken parts. Reassemble correctly, replacing any worn or broken parts.

Shells Are Not Extracted or Ejected: A rough or dirty chamber is most often the cause of extraction problems. However, if the problem persists after cleaning the chamber, look for a worn, broken, or burred extractor. Also check the extractor spring and check for an improperly assembled ejector. Both can cause all sorts of problems in slide-action shotguns.

The chamber may be cleaned with a power drill and a brass chamber brush or bore-polishing rod. Also remove any caked dirt that may be found in the extractor recesses. Burred parts should be smoothed with a file and honing stone. Missing, broken, or worn parts should be replaced.

Two Shells Fed into Receiver at Once: Double-feeding is usually due to a bent, sticking, or broken shell stop or else a loose shell-stop screw. Caked debris in the shell-stop seating grooves can be the cause of the problem.

If the problem persists after thoroughly cleaning the gun, straighten a bent shell stop by hammering it against a flat steel block (anvil). Replace it if it is broken or badly worn. If replacement parts are not available, sometimes the part can be repaired by brazing. Check the shell-stop screw and tighten it if necessary.

Shells Stick In Magazine: A corroded or bent magazine follower is the most probable cause of this malfunction, but a dented tube, broken or weak magazine spring, or dirt in the magazine are all possibilities.

Clean any corrosion from the magazine and remove any dents. The magazine can usually be straightened by driving a dowel (slightly undersized) into the magazine tube. Dents are removed as discussed previously, and worn or broken parts must be replaced.

Trigger Safety Sticks: If the problem isn't caused by gummy residue in the safety slots, the problem is usually caused by a worn or burred carrier plunger spring. A jammed or rusted trigger spring can also cause the hang-up.

After cleaning the safety and related parts, check the areas for burrs. Replace any missing, worn, or broken parts.

SEMIAUTOMATIC SHOTGUNS

Malfunctions in autoloading shotguns may be caused by broken, damaged, or incorrectly assembled parts, faulty ammunition, incorrect operation, or debris in the mechanism. Since the receivers of autoloading shotguns are comparatively open, foreign matter can easily enter and clog the mechanisms. Therefore, a clean, properly lubricated gun inspected at frequent intervals is the best insurance against malfunctions and stoppages.

Malfunctions of autoloading shotguns sometimes occur from obscure conditions that would not affect a pump or other manually operated repeater. Most manufacturers put their guns through severe tests before leaving the factory to ensure that the gun will function properly in the field. However, there may be potential trouble in some guns, undetectable at the factory, which will come to light only when used in the field under varying conditions.

Worn Parts: The remaining causes of malfunctions can usually be traced to worn parts caused by excessive use and firing of the gun and, in some cases, mistreatment. For example, Franchi autoloading shotguns often develop feeding problems after several years of use. This problem can usually be traced to a worn carrier latch made of formed sheet steel, its edges turned to form flanges that contain the opposite holes for its pivot pin. Since this latch is under considerable repeated stress and the outside loop of the pivot holes is fairly thin, the holes will eventually begin to enlarge and finally the bridge of the loop will break, causing the gun to misfeed.

To correct this problem, raise a bead of steel weld at the pivot holes, leaving the walls of the latch thicker at that point, then redrill the holes to the proper size. Be sure to leave room for the latch spring. This extra thickness will give the additional strength necessary to eliminate future problems.

Another commonly worn part is on the Remington Model 1100 shotgun. This model utilizes a small ring of special rubber that fits into a groove on the magazine tube just forward of the piston and the piston seal ring. After many shots over a period of years, the rubber ring can become worn and lose some of its sealing qualities, causing a malfunction. Every gun shop should keep a few of these seals on hand at all times. They may be purchased from Remington Arms Company Inc.

Autoloading shotguns also develop feeding problems from worn magazine springs. During the firing and feeding cycle, the carrier latch is activated by being struck by the head of the next unfired shell from the magazine. If the magazine spring is weak, the fed shell may have inadequate energy when propelled back against the latch and may fail to disengage it. The simplest way to correct this problem is to replace the magazine spring with a full-strength one. A temporary solution is to stretch the magazine spring or to adjust the carrier latch by bending it forward slightly.

The best way to troubleshoot these problems is to learn to recognize these worn parts when inspecting the group of parts where the problem is most likely to occur. When cleaning the gun, examine every part closely. Look for bright spots, rounded corners that should be sharp, out-of-round holes, and broken parts. Also check an exploded view of the gun to make certain that no parts are missing. This inspection alone should uncover any worn, missing, or broken parts. If none are found, chances are the malfunction was caused by dirt or debris in the action, which is already remedied since you have thoroughly cleaned the gun.

General Malfunctions

The autoloading guns covered in this section are generally similar in basic design, operation, and functioning. However, certain parts will naturally vary somewhat. Malfunctions will therefore be covered generally as a guide only to be applied to the specific gun if and when applicable. The main concern is to learn how the guns function.

A malfunctioning gun should first be cleaned before inspecting the firearm or any repairs are made. This is especially true of any semiautomatic weapon.

In climates where the temperature and humidity are high or where salt air is present or during rainy seasons, the shotgun should be thoroughly inspected at frequent intervals and kept lightly oiled when not in use. In extreme climates the various groups of the shotgun should be disassembled for drying and oiling parts.

See that unexposed parts and surfaces are kept clean and oiled, such as the underside of the barrel, magazine tube, inner surface of the slide handle tube, interior of the magazine tube, slide handle bar, interior of receiver, operating parts, trigger group, spring wells, and similar parts and surfaces. Light oil should be used for lubricating.

All wood surfaces should also be inspected frequently to see that swelling due to moisture does not bind any working parts. If linseed oil is used on the gun stock, be careful not to let any of the oil seep into the working mechanism or it will gum the parts when it dries.

Failure to Fire: As with other types of guns, when a semiautomatic shotgun fails to fire, the cause is most often gummy residue in the bolt, which prevents the firing pin from moving forward the proper distance and/or at the proper speed. In shotguns using the short-recoil system, a light pull on the trigger can tip the sear against the second notch on the hammer, killing its inertia. An improper adjustment between the hammer catch and hammer can also cause misfires.

Firing-pin length is especially critical in an autoloader, and at the first sign of a misfire, the bolt assembly should be disassembled and thoroughly cleaned and inspected. If the pin is impeded in its travel to the rear for any reason, the gun can fire automatically, slamming the bolt back and forth until the magazine is empty.

A broken firing pin or firing-pin spring should be obvious upon inspecting the disassembled bolt assembly. If at all possible, replace these with new factory parts. If this is not practical, new ones can be made or the broken one can be repaired by welding, but use extreme caution to obtain the original dimensions. To insure that the firing pin is not too long, tape a piece of electrical tape over the primer hole of a *fired shell*. Insert this empty shell with the tape into the chamber and let the bolt assembly slam home as if operating during actual firing. If the piece of tape is indented at all, the firing pin is too long and must be shortened.

Bolt Fails to Close Fully: This problem can be caused by a lack of lubricant on mating surfaces, but more than likely the fault lies with burrs or foreign matter in the locking recesses in the receiver raceways. Stone all burrs and sharp edges on the hammerhead contacting link and check for sharp corners on the rear of the chamber. Should

the chamber rotate slightly, the slides can hang up on the sharp edges.

Sometimes a broken, rusted, or improperly engaged recoil spring can cause the action not to lock up properly, as can a damaged carrier or carrier latch.

When the reason for a bolt's failure to close fully is not readily apparent, remove the appropriate groups from the gun, then clean, inspect, and test them (in that order). Old shells may be the cause of the problem, so don't overlook this. Also inspect the shell seat in the barrel.

Failure to Feed: The problem of improper feeding in autoloading shotguns will probably be the one most often encountered . . . or at least this has been my experience. In general, feeding problems may be due to a faulty magazine (and components), a faulty carrier, malfunction of shell stop(s), or a dirty action — preventing the appropriate parts from functioning correctly. Of course, if the fired shell fails to eject, a new shell cannot be fed into the chamber and feeding is again a problem.

Magazine tubes under the barrel of a shotgun are located in an ideal place to get banged against all sorts of objects. When dents, gashes, and bends occur, feeding problems almost always arise from binding of the magazine spring of crimping the shells within the tube. In most cases, dented magazine tubes can be repaired by inserting an expanding dent plug.

All autoloading shotguns use two shell stops positioned on each side of the receiver wall. The primary shell stop delays the shell at the mouth of the magazine until the lifter or carrier accepts it. The second shell stop holds back the other shell while the first shell is being lifted by the carrier. Once the first shell is chambered, the second shell stop releases the next shell, which is then held in position by the first shell stop. Should this second shell stop miss or release too soon, the shell in the magazine ends up on the ground. On some guns, this can be caused by the carrier lock head being too low, thus allowing the rim of the shell to pass through the cutoff. The problem may be solved by installing a new carrier lock, but usually the repair can be made by inserting the carrier lock in a vise with the button and head protruding and then striking the button lightly with a hammer to bend the carrier lock in slightly. Assemble and check your work carefully to see that the shell head does not pass through the carrier lock. Finish up by feeding a shell from the magazine tube and adjusting the carrier lock. To do so, remove the trigger guard and slide a shell in and out of the magazine tube. If the front end of the carrier lock scrapes the shell, it should be stoned until it just clears the shell case.

The second shell stop seldom gives trouble except for occasionally burring at the edges after heavy use over a period of years. This problem can normally be dressed out by stoning.

Shell lifters are another source of trouble when feeding is a problem. If a shell lifter is badly worn or bent, it will not fully lift the shell and a replacement is about all that can be done to remedy the situation.

Defective Safeties: Most autoloading shotguns employ trigger-block safeties, which utilize a spring-loaded plunger that works in two notches. When the safety button is pushed from SAFE to FIRE, the plunger is depressed and rides over a hill that separates the two notches. This hill, after years of use, can become rounded and can then slip easily from one notch to the other, rendering the safety feature worthless. Sometimes the safety can be corrected by grinding the notches deeper, but a replacement of this critical device is recommended. Also, if the plunger or its spring become worn, replacement must be made.

Miscellaneous Malfunctions: The problems of extracting, ejecting, rough trigger pulls, etc., are essentially the same for autoloading shotguns as for other types of shotguns and rifles, so there is no need to mention them again under this chapter. Again, to be able to adequately troubleshoot any firearm, you must first understand how it functions, and exactly how each part is used to make the gun work properly. Once this is learned, you will have little difficulty troubleshooting the weapon. Once you have the problem isolated, it is simply a matter of repairing worn parts or installing new ones.

Chapter 11
Soldering and Brazing

Anyone seriously interested in gunsmithing should obtain a good knowledge of soldering and brazing as soon as possible, especially since it is becoming extremely difficult to obtain many parts for obsolete firearms.

With this knowledge and the proper equipment, the gunsmith can make all sort of repairs on many broken gun parts that will last as long or longer than the original, in many cases.

Soldering can prove useful for mounting sight ramps, and for resoldering old double-barrel shotguns when the old solder deteriorates to the point where parts might come apart upon firing. This latter technique is not for the amateur; the job takes a set of special barrel wedges, clamps and the professional skill that few gunsmiths possess.

It is best not to apply heat to any part of a gun until the person planning to do it is absolutely certain that he or she knows what is going on. The experienced hobbyist, however, can make repairs on certain non-critical parts by silver soldering, if care is exercised. For example, the thin, semi-fancy trigger guards of certain double-barrel shotguns are subject to breakage; these may easily be repaired by silver soldering, and then rebluing. Tangs on some of the older Winchester Model 92s and 73s

are often found broken, and can be helped by silver soldering. So can many other non-critical parts found on firearms — hammer spurs, triggers, and swivels, for example.

Regardless of the type of metal joining — soldering, brazing, or welding — there are certain requirements common to all three; namely:

- Cleanliness.

- Flux.

- Proper amount of heat.

The first, cleanliness, means that the metal to be joined must be absolutely free of scale, grease, oil and dirt, and clean and bright. This could mean, in some cases, that the bluing should be removed, such as at the muzzle of a rifle barrel prior to sweating on a sight ramp. The main purpose of flux is to prevent oxidation. When metal is heated, it will oxidize to prevent the formation of a good joint; flux, when properly applied, will help prevent this. The third, heat, must be sufficiently high to flow the joining metal, and also to raise the temperature of the parts to be joined. If you can meet these three requirements, you are well on your way to becoming an expert at soldering, brazing and welding.

Soft Soldering

Sight ramps, shotgun barrels, rimfire barrel liners, scope sight bases, and some other firearm accessories can be satisfactorily attached by soft soldering. Most solder found in your local hardware store, however, is designed for electrical and plumbing applications, and is not the best for use on firearms. Hot caustic bluing solutions attack the soft-soldered joints, and in some cases will render the joints useless, requiring that they be re-soldered.

Brownells of Montezuma, Iowa, has solved this problem with their *Hi-Force 44* solder, which contains 4 percent silver and 96 percent tin, and can be used on all types of gunmetals except aluminum. Best of all, users have reported that parts joined with *Hi-Force 44* showed no effects when immersed in the hot caustic bluing solution.

When the areas on both pieces to be joined have been thoroughly cleaned, the areas are then "coated" with solder; this process is called tinning. Heat the areas with a torch — propane will do — to a temperature high enough to melt the solder; but first apply soldering flux, such as No. 4 Comet. Spread a thin coat of melted solder completely over the areas to be joined. This is accomplished by heating the metal — not the solder — with the torch. By doing so, the metal will melt the solder when it reaches the proper temperature. If the solder is heated and melted onto the surfaces, it will not make a good bond, and most of the time, none at all. While the surfaces are still hot, take a thick rag, and with a quick swipe, wipe off all excess solder; the thinner the better. A good joint cannot be had if too much solder is in between the two pieces to be joined. Then let the parts cool at room temperature until they can be easily handled.

Once cool, the parts can be located exactly in position and then clamped securely. Heat the parts again with a propane torch, to a point where the solder flows freely. Additional solder may be fed to the two joining areas, either around the edges of

Figure 11-1: Soft-soldered double-barrel shotguns that have defective solder can be re-soldered, but the defective areas must first be carefully cleaned and degreased. Care must also be exercised, so as not to allow the good areas to become unsoldered.

the objects or possibly through screw holes that may be in the pieces. Be careful not to clog the holes if this latter route is taken. Any excess solder should be wiped off immediately with a dry cloth, before they solidify.

If you are soldering a part on a blued surface, the bluing should be removed only where the parts will join, so that all surfaces that can be seen will retain the blue. Be extremely careful not to apply too much heat, so as not to discolor the surrounding blued surfaces. Parts that have been properly cleaned and tinned with the *Hi-Force 44* solder, and then joined together, will be permanently attached and take just about any treatment one would normally give a gun. It is not recommended for repairing broken parts that will be exposed to strain even the slightest bit.

Silver Soldering

This technique will find the most uses around the gun shop. Silver solder becomes fluid enough with heat to flow through small cracks and, although it requires more heat than soft solder, it normally requires less than conventional brazing. For gun work, a solder that flows between 1,000 and 1,200 degrees F. is best; anything higher will render some metals useless for gun work. In general, the parts to be joined must be cleaned as described previously, and then held in position. Apply flux to the

Figure 11-2: Sears on many double shotguns — especially some of the inexpensive foreign models — were often made of relatively soft metal, which eventually wore and usually resulted in both barrels firing simultaneously. One solution to this problem is to cut off the tip of the sear, and silver solder another piece of good hardened steel in its place.

joining surfaces. Both are then heated to a dull red to bright red — depending upon the metal to be joined — and when hot enough, the silver solder is touched to the joint, which will "suck" in the solder between the pieces being bonded.

Since the gunsmith will encounter many types of metals and alloys during the course of his or her work, selecting the proper solder for a particular job is often difficult. Knowing the exact proportions of solder and flux — and the right solder and flux — requires considerable experience. *Fusion*

solders come already ground in their own special flux in the right proportions. Because of this, practically anyone with a minimum amount of experience can do top-quality soldering with the following types:

S-4 1000 Silver Braze: This is a low temperature, high-strength brazing alloy for use mainly where tight-fitting joints, with a minimum amount of fill are desired. It melts at 1,000 degrees F. When using, however, make sure that you mix it well and keep the container tightly closed. The first time I tried this solution was on a recoil spring for a Remington autoloading shotgun. It was the first day of the rabbit season and the customer had to have his gun fixed quickly. I had no parts on hand, so I used *Heat Stop* on either side of the break, and silver-soldered the joint. Actually, I did not expect the joint to hold, but it would allow him a few shots at the running bunnies. I then ordered another spring for his shotgun. This was more than five years ago, and the joint is still holding. The part that I ordered is still in my parts bin.

S-4 1200 Silver Braze: This solder closely resembled S-4 1000, but has a wider melting range and higher flow point for better filling characteristics. This is the solder to use when putting on front ramps that do not match the barrel exactly. It can also be used for joining small parts where chips of steel have been broken, or where it is impossible to hold parts together for brazing.

DMS-1200-750 Non-flowing Silver Braze: This solder does not flow when it melts. It can prevent runny solder, and helps keep you from losing your alignment in jig setups, which can happen when solder begins to run. It is excellent when used for ramps, ribs, sights and repairs where the fit does not have to be perfect.

For most silver soldering in my shop, I use Brownells *Silvaloy,* which melts at about 1,100 degrees F. and flows at around 1,150 degrees F. This has about the lowest melting point of any commercial silver braze, and is excellent for use on gun parts. It comes in both wire and ribbon forms, to take care of most gunsmithing applications.

Welding

Acetylene Welding: An oxyacetylene welding outfit is one of the most useful pieces of equipment for the gun shop. The acetylene torch alone may be used for bending, forging, hardening and tempering, and soft soldering. With the oxygen added, it can be used for silver soldering, brazing, and welding. Most any good set will suffice for gun work, but my preference has been the smaller units (tanks) that can be easily rolled or carried to various locations. Mine happens to be manufactured by Uniweld of 2850 Ravenswood Road, Fort Lauderdale, FL 33312. It is known as an aircraft welder, and comes in kit form with regulators, hoses, tips and tanks. The tanks are placed in a rolling carriage, and can easily be rolled from one area in the shop to another.

Tip sizes are important and should be selected for the type of work that will be encountered. For example, size 0 is small and good for spot annealing on some casehardened receivers prior to drilling and tapping for scope mounts. Size 4 is used when bending bolt handles to accept telescopic sights, while those sizes in between are used for various welding and brazing applications.

Certain safety precautions must be followed when using welding equipment. Eye protection is absolutely necessary. I use a pair of colored goggles for most work. Another important thing is the method of lighting the torches. Never use a cigarette lighter. I have heard of people who have had their hand blown off during this practice. Use a flint-type torch lighter, designed especially for lighting acetylene welders. You also should have some type of body protection, such as welder's gloves and a leather welder's jacket. The latter is rather costly, so many gunsmiths wear cotton overalls, or a blue jean jacket, instead. Be extremely cautious about the surrounding atmosphere. Obviously, you don't want to use the torch around any combustible materials or fumes; these can be disastrous. Many auto mechanics have lost their lives when repairing gas tanks. They drain all the liquid gas out, but forget about the fumes. When the torch is applied, an explosion results.

For welding and brazing, the gunsmith will need an assortment of welding and brazing rods. In my work, I've found one type to fulfill all my needs to date: the 3 percent nickel steel welding rods. If I should ever obtain a TIG outfit, I definitely will need Certanium TIG welding rods. These rods respond to heat treatment with the base metal, and will weld most grades of steel such as AISI-SAI 4130, 4340, 4140, 80, 20, 6150, 40 and others.

I hesitate to get into actual welding techniques because the subject really requires a complete book on the subject. Actually, the best way to learn welding is to attend one of the many classes that are held in communities all over the United States. Most are given at night, so as not to interfere with most people's work. Under a good instructor, the student can learn a great deal about welding in a relatively short period of time.

When welding, your work must be securely clamped before applying the torch. Many gunsmiths have an assortment of jigs suitable for practically any job that might be encountered. For welding small parts, I use two conventional vises for holding the work, one half of the part in each vise. The vises are then swiveled until the joint is in perfect alignment. If the parts are very small, use alligator clips with *Heat Stop* to prevent the springs from losing their temper too quickly. Have plenty of such clips on hand, because after each weld the springs will be of little use, and will have to be discarded due to the high heat used in welding.

Each welding torch tip normally comes with recommendations for the proper gas pressure (set the regulators accordingly). These should be followed, until you have reason to do otherwise. The chart in Figure 11-3 should be helpful.

Tip Size	Drill Size	Min. Oxygen Pressure (psi)	Max. Oxygen Pressure (psi)	Min. Acetylene Pressure (psi)	Max. Acetylene Pressure (psi)	Min. Acetylene Consumption	Max. Acetylene Consumption	Metal Thickness
000	75	½	2	½	2	½	3	Up to $1/32$"
00	70	1	2	1	2	1	4	$1/64$ -$3/64$"
0	65	1	3	1	3	2	6	$1/32$ -$5/64$"
1	60	1	4	1	4	4	8	$3/64$ -$3/32$"
2	56	2	5	2	5	7	13	$1/16$ -$1/8$"
3	53	3	7	3	7	8	36	$1/8$ -$3/16$"
4	49	4	10	4	10	10	41	$3/16$ -$1/4$"
5	43	5	12	5	15	15	59	$1/4$ -$1/2$"

Figure 11-3: Tip sizes and recommended gas pressure.

To use the torch, first turn on the acetylene and ignite it with the flint-type "striker." This will give a dirty, sooty flame. Then turn on a small amount of oxygen and the flame will clear. If the oxygen is below normal requirements, the light-colored inner portion of the flame will be long, or "fishtailed." This is known as a reducing flame, which has an excessive amount of acetylene. As the amount of oxygen is increased, the light-colored inner portion, or oxygen cone, will shorten and become clearly defined. This is known as the neutral flame, or one which contains enough oxygen to burn all the acetylene, and will see the most use around the shop. If the oxygen is increased still further, the oxygen cone will grow very short, and there will be an excess of oxygen known as an oxidizing flame.

Too much of either gas does steel no good. For example, the reducing flame will carburize the metal and harden it. It is, however, recommended for brass, as it will not burn it. The oxidizing flame will burn the carbon out of the steel and ruin it. Remember, when welding or bending bolt handles, never let the oxygen cone in the center of the flame touch the metal, as it will quickly burn out the carbon in the steel.

When welding, the general principle is to heat the two parts hot enough, so that they begin to flow and fuse together. Then use the welding rod to fill in the gaps. This is easier said than done, and much practice should be done on scrap metal before attempting work on good parts.

In addition to repairing small parts, the welder is frequently used in the gun shops to weld on new bolt handles. These new handles may be purchased from various sources for only a few dollars apiece. The bolt ends are normally cut at an angle; when cutting off the original bolt — prior to welding on the new one — this should be cut at an angle, too.

There are bolt welding jigs available, but many gunsmiths prefer to use two vises — one fixed and one portable — to hold the bolt and bolt handle. The steel vises draw off sufficient heat from the lugs, provided they are placed correctly, then, by "playing" the flame of the torch away from the bolt body, the job can be done in a relatively short period of time. The usual procedure is to "tack" the two pieces first, then let them cool slowly at room temperature. Before doing this, however, some gunsmiths pack the inside of the bolt body with wet asbestos, to help keep the temperature down. The entire bolt body and accessories must be completely stripped before any heat is applied; this includes the firing pin (striker), striker spring, extractor, and ejector.

When the part has completely cooled, the two parts are once again heated and the voids filled in with 3 percent nickel steel welding rod. If you have never done this, or if your welding experience is limited, it is strongly recommended that you do your first couple of jobs under the supervision of a professional — one who knows what he is doing. The locking lugs on any bolt are hardened and heat-treated to stand a given amount of pressure. Any heat that will color the steel will do damage to these lugs, so use extreme caution when applying heat to the bolt handle.

Electric Welding: Some gunsmiths maintain that electric welding is better than acetylene welding for gunsmithing work. For me, however, if I could only have one, it would be the acetylene welding outfit.

The main advantage of the electric welder is that it works so fast that heat is spread over only a very small area, compared to the same job using acetylene. When this type of welder can be used with a TIG attachment, then I might agree that it would be the best outfit to have, especially for welding bolts, receivers, and other heat-treated parts of a gun. Any of these three types of welding are definitely not for the beginner; all, if done incorrectly, can damage the gun beyond repair; and, if the gun is fired, it can cause serious injury.

Any of the welders offered by the mail order houses that are of good quality should suffice for the gun shop. However, if you do purchase one, make sure that it has both AC and DC modes. The cheaper AC welders are very difficult to hold an arc with, so get a good one if you are going this route. Special rods are required for AC welders; the one most used around the shop will be a mild steel rod. If the part being formed or repaired is heat-treated, you will want to go with a rod that allows this. One of the older rods was called "Toolweld," but I'm not certain if these are still going by that name. I have not seen them around for some time. For

extreme hardness, there are other rods, but they will not take bluing, at least not by ordinary methods. So if the part is exposed, it will have to be blued. For stainless metals, stainless steel rods must be used.

Arc welding, like acetylene welding, requires much practice to master sufficiently for practical use in the gunshop. The machine must be set at the proper voltage and amperage. Each type and size of welding rod carries with it complete specifications for setting various machines. Settings will vary with the type of rod and the thickness of the material being welded.

The rod is placed in the rod holder, with the ground clamp on the piece to be welded, and then touched to the metal, in a way similar to striking a match. It is touched only for an instant and then withdrawn, leaving the tip close to, but not touching, the work. As the rod melts, it will naturally get shorter, and the operator must lower the tip to maintain this exact distance. If not maintained at the proper distance, the result will be either losing the arc or burning holes in the work.

Since arc welding will not penetrate cracks to any appreciable depth, the joint must be scarfed; that is, cut out with a grinder at a 45-degree angle to the depth to be welded.

With the amount of intense heat generated by an electric welder, it is easy for the metal to warp or expand out of position. Therefore, each piece to be welded should be securely clamped in place. When welding relatively thick pieces, weld only a small amount at a time, first on one side and then on the other, so that expansion will be even.

Remember that extreme care must be taken in doing or watching arc welding, because the eyes can be damaged by the ultra-bright arc. Special colored goggles or a face shield must be used to filter the harmful ultra-violet rays from the eyes. One glimpse can damage the eyes seriously, causing much pain, if not permanent damage.

Chapter 12
Metal Hardening and Tempering

Many parts of firearms have been casehardened, especially receivers of shotguns and early repeating rifles, such as the Winchester Model 1886.

Frames for the Colt Single Action Army revolver were also once casehardened, as were trigger guards, buttplates, hammers, triggers, and similar parts for other arms. The main purpose for this hardening was to increase the life of the part, and prevent it from wearing so quickly. Color casehardening also enhanced the beauty of the metal, and helped keep it from rusting.

The person who knows how to harden metal properly can turn out pieces of work that will last and wear just about as long as the hardest steel. In examining a properly casehardened piece of metal, the surface will have a fine grayish appearance, and in many places, mottled with colored tints that are pleasing and beautiful to the eye. It can be further observed that the hardening is of such depth that it will wear for a long time.

While the majority of gunsmiths in the United States perform hardening and tempering of gun metal to some extent, few perform any color casehardening. In fact, color casehardening is almost becoming a lost art. The reason is simple. Few gunsmiths know anything at all about the process,

except what they have heard from others, who probably knew even less. These same gunsmiths will then claim that the practice is beyond most people, and that it should definitely not be practiced by the hobbyist. They reason that the very deadly chemical, potassium cyanide, must be used to color caseharden, and a speck of this powder in the eye can kill instantly. Furthermore, many claim that warpage is a problem, sometimes causing much work to reassemble the gun. In questioning some of these "gunsmiths" further, I found that none had actually tried color casehardening themselves, probably due to the rumors they had heard.

Cyanide is about the most deadly chemical obtainable, and should therefore never be used by amateurs or hobbyists for any reason. In fact, few professionals should try it either; it's just too darn risky. While cyanide can be used in some casehardening applications, it is not absolutely necessary.

It is also possible for warpage to take place in some receivers; this is usually caused by the heat being too high, or held at a certain temperature for too long, or both. Those experts who can obtain a basic gray appearance with pleasing reds, yellows, browns, and blues thrown in seldom have any serious warpage problems. Those whose work normally comes out with a basic dark blue background, with streaks of gray and few other colors, sometimes do have problems. The beginner should not attempt to color caseharden receivers. He or she should stick to such non-critical parts as hammers, triggers, trigger guards, and buttplates. Then, once experience has been gained, the home gunsmith may wish to advance to color casehardening receivers for rifles and shotguns.

Color casehardening can be quite time-consuming, especially at the outset, and this is probably the main reason why few gunsmiths even attempt such a project these days. When the need for such work arises, they merely send the part or parts to a company that specializes in such work, proclaiming that the practice is too complex for the average gunsmith, not to mention the amateur. This is not quite true, in my opinion. Amateurs have been able to easily obtain a hardened surface on metal; it's a good color that seems to be the difficult part . . .and those who are good at it are reluctant to give up their "secret."

If your first attempt at color casehardening is not a success, welcome to the club. Neither was mine, nor was my second attempt, or third. It took four tries for me to start getting colors I liked, and each try took another couple of hours of preparation. From this, it would seem a little useless to even try to color caseharden, but not really. It is an excellent project for the amateur, since the initial equipment, if you already have a shop, is not too expensive and the practice provides excellent experience. Most professionals don't have the time for much experimentation, and therefore never learn how to caseharden.

While there are several methods of color casehardening — many of which are included in this chapter — the basic essentials are the correct heat for the right amount of time and bubbles in the quench bath. When any of the methods listed in this chapter are tried, and you don't get good colors, the reasons could be:

- Metal not properly polished.

Figure 12-1: The main ingredients for a simple casehardening operation are bone meal, charcoal, and leather.

- Part heated above 1,400 degrees F.
- Quench bath not agitated enough.

Even when these methods have been followed to the letter, varying results will be obtained; so you might have to do some experimenting on your own to obtain the desired results. Such items as type of metal and the exact degree of heat, along with the exact time, will all affect the final outcome of the casehardening job.

You will need a cast-iron container large enough to hold the part to be hardened; allow for at least one inch space on all sides. If you can't find a suitable container, you might find suitable electrical outlet boxes made of cast iron that will suffice. Some, however, are cast aluminum and these will not work. This type of electrical box is used for wiring in hazardous areas in service stations, airplane hangers and grain bins. They come in different sizes, from those suitable for a duplex receptacle to large junction boxes. If you have to buy the larger ones, however, they're going to cost a pretty penny. Perhaps you can search a building that is being torn down; if any are available, the contractor handling the demolition job will probably give you one, or at least sell you one for a dollar or two.

The best container is an iron box made especially for the purpose with a loose fitting lid that can be opened quickly so the contents can be dumped into the quench solution while still at the desired temperature. I have no idea where these can be obtained, unless you contact a foundry and have one made. A box about 5" x 5" x 10" long — with walls about ¼" thick — should suffice for most gunsmithing applications. I used an old Dutch oven for my initial experimenting.

Other necessary ingredients include granulated raw bone, granulated charcoal, hydrocarbonated bone, and charred leather. The professional who already has a heat-treating furnace is well on his way to casehardening. The bone meal can be purchased from a gardening supply shop and granulated leather can usually be obtained from a leather tannery or shoe shop; or you can cut up some old leather items such as shoes, then char and pulverize them.

A suitable furnace can be made from fire bricks; then, by using a propane torch and air from a vacuum cleaner (in the blowing mode), you can create enough heat for casehardening. I've had reasonably good results by burying the container in burning charcoal, and letting it cook for a while.

To obtain the brilliant colors often desired for casehardened parts, it is essential that the parts be well polished. The better the polish, the more brilliant will be the colors. Then clean the parts by boiling them in a commercial cleaning solution, such as Brownells Dicro-Clean No. 909, for about 15 minutes. After cleaning, the parts should not be touched with the hands, else the oil from the skin will leave spots on the finished work. Handle the parts only with clean tongs or clean rubber gloves. Work quickly from now on.

Figure 12-2: Once mixed, the ingredients should be charred and pulverized before packing the part in them.

Pack the parts to be hardened in an equal mixture of charred bone meal, charred leather, and charcoal; be sure that at least a one-inch thickness of these materials surrounds the parts to be casehardened on all sides. This packing is done in the cast-iron box previously described. When properly packed, place the lid in position and seal the seam with furnace cement or fire clay. If more than one part is in the box, make sure they don't touch each other. Place the packed cast-iron box with the part in a heat-treating furnace, and bring the box to a temperature of about 1,200 to 1,300 degrees F. If you don't have a thermometer, polish a spot on the container and watch the metal change color. When it becomes a dark to cherry red, hold it at this heat for about 30 minutes.

While the iron container is "cooking," fill a container with clean, cool, soft water (distilled will be fine) and arrange a wire mesh screen about eight inches below the surface of the water to catch the small parts as they are dumped. A small pipe should also be inserted in the bottom of the container, so that a strong jet of air can be injected into the water while the parts are being dumped. Actually, an air hose in the top of the container, with the nozzle extending down to the bottom, will work just as well. Make sure that the hot parts do not burn the hose as they are being dumped. This saves time in fitting a pipe through the bottom of the container.

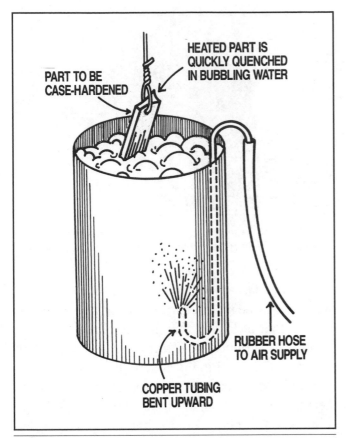

PART TO BE CASE-HARDENED

HEATED PART IS QUICKLY QUENCHED IN BUBBLING WATER

RUBBER HOSE TO AIR SUPPLY

COPPER TUBING BENT UPWARD

Figure 12-3: Here is one way to make a suitable "dip" bath of the casehardened part. The air bubbles have a lot to do with the mottled colors obtained.

If you plan to do considerable casehardening, it would be best to make a suitable container to be used especially for the purpose.

Once the heated container has "cooked" for about 30 minutes, grasp it with suitable tongs and hold it near the surface of the water, which should now be agitating via an air jet from the hose. Gently knock off the fire clay, quickly remove the lid, and dump the entire contents into the bubbling container of water. The wire mesh should catch the parts, while the charred materials drop through the mesh to the bottom of the tank. Sometimes, these materials will "weld" into a solid ball around the parts. If so, use the tongs to gently break up the ball, being careful not to scratch or otherwise harm the part being hardened. Make sure the air bubbles are really prevalent, as these are what give the fine

mottled effect on the metal which is so admired in casehardened objects.

When the parts have cooled, they should be taken out of the water and boiled in clean soft water, dried in sawdust, and oiled. If done properly, the parts should be tough skinned with highly desirable colors.

If the part comes out a very light gray with no color, chances are you let the temperature get too hot. On the other hand, if the parts are a blue-black color, they may not have been hot enough. But the reverse could be true, depending upon the metal and the length of time it remained at a given temperature. Some experimentation may be necessary, but once you have the technique mastered, you will find that your work will be 100 percent right all the time.

This brings us up to the point about cyanide. It was not mentioned in the previous method, so some gunsmiths who have heard that cyanide must be used might question this method. The U. S. Government Ordnance Manual of 1862 cites the following information on casehardening:

"casehardening — This operation consists in converting the surface of wrought iron into steel, by cementation, for the purpose of adapting it to receive a polish or to bear friction, etc.; this is affected by heating the iron to a cherry red, in a closed vessel, in contact with carbonaceous materials, and then plunging it into cold water. Bones, leather, hoofs, and horns of animals are generally used for this purpose, after having been burnt or roasted so that they can be pulverized. Soot is also frequently used."

Note that cyanide was not mentioned in this technique, yet excellent results were obtained with very pleasing colors, as can be seen on some Springfield muskets of the period.

One of the easiest, and perhaps the best way to caseharden metal gun parts is to obtain a short length of common black iron pipe, of a size that will accommodate the pieces to be hardened, and weld a cap on one end of the pipe; or the end can be threaded and a conventional end cap screwed on. The other end should have a hinged "door" with a catch, so that the pipe may be readily opened.

The pieces of metal to be casehardened are then placed in these pieces of pipe, packing each with fine bone meal, such as is used by gardeners for fertilizer. During this packing, be sure to arrange the different pieces so they do not touch each other. When packed solidly, close the hinged cover and place the pipe and its contents in a fire or heat-treating furnace, heating it at a temperature of between 1,200 and 1,400 degrees F. for 15 minutes or more, depending upon the thickness of the parts and the depth they should be hardened. With tongs, remove the pipe from the fire and quickly empty the contents of the pipe into a pail of cold water that is agitated by an air hose. When the pieces are cool, remove and boil them in clean water; then oil them thoroughly.

For casehardening, bone meal is the substance most readily obtainable. It is clean and neat to use, but it will not produce the mottled tints that charred or burned leather will give. The leather may be prepared by cutting up old shoes or boots, putting them in an old pan and setting the batch aflame. Let it burn until it is a charcoal that will readily crumble in pieces by using a little force. Grind this charcoal to a fine powder by pounding in a mortar, or by running it through an old coffee mill. Pack the parts to be casehardened in the burnt powder the same as you did with the bone meal. Gun guards, straps and long pieces of work will become shorter by case-hardening, and it is best not to fit such pieces into the stock until after they are hardened. If it is desired to have a portion of the work left soft, and the other parts hardened, securely cover the places to be soft with a coating of moist clay; this will prevent the hardening material from coming in contact. Consequently, it will have no opportunity

to absorb carbon, and harden when put in cold water.

If the parts are thin and there might be a chance of their cracking by a sudden chilling action, the water may be warmed somewhat, or a film of oil may be spread on the surface of the water, which will tend to prevent a too-sudden contraction of the parts while cooling.

The surface of the metal to be casehardened should be polished before being packed in the burnt leather. You will also want to buff and burnish the metal; the higher the shine on the bare metal, the more brilliant will be the colors.

Polish the parts to be hardened to a high luster and place them in an iron box or black pipe. Make sure the parts are completely surrounded by the charred leather, and that they do not touch each other. Use a saturated solution of common salt and water — enough to float an egg — and pour this solution into the container until the powder is made moist. If you don't have any salt, do what the old-timers did: urinate into the container. It got the job done!

Next, close the container and seal it airtight with wet and well-worked furnace clay; then, put the container and its contents into a furnace or fire to heat. Try to keep the container at a dark red temperature for about five minutes. Then dump the contents immediately into a tub or bucket filled with water and slaked lime. This method produces extremely hard steel.

In earlier times, when guns were more in use than either agricultural or mechanical implements, there was a gunsmith in almost every village. Casehardening in those days was even simpler than the methods I've described. Scraps of old leather, cut from old boots or shoes, were tightly wrapped and tied around the piece of metal to be hardened; several thicknesses were used. A half-inch layer of sand and salt, in equal proportions, was placed around the wrapped part. This mixture was dampened with water to make it stick together. A layer of furnace cement, an inch thick, was then worked around the part and heated to about 1,200 to 1,300 degrees F., just long enough to consume the leather. Then the parts were dropped into a slack-tub.

This method produced a hard surface, but few colors developed. It was used mainly to harden frizzens, hammers, and similar gun parts that were subject to hard use, and would therefore be subject to heavy wear. When the mottled colors were desired, such as on the side lock, one of the other methods—or something similar—was used.

Hardening Without Color

When gun parts are to be hardened without colors, there are several easier methods than those described. Commercial hardeners are probably the simplest to use, and anyone capable of disassembling a firearm is capable of using them. All you need is the chemical, a small propane torch, and a container of oil or water in which to quench the parts.

Two of the most popular compounds for hardening steel are Brownells *Hard 'N Tuff* and *Kasenit Surface Hardening Compound.* Both are nonpoisonous, nonexplosive, nonflammable, and produce an extremely hard surface.

The Kasenit compound (No. 1) is a refined, rapid acting powder suitable for delicate and highly finished work, such as would be the case with firearms. It carburizes the work quickly, to a uniform depth. After quenching, the surface of the work will be clean and extremely hard. To use, heat the part to a bright red— between 1,650 and 1,700 degrees F.; remove any scale with a wire brush, and dip the part into the powder. The Kasenit powder will melt and adhere to the surface, forming a shell around the part being treated. Then, once again, heat the part to a bright red and hold this color for about three or four minutes. Now, quickly quench into clean, cold water. This will give the part a completely hard case of uniform character and depth. The Brownells compound is almost identical.

In using this and any other hardening compound, remember that you are using high temperatures around an open flame. Do not perform the operation around any flammable or combustible items. Wear protective goggles, gloves and protective clothing to guard against splatter from the hot compound, and the hot object itself. Use adequate tongs to handle all parts until they are cool.

Prussiate of potash may be used to caseharden gun parts, and will work similar to the Brownells or Kasenite compounds. When using, remember that the potash must be finely powdered, and the work heated and dipped into the potash contained in some type of vessel. If the piece is large, the potash must be spread entirely over it, and then heated. The part being hardened must be hot enough to fuse the potash. If it becomes cold before removing from the heat, it must be reheated, removed quickly from the fire and quenched in cold water.

Annealing Tool Steel

When altering or making a new part from existing tempered steel, it will usually be necessary to anneal it making it softer, before any work on it can be done. Annealing consists of heating a piece of steel to a predetermined temperature, then letting it cool slowly. Most steel can be adequately annealed by heating it to a bright cherry red, then letting it cool slowly at room temperature; or else burying it in sawdust. On some steels, you may wish to try heating it first to a dull blood red; if this doesn't work, you will have to go to full cherry red.

Sometimes it is desirable to partially soften a piece of metal—if you don't plan to reharden it—to allow it to be filed or drilled. In this case, heat the part in a dark corner of your shop to a cherry red; then allow it to air cool until it is no longer red. Drop the part into warm to hot water. This method will usually not remove all the temper, but it will soften the steel, so that it can be worked.

Preventing Scaling

When heating metal, it usually forms a scale that will later have to be removed. This can be quite annoying, especially on hammers with sear notches. To prevent this scale from appearing, obtain some old leather, char it with a propane torch and then pulverize it to make about one pound. Add 1½ pounds of flour to the pulverized leather; also add two pounds of common table salt. Mix the ingredients dry, then add water slowly to make a stiff paste. Add more water until the mixture can be painted onto the steel parts to be treated.

To use this mixture, spread a thin coat of it evenly over the part to be treated and let it dry slowly, but thoroughly, over a low heat. You can then heat the part to a bright cherry red, without having to worry about scale forming on the part. There are also commercial mixtures available to help prevent scale forming on metal during heating.

More on Hardening

Practically all gun parts made from high-carbon steel should be hardened at a low red stage, or a dark, blood red, to as high as a cherry red (which is around 1,350 degrees F.). In heating parts to be hardened, be aware that smaller parts take less time under heat, while large parts take longer, because the latter retain the heat longer. When quenching, the beginner should stick with an oil solution; water will, when improperly used, make the metal brittle, and therefore is useless for most applications.

There are certain techniques that will be developed as experience is gained. Set rules are difficult to describe, since there are so many variables with which to contend.

Hardening consists of heating the part to a cherry red and then quickly quenching it in a container of oil to cool it. The part is once again polished and heated (drawn) to a straw yellow color, to take away any brittleness and to give it added strength. This can vary with different types of steel, and under different applications.

One word of caution: the application of heat to a gun part can be extremely dangerous. The amateur should never apply heat to any critical area of a firearm, such as the breech end of a barrel, the locking bolt, locking lugs, or the receiver itself. Incorrectly applying heat to these areas can weaken the steel, causing it to shatter under the pressure of a fired cartridge or shotshell. In doing so, not only is the gun ruined, but the explosion could injure the shooter or bystanders.

For these and other reasons, it is recommended that the amateur restrict his hardening operations to such items as firing pins and trigger sears, until sufficient experience has been gained. It is also recommended that books on metallurgy be studied to acquire a good working knowledge of the subject. When you feel it is time for you to advance, do so only under the supervision of a qualified professional, so he can make sure that you get started on the right foot and correct your mistakes as you go along.

Chapter 13
Replacement Parts

There are millions of obsolete firearms needing repairs and replacement parts. Some parts are available from manufacturers; others are available from dealers who specialize in obsolete gun parts; others simply are not available at all. In fact, in the near future, much of the professional gunsmith's work probably will consist of manufacturing parts to repair obsolete firearms. In many cases, however, the time and cost of making a replacement part is worth more than the gun, so the firearm remains in poor condition. This is where home gunsmithing can pay off. Make the part yourself!

Using a metal file, you can shape almost any gun part by hand from a piece of metal stock, but this takes time and patience. This practice is usually too time-consuming for the professional, but not for many hobbyists and home gunsmiths. Even with power tools, turning out a single gun part can take a lot of time. Therefore, whenever available, a replacement part should be purchased.

Most metal components that combine to make a complete firearm, including screws like the ones shown in Figure 13-1, must be made to highly accurate dimensions for the gun to function properly. However, regardless of how accurately and nicely finished they are, most gun parts will be of little value if they are not heat treated properly before their installation. Such treatment can include hardening, tempering, annealing, forging,

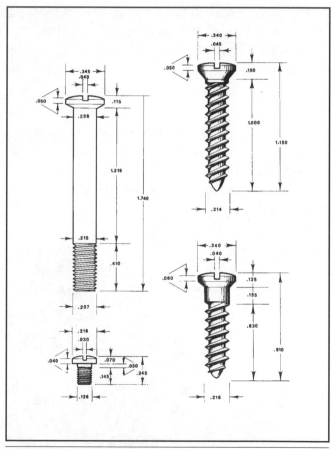

Figure 13-1: Gun screws, even those turned to exact dimensions, would quickly become worn if they were not heat-treated before being placed in a firearm.

normalizing, and carburizing. In general, heat-treatment is applied mostly to carbon and alloy steels. See Chapter 12 in this book.

LATHE LORE

If very many parts are to be made, a metal-turning lathe with a milling attachment is almost essential. While it is not the intent of this book to give a crash course on lathe operation, a brief review of lathe lore is in order.

The screw-cutting metal-turning lathe is the oldest and most important machine tool, and from it practically all other machine tools have been developed. Lathes vary in size from the small jeweler's or clockmaker's lathes for making miniature parts, to the large gap-bed lathes and special-purpose lathes used in high-production work. In between these extremes are many models of varying lengths and capacities.

The maximum size — that is, the diameter and length — work that can be handled by the lathe is used to designate the size of the lathe. For example, a 9 x 36 inch lathe is one having a swing over the bed sufficient to take work up to 9 inches in diameter and a distance between lathe centers of 36 inches.

When selecting a lathe for gunsmithing work, careful consideration must be given to the size and amount of work that the lathe will be required to handle. Ideally, the lathe selected should have a swing capacity and distance between centers at least 10 percent greater than the largest job that is anticipated.

Parts Of A Lathe

A lathe is made up of many parts. The principal parts are shown in Figure 13-2 and include bed, headstock, tailstock, carriage, feed mechanism, thread-cutting mechanism, and others.

Bed: The bed is the foundation on which the lathe is built, so it must be substantially constructed and scientifically designed. The two types in common use are flat and prismatic V-ways.

Headstock: The headstock is on the left-hand end of the bed and is one of the most important parts of the lathe; it should be back-geared for more versatility. The backgear provides a means of controlling the spindle speed. A lever engages the backgear for slow spindle speeds (75 to 280 rpm) or disengages

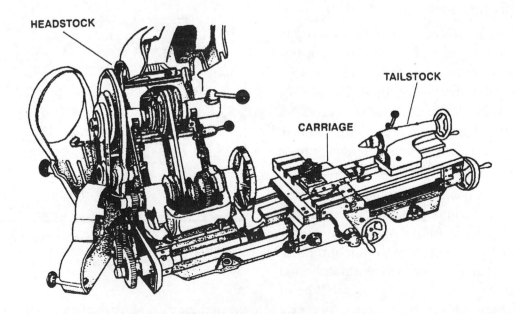

Figure 13-2: The Myford Super 7 is a high-quality lathe, ideal for gunsmithing gun parts in the home shop.

it for high spindle speeds from about 300 to 1100 rpm or more.

Tailstock: The tailstock assembly is movable on the bed ways, and carries the tailstock spindle. The tailstock spindle has a standard Morse taper, in most cases, to receive various types of lathe centers. The tailstock handwheel is at the other end to give longitudinal movement when the workpiece is mounted between centers. The tailstock can also be used for drilling operations when the work is held in a gripping device, known as a *chuck*, or bolted on the face-plate so the work revolves and the drill remains stationary.

Carriage: The lathe carriage includes the apron, saddle, compound rest and tool post. Since the carriage supports the cutting tool and controls its action, it is one of the most important units of the lathe.

Feed Mechanism: Quick-change gear lathes are preferred in gunsmithing shops where frequent changes of threads and feeds are required. On most lathes, the quick-change gearbox is located directly below the head-stock on the front of the lathe bed. A wide range of feeds and threads per inch may be selected by positioning the gears. The index plate is an index to the lever settings, required to position the gears for the different feeds, and inches that the carriage will move per revolution of the spindle.

The reversing lever is used to reverse the direction of rotation of the screw for chasing right- or left-hand threads, and for reversing the direction of feed of the carriage assembly. Levers on the quick-change gearbox should never be forced into position.

Centering Work

Both centers of a lathe must be in perfect alignment. One way to check center alignment is to use a test bar such as the one shown in Figure 13-3. This can be a 12-inch length of round stock, 1 inch in diameter, and must be concentric and straight to

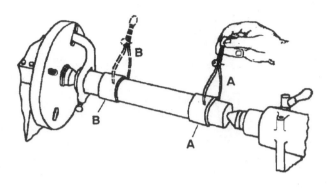

Figure 13-3: A test bar being used to check lathe centers. A test bar must be concentric and straight to within 0.001 inch.

within .001 inch. By using a bar of this type, the centers can be aligned easily.

One favorite method used to align lathe centers is the "trial cut" method where a light cut is made on the workpiece. A measurement is then taken at the tailstock end of the work piece and at a point midway between centers. If there is a difference in the two readings, then the tailstock is moved an amount equal to the difference. If the tailstock end is the larger of the measurements, the tailstock is moved toward the operator; if the tailstock end is smaller, it is moved away from the operator.

A more sophisticated method is to use calibrated centering gauges available from Brownells.

Taper Turning

One of the operations that often confronts the professional gunsmith is tapering a rifle barrel from a barrel blank. In general, there are at least three methods in common use for taper turning on a metal-cutting lathe. The simplest method is performed by swiveling the compound rest to the required angle and traversing the top slide by hand. Naturally, this method is limited to short taper parts such as lathe centers to hold the barrel blank because the top slide is limited to only a few inches of travel. *See* Figure 13-4 on the next page.

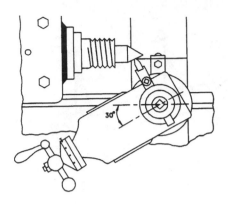

Figure 13-4: The degree setting on a compound rest for turning 60° lathe centers.

Tool Setting

When conventional cylindrical work is being turned, the height of the cutting tool has little effect on the accuracy of the work, although it may affect the quality of its finish. On the other hand, when tapering on the lathe — especially when making lathe centers — the cutting tool must be exactly on the centerline of the work, otherwise a true cone cannot be obtained. This fact may be observed in Figure 13-5. The full lines represent the small and large ends of a taper surface. The cutting tool will have moved outward the distance A as it travels along the workpiece. If, however, the tool had been set at the height B, touching the small end of the taper and then traversed along, it would still move outward the distance A, but terminate at the dotted-line position, making the large end of the taper much too small. In addition, in the operation of turning work to a fine point, like the lathe center, it will be discovered that if the tool was set either above or below the work-center, it would leave the work before a point was produced. Therefore, aside from making inaccurate work, it is impossible to produce a pointed workpiece unless the tool is set correctly.

One of the simplest methods of insuring this is to set it by comparing the height of the cutting edge with one of the lathe centers before placing the work in the lathe. This method of turning tapers by swiveling the compound rest is applicable to short tapers on work mounted between the centers, or either turning or boring tapers on work held in the chuck.

Offsetting Tailstock

One of the most popular methods of tapering long workpieces is offsetting the tailstock as shown in Figure 13-6. When the tailstock is offset, the angle of the taper will vary with the length of the work. The amount of setover depends on the amount of taper per foot and also the overall length

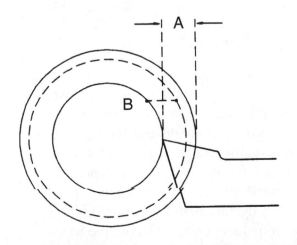

Figure 13-5: The cutting tool point for taper turning must be exactly on the centerline.

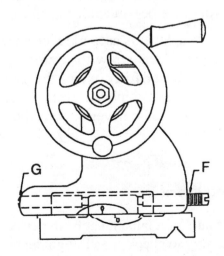

Figure 13-6: A tailstock showing adjusting screws (F and G).

of the work. With the same amount of setover, pieces of different lengths will be machined with different tapers.

Setting the tailstock toward the operator (or tool post) results in a taper with the smaller diameter at the tailstock, while setting the tailstock in the opposite direction results in a smaller diameter at the headstock end of the work.

In determining the proper amount of tailstock setover, bear in mind that the tailstock center is set over one-half the total amount of the taper for the entire length of the work. To calculate the amount of setover, the following equations may be used:

When the taper per foot is given, such as inches per foot, the equation used is

$$Setover = taper\ per\ foot \times length\ of\ taper\ in\ inches/24$$

To demonstrate the use of this equation, assume that a piece of stock is exactly 1 foot long and is to be tapered ½ inch per foot. Substituting these values in the equation, we have

$$Setover = .5 \times 12/24 = .250\ or\ ¼\ inch$$

To obtain the required taper, the tailstock should therefore be set over ¼ inch. If the piece were only 10 inches long, then the setover would be

$$Setover = .5 \times 10/24 = .208\ inch$$

When the entire length of the piece is to be tapered and the diameters at both ends of the tapers are known, divide the large diameter, less the small diameter, by 2 to obtain the amount of setover. For example, a piece of stock 1 foot long with a 1-inch diameter at one end and ½-inch diameter at the other, should have the tailstock set over the following amount:

$$Setover = 1 - .5/2 = .250\ or\ ¼\ inch$$

When a portion of the stock is to be tapered and the diameter at ends of the tapered portion are known, divide the total length of the stock by the length of the portion to be tapered and multiply this quotient by one-half the difference in diameters; the result is the amount of setover; that is,

$$Setover = total\ length\ of\ work/length\ to\ be\ tapered$$

$$X\ large\ diameter - small\ diameter/2$$

The method of adjusting the setover will vary slightly with the make of lathe, but in most cases all that is required is to loosen the clamping nut or lever and back off one of the setover screws which are located on each side of the tailstock body; then screw in the opposite setover screw until it is tight and reclamp the tailstock to the lathe bed. A zero mark is usually engraved at the end to assist in returning the tailstock to its normal position for parallel turning.

To measure the setover of the tailstock center, place a metal scale having graduation on both edges between the two centers, as shown in Figure 13-7. This will give an approximate measurement.

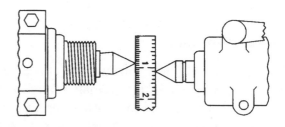

Figure 13-7: Approximating the amount of tailstock offset using a metal scale.

The best way to machine an accurate taper is to fit the taper to a standard gauge. To test the taper, make a chalk mark around the entire length of the taper gauge and then place the roughly tapered work into or onto the gauge or the tapered piece the work is to fit. Revolve the work carefully by hand. Then remove the work and the chalk mark will show where the taper is bearing so that adjustments can be made.

If the taper is a perfect fit, it will show along the entire length of the chalk mark. If the taper is not perfect, make the necessary adjustment, take another light chip and test again. Be sure the taper is correct before turning to the finished diameter.

The alignment of lathe centers should be checked at regular intervals, so as to maintain accuracy of long cuts, even though the tailstock might not have been purposely moved.

Where greater accuracy is required, a special headstock may be used. This arrangement necessitates a swivel slide between the base and the spindle section, so that prior to offsetting the tailstock, it can be swiveled by loosening the bolts and pulling the spindle around to the angle required. Most of these headstocks are indexed in ½ degrees, while a micrometer collar on the transverse screw is graduated to read in .001-inch intervals, so that a very accurate setting in two directions is possible. This arrangement takes all strain from the dead center, which bears fully in the end of the work, and while the live center still bears only on one side, the conditions are not so severe at that end.

Taper Attachments

Many lathes are fitted with a taper attachment that permits the lathe centers to remain in alignment just as if for conventional cylindrical turning, but causes the tool to traverse in a tapering direction as compared to the setting of the lathe centers. This arrangement is considered to be the best method of taper-turning by many machinists. A typical taper-turning attachment is shown in Figure 13-8. This

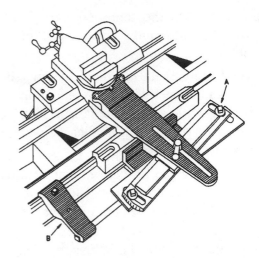

Figure 13-8: With a taper-turning attachment, the lathe centers remain aligned, but the tool traverses in a tapering direction according to the setting of the centers.

device is fitted to the back of the lathe saddle and to the rear slide of the bed. A slotted bar is fixed to the tool post, and can be clamped to a short slide on the swivel bar *A*. For plain turning the swivel bar is set in alignment with the slides of the bed, so that the tool follows a longitudinal path only when the sliding feed is engaged; but if the bar is swiveled, then the tool follows a tangential path, in or out as well as along the bed. Such taper-turning attachments may be placed on any part of the bed by merely relocating it by its clamps or screws.

Fine setting for either turning or boring is obtained by the end graduation giving the inches per foot of taper. Sometimes shop drawings and/or specifications give the taper in angles, or the taper per foot. While the converse would be more useful, the following table may be used to convert from one to the other.

TAPERS PER FOOT WITH CORRESPONDING ANGLES

TAPER PER FT. IN INCHES	INCLUDED ANGLE	ANGLE WITH CENTERLINE
⅛	0°36'	0°18'
¼	1°12'	0°36'

TAPER PER FT. IN INCHES	INCLUDED ANGLE	ANGLE WITH CENTERLINE
3/8	1°47'	0°54'
1/2	2°23'	1°12'
3/4	3°35'	1°12'
1	4°46'	2°23'
1 1/2	7°09'	3°35'
1 3/4	8°20'	4°10'
2	9°31'	4°46'
2 1/2	11°54'	5°57'
3	14°15'	7°08'
3 1/2	16°36'	8°18'
4	18°55'	9°28'

MAKING SPRINGS

Whenever possible, it is best to obtain a ready-made spring. Those that are available are inexpensive, when compared to the time spent in making one from scratch. Manufactured replacement springs, however, are not available for every firearm, which means that they must be hand-fashioned if the firearm is to be put back into service.

It is not difficult to make a useful replacement spring for a firearm, provided certain basic techniques are fully appreciated and understood.

The type of spring that will most often have to be handmade are the mainsprings used in some of the older sidelock shotguns. There is so much variation in these that it is extremely difficult to find factory-made replacements that will always fit exactly. Even the replacement springs that are manufactured for a specific gun will usually have to be modified, and fitted to the individual gun.

Next in line are the springs for boxlock shotguns, which are also difficult to obtain these days. Then come the frizzen springs, sear springs, and trigger springs. The techniques in this section will show how to make most of the them.

Spring Stock

Various assortments of spring stock are available from gunsmithing supply houses, such as Brownells Inc. and Frank Mittermeier, Inc. Coil or compression gun springs are normally available already tempered, requiring the user only to cut them to the required length. For example, Brownells No. 69 coil springs are packed several sizes to the carton, and are cut in 12-inch lengths. This assortment is designed primarily for the softer-acting gun springs.

Next in line comes their Brownells No. 150 kit, which contains small spring wire in diameters from .020 to .120 inch. The spring stock in this assortment is ready to make into springs, or any piece can be annealed and retempered.

Brownells No. 152 kit contains round oil-tempered spring stock, in diameters from .062 inch to .120 inch. The stock in this assortment is ready to make into springs, or any piece can be annealed and retempered.

Flat spring stock is available in Brownells No. 149 Kit, which contains 12 assorted pieces in widths from 3/16 inch to 3/8 inch, and in thicknesses from 1/16 inch to 1/8 inch. This assortment is annealed and in a soft state as purchased, but forges and tempers to gun-quality springs.

Brownells also carries extra-wide flat spring stock and music wire spring stock in a variety of

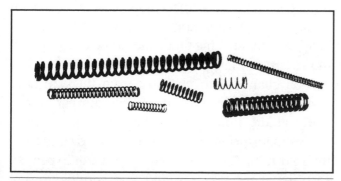

Figure 13-9: A few of the many types of coil gun springs sold by Brownells.

sizes. These combinations should suffice for 99 percent of the gunsmith's needs.

You should not overlook the possibility of good spring stock lying around your shop, home, or in junkyards. Old wagon springs and clock springs, for example, may be used as raw material for gun springs, once they have been cleaned up and annealed. They can then be used as raw materials to be forged and tempered for practically any requirement. Be cautious of modern springs such as those used in automobiles. Modern metallurgy has developed certain steels for specific applications, many of which are not suitable for gun springs. Regardless of the type of raw material obtained, it will have to be annealed or softened, so it can readily be worked with a file, hacksaw, and other tools necessary to obtain the required shape prior to tempering.

Initial Preparation

It is always best to have the broken spring close at hand when preparing to make a new one. If this is not possible, be prepared for a lot of time-consuming research and work that must be done on a trial-and-error basis. Here are a few suggestions.

- Try to locate a drawing of the spring, in either sectional or perspective views, that can usually be found in old parts catalogs. Back issues of the *Shooter's Bible* are good sources for these drawings.

- Determine the approximate physical dimensions of the spring you need. For example, if a sidelock on a double shotgun on which you are working is four inches in actual length, and the length of the same sidelock in the drawing is, say, one inch, then the drawing has been reduced in scale to one-fourth of the original. Keeping this in mind, you can obtain the approximate dimensions of a spring in a drawing; that is, obtain all actual dimensions in the drawing and then multiply each by four (in this case). Of course, there still will be some trial-and-error fitting, but at least you will have a starting point.

- On many sidelock shotguns requiring the replacement of a broken mainspring usually one of the mainsprings will still be intact within the mechanism. This is also true for boxlock actions. The remaining good spring can be used as a template to make a duplicate of the broken spring. In this case, curvatures and retaining nipples, for example, will have to be reversed (like a mirror image); however, anyone capable of making a spring should experience little difficulty in laying out these changes.

- Try to find another firearm like the one you're working on. Disassemble the good weapon, then take measurements of the good spring to use in making a new one for the broken gun.

Assuming that all the pieces of the broken spring are in your possession, reconstruct them — using epoxy glue to hold them in place — to obtain the overall shape to act as a guide for making the new spring. Study the broken spring carefully, observing the shape of the taper. In the case of a flat leaf spring, the arms are tapered to withstand considerable movement. This taper should be even, so that the strain on the whole arm will be constant. If a section changes too abruptly from thick to thin, then all the strain will fall on the thin part, especially at the point where the difference occurs. Heavy mainsprings must always taper evenly from the fold to the hook, otherwise you can expect an early breakage. Frizzen and sear springs are not quite as critical; the arms on these springs do not receive the great amount of deflection that the arms on mainsprings do.

An experienced springmaker can apply a quick heat, give two or three blows with a hammer and he's formed a hook or an eye that will make up part of a flat spring. It looks easy, but it is extremely difficult to accomplish without many years of experience. The beginner will need considerable time to accomplish the same thing, and should expect many failures at the outset.

Making The V Spring

Two types of stock may be used to make a V spring; flat stock and drill rod of high carbon content, so either can be hardened and tempered. If the latter is used, select a rod of sufficient diameter to allow for the round edges to be squared off with either a grinder or a file. Once selected, measure the distance from the end of the broken spring arm (the one you are copying) to the bottom of the V. Then, with a hacksaw, slit the rod to a little more than the depth required; that is, if your measurement was, say $1\frac{3}{4}$ inch, make the slit about $1\frac{7}{8}$ inch, so as to have a little to spare.

Again, measurements of the existing broken springs are taken and the rod with the slit is then squared up on a grinding wheel to within about $\frac{3}{32}$ inch of the finished width and thickness at the bottom of the V. In doing so, be careful not to overheat the metal. This calls for very slow grinding; if you see any colors start to form, stop immediately and let the steel cool.

You will now want a pair of calipers to constantly check the width and thickness at the bottom of the V; or you might wish to use a combination of grinding and filing, as the situation dictates.

At this point, the arms of the new spring, formed by the slit down the middle of the rod, are bent outward and cut to the exact length. Some like to do this bending hot, but usually it can be done cold, if care is exercised. Frequently match the existing broken spring to ensure that the arms, or leaves, are

bent to the exact same shape as the original. To ensure even pressure throughout the entire lengths of these leaves, the arms must be tapered evenly. For this operation, the use of flat files and a small grinding wheel in a Dremel Moto-Tool is ideal. Take care not to heat or burn the metal. Try to obtain the exact taper (or close to it) of the original spring. When the leaves have been shaped and tapered, and all dimensions have been double-checked, cut the spring from the round stock, leaving plenty of metal for shaping the butt of the spring, behind the V notch.

Next comes polishing. This may be done with abrasive paper wrapped around files, or with a power buffing wheel, or with a combination of the two. There are many reasons for polishing the spring at this point. First of all, if tool marks are allowed to remain, chances are the spring will break from a stress concentration around such a mark in the surface of the spring. Also, the metal must be polished to allow the colors to show through readily during the heat treatment.

A temperature-controlled furnace is the best in such cases. Few professionals and practically no beginners, however, have such an apparatus, so an improvised method will have to be used. Set up some fire bricks on your bench. A small stovepipe wire is used to hold the spring against the bricks

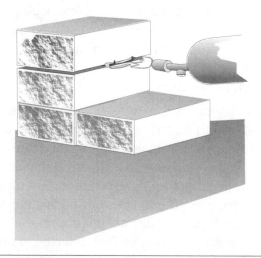

Figure 13-10: Arrangement of fire bricks for tempering gun springs.

during the heat-treating process as shown in Figure 13-10. Anything larger than these pieces of wire will draw heat away from the workpiece, and cause it not to temper equally. Result: a poor spring that more than likely will break after only a few compressions. You'll also want another piece of thin wire to lift the spring when it reaches the right temperature in the correct length of time. Immediately quench it in the recommended solution, which will vary depending upon the type of drill rod used. Usually, drill rods from $\frac{1}{4}$ inch to $\frac{3}{4}$ inch are designed for quenching in oil, while those smaller do best when quenched in water. Some like to use water with a light quenching oil floating on top. It may take some experimenting to determine which solution is best for the spring stock you are using.

With the solution in a suitable container close by, and the spring in position on the wires against the fire bricks, heat the metal as evenly as possible with a propane or similar torch. When the spring reaches a cherry to bright cherry color (1,400° to 1,500° F.), hold this color for about 20 seconds; then immediately quench in the chosen solution, holding the spring by the long wire attached to the spring before heating it.

At this point, the little spring is hot, and you certainly don't want it to come into contact with anything it can harm, especially your skin. Be careful if you are using an oil-quenching bath. Some have a low flash point, and will ignite when hot metal is dropped in it. If you can work outdoors in the shade, it is safer than performing the operation within a building.

After the heated spring cools in the quenching solution, it will be strong, hard, and brittle, and is easily broken at this stage. So handle it with care, the way you would handle a glass rod. It must now be drawn — tempered — to produce the toughness required for a good gun spring. But first the metal must be polished again, so the colors the metal takes on during heating can be detected. You can use the power buffer you used to polish the spring prior to heating; but since it is now very brittle, it is recommended that you do the polishing by hand, using abrasive paper, and exercise extreme care not to break the spring.

Tempering temperatures will vary with the type of spring stock used, the length of time the hardening temperature was held, and the temperature used in the hardening. Most texts recommend a temperature between 600° and 650° F., which should give a color of between dark blue and gray.

A dark straw to yellow brown works best on some steels, which is produced at between 465° to 500° F. You might have to do some experimenting, especially if you don't have a temperature-controlled furnace. There is one good thing about such experimenting, if you don't get it right the first time, reheat the part to cherry red, and try it again. As long as you don't break the brittle part, and it is polished each time it is heated, you can probably try different temperatures many times without having to shape an all-new spring.

Assuming the piece has been polished brightly, and it again is in position on the wires against the fire bricks, use the torch to heat the spring evenly and slowly, until it reaches the desired color. Keep the flame moving all over the piece (at this color) for about 15 seconds, then slowly remove the flame and let the piece cool. Protect it against any breeze that might cool it too quickly. Some gunsmiths like to completely cover the spring with lime, and let it cool slowly this way.

When the spring is completely cool (the same as room temperature), again remove all scale and polish the spring. Check the measurements, especially the distance between the two leaves.

Use a bench vise and completely compress the spring between the vise jaws, then release the pressure. Once more, check the distance between the two leaves of the spring. If the leaves return to their original distance and the spring didn't break, you have a perfect spring. If not, give it another try. Should you happen to get this right on the first try, you did better than most.

Another approach to this tempering is to use molten lead. Many shooters cast their own bullets and have an electric melting pot on hand, or at least a ladle which lead can be melted in. Pure lead melts at 620° F., so if you heat the lead until it just melts, or becomes liquid, you should be just about right. At this point, remove the lead from the heat and use a wire to submerge the spring into the molten lead. Be careful not to let the spring touch the sides of the melting pot; the temperature might be hotter there. Hold the spring under the lead for about 15 seconds; then remove it and let it cool slowly at room temperature.

Depending upon the metal used to make the spring, a better temper might be obtained by dipping the spring in water after removing it from the lead. Some experimentation may be necessary. We offer these different techniques to be tried by you, so you can find the one that works best for your individual needs. Nearly every springmaker has his own techniques, one that works the best for him. All will make a spring, but one technique might suit your situation better.

V-type mainsprings can be made from flat spring stock, such as that offered by Brownells. Examine the broken spring carefully, taking required measurements as to thickness, width, and length. Then select a spring stock that comes closest to your measurement to minimize the labor required to shape the spring.

The sharp bend required for the V notch in the spring is difficult to bend cold without cracking or breaking, so it's best to grip the stock in a bench vise and heat the area to be bent to a cherry red; partially bend the V with pliers. Complete the bend by holding a torch to it, and forging it with a hammer. Thus formed, it must be slowly air-cooled to remain soft enough for the remaining forming and polishing.

The curved profile required for the spring can then be easily formed by cold bending. The spring at this point should roughly resemble the finished spring, with the exception of being slightly over-size in thickness, width, and length. Now comes the final shaping to obtain exact dimensions and, most importantly, the proper taper. This portion of the project can be done entirely by hand, using files, a bench grinder, and abrasive paper. Some professional shops use the milling machine for this operation, which is fine if one is available. Once exactly shaped, the entire spring must be polished and free from defects.

Heat treating is now necessary to produce elasticity and resilience in the spring. Should the spring crack while testing, try again, using a little higher temperature. If the spring remains bent rather than springing back after compression, the spring stock may have too low a carbon content, in which case you'll have to look for a different metal. It can also indicate faulty heat treatment: quenching from too low a temperature, quenching too slowly, or tempering at too high a temperature. Fortunately, a soft spring is not a complete waste; it can be heat-treated again and again until the correct results are obtained.

Making Complex Springs

Up to this point, only simple V-type mainsprings have been discussed. These will suffice for many makes of boxlock actions; but mainsprings for sidelocks will be more elaborate. They contain hooks, crooks, pegs, slots, and eyes, all of which seem complicated. After gaining some experience, however, you should be able to shape practically any design. The process is going to be time-consuming, but with patience and know-how the technique can be perfected.

Upon examining designs of sidelock mainsprings, you may find one where the anchor eye is at right angles to the leaves. This type of spring can be made by first making two cuts on each side of the flat stock, heating the area to cherry red, and then turning the end piece 90°. If careful measurements are taken and your planning is correct, you will have the leaf just the right width after allowing

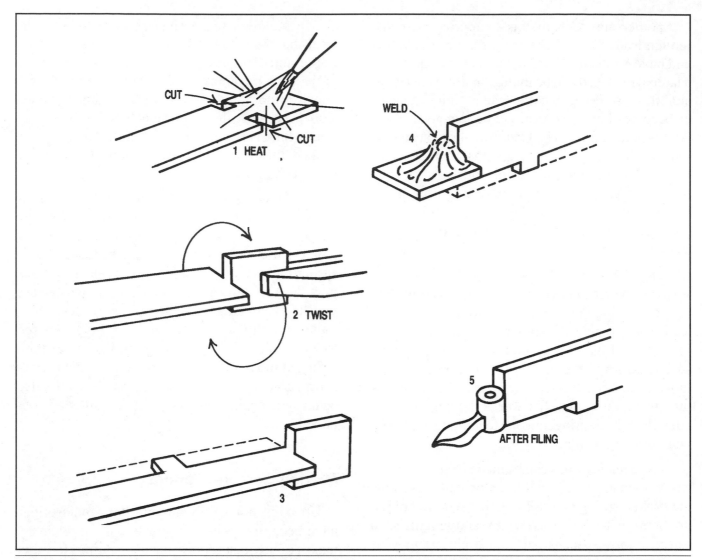

Figure 13-11: With a little thought, almost any shape of gun spring can be fashioned. Here, a piece of flat stock is first notched and heated; the end of the stock is twisted, as shown. Then the stock is removed to match the spring needed, and the weld is built up, then filed to exact shape. Note that a small hole has been drilled in this spring to match the original.

for the removal of the unwanted part of the back strip, which is removed to form a peg on the side of the spring.

Some of the embellishments found on mainsprings are not really necessary. Many will function normally without them. So try to understand the reasoning behind certain shapes, and then simplify your design as much as possible. For example, on certain frizzen springs, the eye is normally as deep as the leaf, but in many cases, the depth is not necessary. Try one with a shallow eye, the thick-

ness of the steel strip. Chances are it will work just as well, and is obviously much easier to make. If oxyacetylene welding equipment is available, twist the eyepiece, drill the required hole, and then use a welding rod to build up around the eye, giving it the depth wanted. Allow it to cool slowly, so it will anneal properly. Then redrill the hole and shape the area with files.

Many professionals balk at the word welding on springs. but it can be done, provided the spring is retempered. Even springs that have been in a fire can sometimes be brought back to life by further hardening and retempering. Similarly, a broken peg can be effectively repaired by silver soldering. Merely anneal the spring, drill into the leaf with a slightly smaller drill bit size than the old peg (about one-third the depth of the leaf width), turn or file a new peg, and silver solder it in place. You'll need a relatively high melting point solder for this operation, one that has a melting point above 1,500° F. Then the entire spring can be re-hardened and tempered.

We once had a broken recoil spring for a Remington Model 58 Sportsman semiautomatic shotgun brought in for replacement. Since it would take a couple of weeks to order a replacement spring, and the customer wanted to use the gun the next day, we tried putting a dab of Brownells Heat Stop on each side of the break, placed the ends of the coil spring together, and successfully joined the break with a low-melting temperature (1000° F.) silver solder without losing any significant amount of temper in the remaining part. The customer was using this repaired spring several years later and so far as we know, it is still working.

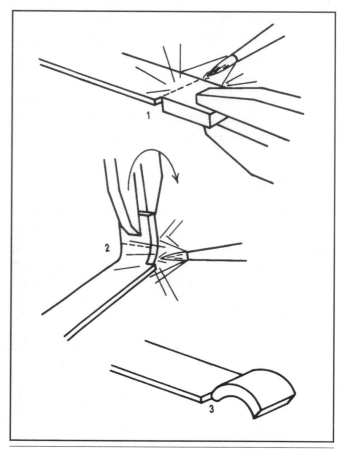

Figure 13-12: To make an eye on the end of flat stock, first heat the piece and bend upward with pliers; then apply heat to the center and bend downward. File to exact size and shape.

Forming Hooks

Many mainsprings contain hooks at the end of one leaf. Forming them can be a bit complicated. Once the basic spring has been formed, leave some extra metal on the end of the leaf where the hook will be located. This widened area should then be further narrowed, so that it is the same width as the tumbler. To make the hook, heat the leaf at the end of the taper and turn the thick stub upward. Then heat the upright piece, keeping the actual bend as cool as possible. Next, pull the tip of the metal back down again. The method is similar to forming an "eye" in the end of an electrical wire for connection to a terminal. It will require some practice to master this technique. Remember, since you have left some extra thickness in this portion of the leaf, the arc or bend does not have to be too great; you can

obtain further roundness when you shape the hook later on with a file.

Cut off any surplus steel from the point of the hook and try the resulting shape with the existing spring. The hook can be adjusted somewhat by heating the toe of the hook and then using pliers to close it in or out.

Some hooks also contain a notch. Before the spring is hardened, use a small drill bit, with light pressure, and drill a row of holes at the required location. Then use a set of Swiss files to smooth the interior of the slot.

Mainsprings with lugs on the ends of the leaves are best formed from a solid piece cut completely with the lug intact. Further shaping can be done by forging, using a vise, anvil, or swaging blocks. This takes much practice.

Bear in mind that, like nearly all gunsmithing techniques, springmaking takes considerable practice. Seldom will the amateur meet with perfect results on his first attempt. Once the technique has been learned, however, it is seldom forgotten.

Summary

Gun parts, other than springs, are usually made on machine-shop tools such as the lathe, milling machine, etc., but if you have patience, almost every small part for any gun can be made with a set of metal files. The main thing is to know the shape and dimensions of the part(s), and how to take and transfer correct measurements.

When planning to make a new part from scratch, it is always best to have the old part available. If this is broken, use Krazy Klue to temporarily hold the parts together for measuring. If the part is missing, refer to old parts catalogs for the general shape and appearance, the same as explained for springmaking. Dimensioned drawings are also available for a few gun parts.

Chapter 14
Metal Polishing

The quality and beauty of any gun finish depends a great deal on the preliminary preparation of the steel before the finish is applied. Metal coloring will not hide pits and blemishes, which will only be colored and, in many cases, will show up even more once the bluing or other finish has been applied.

Ideally, gun metal — whether new or refinished — should retain the original contours, corners, and planes, with no rounding-off of sharp edges or loss of outline and serial numbers. Care should be taken so that screw holes will not be funneled or otherwise disfigured during the polishing process. The texture of the steel should be smooth and even, and show no tool marks, nicks, or polishing scratches.

There are four popular methods of finishing gun metal prior to bluing, plating, parkerizing, and the like: hand-polishing, power buffing, mass-finishing, and sand blasting. Of the four, the beginner should stick to the hand-polishing methods until they are thoroughly mastered. Then, and only then, should the beginner think of using a power buffing wheel on a firearm of any value. Practice on some scrap pieces of metal. This procedure is encouraged, but not until sufficient experience is had to insure a good polishing job, without changing the contours of the metal being polished.

BASIC POLISHING

Aside from keeping the metal surfaces free of oil, polishing is the most important step in obtaining a rich, velvety finish on your gun parts. Without proper polishing, you might as well forget bluing the gun and leave it as is. The coloring of the metal will never cover up pits, scratches, and the like. The surface of the metal must be perfect before the bluing solution is applied. Nothing else will do.

Many professional shops utilize power for buffing or polishing the metal parts. However, it takes lots of experience and practice to do a good job of power polishing without rounding sharp corners, funneling screw holes, or otherwise "grinding them up" too much. The beginner will do well to stick with hand polishing. Hand polishing will insure that all contours, lettering, markings and square edges will be properly preserved. About 12 hours of hand polishing are required to complete all parts on the average rifle or shotgun. If many pits are present, this time may be doubled.

Roy Dunlap points out in his book, *Gunsmithing,* that a hand-polished gun looks better than a power-polished one, since corners and angles can be maintained with no loss of outline. An excellent final finish can be obtained on metal when polished by hand to a high degree of smoothness. Metal polished by power, to the same degree of finish before bluing, will not turn out as well.

The first step is to disassemble the gun completely down to the last screw and drift pin. If you are unfamiliar with the takedown procedure, exploded views and instructions are available from various sources for most firearms. When you have no printed instructions, jot down notes as you disassemble the gun and perhaps even take close-up photos of intricate parts. Then you'll have some reference to follow when you are reassembling the firearm. *See* Chapter 7, Firearm Disassembly.

Wipe the parts clean, examining each for wear and ensuring that no aluminum alloy parts are present. This can easily be determined by using a small magnet. If the magnet doesn't react, then the part is nonferrous — aluminum, brass or similar alloy — and these parts should be set aside with others not to be blued. Besides the nonferrous parts, other parts will include springs and other small elements not visible in an assembled gun.

With all pieces to be blued in one pile, thoroughly clean each one with a solvent such as acetone or AWA 1-1-1. Then, start with the barrel or barreled action; clamp this assembly in a padded vise. Care must be taken, however, not to "clamp down" too hard and damage the gun parts.

If some of the parts have pits, nicks, or scratches that are too deep for the abrasive paper to remove, use a 10-inch bastard file to smooth all metal surfaces. With the tang of the file in the left hand and the tip in the right hand, "draw" the file toward yourself over the metal surface to be smoothed as shown in Figure 14-1.

The amount of pressure you use on the file is very important; too little will scratch the metal, while too much will clog the file and cause deep gouges in the metal. On the return stroke, do not let the file touch the metal; cutting should be done only on the "draw" stroke. In other words, with the file positioned at the most distant spot on the barrel, draw the file smoothly toward you, using enough pressure to smooth the metal without scratching it. At

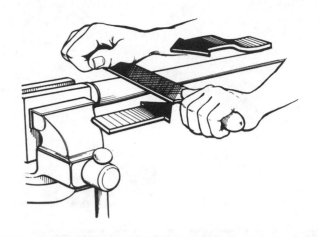

Figure 14-1: Draw-filing will quickly remove pits from gun parts, but caution must be taken not to scratch the metal surface or take off too much metal.

the end of the stroke, lift the file from the metal and sort of arc it back to its starting position; then again use pressure and draw the file toward you. Repeat this procedure until all pits and scratches are removed. However, you must be cautious so as not to take off too much metal — especially on thin shotgun barrels and locking points on receivers.

The barrel is now ready for cross-polishing to remove the many "flats" that will be left after draw filing. With a pair of scissors or a bench knife, cut a strip of 80-grit abrasive paper about $1\frac{1}{2}$ inches wide (cut the long way) and polish the barrel as though you were shining a pair of shoes, and as shown in Figure 14-2. Your first few strokes will reveal the flats left by the draw filing. Continue this operation over the entire length of the barrel with the 80-grit paper until all of the flats disappear and the barrel looks like it has just been "turned" in a metal-turning lathe. You may have to use several pieces of the abrasive paper to achieve this polished condition.

Next cut a $1\frac{1}{2}$-inch strip of the 150-grit paper and fold it a couple of times so that it fits the palm of your hand as shown in Figure 14-3. With the open edges in the direction of the axis of the bore, start polishing the barrel lengthwise (Figure 14-4). Continue polishing in this manner until all cross-

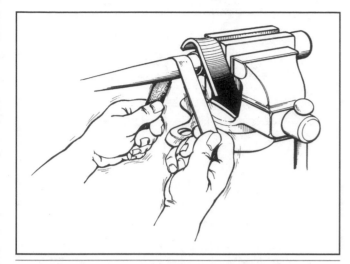

Figure 14-2: Use 80-grit abrasive paper to remove the flats left by draw-filing. Notice that the barrel polishing procedure is similar to shining a pair of shoes.

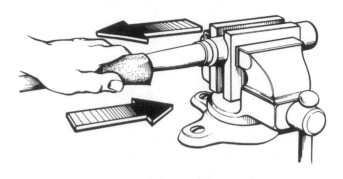

Figure 14-4: When draw-polishing, move the folded abrasive paper back and forth, up and down the barrel to remove the marks left from the previous cross-polishing.

polishing marks from the previous operation are removed. Instead of the palm of your hand, some gunsmiths like to use styrofoam as a backing for the abrasive paper; the styrofoam will mould to the contour of the barrel.

The above procedures should be repeated alternately, using progressively finer grits of abrasive paper. Make sure all polishing marks from the previous polishing are removed before proceeding to the next finer grade of paper.

Once the barrel has been polished, the position of it in the vise should be reversed and the receiver

polished in a similar manner, but make certain that the newly polished areas are well protected from the vise jaws. Heavy leather padding offers good protection. Then continue with the trigger, lever or trigger guard, and the like. Most of the smaller parts, however, because of their shape, will be most adaptable to cross-polishing. Just be sure that all polishing marks from the previous grit size are completely removed before using a finer grit size. Protect all of the newly-polished surfaces from rusting with a light coat of oil until you are ready to apply the bluing solution.

Screw heads (Figure 14-5) are best polished by securing them in the chuck of an electric drill or

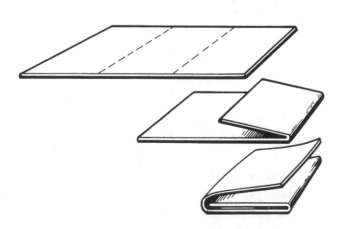

Figure 14-3: Method of folding abrasive paper for draw-polishing. Styrofoam backing is sometimes used because it will mold to the contour of the barrel or gun part.

Figure 14-5: Damaged screw heads, like this one, can be repaired easily by polishing. Use a screw holder and power buffing wheel for the best result.

drill press. While the screws are rotating, run a file over the head (if pitted), then complete the polishing this way with the various grit sizes of abrasive paper. In doing so, however, try to maintain the original contour of the screw head. The file especially can take off a lot of metal quickly, so be cautious.

Once all the parts are polished, you are ready to start heating up your tanks. However, if there is going to be any delay between the polishing and bluing, certain precautions must be taken. A freshly polished gun is a prime target for surface rust if it is not going into the cleaning or hot-water tank immediately. A delay of a few days or even a few hours under some conditions between final polishing and bluing can result in fine "silver" spots showing up on the gun after it has been blued. These are the result of microscopic rust spots developing while the gun is being held after polishing and prior to bluing.

Power Buffing

The equipment required for power buffing can vary tremendously, depending upon the amount of work that has to be done and the amount of money allotted for the equipment. Many professionals start out with only a bench grinder. Others start out with many power buffers (Figure 14-6) to save time in changing wheels.

Cloth or loose buffing wheels come in a large number of sizes and special shapes to quickly buff special contours. They are really a series of muslin discs sewn together. *See* Figure 14-7. Some wheels may have only a few pieces of cloth while others may be so thick that they involve hundreds of layers. These wheels, although extremely soft, revolve at high speed and the resulting centrifugal force is constantly at work tending to keep them "flat" against the surface being buffed.

When using a bench grinder, one end of a double-ended shaft contains a conventional grinding wheel, while the other grinding wheel is replaced

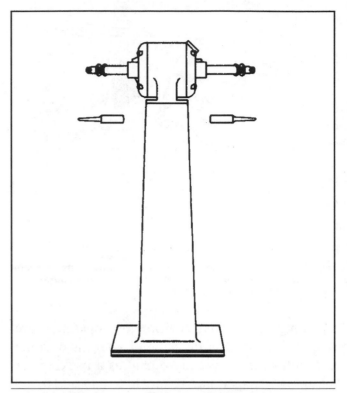

Figure 14-6: The power buffing motor mounted on a metal pedestal is the ideal setup for power buffing metal gun parts.

with a muslin buffing wheel. Therefore, the one machine may be used for both purposes. The main disadvantage is that each time a new grit size is required, the buffing wheel has to be changed. With only this arrangement, some buffing compound, and a barrel-spinning fixture, many guns can be polished for bluing at very little cost.

On the other end of the ladder is what might be considered the ideal setup for the professional gunshops. Several Baldor pedestal buffers should be installed in the buffing area of the shop. Stitched and loose muslin wheels, each containing different size of buffing compound, are installed. Number 555 gray and white polish is normally used on felt polishing wheels. Other specialty wheels may include those that have been grooved to accept curvatures of gun barrels and receivers.

The buffing room should also contain a belt sander and an assortment of belts from 60 to 400 grit, along with smaller wheels for polishing trigger

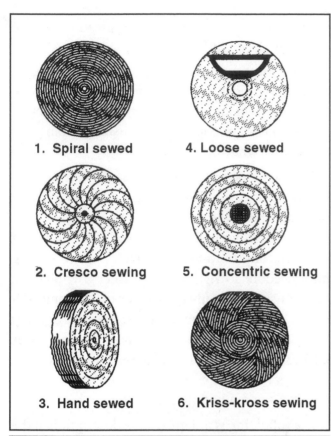

Figure 14-8: A belt sander has many uses in the gunshop, especially for polishing gun metal.

Figure 14-7: Various types of power buffing wheels. The spiral sewed (1) will hold uniform face longer. The cresco sewing (2) will wear down in layers. Hand sewing (3) is used on very thick wheels. Loose wheels (4) are used for high luster and will follow the contour of an object being polished. These wheels will also funnel screw holes, so be careful. Concentric sewing with hard center (5) is used for fast cutting; the hard center is used on tapered spindles. Kriss-kross (6) sewing gives almost the same results as spiral sewed wheels except the action is slower.

guards and similar items (Figure 14-8). These can be mounted by means of a special adapter on the Baldor buffers, or used in a Dremel Moto-Tool. A bead- or sand-blasting cabinet (Figure 14-10) and apparatus should also be on hand in the polishing area.

Some shops even have vibrator buffers set up for final polishing, such as those used by most major manufacturers. The parts to be polished are placed in barrels or drums containing the abrasive; the parts are then left to vibrate overnight. The next morning the parts will be brightly and evenly polished, ready for the bluing tank. Pits and other metal defects cannot normally be corrected in a vibrator polisher, but it does an excellent job on the final polishing.

To illustrate how a professional gunshop may handle the polishing of a rifle or shotgun for bluing, here is the normal procedure:

The firearm to be blued is first disassembled right down to the last drift pin and screw. On ribless single-barrel firearms, the barrel or barrel and receiver are secured between centers on a special barrel-spinning fixture. Up until recently, most shops made their own fixtures out of lengths of pipes, fittings, and lathe live centers. However, in recent years two such fixtures have hit the market and both can be highly recommended. One is manufactured by Clymer Manufacturing Co., Inc.; the other by McIntyre Tools & Guns of Troy, NC. Both are light in weight and can be purchased for a reasonable price; in fact, probably less than you could make one for yourself. The McIntyre spinner has a greater capacity, and includes chamber plugs for shotgun barrels — a big plus. Clymer is a well-known name in gunsmithing circles, due to its excellent chambering reamers.

Once the barrel is positioned between centers in the spinning fixture, and depending upon the condition of the surface, the barrel is then placed

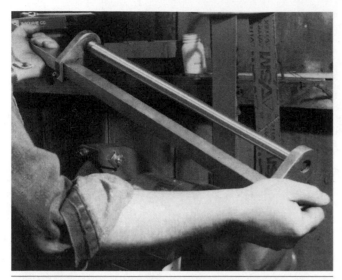

Figure 14-9: The power buffing room should contain a belt sander for quickly removing pits. The operation shown here is called "spinning." The barrel is positioned between centers in a Clymer spinning fixture and rotates with the belt. A good, even finish is assured.

against a polishing wheel or belt and allowed to spin as the barrel is worked up and down along the face of the polishing wheel as shown in Figure 14-9. If the barrel is pitted, the polisher will normally start out with the belt sander, which will cut a lot of metal quickly, and then progress down to about size 320 grit, again on the belt sander. For the master mirror shine, however, the work should be taken down to size 555.

Other parts are polished in a similar way. Receivers and tangs, for example, are usually held in the hands and worked in a circular motion across the buffing wheels, first in one direction and then another. In doing so, care must be taken so as not to polish out serial numbers and other lettering that is found on the typical firearm. Make sure that all corners are kept sharp and not rounded, and that the original lines of the part are maintained. If in doubt in a particular area, go to hand-polishing.

One of the most common faults with power-buffing is the funneling of screw holes. Even experienced polishers will have this happen if the holes are not protected. Many shops keep a set of extra screws for most firearms to be inserted into the vacant holes. For holes in the receiver that are not

threaded, use spring clips or locknuts to secure the screws in place while polishing.

Power-buffing takes considerable practice to master, and most beginners will do well to stick with hand-polishing on gun parts until enough practice has been obtained in polishing scrap parts on the power buffer.

In general, power polishing entails starting with the coarsest grit and polishing the surface of the metal in a given direction; then, with the next finer grit on a different buffing wheel you polish at 45-degree angles to the first "pass." By following this procedure down through the finer grit numbers, the final surface is unequaled for quality and perfection. When playing football, there are many different ways to score. The same is true of power buffing or polishing; that is, there are many different ways to obtain good results. Experiment until you find one method that suits you the best.

The following is a step-by-step description of the methods used by one gunsmith to prepare the metal for rebluing a Savage .22 single-shot barrel/action:

- The first step was to completely disassemble the barrel/action.

- The first polishing pass was made with stitched muslin wheels using 140 grit polishing compound. The barrel was held at a 45-degree angle to the bore and all old blue and rust pits were polished away. No polishing was done to the lettering.

- The next pass was made with loose muslin wheels using 240 grit. The barrel was held so that polishing marks with the 240-grit polishing compound were at a 90-degree angle to the 140-grit polishing marks. This pass completely removed the polishing marks made by the 140-grit compound. No polishing was done to the lettering.

- The last pass was with 400 grit. First the lettering was polished using a hard felt wheel. Then, with the loose muslin wheel, the barrel was held with the bore at a 90-degree angle to the polishing wheel and polished from one end to the other, turning the barrel slightly as each end was reached until the whole surface was polished.

Before beginning any work on the metal buttplate for this rifle, the metal was first inspected to evaluate the condition of the engraving and lettering and the severity of the blemishes that were to be removed.

In evaluating this buttplate, it was found that the engraving would need to be recut before polishing to prevent any loss of lines to the engraving.

Once recutting was completed, draw filing was used to remove deep pits in the metal; care was taken to avoid the engraved area and to maintain proper contours. Once draw filing removed all major blemishes, the surface was then hand polished using 180 grit in the opposite direction until all previous lines and marks were removed. This process was repeated — first in one direction and then in another — using finer grit abrasive cloth until all previous lines and marks were removed.

While polishing or draw filing, it is important that all screw holes are maintained at the proper taper and the holes do not become funneled. Sometimes screw holes become funneled due to improper installation of a screw or poor polishing. When a screw hole is funneled to where it is obviously bad, the hole must be widened (retapered) and a new screw with an oversized head machined to match the new taper of the hole.

Once the polishing on the buttplate was almost complete, using 500 grit paper, 600 grit wet paper was used and finally 1000 grit abrasive paper with oil. At this point, the metal is ready to be engraved and blued by any of the various methods.

Polishing Aluminum

First of all, you must realize that there are many, many different aluminum alloys and also many tempers of those alloys; and they all respond to polishing differently. As a result, polishing time, technique and results will vary from alloy to alloy.

The basic procedure is as follows: Sand as needed to remove scratches, machine marks, etc., finishing up with a worn, greased 400 or 600 grit belt if power sanding or 600 grit wet-or-dry (used wet) if hand sanding. Clean the piece thoroughly to remove any traces of sanding grit and grease. This is a *must* step. Just a wipe with a cloth isn't enough. Use solvent or detergent but get any grease and grit residue off or you'll end up with unexplained scratches later on.

Begin polishing with Brownells 555 Black on a stitched muslin wheel with about a 1-inch wide face (group $\frac{3}{8}$-inch wheels together). The 555 Black will take out the sanding scratches and give the aluminum a nice glow. Depending upon where the piece will be used, and how hard an alloy you are working with, it may be possible to stop after 555 Black. For harder alloys and pieces that will be highly visible, change to a 1-inch wide, stitched muslin wheel and 555 White. This will change the "color" from a glow to a bright, chrome-like shine. For a final touch, use a loose muslin wheel, lightly loaded with 555 White.

Here are some Dos and Don'ts to improve your final results.

- Don't skip grits as you work through the sanding process.

- Don't press the work hard into the buffing wheel. Doing so will build heat in the workpiece and the polish. The result will be streaks of polish deposited on the workpiece. Use a *light* touch.

- Don't overload the wheel with polish.

● Do clean your wheel with a cleaning brick and reload frequently. Minute bits of aluminum will gradually mix with the polish and build up a "glaze" on the surface of the wheel. If glaze is not removed you will end up "polishing" with aluminum residue instead of polish.

Concerning Power Sanding Equipment: The following also applies to disc, belt or orbital sanders. Your last grit MUST have a BELT GREASE applied. There are special belt greases available; many stick-type tapping compounds are also recommended as belt greases; light greases like Lubriplate work well and, in a pinch, you can even apply some 555 White to the belt, disc, or sheet to act as a grease. Why? Power sanding generates a tremendous amount of surface heat and this heat causes aluminum to oxidize instantly forming a hard, oxide coating. Polishing compound 555 Black cannot cut through this layer easily, the wheel will drag and pull and the resulting surface will look splotchy and uneven.

SAND BLASTING

Sand- or bead-blasting gun surfaces is becoming more and more in demand. The process offers an excellent way to "polish" thin, pitted areas such as magazine tubes on rifles and shotguns where the metal is too thin to buff out the pits. The pits will remain, but the matte, non-glare finish that results from bead-blasting will not make them stand out, as they would on a highly polished surface.

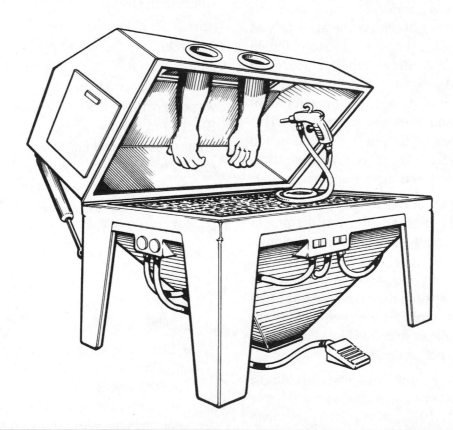

Figure 14-10: A sand-blasting apparatus is a great help in removing rust and preparing the metal surface prior to power buffing. It is an almost essential piece of equipment if you plan to parkerize firearms.

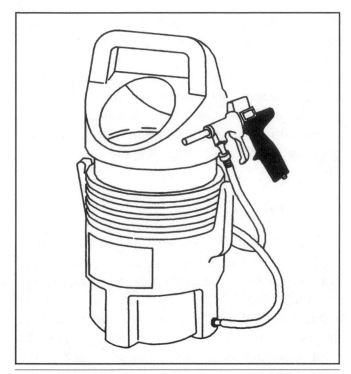

Figure 14-11: Here's a good sand-blasting device for both the small and large gunsmithing shop. Everything needed is included except an air compressor.

The sand-blasting apparatus shown in Figure 14-10 is the ideal set-up for the professional shop, but will cost in the neighborhoood of $800 plus the cost of a compressor. However, there are also portable sand-blasting rigs that are relatively inexpensive — less than $150. *See* Figure 14-11. They will do any pressure/abrasive cleaning, using silica sand, steel grit, aluminum oxide, glass beads, pecan shells or detergent and water. The most expensive item needed for sand-blasting is an air compressor; these will run from $500 to $2,000 or more. For indoor use, a sand-blasting cabinet is needed to hold the abrasive. These are usually provided with a glass door and electric light, to enable the operator to view the work as it is being cleaned. The cabinet also should contain a pair of sand-blasting gloves, so the operator can hold the various objects as they are being worked on. Sand-blasting is recommended for highly pitted areas where removing all the pits is next to impossible. The pits won't show up as much if the area is sand-blasted.

Polishing Small Parts

Inside radius polishing of trigger guards, magazine-tube rings, and similar gun parts, often require much time because of the varied sizes and intricate shapes involved. A Moto-Tool with small revolving polishing disks is one way to solve the problem, but when many polishing operations are required, it is most beneficial and cost effective to install a permanent set-up on a spindle polisher.

An effective unit can be fabricated from a medium-duty, universal motor with a $\frac{1}{3}$ horsepower rating. It may be a single-end shaft model with an output of 1725 to 3450 rpm. It is preferable to have a resilient-mounting system to limit vibration and should have no restrictions on its mounting position. Because of its intended function, the motor should be dust-resistant and drip-proof. The shaft should be prepared to accept a $\frac{1}{2}$" keyed chuck which will greatly facilitate changing mandrels and specialized polishing equipment.

A belt-driven spindle/grinder/polisher is shown in Figure 14-12. Note the spindle chuck on the

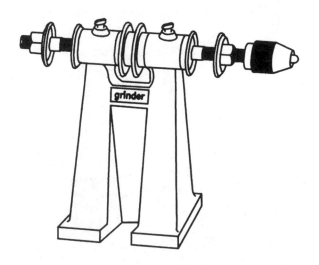

Figure 14-12: A spindle/grinder polisher has many uses in the gunshop, especially for polishing the inside radius of trigger guards, magazine-tube rings, and similar gun parts.

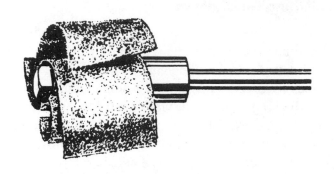

Figure 14-13: A split-shaft mandrel is suited for using abrasive flaps for polishing the inside radius of gun parts. It is also ideal for polishing the bores of shotgun barrels.

right-hand shaft. This is designed to hold small polishing wheel mandrels for polishing the inside radius of gun parts. If a motor shaft is used, the set-up can be enhanced by using a motor-mounted rocker control switch, a reversing switch and a variable speed control. These additional features greatly expand the unit's flexibility but are not mandatory. A split-shaft mandrel is sometimes used to hold polishing flaps of various types and grit sizes as shown in Figure 14-13.

A 1-inch belt sander like the one shown in Figure 14-14 is another power tool ideally suited for pol-

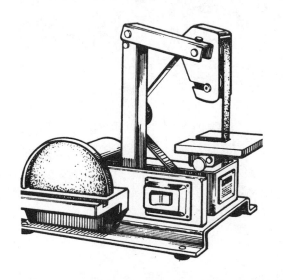

Figure 14-14: Typical 1-inch belt sander. The narrow belt is ideal for polishing the inside radius of small gun parts.

ishing small parts. The unsupported belt spans may be used to contour and polish irregularly shaped parts. Using the table in conjunction with the backed-up area of the belt, flat and square profiling may be accomplished. Controlled radius polishing is made possible by using the exposed upper carrier wheel with more than 40 percent of its circumference available for profiling and polishing.

Summary

Regardless of the type of finish you intend to apply to the gun metal — bluing, parkerizing, browning, etc. — the metal must be properly prepared to accept the finish. Sand or bead blasting is a quick method that leaves a dull, matte finish on the surface. However, polishing and buffing is the most popular way to prepare metal to accept the desired finish.

Cloth or loose muslin buffing wheels come in a large number of sizes and special shapes to buff practically any shape of metal object prior to coloring or plating. Most are extremely soft, but when revolving at high speed (from 1700 to 3600 rpm) centrifugal force continually acts to keep them "flat" against the surface being buffed, permitting a relatively great amount of pressure to be applied.

Depending upon the size of the buffing wheel, it may be used in a small hand grinder (Moto-Tool) for polishing small gun parts, or on a large double-shafted motor, or on large revolving shafts containing many buffing wheels. The most practical size for shop use, however, is about a 1-horsepower double-shafted motor that can contain two buffing wheels — one on each shaft end.

What is known as a packed buffing wheel is sometimes used for color-buffing nickel, gold, and silver. It is formed by placing cardboard discs of smaller diameter in between the cloth discs.

Pieced buffs are made of remnants smaller than ordinary full discs and these are held together by continuous spiral stitching over the entire surface.

This results in a wheel that is somewhat more unyielding than buffs assembled by other means.

The form of sewing on a buffing wheel is most important, as this determines the hardness of the wheel in most cases. The stitching can be spiral, crescent, radial, or other — each of which has its particular use in certain buffing applications. The speed of the buffing wheel is also important. A rule of thumb is, the larger the wheel, the slower the speed. That is, the larger-diameter wheels should operate at a slower rpm to acquire the same speed in feet per minute of the smaller wheels.

In general, the worker starts at one area of the wheel and then pulls the parts upward against the wheel and with a pressure that will depend a great deal upon the ease with which the particular metal cuts. Very little pressure in polishing will be needed for anything but steel. For removing pits in the surface of the steel, the polishing wheels cut more quickly if the part is moved in a circular motion as the part is moved upward or across the wheel. Where deep pits are involved, it is usually best to first cut these out with a belt sander using progressively finer grit sizes until the metal is smooth. Then it can be finished on the buffing wheel.

When polishing round, hollow objects, such as a gun barrel or magazine tube, much time can be saved by using a spinning fixture. The finish will also be smoother, with practically no visible abrasive marks when taken down to, say, size 400-grit buffing compound.

Polishing Precautions

Although it is a normal practice in gunshops, using the lathe for polishing and grinding is not recommended. Under such conditions, fine abrasive dust will gradually find its way into the lathe bearings, and eventually cause trouble. This dust also accumulates on the lathe ways and can scratch them, which will affect the lathe's accuracy.

When buffing, always wear a face mask and have adequate ventilation. It is also advisable to use a vacuum tool rigged to the wheel guard to carry off dust that forms from the buffing and polishing operation. A pair of leather gloves is also essential to protect the hands from bad wheel burns.

The operator must be careful of sharp edges on objects being polished. A buffing wheel will rip a piece out of the hands instantly if caught just right and will sling the piece against the floor or across the room with great force. Obviously, this can damage the workpiece and also people who may be in the area. Never buff a gun part that contains wires such as those used for hanging the parts in the bluing solution. Always remove the wires before buffing. To do otherwise is dangerous. Should the wires become entangled in the revolving shafts, and the wires are near your hands, the force of the wire wrapping around the revolving shaft can quickly cut off fingers.

MASS FINISHING

Many of the firearm manufacturers — and even some private gun shops — use barrel tumbling and vibratory finishing methods to prepare metal parts for bluing. Yes, mass finishing, the multi-operational process has come to stand alone in its ability

Figure 14-15: Vibrator cartridge-case polishers are being used in gunshops for polishing small gun parts prior to bluing. Be selective in choosing the appropriate polishing medium.

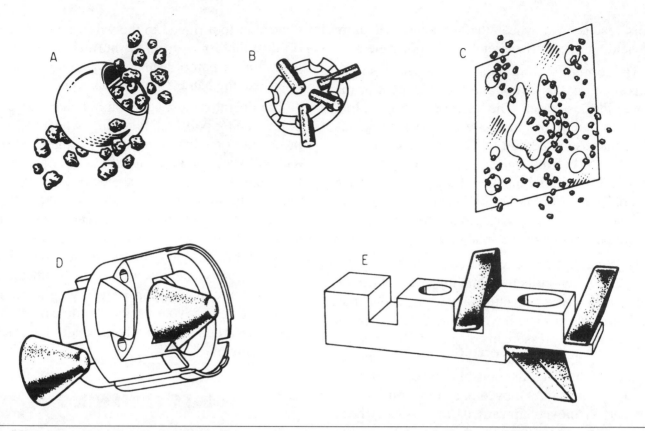

Figure 14-16: The abrasive media should match the job. Here are just a few of the many shapes of media available. They are designed to reach in every crevice and slot, and will do a fine job of polishing with the least amount of effort.

to perform a multitude of processing steps at one time. Media compositions and shapes along with improved equipment have evolved to the extent where it is now possible to perform upwards of ten operations simultaneously on gun parts.

A vibrator sanding drum large enough to hold a complete gun can be very costly, but many gunsmiths have had good luck polishing small parts with a vibrator designed to polish brass cartridges for reloaders. *See* Figure 14-15. If these are used, however, remember that the walnut shell abrasive that comes with them are virtually useless for polishing steel parts; they are okay on brass, but not steel. One with more cutting abrasives should be used. These are available from a local body shop supply house, or an industrial supplier.

The workpieces may be, for example, a batch of magazine-tube rings for a .22 caliber semiautomatic rifle. In a single finishing operation, the media can remove die marks, generate external and internal radii on edges, improve metal fatigue life, and impart a high-luster and low-microinch finish. Performing each job separately would obviously be uneconomical by today's metal-working standards. This is why the mass-finishing process is growing at a rapid rate.

Paramount in the success of mass finishing is the consistent finishing action which guarantees uniformity of surface finish of every workpiece in the work load time after time. Proper selection and control of all elements involved in the process — equipment, media, compounds, water, and time cycles — must be correctly synchronized, for one complements the other in producing the best results.

Conventional mass-finishing equipment can be categorized by the purpose and function it performs according to the following:

• Conventional barrel equipment should be operated at proper speed levels to achieve the optimum slide pattern. For stock-removal applications, equipment manufacturers recommend 120-200 sfm as opposed to 75-100 sfm for polishing.

• Vibrators should be operated at the frequency and amplitude that provides best movement of the work load.

• High-pressure-force equipment should be set for the proper "G" force for the given application. "G" forces of 25 or greater are recommended for the fastest stock removal, 10 to 20 G's for intermediate action, and 5 G's for polishing.

• Spindle-type machines. The speeds of the spindles holding the workpieces and the tub spindles must be synchronized to provide the surface speed required for "plowing action" between the media and the workpieces.

Media Development

During the past 20 years of rapid development in equipment, media technology grew with improvements in compositions to be used in the more aggressive vibrators and high-pressure-force equipment.

Preformed ceramic bonded shapes such as triangles, starts, spheres, cylinders, and diamond shapes have appeared in the marketplace. Since their inception, a large variety of these shapes and compositions have been developed to finish parts with a minimum amount of wedging problems. *See* Figure 14-16. Ceramic preforms are now available with compositions of aluminum oxide, silicon carbide, natural abrasives, or without any abrasive content.

Within the past decade, media manufacturers introduced lightweight, preformed resin-coated media to remove burrs, flash, gates, and parting lines while maintaining smooth microinch finishes on soft ferrous and nonferrous parts. This process is often referred to as producing pre-plate finishes and is most often used on zinc and aluminum diecastings.

Prior to the introduction of resin-bonded media, it was difficult to restore smooth surface finishes after cut-down operations. The future will bring new metal alloys and synthetic resins that will challenge machine and media manufacturers to produce equipment and new media products for finishing these materials quickly.

Media Selection

The scope of mass finishing is large and diverse, necessitating quite a number of various media specifications to accommodate the many finishing requirements. Manufacturers and suppliers are well qualified to advise users on the proper recommendations for finishing their products.

Because of the many considerations in selecting the type of abrasive media to fit a particular job, it is important that users familiarize themselves as much as possible with the different abrasive materials available — what they are and what functions they perform under various conditions.

The first prerequisite is to review the workpiece: its material, shape, size and weight. Also determine the part requirements: removal of burrs, sharp edges, tool marks, flash, grinding lines and heat-treat scale; forming or radii; producing surface finishes to specific microinch requirements; and improving metal fatigue life.

A systematic approach should be used in selecting the composition, shape, and size of abrasive to process a particular part. The abrasive compositions are generally classified as aggressive, intermediate, or mild acting. Aggressive abrasives are used when maximum stock removal is required.

Intermediate abrasives are used when a combination of stock removal and smooth surface finishes are necessary. Mild abrasives are employed when minimum stock removal and high luster are desired.

With synthetic abrasives, the aggressiveness can be controlled accurately. Crystal structure and density will determine the aggressiveness of the random-shaped abrasive media. The type of abrasive, the amount of abrasive in relation to bond, abrasive density, and bond hardness determine the aggressiveness of the ceramic and resin-bonded media.

Composition: Those familiar with grinding operations usually associate the use of aluminum oxide with ferrous metals and silicon carbide with nonferrous metals. But this isn't true in mass finishing; aluminum oxide is used in most applications, regardless of the type of metal being processed. Other abrasive materials employed include silicon carbide, corundum, quartz, pumice, and garnet.

Shape: The shape of the media to be used is determined by the shape of the part being processed. Slotted parts are best finished by triangular-shaped media. Parts with holes or rounded areas would be best processed by round-pin or spherical-shaped media. In most instances, stampings or parts that have plain basic shapes with few areas for the media to lodge in are best processed with random-shaped media.

Size: The size of the media to be used is determined by the size and weight of the part being processed. The larger the part, the larger the media. The reason for this is to displace the weight of the parts, which aids in keeping the parts in a homogeneous mixture and prevents nicking. The areas of the part which require processing also determine abrasive media size. If the area is restricted or not easily accessible, it becomes necessary to use media small enough to reach into this area.

Another very important consideration in selecting the best size and shape of media is the ability to separate the media from the parts when the job is completed. Abrasive size isn't too critical when processing ferrous-metal parts, for they can be separated magnetically. But with nonmagnetic parts which require screening or dimensional separation, media size determines the ease of separation.

Another factor in selecting the size of media is the amount of stock removal required. The larger the size of the abrasive media, the more weight and energy generated, and, consequently, the greater the stock removal. This also means that the amount of stock removal can be controlled simply by selecting different sizes of media.

There are additional benefits in knowing how much stock can be removed by the various compositions and sizes of media. A very important benefit is the control of dimensional tolerance. Today, dimension is so important that it is not uncommon to see dimensions controlled to millionths of an inch. Time cycles are the counterpart to abrasive media in the control of dimensional tolerance.

The type of machine being used also dictates media selection. It is quite common to use the most aggressive abrasive media in tumbling barrels and the more durable media in vibratory and centrifugal machines. All of the abrasive compositions can be used in all the various types of machines.

Frequently, a manufacturer's equipment capacity and production requirements influence the abrasive composition used. If a manufacturer's production exceeds his machine capacity, he must use the most aggressive abrasive media available. He will be able to keep his mass-finishing time cycle to a minimum and get maximum production from his machines.

Some manufacturers have an excess of machine capacity over production volume. This allows the use of a more durable, less aggressive abrasive media. The time cycles are increased, but these manufacturers have the advantage of a lower cost per part finished because of longer media life.

Cost Savings

The reason a manufacturer turns to mass finishing is to eliminate the necessity of handling each individual part. He can produce a finish not obtainable by any other method at a cost considerably lower than that of his present process. The amount saved depends, naturally, on the cost of the abrasive media and compound used. From a cost standpoint based on lowest cost per pound of media (which is also affected by media weight and wear rate), the following guidelines are recommended:

- Use a random-shaped media as first choice, provided it doesn't lodge in the part.

- If the part presents a lodging problem, then the second choice is the preformed ceramic bonded media.

- If the part cannot be processed with either of the first two materials, use preformed resin-bonded media.

Wet Finishing

Water levels are extremely important in industrial mass finishing because a high percentage of all operations are done with wet solutions. In rotational barrel finishing, low water levels are recommended for fast cuts. For polishing, the water should be level or slightly over the top of the mass. With vibratory equipment, "flo-thru" water systems should have a constant water stream to produce optimum results. Low water levels are recommended in a "captive" solution where there is no "flo-thru" system.

The water level should be over the top of the work-load when using high-pressure-force equipment, because the water helps dissipate the heat generated by the high frictional forces. Low water levels — just high enough to form a slurry — are recommended for spindle machines.

Abrasive or grinding compounds are finding wider use because they can increase the cutability of the media charge and because they can be used in self-tumbling applications (part on part — without conventional-type media). These compounds are classified as either abrasive or nonabrasive. The nonabrasive compounds, for example, come under three general classifications: alkalis used as rust inhibitors, descaling compounds used for removing heat-treat scale, and burnishing compounds for imparting color and luster to parts.

For general gun work, however, most gunsmiths seldom use mass-finishing exclusively. Gun barrels, for example, are normally polished on a spinning fixture, using either a belt sander or polishing wheel. Small, hard-to-polish parts, such as trigger, pins, and the like are often placed in a polishing media inside a tumbler at night, and the next morning they are ready for the bluing tanks. Others use the mass-finishing system exclusively with the exception of removing pits. Areas containing pits are first draw-filed and polished in a conventional manner. Then all parts are placed in a vibratory barrel and allowed to vibrate, and consequently receive a polish, for from six to 12 hours. They are usually ready for the bluing tanks after this time.

Chapter 15
Rebluing at Home

Firearm refinishing is one of the most rewarding phases of gunsmithing work. Besides its monetary rewards, gun bluing also enables the gunsmith to derive many by-products. First, as the guns are being disassembled to prepare them for polishing and bluing, the operating characteristics of each gun become instilled in one's mind. Further handling of the more popular guns soon leads the gunsmith to know — almost instantaneously and without thinking — just what parts are worn, broken or need replacing.

Also, few gunsmithing operations are more pleasing than to see a rusted and badly-abused firearm turn into a thing of beauty with a rich, blue-black finish instead of the reddish rust. For those unfamiliar with the firearm bluing operation, the process may seem like magic; that is, turning a worn firearm into one that looks brand new. But for the person doing the work, he or she knows that the process was not an act of magic. Rather, it was accomplished by knowing what to do; that is, a masterful job of polishing all the surfaces true and bright, keeping the corners sharp, and not funneling the screw holes. Furthermore, the gunsmith made certain that all parts were thoroughly cleaned with a degreasing solution before bluing. The results were rewarding — a perfect blue-black finish on the steel that will last for years to come.

BASIC BLUING

The earliest bluing solutions consisted of a mixture of nitric acid and hydrochloric acid with steel shavings or iron nails dissolved in them. The process used in applying solution to the gun metal is generally known as the slow rust bluing process.

In general, the slow rust process consists of polishing the metal parts to be blued to the desired lustre and then degreasing the parts by boiling them in a solution of lime and water or lye and water. Without touching the metal parts with bare hands or otherwise letting them become contaminated, the metal is swabbed with the bluing solution in long, even strokes until all parts are covered. The metal is then allowed to stand and rust from six to twenty-four hours. After this the rust is rubbed off with steel wool or a wire brush to reveal a light gray or bluish color underneath.

The surface, still free from oil, is again swabbed with the solution and allowed to rust another day. When this second coat of rust is carded off, the metal beneath is an even darker shade of blue. The process is repeated until the desired color is obtained, taking anywhere from one to two weeks on the average, depending upon the metal and the humidity in the air. The parts then are boiled in water for about fifteen minutes, to stop further rusting action, and oiled. The result is a beautiful, long-wearing metal finish.

A. F. Stoeger (later Stoeger Industries, Inc.) manufactured and distributed one of the better slow-rust bluing solutions for decades. It was called Stoeger Gunsmith's Bluer. This product, however, was discontinued for the second time in the 1980s and is no longer available.

The time required to obtain a perfect finish by the slow rusting process forced gunsmiths and manufacturers to seek a faster and easier process. The one developed has been called many names such as 20-minute blue, express blue, but hot water bluing is generally the accepted term.

Hot water bluing is based on the fact that steel, when heated, rusts more rapidly than when cold. This is due to a more rapid absorption of the oxygen that forms ferric oxide or red rust. Therefore, new formulas were developed that reacted favorably on metal that was polished, degreased, and then heated in boiling water. Once boiled for five or ten minutes, the metal parts are lifted from the boiling water where they dry almost immediately due to the heat of the steel. The bluing solution (often heated also) is applied to the hot metal in long even strokes. Rust forms immediately on the metal, but before carding, the parts are once again dunked into the boiling water for another five minutes. The first carding should turn the metal parts a light gray color, and each successive coat should deepen the color until it is a deep, velvety, blue-black color. Depending upon the metal, it may take anywhere from four to twelve coats to obtain the desired finish.

Other bluing methods were developed — nitre bluing, charcoal bluing — but the major development in gun bluing occurred around the turn of the century when the black oxide (hot caustic) process of bluing was patented. This method requires that the parts be polished in the conventional way, but instead of applying the solution to the metal parts, the parts are dunked into a tank of the boiling solution. Once in the tank, the bluing process is

Figure 15-1: Catalog listing of Stoeger Gunsmith's Bluer, from the 1946 *Shooter's Bible*.

REBLUING AT HOME 189

essentially a fifteen to thirty minute process of boiling the parts in a strong alkaline solution. The process works exceptionally well on a wide variety of steel and is much more economical for mass production than any other process. Another advantage of this method is that the number of guns that can be blued at one time is limited only by the size of the tank and the heating facility.

During the early part of the twentieth century, an instant or cold bluing process became popular with do-it-yourselfers. The trend is still popular today. The cold bluing solution is a mixture of acids and copper nitrate. The copper nitrate forms a plating on the metal and the acids turn the copper black the instant it touches bare metal that has been degreased.

There are many kits on the market that contain everything necessary to blue guns at home. If care is taken, the result can look quite pleasing. The main problem is durability. None of these cold bluing solutions will hold up for any length of time, and eventually the gun will be coated with red rust and no blue.

These cold bluing solutions do have a place, however, in every gun shop — for touch-up jobs. The cold bluing solutions on the market will most definitely blacken metal, if the metal is properly prepared. Of these solutions, Brownells Oxpho-Blue seems to be the most durable, but the application is a little tricky, so it is probably not the best choice for the beginner. Birchwood-Casey's Perma-Blue Paste or G96 Gun Blue Creme are better choices for a first attempt at touch-up gun bluing.

Cold Bluing Techniques

Cold bluing chemicals will not blue casehardened steel, stainless steel, aluminum, or other nonferrous metals. Casehardened steel can be readily detected by the mottled colors running through the surface of the steel. If these colors have faded, the metal will usually have a chrome appearance.

Figure 15-2: Basic items required for cold bluing: cleaning solution, steel wool, applicators, oil, and the cold (instant) bluing solution.

Stainless steel barrels are usually marked as such. Aluminum or other nonferrous metals will not react when touched with a magnet.

The chemicals used in cold bluing solutions are poisonous and should be treated accordingly. Many of the chemicals will affect the skin, so it is recommended that gloves be worn when using them. Skin-tight surgical gloves, available from drug stores or medical suppliers are ideal for cold bluing. They allow free movement and feel, yet give adequate protection from harmful chemicals.

There are several cold bluing solutions available on the market, and, because many of them vary in strength and application technique, the manufactur-

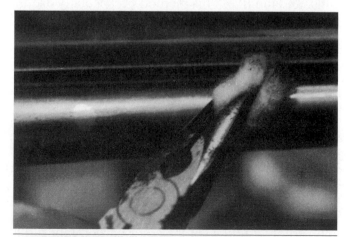

Figure 15-3: Once the metal is perfectly clean, the bluing solution is applied to the metal with applicators; here a cotton swab is held with clean long-nose pliers.

ers' instructions should be followed in all cases. In general, no heat is required to apply the bluing solution, but the metal surfaces must be free from oil for best results. After cleaning the surface to be blued with a solvent such as AWA 1,1,1, the bluing solution is applied in even strokes over the surface with cotton swabs, left on for a few minutes, and then wiped off. Successive coats are applied until the desired finish is reached. Then swab the area thoroughly with gun oil.

As mentioned previously, the cold or instant bluing method is recommended only for touch-up jobs. In a pinch, it will produce a nice-looking, complete blue job if correct procedures are followed — proper polishing, removing all pits and scratches from metal, degreasing, and applying the solution evenly. When completed and oiled, the final result will appear quite similar to a factory hot-caustic bluing job, especially immediately after the job is finished and the metal surfaces are oiled. However, this appearance does not last as long as some of the other methods.

HEAT BLUING

Heat bluing is used extensively in the gun shop — mainly to blue small parts such as screws, drift pins, and the like. This method is especially useful when replacing one screw or drift pin that would not warrant "firing up" the hot caustic bluing tanks. The oil-and-heat method is one of the favorites for bluing such parts and the procedures are simple.

Polish and degrease the parts to be blued in the usual manner. Use a piece of stovepipe wire or a pair of degreased long-nose pliers to grip the part to be blued and heat the part with a propane or similar torch until it is a dull red in color. Then quickly plunge the part into a small container of oil or transmission fluid. It should turn a nice temper-blue color. If you want the color darker, repeat the operation. Be careful of the oil igniting, and don't touch the heated part while it's still hot.

Nitre Bluing

Heat or temper blue was used extensively on some parts of the earlier firearms manufactured by Winchester, Marlin, and others. To obtain this temper blue, such methods as torch heat, charcoal, sand and nitre were used as the heat-transfer media. The excellent finish found on Winchester firearms, however, was a result of good steel and perfect polishing of the parts, rather than the bluing process.

The nitre process of bluing steel is a quick and easy method for bluing small parts such as screws, triggers, hammers, and the like. Of course, it can be used for receivers and other large parts also, but the expense of setting up for the larger parts will far outweigh the cost of having the parts done by a professional or using the money to purchase equipment for the hot-caustic bluing method.

In using this method, there are several precautions that should be followed to prevent bad burns and/or damage to eyes. Always wear a face shield or safety goggles, and also heavy clothing and gloves to protect the skin. The main reason for this protection is if any oil or water (just one drop) should fall into the hot nitre mixture, 700-degree molten lava will fly all over creation and can cause severe burns. The next precaution is to make absolutely certain that the parts to be blued are free of water and other liquid before placing them into the solution to be blued.

To begin, you need a cast-iron container large enough to hold the parts so they will be completely covered by the bluing solution. *See* Figure 15-4. A lead-melting pot is okay, as long as it is completely clean. A small gas or electric hot plate will serve for the necessary heat. You will then need enough potassium nitrate (common saltpeter) to fill the melting container.

The parts to be blued are polished and cleaned to remove all traces of grease. Usually, AWA 1,1,1 (found in most hardware stores) will suffice for degreasing or a commercial degreaser may be used.

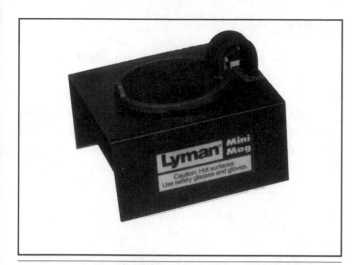

Figure 15-4: A lead melting pot or furnace will suffice to hold the nitre bluing solution when bluing only small parts like screws and triggers.

Just be sure that the parts are completely dry before immersing in the bluing solution; especially check blind screw holes for possible trapped liquid.

Set the melting pot onto the source of heat, and sprinkle a little of the potassium nitrate in the pot. It will melt in due time, and when melted, sprinkle more in. Continue this until you have enough melted potassium nitrate or nitre bluing solution. Attach a black iron wire to each small part to be blued, and once you are certain that no liquid is present on the part, gradually lower it into the melted bluing solution.

Let the part remain in the molten solution until a uniform color of the desired shade is obtained. This usually takes from 10 to 30 minutes, depending upon the size of the part. The part is then removed from the solution, and plunged immediately into warm water. In a few seconds, the part will cool; then wipe the part off and oil thoroughly.

If you have done your part on the polishing and degreasing, you should have a nice, rich blue-black finish on the gun part.

The original Winchester nitre bluing formula calls for a small amount of manganese oxide to be added to the potassium nitre, but in trying this addition some gunsmiths have had adverse results; that is, spotted finishes, extreme heat, etc. Therefore, the addition of manganese oxide to the saltpeter is not recommended.

Charcoal Bluing

Charcoal bluing, as used to color some metal parts on early firearms, is another form of temper or heat bluing. The color could be varied from a light blue to a dark blue black, depending upon the temperature of the charcoal. This bluing method, according to research, was used mainly on small parts such as screws, pins and similar parts that did not lend themselves to easy bluing of larger parts.

Your first attempt at charcoal bluing can be done with a small cast iron melting pot over a gas camp stove. A few bricks of commercial charcoal are placed in a cloth bag, and then pulverized with a mallet until small granules about the size of pea beans remain. These are then dumped into the melting pot to be heated. You don't want to get these coals red hot; just enough so that an even temperature of about 600 to 700 degrees F. is held.

The parts to be blued are polished as usual and degreased. Use black iron stove pipe wire around each part so that it could be removed from the charcoal without having to touch them with any other object. If the temperature is correct, the parts should be ready in about 10 minutes after being placed in the heated granulated charcoal.

Purchase a can of regular car transmission fluid, and pour this into a separate container large enough so the fluid will completely cover the objects being blued. Using the wire so as not to burn yourself, lift one of the parts from the charcoal and inspect it. If it has taken on the proper blue-black color, then quickly immerse it into the container with the transmission fluid; wait until it cools, then remove and place aside.

Repeat this procedure with all the parts. If the initial inspection shows an improper color, place the part back into the charcoal for a while longer. However, once the part has been dipped into the transmission fluid, it will have to be degreased before returning it to the charcoal.

The process is completed by wiping off the parts with a clean rag and then oiling.

If care is used in the polishing, degreasing, and the preparation of the charcoal mixture, you should have a nice, authentic-looking satin blue-black finish when completed.

Clyde Baker, in his very comprehensive book, *Modern Gunsmithing* gives a slightly different method: Make a container of heavy sheet iron large enough to hold the largest part to be blued. Since no liquid will be used in the container, it is not necessary to have tight seams; merely fold the corners. Fill the container with pulverized wood charcoal in lumps about the size of a small pea, and heat the container until the charcoal is partly burning throughout, but not red hot. Attach a rod or wire to the part to be blued and bury it in the glowing mass, allowing the rod or wire to stick out to be used as a handle. In 5 or 10 minutes, lift the part out and examine it. If the color has started, take a large, clean cotton rag, balling it up, dip it into some powdered lime and thoroughly rub the part vigorously all over.

Get the part back into the glowing charcoal as soon as possible. Repeat this treatment every 7 to 10 minutes, using plenty of lime and rubbing it into every part of the gun, working very quickly. Be extremely cautious so as not to burn yourself. Continue this treatment until a rich blue-black color has appeared, then let it cool in the air before applying a light gun oil to the part.

Of course, the parts have to be polished and cleaned as for any type of bluing.

Either one of these methods will work fine on small gun parts. If you have complete control of the temperature, an entire gun may be blued this way, but to get an even color throughout is not an easy task without the proper equipment. Therefore, we recommend this method only for screws, triggers, pins and the like.

Imitation Heat Blue

Most gunsmiths now use the hot caustic bluing method almost exclusively and seldom have the time to experiment with alternate methods. However, these same gunsmiths are often called upon to restore older firearms on which the owner wants an authentic-looking metal finish. One hot caustic bluing formula that gives results close to the original nitre blue is as follows:

To each gallon of pure water add a mixture of:

- 65 ounces sodium hydroxide
- 30 ounces sodium nitrate
- 5 ounces sodium nitrite

To mix, first determine the size of your bluing tank and the amount of water required to bring the water level up to about the half-way mark. Let's say this requires four gallons of water. Therefore, you would need four times the amount of chemicals as described above; that is, 260 ounces of sodium hydroxide, 120 ounces of sodium nitrate, and 20 ounces of sodium nitrite. Mix these ingredients dry. Add the four gallons of pure water to your bluing tank, turn the heat on low and slowly add the dry powders, a little at a time, stirring the solution to help the chemicals mix with the water. Be sure to use all safety precautions as with any type of bluing; that is, face shield, rubber gloves, apron, etc. If you add the chemicals too fast, the solution will heat too quickly and erupt or boil over. Let the chemicals dissolve slowly. The solution should start boiling at about 285 degrees F. If not, add a little more water; if the solution boils at a lower temperature, add more bluing salts. When adding water, however, use a water shield and let the water trickle into the tank; too much will cause the solution to erupt — causing bad burns and damage to clothes or leather shoes. Always be cautious when adding either water or salts to the tank — especially water.

Once the solution is at a rolling boil, and the temperature is between 285 degrees F. and 295 degrees F., degrease the parts to be blued and suspend them in the bluing solution with black iron wires or in a suitable parts basket. Make sure all parts are at least one inch from the tank sides and bottom, and that the temperature of the solution does not get above 295 degrees F.

The time required to obtain the desired finish will vary with the type of steel. Some gun metal will color within five minutes, but some parts may take as long as 30 minutes. Inspect the parts about every five minutes until the desired color has been reached.

When the color is deep enough, remove the parts from the bluing solution and immerse in clean boiling water for about five minutes, let cool, and then oil with any conventional gun oil. You should have a rich blue-black finish very close to the original nitre blue found on some firearms manufactured some 50 to 100 years ago.

This solution, like most hot caustic solutions, will destroy solder, brass, aluminum, etc. The action of non-ferrous metals will also destroy the effectiveness of the solution. Small traces of sulphur in the water will do the same thing.

Be sure to take all precautions and use the recommendations for conventional hot caustic bluing when using this method. Instructions and precautionary measures are normally included with commercial bluing solutions and outfits. Detailed information on hot caustic and other bluing methods — including the equipment needed — is covered later in this chapter. Always wear goggles or a face shield when handling any chemicals. Furthermore, rubber gloves should be worn as well as proper clothing for skin protection.

HOT-WATER BLUING

The hot-water bluing formulas were jealously guarded by professional gunsmiths of the day. It seemed that each gunsmith had developed his own formula. Even different foremen in the larger manufacturing plants had their own "secret" method of getting the desired results. Most of the formulas, however, were based on a solution consisting of sodium and potassium nitrates, potassium chlorate, and bichloride of mercury, mixed in distilled water. One well known formula is as follows:

- ¼ oz. potassium nitrate
- ¼ oz. sodium nitrate
- ½ oz. bichloride mercury
- ½ oz. potassium chlorate

Mix the above ingredients in a clean, wide-mouthed glass jar and then add 10 ounces of slightly heated (120°F) distilled water, poured slowly into the container holding the mixed dry chemicals. Stir with a glass rod continually until almost cool, then pour the contents into a dark brown glass or plastic bottle with a tight plastic cap. Keep the mixture in a dark, cool place the same as you would store photography chemicals.

However, chemicals are expensive these days when purchased in small quantities, and you will be money ahead by purchasing one of the commercial bluing solutions. Brownells sell Belgian Blue or you can order this hot-water bluing solution directly from sources listed in Appendix I of this book. Most of these solutions are excellent and you should experience very few problems, provided instructions are followed exactly, and all parts to be blued are absolutely clean.

Polishing Equipment

To begin preparing the metal for bluing, all pits should be removed, and the metal then polished to the desired sheen. A 10-inch mill bastard file and file card are needed if the gun has rust pits, nicks or scratches too deep for abrasive paper to remove. Otherwise, these two items may be eliminated.

Purchase at least three sheets each of the following grits of open-coat aluminum oxide abrasive paper. If your local hardware or automotive supply store doesn't have them, order from Brownells Inc., 140 S. Front St., Montezuma, IA 50171.

80 grit	240 grit
150 grit	320 grit
400 grit	500 grit

The 400- and 500-grit silicon "wet/dry" paper is used for the final polishing.

Bluing Equipment

If you already have a bench vise and two water-tight metal containers large enough to hold the parts to be blued, you already have much of the material needed. However, if not, get two 6" x 6" x 40" bluing tanks. One will do, but two are better, and the Heatbath three-tank system shown in Figure 15-5 is ideal. Make sure the tanks are made of ferrous metal or stainless steel; never galvanized.

A package of 00 steel wool and a stainless steel brush made of .005" hand-tied stainless steel wire are necessary for carding the rust from the gun. Clean rubber gloves are recommended during the bluing operation to insure that your skin will not come into contact with the metal. The inexpensive surgeon's gloves found in any drug store work fine.

Several good degreasing solutions are available but a can of household lye (sodium hydroxide) will do the job adequately. If you use a commercial cleaner, always follow the directions on the package.

A source of heat can be the kitchen range, but to keep peace at home, you'll do better to take the work to the basement or garage and use a camp stove or gas-fired hot plate for your heat source.

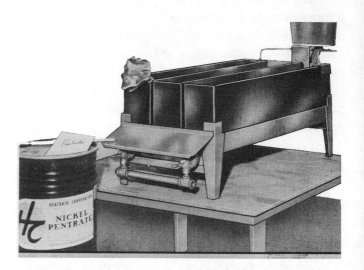

Figure 15-5: The Heatbath Corp. three-tank bluing system is ideal for hot-water bluing. The system may also be used for hot-caustic bluing when the need arises.

Chemicals added to city water supplies will sometimes have an adverse effect on the final bluing job. Some "hard" well water can do the same thing. Therefore, either buy distilled water from your druggist, or else try catching 8 to 10 gallons of rain water in plastic dish pans.

You will need some tapered dowels to plug the bore of the barrel and also some black stove pipe wire to attach to each part during boiling. The dowels may be made of wood, plastic, or similar material. A pack of cotton balls and a wooden clothespin or two for holding the cotton should just about complete the initial equipment.

With the material at hand, get ready for some hard work, but don't get discouraged; remember that you are getting a bluing job that should be superior to many factory finishes.

Procedure For Hot-Water Bluing

Regardless whether you use a commercial bluing solution or mix your own formula, the procedure is the same.

Polishing: Aside from keeping the metal surfaces free of oil, polishing is the most important step in getting a rich, velvety finish on your gun parts. Without proper polishing, you might as well forget bluing the gun and leave it as is. The coloring of the metal will never cover up pits, scratches, and the like. The surface of the metal must be perfect before the bluing solution is applied. Nothing else will do.

Many professional shops use power for buffing or polishing the metal parts. However, it takes lots of experience and practice to do a good job of power polishing without rounding sharp corners, funneling screw holes, or otherwise "grinding them up" too much. The beginner will do well to stick with hand polishing. Hand polishing will insure that all contours, lettering, markings and square edges will be properly preserved. About 12 hours of hand polishing are required to complete all parts on the average rifle or shotgun. If many pits are present, this time may be doubled.

The first step is to disassemble the gun completely down to the last screw and drift pin. If you are unfamiliar with the takedown procedure, exploded views and instructions are available from various sources for most firearms. When you have no printed instructions, jot down notes as you disassemble the gun and perhaps even take close-up photos of intricate parts. Then you'll have some reference to follow when you are reassembling the firearm.

Wipe the parts clean, examining each for wear and be sure that no aluminum alloy parts are present. This can easily be determined by using a small magnet. If the magnet doesn't react, then the part is nonferrous — aluminum, brass or similar alloy — and these parts should be set aside with others not to be blued. Besides the nonferrous parts, other parts will include springs and other small elements not visible in an assembled gun.

With all pieces to be blued in one pile, thoroughly clean each one with a solvent such as ace-tone or AWA 1,1,1. Then start polishing the parts as discussed earlier.

Once all the parts are polished, you are ready to start heating your tanks. However, if there is going to be any delay between the polishing and bluing, certain precautions must be taken. A freshly polished gun is a prime target for surface rust if it is not going into the cleaning or hot-water tank immediately. A delay of a few days or even a few hours under some conditions between final polishing and bluing can result in fine "silver" spots showing up on the gun after being blued. These are the result of microscopic rust spots developing while the gun is being held after polishing and prior to bluing.

Cleaning: Once the parts have been masterfully polished, pour enough clear water into one of the tanks to completely cover the gun and all its parts. Add the right amount of cleaning solution — Di-cro-Clean No. 909 or 1 tablespoonful of household lye — to 2½ gallons of soft water. If you don't have rain water, you can purchase distilled water from you local drug store or supermarket. Then suspend the gun and gun parts by black iron stove pipe wires. Make sure that all parts are at least 1 inch away from the bottom of the tank and also away from the tank sides. Otherwise, "hot spots" and blotchy bluing will be the result. Small parts can be individually suspended by black iron wires or else placed in a black iron or stainless steel basket which is then suspended in the tank. Let the parts "cook" in the cleaning solution for about 5 minutes.

Boiling the Parts: While the parts are being cleaned in the alkali cleaner, a tank of clean rain or distilled water is being heated in another tank. A clean glass jar containing the bluing solution is suspended in one corner of the tank so that part of the jar is underwater (heating the bluing solution). Be careful not to let any water in the bluing tank splash into the jar; this will weaken or contaminate the bluing solution.

After the cleaning period is completed, remove the parts from the cleaning tank and quickly trans-

Figure 15-6: A glass jar containing the bluing solution and suspended in the hot water will keep the solution at the right temperature during the bluing operation.

the largest of the parts out of the boiling water. The part should dry in a split second if it has been heated enough. If not, put it back into the boiling water and boil it a little longer. Don't worry about getting the parts too hot; the only danger is not having them hot enough.

Applying Solution: When the part dries in a split second after being lifted from the water, suspend the part in mid-air with wire, or in the case of the barrel which should have wooden or plastic dowels in each end as holding plugs, rest one wood plug on a table holding the opposite plug in your gloved hand. Then, as quickly as possible — before the part cools too much — dip a swab into the hot bluing solution in the suspended jar and dampen the swab. Don't "load" the swab, just dampen it. Apply the solution in long even strokes. The parts should be hot enough so that when the solution is applied, it dries immediately and leaves a light grayish brown coat on the parts.

After all parts have been coated, return all parts to the boiling water for about 5 minutes. Again, remove the part and swab more of the solution onto the hot metal surfaces. Do this to each of the other parts in turn.

fer them to the rinse tank (again containing clean, cold rain or distilled water) and then immediately put them into the hot water tank. The water must be kept at a hard, rolling, bubbling boil from here on out. Nothing else will do if best results are to be obtained.

Let the parts boil for a full 15 minutes the first time to insure an even heat throughout and then lift

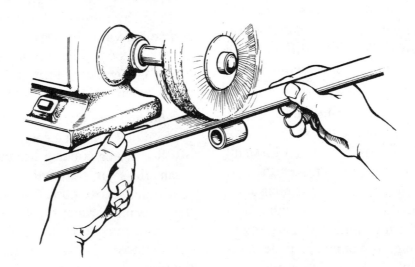

Figure 15-7: To card off the light coat of rust that forms after applying each coat of bluing solution, use steel wool, a stainless steel brush, or a motor-driven wire wheel. Be sure to remove only the loose rust and not the thin coats of color underneath.

Carding: Following the second application, you will see a darker coat of gray, flecked with rust, forming on the metal. Before returning the part to the hot water tank, rub the parts with clean 0000 steel wool to remove the rust particles. Do not rub the parts too vigorously. That could remove the thin coat of light grayish brown blue.

After all parts have been carded, return them to the hot water tank for another 5 or 6 minutes, and repeat the previous steps. As you put on more coats of the bluing solution, the brown or grayish-brown gradually turns to a rich velvety blue-black color. This might require as few as 4 coats (on, say, .22 rimfire barrels) or as many as 10 or 12 coats on harder steel. According to Clyde Baker, the famous gunsmith/author of the last generation, he has blued stainless steel with this method, but it required 30 or more coats of bluing solution.

Final Boiling: After the last coat of bluer has dried on the parts and has been removed with steel wool, wire wheel, or stainless steel brush (for tight places), place the parts in the boiling water once more and boil them for about 20 minutes to stop all further rusting. The parts will dry almost immediately upon being lifted from the water. When cool, oil all parts or boil them in a water displacing oil for the final oiling. Other than assembling the various parts, the job is finished.

To etch the metal surfaces, heat the gun and gun parts in the boiling water (prior to applying the bluing solution). When hot, lift them out and quickly coat each part with the etching solution, using a clean sponge or rag. Work very quickly. Splash on plenty of the etching solution and try to cover the entire surface in one or two strokes. Keep going over all the parts (keeping them wet). In a very short time (usually only a few seconds), the surfaces will take on a slightly frosted silvery appearance. Inspect each part carefully. If any areas seem to be uneven, coat these again and hold a few seconds. Otherwise, plunge the parts instantly back into the boiling water and continue the bluing procedure as discussed previously.

NOTE

On some metals, especially those blued for the first time, an etching solution might be needed to open the pores and permit the color to "take" properly. For most purposes, a solution of one part nitric acid to seven parts distilled water works fine — even on hard steels. When bluing stainless steel barrels, use "Spencer Acid" obtainable from jewelry supply houses or chemical distributors instead of the etching solution, or you can mix your own. First mix $\frac{1}{2}$ ounce silver nitrate with $13\frac{1}{2}$ ounces of distilled water. Never pour water into acid. It will erupt violently. Then add $\frac{1}{2}$ ounce mercurous nitrate, and finally $5\frac{1}{2}$ ounces of nitric acid. Put the solution into a brown bottle and do not expose it to light any more than is necessary.

Bluing Small Parts: Small gun parts such as screws, drift pins and the like are sometimes more difficult to blue than the rest of the gun because they lose their heat quicker when lifted from the hot water bath. One way to overcome this is to have your swab damp with the bluing solution before lifting the parts out of the water. Then, immediately upon surfacing, quickly coat the part with the solution. Try to coat them when they are no more than an inch out of the water.

Safety Precautions

Like most firearm coloring methods, the chemicals used for hot-water bluing can be dangerous. Most formulas can be fatal if swallowed and many cause severe burns. Therefore, be extremely careful when working with any of these chemicals; wear rubber gloves, safety glasses and avoid inhaling any of the fumes.

In case any of the chemicals come into contact with the eyes, flush with water for at least 15 minutes and get medical attention immediately thereafter. If swallowed, give water or milk and egg whites if available. Repeat if vomiting occurs and get medical attention immediately.

Keep these chemicals in a safe place away from children or pets or where they may be mistaken for something else. If you mix your own solution, be sure to label the container *POISON* and keep it in a safe place.

Troubleshooting Hot-Water Bluing

Hot-water bluing solutions depend upon heat for their action. Therefore, the solution and metal must be kept hot during the entire operation. Work as fast as possible in applying the solution, so that the temperature will not drop rapidly. When the bluing solution is applied, it should dry almost instantly. In case it does not, either the solution or the steel is not hot enough. The obvious correction is to raise the temperature of both, but once water boils, that is the highest temperature it can reach. So leave the metal parts in the boiling water longer if they appear not to be hot enough.

Small parts that do not "take" the bluing solution readily should be held an instant over an open flame before applying the bluing solution. Small pins and screws may be dipped into the hot solution rather than trying to swab it on. Very thin parts such as magazines will not hold the heat long enough as they are, so it is recommended that they be filled with metal blocks, rods, or other clean metal objects to help hold the heat longer.

Steel varies in different guns, and in some cases the bluing solution will be too strong for the gun metal. In this case, when the solution is applied, a heavy brown rust will appear. To correct this condition, weaken the solution with a few drops of distilled water. If too weak, after being set in boiling water for several minutes, discard the solution and add fresh to the clean jar suspended in the boiling water.

One of the worst problems with hot-water and slow rust bluing is the bleed-out of water onto the surface of the metal. Blind screw holes, dovetail notches, and the like will retain water when the parts are lifted from the boiling tank. This water will eventually dissipate onto the metal surfaces and thin the bluing. Compressed air is the best remedy for this situation. Merely give the trouble spots a shot or two of compressed air to force the trapped water out.

Remember, a good hot-water bluing job can be obtained only if everything is just right. The main secret of successful hot-water bluing is cleanliness and heat. Therefore, special attention should be given to both.

SLOW-RUST BLUING

Most experts agree that slow-rust bluing is the most durable blue-black finish obtainable on gun metal. In fact, many manufacturers used this type of finish on all their guns prior to World War II. Then, as mentioned previously, the hot caustic bluing method became the most logical for mass production. The main problem with slow-rust bluing was the time element. It takes from three to 10 days to obtain a good slow-rust finish on firearms. In this day and time, it takes too long and is consequently too expensive for most gunsmiths and customers. There are, however, some custom-built rifles that still boast the coveted slow-rust finish. Here's how to obtain it:

Use the same preliminary procedures as discussed for hot-water bluing; that is, metal preparation, cleaning, etc. Then fill each of two bluing tanks with enough water to cover all parts completely. In one tank, add a cleaning solution such as

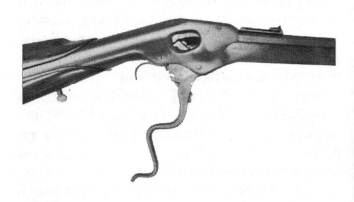

Figure 15-8: If antique firearms are to be restored, a thorough knowledge of slow-rust bluing is essential.

Figure 15-9: This custom rifle was slow-rust blued to give the gun metal a durable satin finish, a finish that is currently unobtainable from most factories.

Brownells Dicro-Clean No. 909 according to instructions on the package, or conventional household lye in the proportion of two tablespoons of lye to each gallon of water. Either of these solutions will degrease the parts to be blued. Bring the solution to a boil and then insert all parts into the tank and suspend them so that none touches the bottom of the tank. Leave the parts in the boiling solution for about 5 minutes; too long a time will cause premature rusting. Then immediately transfer the parts into the tank containing the clean boiling water. Let the parts remain in the clear water for two minutes, remove them, then hang them up to dry and cool. At this point, your hands must never touch any portion of the metal which is to be blued. Also make sure that the clean boiling water is kept at a hard rolling boil — nothing else will do.

When the parts are dry and cool, take a clean cotton swab, saturate it with a slow-rust bluing solution. Which one? This is a good question. In recent times there have been so many different slow-rust bluing solutions out — only to remain on the market for a short time — that it is difficult to recommend any one brand. Stoeger's Gunsmith's Bluer was a favorite for years before it was discontinued. Then it was once again placed on the market in the early 1980s, only to be discontinued again in 1987. You might try Brownells and Dixie Gun Works for the ones currently available. The one that most gunsmiths use at the present time is Pilkington Classic American Rust Blue which is available from Brownells Inc.

Regardless of the solution used, most work exactly alike. Therefore, apply some solution to the swab and then squeeze out any excess. With long, even strokes and moderate pressure, swab all areas to be blued. Do not use an excessive amount of solution. The rust bluing solution will also act as a rust remover if too much is applied. After all areas have been covered, hang the parts to rust in a damp, humid place for a period of about six hours. In some areas, the air is too dry for the gun to rust properly. Therefore, a steam cabinet must be made to help this rusting process along. The cabinet may be kept simple. One type was made from ¾-inch plywood with a hinged door. A lamp-holder and a 100-watt incandescent lamp was used to heat a coffee can filled with water. The gun parts are then placed in the cabinet above the steam (see Figure 15-10) to

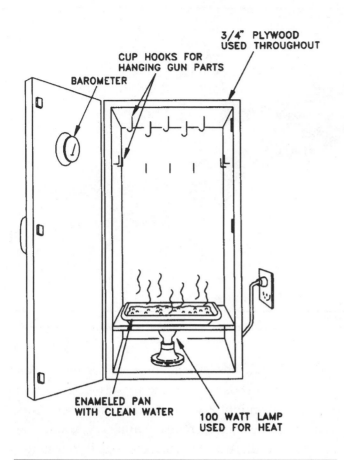

BAROMETER

CUP HOOKS FOR
HANGING GUN PARTS

3/4" PLYWOOD
USED THROUGHOUT

ENAMELED PAN
WITH CLEAN WATER

100 WATT LAMP
USED FOR HEAT

Figure 15-10: Details of slow-rust bluing cabinet — necessary in climates with insufficient moisture.

clean steel wool or a powered wire buffing wheel. For tight places, use a clean stainless steel brush. This process is called "carding." This first carding may give you any color from a light gray to a light blue; it may be splotched, or uniform. Don't let this bother you. Each succeeding pass will deepen the color and make it more uniform. When all parts are thoroughly carded with steel wool and the brush, repeat the application with the bluing solution; that is, boiling, applying the solution, rusting, boiling, carding — as before.

The number of passes necessary to obtain the desired depth and uniformity of color will depend on the hardness of the metal. You may get by with as few as three passes on .22-caliber rimfire rifles, while nickel-steel barrels might require as many as 10 or 12, but the average will be five passes. After the metal reaches the depth of color desired, give the just-carded parts one more carding — this time using a steel-wool pad saturated with an oil such as WD-40. Don't be afraid of wearing off the bluing with steel wool — this bluing is so tough you won't disturb it even with 00 steel wool. If it does, your job is faulty. Then you are done.

For easy reference, here is a checklist of steps to follow when slow-rust bluing:

- Disassemble gun, separating parts to be blued from those that are not to be blued.
- Remove all pits and deep scratches by draw filing.
- Polish the metal parts using abrasive paper from size 80 grit to 500 grit. See instructions under hot-water bluing.
- Degrease the parts in a hot lye or other cleaning solution.
- Boil the parts in clean water.
- Apply the bluing solution evenly and allow parts to rust from four to six hours

accept the heat and steam. About 1½ hours is all the time necessary to get the parts to rusting properly when the steam cabinet is used. However, take the parts out of the cabinet after this amount of time, and let them continue to rust for a few more hours outside the cabinet. Applying more bluing solution too soon will cause pitting. Wait at least three hours between coats.

Fill one of the tanks with clean water and again bring it to a rolling boil. Then all parts coated with the bluing solution, and allowed to rust the required length of time, are returned to this tank of boiling water for about 20 minutes. After boiling, they are hung up to dry and cool, but all accumulated water droplets in corners, screw holes, etc., should be blown away with compressed air. When cool, all of the oxide covering (rust) is removed with new, (more if necessary), but never overnight or longer than 12 hours.

● Card off rust with steel wool, stainless steel brush, or soft carding wheel on power buffer.

● Repeat the last three steps until the desired finish is obtained.

When the job is completed, you will know how much hard, meticulous work was required; and if you did your part well, you will also know that the finish on the rust-blued firearm equals, if not surpasses, the finest finish on any factory-blued model.

Once you have mastered the previously mentioned bluing methods, you will find the popular hot caustic bluing method a breeze to master. However, the other methods will still have a place in the gunshop.

HOT CAUSTIC BLUING

Unless you choose to be highly specialized in your gunsmithing work, and you plan to do commercial bluing, you will eventually go to the hot caustic method of bluing firearms. This is the process used by the majority of firearm manufacturers, as well as most professional gunsmiths. The number of firearms that can be blued at one time — using this method — is limited only to the size of your bluing tanks.

Bluing Equipment

Each tank should be a minimum size of 8" x 8" x 40" for the most efficient work. The tanks should be made of 11 to 14 gauge black iron or steel welded (not brazed) at the seams. Each tank should also be flanged around the open edges to prevent excess dripping or "creep." The oil tank must have

Figure 15-11: The Heatbath Corp. six-tank bluing system is ideal for the professional shop. The same system can also be used for hot-water bluing and browning.

a drain board attached to it and also a rack on which to hang guns and parts while the excess drips off.

A good quality drain plug on each tank is also a help to enable easy cleaning. If possible, each tank should be connected to a drain. The cold water rinse tank should have an overflow pipe and a water inlet pipe to provide the best possible work by providing a constant flow of fresh clean water during the bluing operation.

The operator will also need safety goggles or a face shield, a suitable apron, and rubber gloves. Black iron stovepipe wire is the favorite for suspending the parts in the bluing tanks. Never use galvanized wire. You will need an accurate thermometer that reads temperatures from 0° F. to at least 310° F. A sufficient quantity of bluing salts, alkali cleaner, and hot soluble oil will just about complete the basic setup. In choosing the oil, be extremely careful to obtain the correct type. Some oils will ignite and are unsafe for heating. At least one gunsmith's shop has burned to the ground due to the oil in the tank igniting. Therefore, use only oils that are designed for the purpose and follow the direction supplied by the manufacturer or distributor. Of course, new ideas and techniques are conceived often, but all should be approached with caution until they have been proven.

When using the six-tank system, the work progresses from left to right and the sequence of operation is as follows:

- Hot alkali cleaner tank

- Cold water rinse tank

- 285° F bluing tank

- 300° F bluing tank

- Cold water rinse tank

- Hot soluble oil tank

The hot caustic bluing process produces a black to blue-black finish on gun steel. The surface condition of the gun part will be the determining factor of the quality of the ultimate finish. Parts to be finished must be absolutely clean and free from oil, grease, and rust.

The gun parts may be cleaned by scrubbing with any good cleaner and hot water. If mild acids are used to remove rust or scale, the parts should be washed in soap and water to neutralize the acid.

With the six-tank system, cleaning is accomplished in Tank No. 1, followed by a cold water rinse.

Making Up the Bluing Solution: To make a 6-inch depth of bluing solution, proceed as follows:

- Start with about 3 inches of cold water in each bluing tank.

- Add bluing salts in small quantities, allowing each quantity to dissolve thoroughly before making further

additions, until about 30 pounds of material have been added to each tank.

- Light gas burner (half capacity at first, increase as temperature approaches working temperatures).

- Add cold water slowly through the splash guards (from the reservoir) until the depth of solution is approximately 5 inches, and allow solution to come to a boil.

- Continue to add bluing salts to each tank until a boiling temperature of 285° F is obtained in the first tank with bluing salts (tank No. 3). Also add salts to tank No. 4 until the boiling temperature reaches about 300° F.

- After these temperatures have been reached, they are maintained by adding water slowly from a reservoir to compensate for the water lost through evaporation, making sure a good rolling boil is maintained at all times. Additional bluing salts is added only to maintain the desired working level of the solution.

Operating Procedure: Clean the parts to be blued by hand or immerse in hot alkali cleaner. If using the alkali cleaner, never leave for more than one minute; too long will cause rusting. The same is true for the cold water rinse; never leave for more than 30 seconds in the cold water rinse; too long will cause rusting. After the parts to be treated have been properly cleaned by hand, or with the alkali cleaner in tank No. 1, and rinsed, they are immersed in tank No. 3 (285° F. tank) for twenty to thirty minutes. The parts are then removed from this tank and transferred to tank No. 4 for another twenty to thirty minutes. Do not let the parts dry off between tank No. 3 and tank No. 4. The work is then removed and rinsed immediately in cold water (tank No. 5) before placing in tank No. 6 for immersion into the oil bath. After boiling in the oil bath for about twenty minutes, remove the parts. When cool enough to handle, wipe off with a clean shop cloth. Reassemble the gun and the job is done.

Barrels, magazine tubes and similar parts may be suspended in the solution with black iron stove pipe wire. Smaller parts such as screws, pins, etc. may be placed in a black iron basket and immersed in the bluing solution. Make sure the basket is not soldered; it must be welded and do not use galvanized or nonferrous metal.

Caustic bluing solutions are designed for bluing ferrous metals and their alloy only. Aluminum, magnesium, die-cast parts (including most of the investment casting receivers and frames), tin, galvanized metals, brass, and copper CANNOT be blued with this system. Furthermore, parts that are soldered with lead-tin solders, such as many of the double-barrel shotguns, cannot be blued by the hot caustic method.

If brass sights are attached to the barrel, they can be immersed without problems, but it is still best to remove them if at all possible.

Troubleshooting Caustic Bluing

U.S. Krag, Mauser and some other receivers will often come out of the bluing solution with a reddish or purple tint. To avoid this, first bring the bluing salts up to normal operating temperature. This is to make sure that the salts are of the correct concentration. Then lower the temperature of the bath by cutting back the heat of the burners and allow the solution to cool down to about 235° F. When this temperature is reached, immerse the barrel/receiver and other parts into the salt bath. Then turn the heat up slightly and bring the temperature of the bath back up to the normal operating temperature, but make certain this is done very, very slowly. The receiver and other hard parts will blue at the lower temperature and the softer parts at the upper temperature. After the receiver has blued at the lower temperature no harm is done to the surfaces by the higher temperature.

Frequently a green scum will form on the surfaces of the metal parts, caused by the bath temperature being too high for a particular type of metal. This scum can be removed by gently carding the metal surface with 0000 steel wool and water while the parts are held over the cold water rinse tank. Once removed, the parts may then be put back into the hot bluing tank and continued to blue after lowering the operating temperature.

To ensure the best possible bluing jobs, closely adhere to the following:

- Clean oil and scum from top of water tanks.
- Use magnet to check if part is steel.
- Keep baskets and black iron wire clean; do not set in oil.
- Avoid bluing springs if possible.
- Wear safety goggles or face shield at all times.
- Do not allow metals to stay too long in cleaner or hot rinse; doing so will cause rust.
- Do not plug barrels when bluing by the hot caustic process.

Chapter 16
Browning Gun Metal

The earliest guns used in this country (and other countries as well) formed a brown coating when exposed to the elements. The cause was ferric oxide or plain old red rust. The owners of these guns probably tried to rub off the rust from time to time. Although they succeeded in removing the loose top layer, the stained metal remained brown underneath. As further attempts were tried, the brown stain became even deeper and more even — offering a relatively pleasing appearance. This brown coloring of the metal also dulled the flashy shine to the new metal and no longer spooked game while hunting or alerted the enemy when in battle.

Therefore, the browning concept caught on and by 1700 nearly all gunsmiths had perfected the process of obtaining a rich, deep brown color on all their firearms. The rusting process was hurried by using a salt and water solution on the metal. This rust was carded off, more solution was applied, this was coat-carded off, and so on, until the preferred finish was obtained.

This basic browning process is still used today to restore old firearms to their original finish. This is especially true for shotguns with twist steel or damascus barrels (Figure 16-1) or nearly all muzzleloading firearms (Figure 16-2 on the next page).

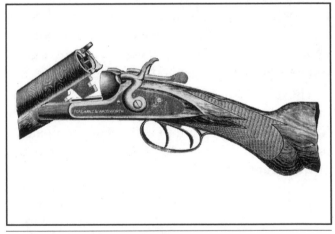

Figure 16-1: Early double-barrel shotgun with damascus barrels.

The browning process is also used quite extensively for refinishing blackpowder guns of recent manufacture. Many of these are sold in kit form and assembling them is within the capabilities of the average gun crank. Many shooters prefer to blue these firearms, but some try to be as authentic as possible and use the browning process to color the metal.

Therefore, the home gunsmith should have a good knowledge of browning techniques. This chapter describes several browning techniques that may be used with very little investment.

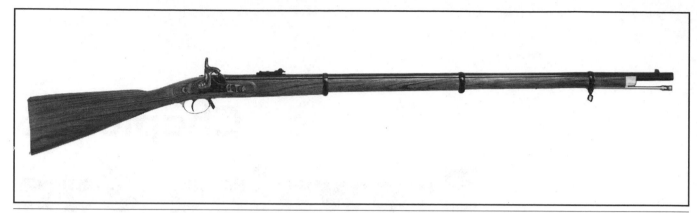

Figure 16-2: Almost all muzzleloading firearms manufactured prior to about 1865 were browned rather than blued.

BASIC BROWN

Here is a technique that you can use almost immediately. All of the necessary materials are readily available. Obtain a pint of distilled water from your local druggist and add 5 tablespoons of common table salt to this water. Mix with a glass rod and store in a clean bottle or jar.

The metal to be browned is prepared as described previously; that is, remove all the old rust and finish (in the case of refinishing) and polish the metal to the preferred luster either by hand or by using power equipment.

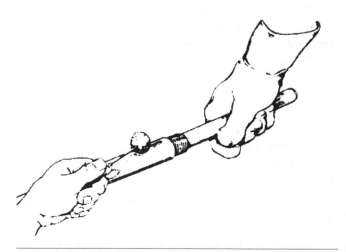

Figure 16-3: Barrels should be plugged with tapered hardwood dowels to prevent water from entering the bore and to allow a means for holding the barrel during the browning operation.

Make two wood dowels so they will fit in both ends of the barrel. But first thoroughly grease the bore with gun grease, pump grease, or similar grease to prevent the inside of the barrel from rusting during the browning process. Once greased, the wood dowels are snugly driven into the ends of the barrel. In the case of thin shotgun barrels, do not drive the wooden plugs in too tight; you might split the end of the barrel.

Next, the metal parts are degreased with a commercial cleaner like Brownells No. 909, AWA 1,1,1, or similar cleaner. Once this is done, your bare hands should not touch the parts until the process is completed. Wear rubber gloves just to be sure, but handle the parts only by the wooden dowels or else by black iron wires attached to the parts. The parts can be degreased by boiling in a solution of commercial cleaner and water as discussed previously. If you want to do it like the early gunsmiths of the last century, make a paste from slaked lime and water and brush this solution onto the surface of the parts and allow to dry hard. This coating is then brushed off with a grease-free paint brush. As the crust of lime is removed, it will carry the grease and oil with it.

If you have iron tanks large enough to hold the parts to be browned, the grease and oil can be removed by boiling the parts in a solution of water and regular household lye. About 1 tablespoon per gallon of water should do the job.

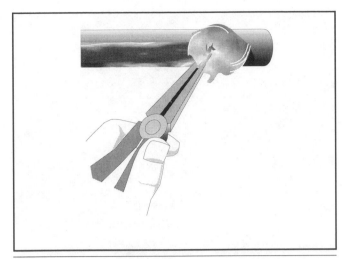

Figure 16-4: A pair of long-nose pliers is used to hold a clean piece of cotton to apply the browning solution.

Once cleaned, swab on the salt solution liberally with a cotton pad or sponge as shown in Figure 16-4; make sure that all surfaces are covered. Try to avoid runs and streaks as these will show on the final job in most cases.

The metal parts are now left to rust. If your basement is cool and damp, merely hang the parts there and let them rust for about 12 hours or more or until a coat of coarse rust is formed on all metal surfaces. If the rusting is uneven, you didn't apply the solution evenly. If you live in a relatively dry climate, then you'll have to help the rusting process along. Build a small wooden box large enough to hold the metal parts and line this box with wet burlap sacks. Place the parts in the box so that they are suspended in mid-air and not touching the sides or bottom. Cover the box and let the parts rust until the desired coarse rust is formed. This usually takes from 6 to 12 hours.

Use 00 steel wool that has been cleaned and freed from the oil that usually is applied at the factory to prevent rust during shipment and card off the rust that has formed on the metal parts. Use a stainless steel brush (that has also been cleaned) to get into tight places. When all of the loose rust has been removed, apply more of the salt solution to the rust

and let it rust again until a coarse rust forms on the surface.

Repeat this process 10 to 12 times or until you get the desired shade of brown. This last carding should be done very thoroughly. Make sure you get every bit of rust off the metal surfaces, around crevices, etc. Then boil the parts in water for about 20 minutes to stop the rusting process. Upon drying, immediately coat all surfaces with a good gun oil. The results will be most authentic and attractive.

The exact shade that you will obtain with the above method will vary. It depends upon the type of metal the solution is used on, but in general, the brown will be about the shade of muddy water. To improve the appearance somewhat, you can soak the parts in a very weak solution of copper sulphate and distilled water prior to oiling the parts. Use a solution of about .02 percent copper sulphate in the distilled water. The resulting finish will be a plum brown which is much desired on antique weapons. For comparison, look at the finish on some of the old Kentucky rifles in museums.

You will sometimes get erratic results with any type of rust bluing. For example, after the last coat of the browning solution has been applied, and the parts are boiled for 20 minutes in water, the parts sometimes turn blue or blue-black. If you want to absolutely prevent the parts from turning this color (it won't happen often) merely pour hot water over the metal parts before oiling and do not boil them as described above. You will have to pour the gun oil to the surface, however, and continually inspect the metal to see if more rust appears. If more rust does appear, card it off and add more gun oil to the metal surface.

Dixie Gun Works Formula

Dixie Gun Works, Inc., of Union City, Tennessee 38261, has a commercial solution available — for a small price — that is very good. It is especially useful on some damascus twist barrels. It's made from a 100-year old formula that was used by many of the gunsmiths of the period. It can be used in a method similar to that described for the salt water solution or a brown finish can be obtained almost instantly by heating the metal parts before applying the solution.

To use the Dixie Browning Solution, first prepare the metal surfaces by polishing. Grease the bore and plug the barrel with wooden dowels. Drive the dowels in tightly, but not so tight you can't get them out. The parts can be degreased with a paste of slaked lime and water as already described or you can use a solution of baking soda and water. Once the parts are degreased, wash with clean water and let them dry. As with all rusting types of bluing, the parts must not be touched with bare hands during the browning process. Handle the parts by the wooden dowels or use iron wires. Wear clean cotton gloves or rubber gloves just to make sure your skin does not come into contact with the parts to be browned.

Take a clean cotton swab or a cotton ball held with a pair of long-nosed pliers or a clothes pin. Dip the cotton swab into the browning solution and squeeze it out against the side of the bottle so that you have only a minimal amount on the swab. Apply the solution to the gun parts sparingly and evenly until all surfaces are covered. In 6 to 12 hours, a thin red rust will form on the metal surfaces in most humid climates. In extremely dry areas, you will have to help the rusting along by providing a "sweat box" as previously described. You can use a covered box lined with wet burlap sacks.

Once rusted, the parts are carded with 00 steel wool and a stainless steel brush until all of the loose rust is removed. Don't remove so much of the rust that you get down to bare metal. Just remove the loose rust. Practice will determine just how much to remove at this point. Repeat the application and carding processes until the preferred shade of brown is reached. However, don't wait as long between cardings as you did for the first coat.

Figure 16-5: Steel wool can be used for carding the loose rust between browning applications, but a power-driven wire wheel is better — especially for the last carding operation.

The final carding (Figure 16-5) should be done very thoroughly. The rusting process is then stopped by boiling for about 20 minutes in water, scalding, or by wiping very carefully with hot soapy water. Let the parts dry and then coat them with lubricating oil. When the parts cool, wipe off excess oil and let them stand in a warm room for 24 hours before handling.

Dixie Gun Works says that with a little practice anyone can turn out a professional-looking job with this browning solution. It is even possible to bring out the twist steel patterns frequently found in old damascus shotgun barrels.

The color and rusting time required will depend on the humidity and room temperature and the type of steel or iron being browned. The process can be hastened by heating the part. Heating the part to be browned will produce an instant brown color, but this color might not be as durable nor as attractive as the slower process.

Laurel Mountain Brown

The Laurel Mountain Forge Barrel Brown and Degreaser is available from Brownells Inc. Although it is easy to use, the metal parts to be browned must first be prepared the same as for any

Figure 16-6: Laurel Mountain Browning Solution and cotton applicators are about all that is needed for browning.

other metal finishes. Parts must be polished. No method of browning will cover pits or scratches. The surface of the metal must be perfect before the browning solution is applied.

In most methods of bluing or browning gun metal, it is necessary to make sure that all parts are absolutely free of grease, oil or foreign matter. Once the procedure starts, be careful not to touch any of the parts to be blued or browned with your hands. The Laurel Mountain solution has a degreaser built in, but it is still recommended to degrease the metal before applying the solution.

Begin by oiling the bore of the gun to prevent the inside from rusting; then seal the bore with tightly fitted plugs, made of rubber, plastic or wood.

To apply the solution, use a piece of cotton cloth folded in a pad four layers thick and about one inch square. Moisten the pad thoroughly with the browning solution and apply it to the barrel. Be sure to apply the solution in long, even strokes from muzzle to breech. After applying this first coat of browning solution, set the barrel aside for three hours to allow the solution to work. Then apply a

second coat; make certain your applicator is only damp. If too much solution is applied after the first coat, it may remove some of the previous coat, causing the finish to be uneven, or spotty.

After letting the second coat work for three hours, rub the surface of the barrel — or other part — with a piece of coarse cloth dipped in hot tap water. This step removes the surface scale that has built up and "evens" the brown; it is a step similar to carding in conventional slow rust browning methods.

After scrubbing the barrel, flood the surface with hot tap water and dry. Do not boil the parts, or the surface will turn black, rather than brown. Repeat the cycle of applying the browning solution, letting it work for three hours, and scaling the barrel until the desired color has been achieved. This will probably take from four to five more coats.

If, for some reason, you cannot get back to the work within three hours, do not apply another coat after scaling. Just scale the barrel and set it aside until you are ready to resume browning.

To stop further action after achieving the desired finish, scrub the surface of the barrel using hot tap water with a little washing soda added. Rinse the barrel with clear warm water and allow to dry. To finish the barrel, apply wax or boiled linseed oil.

If a rougher antique finish is desired on your gun, apply wet coats of the browning solution to the surface at 12-hour intervals. When leaving the solution on the metal this long, usually two to four coats will be sufficient, depending on weather conditions. To maximize roughness, do not scale the surface between coats. After the desired depth of color has been obtained, wash the browned parts with water and washing soda in the normal manner to stop further browning. This method works especially well on small parts.

If a rust blue finish is desired, instead of a brown, the Laurel Mountain solution may be used instead. Just boil the parts in pure water between scalings. Boil each part for about five minutes, or until the finish darkens, then scale as discussed previously. Repeat the process until the desired depth of color is reached.

Browning Old Military Arms

During the mid-1800s, the U.S. armories browned all their rifle barrels prior to releasing them to service. The locks, ramrods, band-springs, triggers, and screws, however, were not browned during this period. Rather, they were normally casehardened and oiled.

The solution used by U.S. armories during this period contained the following ingredients:

- 1½ oz. grain alcohol
- 1½ oz. tincture of ferric chloride
- ½ oz. mercuric chloride
- 1½ oz. ethyl nitrate
- 1 oz. copper sulfate
- ¾ oz. nitric acid

To use this method, mix and dissolve these ingredients in a quart of soft water; store in a dark glass bottle.

In mixing this solution, you may have trouble finding ethyl nitrate, also known as sweet spirits of nitre. For some reason, this chemical has been taken off the market in recent years. Several experts say to omit this chemical, because you get practically the same results without it, but the process may take a little longer. Other gunsmiths claim that a two percent nitric acid solution in distilled water will do the same thing.

Polish the parts to be browned in the usual manner, then carefully clean them. A small quantity of powdered lime rubbed well over the entire barrel will degrease the metal sufficiently. Wooden plugs are used to plug the muzzle of the barrel, and the vent hole.

Apply the solution to the barrel in even strokes, using a clean sponge or rag. Expose the barrel to air for 24 hours, then card it with steel wool or a wire brush, removing all loose rust — but not enough to remove the stain on the metal beneath the loose rust.

The mixture is then applied again to the metal, and in a few hours the barrel will be sufficiently corroded for carding. The same process of carding the metal and applying the solution should be repeated two or three times a day for four or five days, by which time the barrel will be dark brown.

When the barrel is sufficiently brown and the rust has been carefully removed from every part, about

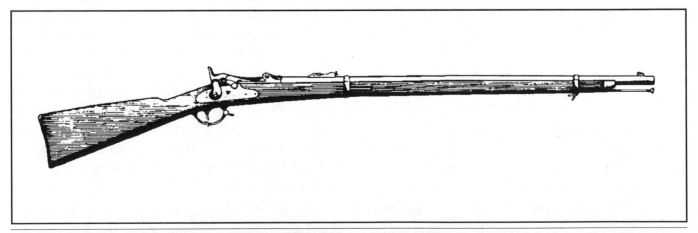

Figure 16-7: This Model 1873 "Trapdoor" Springfield rifle was browned at United States Armories before it was released to troops. If you want to restore such firearms, you must know how to brown gun metal.

a quart of boiling water should be poured over all parts to stop the action of the acid mixture upon the metal, so no more rust forms.

When the barrel cools, it should be rubbed with linseed oil. Be sure to use a scratch brush instead of a hard hair brush, otherwise the browning will not be durable or have a good appearance.

You may wish to varnish the browned gun parts after applying the linseed oil. To do so, mix one ounce of shellac with .1857 ounce of Dragon's blood (resin extracted from the fruit of the Malayan rattan palm) and a quart of alcohol. Apply to the browned metal.

To remove old browning, varnish and grease, plug the vent and the muzzle of the barrels; immerse the browned parts for one hour in boiling lime water or lye (about one tablespoon per gallon of water). Wipe dry and put the barrel and other parts in vinegar, held in a plastic trough, for about 45 minutes. The browning may now be rubbed off with a rag.

Instant Browning Solutions

There are several instant browning solutions on the market and all are used in practically the same way. In general, the parts to be browned are first polished and cleaned. A propane torch or other heat source is then used to slowly heat the parts just enough to "spat" a drop of water. This temperature is just about the same as used for flat or steam irons in the home for ironing clothes. Once this heat is obtained, the browning solution is applied in thin, even strokes with a cotton swab and then left to work for about 15 minutes.

Flush the surface of the metal with hot water. When dry, lightly card off the loose rust that appears. Heat the metal once again, and apply the browning solution as before. Let work for 10 to 15 minutes, flush with hot water, and card. Repeat these steps until the desired finish is obtained.

When using the instant browning solutions, the manufacturer recommends that you don't try to

Figure 16-8: Birchwood Casey Plum Brown Barrel Finish is one of the better instant browning solutions on the market.

cover too large an area at a time because the metal must be evenly warm to accept the finish. One of the best sources of heat is an old kerosene lamp held under the metal parts until they reach the preferred temperature. Sometimes you'll get the part too hot with a propane torch and the finished job will come out spotty.

Remember that most of the chemical browning solutions are poisonous and can be harmful if misused. Read and follow the cautions on the individual containers carefully.

Special Cases

Twist steel or damascus barrels are an ideal candidate for browning. This method brings out the beautiful wavy patterns of the twist. After using any of the slow rusting methods described earlier, the damascus patterns might or might not show as distinctly as you prefer. Sometimes additional treatment is necessary to bring out the full beauty of the twist pattern. This can be accomplished by rubbing the barrels with a linen rag coated with chalk paste or other fine abrasive powder. Then wipe the barrels clean and oil with gun oil or else use conventional paste wax. For such specialized work, however, the operator should gain sufficient experience in doing such work before attempting a really fine arm. There are so many variations that many times you will have to use good judgement to decide which approach should be taken to solve a given problem.

Mark Lee Express Brown

The Mark Lee Express Brown #2 formula is becoming very popular with professional gunshops for obtaining either a soft velvety sheen or a high luster brown on firearms of all types.

To use the Mark Lee formula, first prepare the metal surface as discussed previously; that is, polish and degrease. Degreasing is essential in getting fine results. The parts to be browned should be precleaned by soaking in a solvent such as lacquer thinner. This precleaning is followed by the parts being soaked in an industrial strength alkali cleaner such as Brownells Dicro-Clean No. 909. The parts should be scrubbed with a brush during the cleaning process.

Remove the parts from the cleaning solution with tongs or hooks; never touch them with the bare hands any time during the browning process. Rinse the parts with hot water and then immediately dry with compressed air, a hair dryer, or blot with paper towels. Wear either clean cotton gloves or surgical gloves during the entire operation to prevent body oils from contaminating the metal.

To continue the browning operation, you will need the following:

- Cellulose sponge or cotton swabs
- Small plastic or glass container
- Propane torch, heat lamp, or some other heat source
- Fine steel wire brush (.003" - .005") or very fine degreased steel wool

Pour the browning solution into the small glass or plastic container. Warm the metal parts to be browned to about 200°F. with your heat source. Dip your applicator in the browning solution and apply very thin coats to the warmed parts. A coating of rust will immediately form. Allow the solution to dry (approximately 30 seconds). Now use fine (4/0) steel wool to remove the loose residue on the metal. Make sure all residue is removed, but don't rub so hard as to remove the faint brown color underneath.

Warm the parts again, apply a thin coat of the browning solution, let dry, and then remove the loose residue with steel wool. Repeat this step from 6 to 10 times until the desired color emerges.

Almost any shade of brown through black can be obtained with the Mark Lee formula by using hot water along with varying the number of coats applied. For example, if a plum brown is desired, apply the browning solution to the warm parts as discussed previously. After building up 4 to 6 coats on the metal parts, continue to apply additional coats, but rinse the parts in very hot tap water between each application. If you want black parts, boil the parts for about 20 minutes after the last coat.

Once the desired shade has been obtained on the metal parts, you must neutralize the browning action. To do so, soak the browned parts for 1½ hours in a solution of 1½ pounds of baking soda per gallon of water at room temperature. After this soaking period, remove the parts, rinse with hot water, and dry. If necessary, remove any remaining residue with a terry cloth towel, fine steel wool, or a wire brush. A thorough oiling with a good gun oil completes the job.

In using the slow rusting process of browning, it is recommended that either rain water or distilled water be used. Most other types of water contain impurities or chemicals that can have an adverse effect on your final finish.

Water For Browning

Many experts maintain that pure water is absolutely necessary for the best browning and bluing jobs. Chemicals added to city water supplies are said to have an adverse effect on the final results; namely, lighter streaks will show up in the final finish. "Hard" well water can also do the same thing. This is especially true when using the hot water or slow rust methods for bluing or browning guns. Lesser effects are usually present when the hot caustic method is used.

To obtain rain water for an occasional browning or bluing job, try catching 8 to 10 gallons of water the next time it rains by placing plastic dish pans out in the yard. If you don't want to go to this trouble, distilled water may be purchased at your local drug store.

Another way to get pure water is to have your pharmacist order a water "deionizing column" for you. This is a clear plastic cylindrical container packed with purification crystals. There are couplings at either end for surgical tubing; and, you simply run tap water (slowly) through the column into a clean receptacle — a clean plastic or glass jug works well. Deionizing columns come in various sizes; the larger the column the greater the expense. However, if you plan to do a fair amount of browning or rust bluing, the money spent will be worth it.

A device called H2-OK is available from Consumers Bargain Corp., 404 Irvington Street, Pleasantville, NY 10570 and the filter treats up to 2,000 gallons of water. It costs around $50. The filter removes all chlorine, pesticides, chemicals, sediment, and bad taste from water from any source. You merely pour the water through the filter at the rate of about one quart per minute. This should be ideal for any browning or bluing jobs.

A filter may also be connected in with the plumbing to filter the entire water system for a faster rate of water supply but, of course, greater expense is involved.

For a gunshop turning out many rust blued jobs each week, a cistern might be the answer — provided, of course, you have the space to accommodate such a system. Then you will be assured of a relatively pure water supply for any browning or bluing job that may come along — or any quantity. A cistern, however, is not cheap, and unless you do several hundred bluing and browning jobs each year, it would be best to stick with purchasing distilled water, or else use one of the water columns as mentioned previously.

A cistern may be made by merely digging a hole in clay soil, plastering the sides and bottom directly to the earth, and then pouring a concrete slab, with an opening, over the top. However, the most suitable type of cistern is made with poured concrete walls and bottom of at least 6 inches thick, and a tight concrete top. A manhole should be left in the top to provide access for cleaning. The edges of the manhole should extend about 3 inches above the top of the cistern, and the manhole cover should be made to overlap these edges like the top of a shoe box overlaps the box. This manhole cover may be concrete or $\frac{1}{4}$ inch sheet iron with corners welded. This arrangement prevents any surface water from getting into the cistern through the manhole.

Cisterns of the plastered jug type having walls made up of plastered cinder blocks or concrete blocks are not satisfactory and cannot be recommended. Such a cistern will soon begin to leak and although the leak may not be noticeable by loss of a large amount of stored water, it may be sufficient to let in contaminated shallow ground water that will have an adverse effect on your bluing or browning jobs. Such leaks usually appear in the walls in the upper part of the cistern, above the water line, and are due to the inability of the thin plaster coating to resist the freezing and thawing action in the ground. Also, tree roots will find their way into the cistern and will frequently crack the walls badly.

The only way to assure pure water from a cistern is to keep the rain water free from contamination from the time it hits the roof until it is pumped from the cistern. Assuming that proper arrangements are made to keep the rain uncontaminated from the roof to the cistern, the surest way to get pure water is to have a tight reservoir-cistern built as described earlier with at least 6-inch poured concrete walls and bottom and with a tight top.

The proper size cistern depends on certain conditions such as seasonal rainfall, total roof area, and quantity of water used per month. It will also depend on whether the cistern will be used only for bluing guns or for other uses also. Obviously, going to this much trouble and expense would only be warranted if much bluing or browning operations are performed — usually only on a professional level.

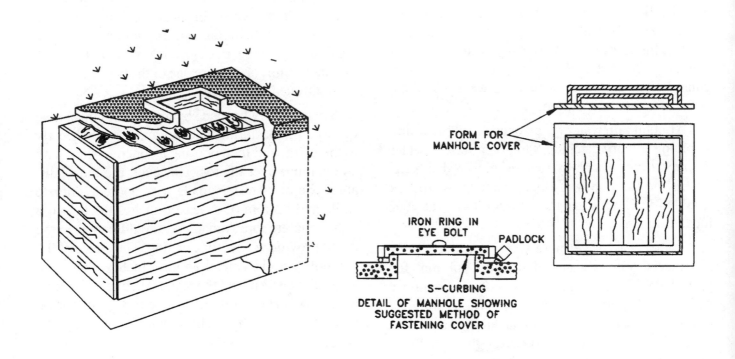

Figure 16-9: Several views of a typical cistern construction.

Chapter 17
Plating and Miscellaneous Finishes

Metal plating has been applied to firearms for quite some time — mainly on handguns. However, with the event of stainless steel handguns and rifles, the metal plating process has lost some ground in the past few years. Still, most gunsmiths will get calls for plating jobs (mostly handguns) from time-to-time, and every practicing gunsmith should at least have a good knowledge of how the various jobs are accomplished.

There are firms that specialize in metal plating, and many gunsmiths merely farm out the work to these firms, rather than setting up for this process themselves, especially if the gunsmith has only a few plating jobs each year.

Parkerizing or phosphatizing is another metal coloring technique that was first used by the U.S. Government on their Springfield service rifles to provide a more durable, rust-preventing finish than was possible with bluing or other metal-finishing processes of the time. The process consists of boiling the gun parts in a solution of powdered iron and phosphoric acid. In the process, minute particles of the parts' surface are dissolved and replaced by insoluble phosphates which give a gray, non-reflecting and rust-resisting finish. When cosmoline is applied immediately after the process, the finish often turned green.

While parkerizing is considered by many to be less attractive than conventional bluing on highly-polished steel, it is far more practical from a military point of view.

Some private firms are now specializing in parkerizing firearms and most are doing a substantial business in restoring military weapons and also to give sporting firearms a non-reflecting matte finish.

This chapter is designed to familarize you with both techniques; that is, metal plating and parkerizing. Furthermore, this chapter will deal with coloring stainless steel and other types of finishes.

METAL PLATING

Nickel plating has long been a favorite finish for many handguns. It provides a decorative effect, protection against rust and corrosion, and a wear-

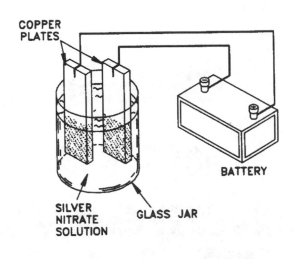

Figure 17-1: When electroplating, anodes are used on all sides of the object being plated so that the electricity may flow from all directions to that object; an even deposit of plated metal results.

resisting surface. Although nickel has been the traditional favorite, other metals have included chromium, gold, silver, brass and copper. Chromium, for example, when applied to metal gun parts provides a surface harder than the hardest steel, which protects the base metal, reduces wear, lessens friction, and at the same time, provides an attractive appearance.

Most metal plating is accomplished by a process called "electroplating," shown in Figure 17-1, which uses an electric current to deposit the plating over the base metal. In general, the object to be plated becomes the cathode (negative plate) in an electrolyte cell that contains (in some chemical compounds) the type of metal which is to be plated onto the base material. Anodes are used on all sides of the object so that electricity may flow from all directions to the article being plated and cause an even deposit of the plated metal. The exact chemicals, currents, voltages, temperatures and general procedure will vary with the kind of metal being plated and the type of method being used. For example, nickel plating often is done with an elec-

trolyte containing nickel sulphate or nickel ammonium sulphate, to which is added ammonium sulphate to increase the conductivity; some acid to help keep the anode rough, and something like glue or glucose to make the plating extra bright. The anodes may be of some material, such as carbon, which is not affected by the electrolytic action. When using this method, all the plated metal must come from the electrolyte and chemicals containing this metal must be added to the liquid at various intervals. In other plating methods, the anode is made of the plating metal. As an example, in plating with brass, the anode is of brass. Then brass dissolves from the anode into the electrolyte which is deposited from the electrolyte onto the cathode or object to be plated. The object of this method is to get metal dissolved into the bath (electrolyte) as quickly as it plates out. As the anode metal dissolves, it generates a voltage just as dissolving a metal generates a voltage in a conventional storage battery. Under ideal conditions, this generated voltage would equal the voltage consumed in depositing metal on the cathode, so the external source would need to provide only enough voltage to overcome the resistance in the cell and the connections.

Before we get into the plating process, it should be observed that you may not want certain areas of a gun plated. A good example would be the sear engagement areas on a handgun hammer and trigger. Until recently, you had to plate those parts and then redress them to work as perfectly as they did prior to plating. Brownells now offers what they call their Stop-Off Lacquer. You simply apply the lacquer to the portion of any part you don't want plated and plate the entire part normally.

When the plating process is done, take some Brownells Stop-Off Stripper and wipe it on to the area lacquered prior to plating — that lacquer and any build up of plating comes right off. It's a super system for keeping the trigger pull "just the way you had it." This method can save you considerable time when plating any type of firearm part.

Stripping

Stripping is used to remove old plating, to brighten up oxidized surfaces and also to clean inaccessible places. In general, there are four ways to take nickel plating off a gun. First, the finish may be removed electrically; that is, the object to be stripped becomes the anode, and a piece of metal such as brass or stainless steel is used as a cathode. Secondly, you can polish it off in much the same way as you would in polishing off old blue on firearms.

Pure nitric acid will also strip nickel from iron or steel without attacking the base metal as long as it is pure. However, such conditions as humidity in the air changes the purity of the acid, and then it can literally dissolve a gun in a very few minutes. Nitric acid is also very dangerous to handle.

The fourth stripping system uses chemicals for the process. It's a companion system to the electroless nickel plating system offered by Brownells. It will not pit or etch steel. It has excellent stability and a long, active solution life. Because of an easy replenishment system, solution life can be further extended which cuts the operating costs. The components contain no cyanide so they can be shipped easily via UPS. The solution operates at a slower rate of stripping than most other systems which gives complete control, and it will remove most nickel plating on firearms.

To strip, the gun should be disassembled and heavy emphasis placed on cleaning. This thorough cleaning prior to beginning the stripping sequence removes all gunk, gun oils and so on. The cleaning must be thorough to allow the stripping operation to work efficiently. The stripping steps are as follows; detailed steps follow the general outline below:

- *Pre-clean:* Use trichloromethane on cotton swabs and brushes to remove as much foreign matter, powder residue, gun oils, etc., as possible. Do not use a petroleum based cleaner such as gas, kerosene, mineral spirits, or gun cleaner; they will leave a residue on the part.

- *Flowing Water:* (Use same tank as used for plating process.) Submerge parts for ten seconds and agitate to float away loosened residue.

- *Acid-Cleaning Tank:* Submerge parts for three seconds and agitate. This further cleans parts and removes foreign residue, especially oil.

- *Flowing Water:* Submerge parts for five seconds to flush acid cleaner from surface of metal.

- *Nickel-Stripping Tank:* Submerge parts in stripping tank until all nickel is removed from the bright steel base metals. The stripping solution must operate at 200-210 degrees Fahrenheit. Water lost by evaporation should be replaced during the stripping cycle in order to maintain the original volume of solution. Parts will have to be removed from the stripping tank to be thoroughly checked to see that they are completely clean of the nickel plating.

- *Flowing-Water Tank:* Submerge parts for two minutes to flush away all of the stripping solution. Allow stripped parts to air dry normally, or use compressed air to speed dry. The gun can now be polished or put back through the plating cycle. If you are not going to polish or plate immediately, be sure to oil gun surfaces with water displacing oil (nye oil, "HOLD," Brownells No. 2 or some other basic rust preventative which does not contain any of the exotic penetrants which could contaminate future bluing or plating of the gun).

Two tanks are required for the stripping operation, and they must be different ones from those used for plating to avoid cross-over contamination. Be sure to mark them plainly "FOR STRIPPING ONLY," and preferably keep them in a different storage area (or on a different shelf). The stripping tanks can be fairly small in size since you will rarely strip more than one gun at a time. The tank can be stainless steel (Grades 304 or 316 only), ceramic, pyrex, quartz or other suitable materials that can withstand the 200° Fahrenheit operating temperature. Because of their convenience and availability, pyrex/laboratory tanks in both round and square styles may be used and are available from Brownells.

If a direct gas flame is used for the heat source, the pyrex tank must be protected from thermal shock. (Special instructions are included with each pyrex tank ordered from Brownells, which explain in detail how to make a "sand bath" to protect the tank and keep it from breaking,) If you anticipate much plating, however, it is recommended that you purchase the Electric Stir/Hot Plate, also available from Brownells. See Figure 17-2. This unit provides a reliable source of constant, even heat plus thoroughly controllable agitation. It is specially designed for chemically stripping gun parts as well as their electroless nickel plating system.

The large $7\frac{1}{8}$ inch square, heavy cast aluminum top has embedded heating elements and is machined flat for optimum heat transfer and uniform top plate temperatures. A "demand" thermostat maintains close temperature control and compensates for room temperature or line voltage fluctuations, holding surface temperatures within 3 degrees C. A heat-indicator light tells when the top is heating.

The stirring part of the unit features an extremely strong stirring torque from 60 to 1000 rpm. The Alnico V-drive magnet is located close to the top plate to assure strong magnetic coupling and to prevent jitterbugging. A solid state speed control gives excellent slow speed control, high starting torque and is independent from voltage changes, maintaining constant stirring action. Controls for the Electric Stir/Hot Plate are up front, easy to use and isolated from the heat of the top plate to assure long trouble-free life. When heating a one gallon jar of solution, the unit is capable of raising the temperature of the solution approximately 1 degree per minute. The unit is fully guaranteed to give excellent service. When using this heating unit, the pyrex tank can be placed directly on the heating plate.

The purpose of the acid cleaning tank is to clean only, and the solution should consist of 50% hydrochloric acid and 50% pure (distilled) water. The tank must be covered when not in use, and must be marked "STRIPPING ONLY" to prevent any mix-up with the plating tanks. To mix one gallon of solution for the acid cleaning tank, measure 2 quarts (64 fluid ounces) of clean water and pour into the tank. Measure 2 quarts (64 fluid ounces) of hydrochloric acid and pour very slowly into the water already in the tank. Remember, always add the acid to the water and not vice versa. When mixing this solution, always wear goggles and rubber gloves.

To mix 1 gallon of stripping solution, first wash the stripping tank with clean water to remove any

Figure 17-2: A heavy-duty plate/stirrer is the ideal heat source for electroless plating operations. The 1320-watt heating element heats a container quickly and then maintains the heat throughout the operation.

residue or possible contaminate. Pre-measure 1 gallon of clean water in the tank, and make note of its depth by measuring it with a dip stick. Measure 51 fluid ounces of clean water (hot or cold) and pour into the stripping tank. Measure 32 fluid ounces of Brownells Concentrate 778-R, and pour slowly into the water already in the tank. Immediately begin mechanical agitation of the solution at a moderate rate. Begin heating the solution, and bring it up 120 degrees F.

Continue by measuring 1.25 pounds (dry weight) of Concentrate 778-R. Slowly add this concentrate to the solution allowing the heat and agitation to dissolve the powder. It will probably take about 10 minutes before the powder is completely dissolved and the bath changes to a clear light-yellow color. Now add sufficient clean water to bring the total solution volume up to 1 gallon, and then bring the solution up to the operating temperature of 200 to 210 degrees F. Do not, however, exceed the 210-degree maximum. Check the thermometer several times to be sure that the heat setting is holding the temperature constant. When it is, the stripping solution is ready for use.

During use, the stripping solution will darken noticeably, and after 2 to 3 hours of use, it will become the color of deep mahogany, or very strong tea. This is normal and doesn't seem to affect anything. Parts should be suspended on iron wire, just as in the plating process to be discussed later. Do not use any other kinds of wire. Once parts are submerged in the stripping solution, they should not be removed until stripping is complete to avoid contamination, which in turn will result in less than a perfect job.

As water evaporates out of the stripping tank, it should be replaced. Use the dip stick method, or make a mark on the side of the pyrex tank. Do not allow parts to stick above the solution level as the fumes from the stripping solution cause very rapid rusting and pitting — which does not happen to parts that are left submerged. The rate of stripping will vary greatly depending upon the type and thickness of plate that is being removed along with other factors. Most will fully strip between 45 minutes and 1½ hours. If parts do not strip in 2 to 2½ hours, the solution is too weak and must be replenished. On some guns the nickel plate is deposited on top of a copper plate which was put on the metal first as an undercoat for the nickel. These pieces will strip slowly, and the solution will turn the copper dark in color. However, as the copper is stripped away, the dark surface will disappear and all the plating will be removed down to the bare steel surface.

Agitation of the solution is important and is done at the same rate as for plating. If the solution is not agitated, stripping will be much slower because the stripping solution, remaining close to the metal, becomes saturated with removed nickel and slows down in removing more. Fresh solution must flow

NICKEL STRIPPING STEPS

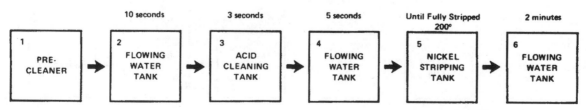

Figure 17-3: Flow chart of stripping operation.

by the metal surfaces at all times to distribute the dissolved nickel throughout the full gallon of stripping solution. One gallon of fresh stripping solution will remove the nickel plating from about four Colt .45 semi-automatic pistols. After this, the solution normally must be replenished. To replenish the stripping solution, first make certain that no guns or parts are in the stripping tank. Then be sure the agitation system is working and the solution is being agitated thoroughly. Also, be sure the temperature is between 200 and 210 degrees F. Add 2 ounces (by dry weight) of Concentrate 778-R to the stripping solution and continue agitation until all the Concentrate 778-R is dissolved.

This replenishment will normally allow the stripping of approximately the same amount of nickel as did the original fresh solution. However, after six replenishments of the stripping solution with Concentrate 778-R, the solution will become super-saturated with dissolved nickel and will fail to strip any more. Dump the solution, wash the tank thoroughly with clean water and mix up a fresh batch. After stripping is completed, turn off the heat, leave the solution in the pyrex tank and allow both to cool to normal room temperature while still sitting on the source of heat. If you take the pyrex tank off the hot plate and set it on a cold bench or counter top, it's possible that the thermal shock will break the tank. Once cooled, do not store the stripping solution in the stripping tank. Pour it into a clean brown plastic chemical jug. Be sure to mark the jug "STRIPPER" and "POISON." Also, label that jug as to how many times the solution has been replenished. To reuse, simply pour back into the thoroughly clean stripping tank, bring up to heat with agitation to correct operating temperature and begin the cycle.

Stripping is a slow process, and of all the sequences involved with nickel plating, it's the most worrisome, so don't expect instant results. It must work slowly so as not to pit or etch the steel.

Plating Operation

Twelve steps are required to properly plate a gun. These are outlined below and in the flow chart provided in Figure 17-4. Do not take any short-cuts. Do each in turn, as given, for the time specified. Then go on to the next step. Layout of the plating room is completely optional, but do try to set up

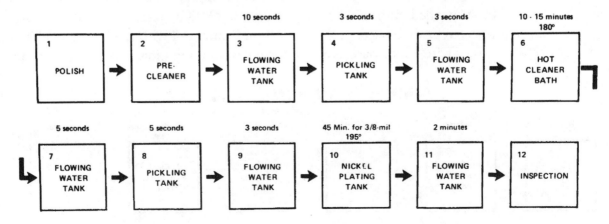

ELECTROLESS NICKEL PLATING STEPS

Figure 17-4: Electroless nickel plating steps.

Figure 17-5: This .32 ACP Colt semiautomatic pistol has been highly engraved besides being nickel plated.

your tanks so a logical progression from tank to tank can be done handily. (The steps to follow are for Brownells Electroless Nickel Plating; however, further information may be obtained from Brownells directly.)

Polishing: Polish and prepare the metal exactly as for bluing. As in bluing a firearm, plating will not hide or fill scratches or pitting. A high gloss nickel finish requires metal preparation equal to "master-grade" bluing preparation; that is, polishing right on down to No. 555 grit. A satin nickel finish can be achieved by using glass beading (very fine sand blasting), or a coarse wire scratch wheel with light pressure on the gun.

Pre-Clean: While this step is not an absolute must, it is highly recommended for best plating results. Use AWA 1,1,1 and saturated cotton swabs to thoroughly clean all surfaces, areas including holes, crevices, and the like. This removes any old grease and accumulated crud, silicone oils and

other gun oils plus polishing residue; especially residue left by wax or grease-based polishing compounds. Do not use petroleum based solutions like gas, kerosene, mineral spirits or gun cleaner. If at all possible thoroughly blow all parts clean with a medium to high pressure air gun to help clean off loosened gunk.

Flowing-Water Rinse: Submerge parts in the flowing-water tank for about 10 seconds to help float away any particles of foreign matter loosened by the pre-clean step.

Pickling Tank: Submerge parts for 3 seconds. The parts will start to "gas" (similar to Alka Seltzer tablets) and this further removes any foreign contamination.

Flowing-Water Tank: Submerge in tank for 3 seconds and agitate to flush pickling solution from surface of metal. This step is extremely important.

Hot Cleaner Bath: Submerge parts in tank for 10 to 15 minutes with operating temperature at 180 degrees F. Agitate occasionally to ensure good surface cleaning.

Flowing-Water Tank: Submerge for 5 seconds and agitate to flush cleaning solution from surface of metal.

Pickling Tank: Submerge for 5 seconds to "activate" the surface of metal for plating. Parts will start to "gas" indicating surface is activated. This step, in addition to cleaning, will make the nickel "strike" the metal surface quickly-assuring a good initial bonding to the surface.

Flowing-Water Tank: Submerge for 3 seconds and agitate to flush pickling solution from surface of metal.

Nickel Plating Tank: First determine thickness of the plate you wish to apply. For optimum results, a 3/8 inch mil plating depth is considered to be the best for guns. This thickness will require 45 minutes of submersion in the plating solution. Start the agitation system and submerge the parts to be plated into the plating solution. (Make sure they do not touch each other or the sides of the tank.) Be sure that agitation is thorough, and that whirlpooling does not develop. The solution must operate between 190 and 195 degrees F. optimum. Once the pieces are in the plating solution, do not remove them until the desired length of time has elapsed. If you do, even for an instant, you will ruin the plating job and have to start over. When the predetermined time has elapsed to plate the thickness desired, remove the parts from the plating solution.

Flowing-Water Tank: Submerge the parts for a minimum of 2 minutes and agitate to flush the nickel solution from the metal surface. There is no maximum time limit in this tank as the nickel plating process has been completed. Remove the parts from the tank and allow them to dry normally or use compressed air for faster drying.

Inspection: Check all parts and components carefully to assure an even plate of all desired surfaces prior to assembly of the gun. However, if a part or component is not nickel plated as desired,

it cannot be put back into the nickel tank. The part must be stripped of all nickel and reprocessed from bare metal! If all parts and components are satisfactory, wipe all parts clean and dry with a soft cloth to remove water spotting or lingering wet areas in holes, etc. If a high-gloss finish is desired, you can buff the parts lightly on a loose muslin wheel to bring up the luster, or use a Professional Nickel Final Polishing Cloth. If the buffing wheel is used, use only No. 555 white Polish-O-Ray and very light pressure as any form of polishing will remove metal, and you will be removing the nickel plate you just put on. Simichrome polish can also be used to increase the luster of a high gloss finish. Reassembly of the gun is the final step.

The complete plating procedure consists of two phases, both equally important. First is a preparation of the metal to enter the plating solution and second, the actual plating of the metal. Any attempt at short cuts in the procedure usually results in a poor plating job and wasted time and material. At first the process will seem lengthy, especially the cleaning steps prior to putting the piece into the plating tank. However, with a little practice you can complete the plating process in about the same amount of time required for a good bluing job.

The preparation phase is a step-by-step sequence in getting the metal absolutely clean of all foreign residue and down to the bare metal. When metal is stripped of all protective coating, it absorbs oxygen and oxidizes very quickly when in the open air. Oxidation on the metal surface prevents good initial bonding of nickel to metal. Therefore, the time between each step should be as short as possible. Work quickly but at a steady pace between each step. Timing in the tanks, in seconds, does not require a stop watch. If you say the words, "One thousand and one" it takes one second. Hence "one thousand and one, one thousand and two, one thousand and three," will take three seconds. Try it, it works.

Equally important is the flushing step between each tank. It prevents the carrying or "drag out" of chemicals from one tank to another tank with resulting chemical contamination of the second tank.

If you can blue guns, you can plate guns. It's only a matter of familiarization and practical experience. The major difference is that plating requires extreme measure to assure parts are clean prior to entering the plating solution. As with all types of metal finishes, it is best to make a test run by using scrap parts until you become familiar with the process instead of making the first plating job on a new gun. According to Brownells, the most common cause of poor plating jobs can be directly traced to lack of cleaning or contamination of so-

lutions, but also see the troubleshooting chart in Figure 17-6. Practically anything that can happen is listed in this chart. If other problems arise, contact Brownells.

It is possible to plate one or two parts for two hours and give them a one-mil plate build-up if desired. This can occasionally be done to tighten up loose fitting screws, pins and other slightly worn parts. Plating past this one-mil thickness is not practical. And be sure to remember that every surface will receive the same amount of plate and increase by the same thickness. So, while you may tighten up threads of a screw, you may also keep

---

TROUBLESHOOTING CHART
Electroless Plating

Malfunction	Probable Cause	Corrective Action
New bath does not plate	1. Improper make-up.	Bring bath into specs if can determine mistake. If not, discard bath.
	2. Incorrect bath volume.	Adjust bath if can do so correctly. If not, discard.
	3. Temperature too low.	Check thermometer; heat source. Must operate between 190° — 200°F with 195°F optimum.
Poor surface activation	1. Acid too old or too weak.	If so, remake
	2. Oil contamination in tanks.	Find source, clean up, then remake all baths.
	3. Poor rinsing between cleaning steps.	Increase agitation or water flow.
	4. No nickel strike on stainless steel or hardened steels.	See special note on "Wood's Nickel Strike" to activate surface.
Smut forms on surface after pickling	Result of over-activation by pickling solution.	Wipe off parts with cloth and repickle for shorter time and/or reduce strength of pickling solution.
Cratered surface	Plating solution agitation too fast.	Slow down agitator with speed control. Part must be stripped and replated. Will not polish out.
Sandy surface	Took part out of plating bath and put back in during plating cycle.	Do not remove parts once put into plating tank. You will get a "false plate" which must be stripped and replated if careful polishing does not remove.
Discoloration on surface	1. Shaded gray streaks caused by parts touching, hanging loops tight, too large a part in too small a tank.	Use larger tank; run more than one batch. Use O-shaped hanging loops.
	2. Adding water during time part is in plating tank.	Water to top-off volume can be done only when no parts are in plating tank; then temperature must be restabilized to 195°F.

Figure 17-6: Electroless plating troubleshooting chart. (Continued on next page.)

Malfunction	Probable Cause	Corrective Action
Smears, streaking	Surface not clean.	Remember, clean — clean — clean and clean again. Strip and replate.
Contaminations	1. Check for galvanized aluminum, copper, or brass in tanks, racks, hanging wires, or stir rods, leaded steel, heavily soldered or brazed parts.	Discard contaminating metals and make baths.
	2. Residual acid left from stripping.	Generally will have to discard bath.
	3. Containers, mixing cups, stir rods, etc. mixed between plate bath, and cleaning bath.	Generally have to discard solutions. Always use separate mixing/measuring cups and label for which bath used.
Rapid depletion of A-1, B-1, 778	Poor chemical reaction, result of storage below 50°F.	Return to solution as described below. Ideal storage is 60° - 90°F.
Working life depletes too soon	Plating solutions stored in tanks, open containers, and not light-proof containers.	Solutions must always be kept in dark brown chemical jugs when not actually in use to preserve working life.
Surface rough with scratches	Probably not polished to fine enough grit before plating.	Plating will not hide anything!
Rough and scratchy surface	Dirt on surface of metal entrapped under plating.	Strip, really clean this time and replate.
Pebbly surface	Plating solution agitation too slow.	Increase speed to just before cavitation or whirlpooling starts. Surface can be cleaned up with 555 white polish on loose muslin wheel and very light pressure.
Plating came off	1. Surface not clean.	Strip, reclean and plate.
	2. Tried to plate stainless steel or hardened steels.	See special note on Wood's Nickel Strike to activate surface.
	3. You took it out of the plating bath to look at it and put it back in for some more plating.	You cannot do this for it will false plate and may come off. Strip and replate.
Plating too thin	1. Tried to plate with depleted solution.	Check mil-usage record on storage jug. Make new solution then strip and replate.
	2. Check surface area-to-volume of plating bath ratio. One gallon does only 114 square inches 1/2-mil thick.	May require larger container and more solution volume.
Plating too thick	Too long in plating bath.	Reduce time in plating bath. One hour gives 1/2-mil, 45 minutes gives 3/8 mil; 1/2 hour gives 1/4-mil. Generally thick plating can be polished off with 555 white polish on loose muslin wheel adjusting pressure and checking fit often. Be sure not to cut through plating.
Casehardened/cast steel plates unevenly	1. Many case-hardened surfaces do not activate as well as unhardened steels.	Leave in pickle longer than normal until good gassing occurs.
	2. High silicone content of some cast steels may inhibit plating.	Pre-clean to the point of "overkill" with trichloroethane to remove silicone.
	3. Cast parts will usually not polish well enough for bright nickel plating.	Suggest sandblasting cast surface before plating for a deluxe satin nickel finish.

Figure 17-6: Electroless plating troubleshooting chart. *(Cont.)*

the head from fitting flush, or fitting the counter-bore at all.

Agitation of the plating solution is critical, for too great an agitation will result in whirlpooling, which draws air into the plating solution. This extra air will "crater" the nickel plating being put on the metal surface and you will have to strip the piece and start over because the poor plating cannot be saved. Too little agitation will result in "pebbling" of the plated surface (little humps and random bumps). This is more easily remedied, for the part need only be polished carefully with 555 white Polish-O-Ray on a loose muslin wheel to remove the "pebbles."

Sand blasting of parts prior to plating is one of the most universally appealing finishes you can give your guns. Especially consider decorative use of sand blasting; for instance, sand blast the entire cylinder, then polish just the outside back up to bright, leaving the flutes sand blasted. Once plated, the contrast between bright and satin is very hand-some.

Polishing prior to plating is more important than you can realize as you read this chapter. Every scratch, rough spot, wobble or nick is highlighted by the plating; it will hide absolutely nothing, not even those things bluing will sometimes hide. So, consider the stain finish if you don't want to go to the trouble of doing the high degree of polishing required for a mirror-bright finish. Many shooters prefer the satin finish anyway.

Do not mix and add more fresh plating solution to a partially used batch. This is a tempting idea but don't do it, for you then lose track of the plating capacity of the total solution.

Solution heat-up in the pyrex tanks can be greatly hurried by making a "tank jacket" from fiberglass furnace duct insulating panels. Cut those panels to fit like an open-ended box and seal the corners with duct tape. Make a lid from a pyrex glass sheet or hi-temp plastic, and be sure to use that lid on any enamel tanks. It will cut evaporation and shorten heat-up time.

Because of the acids used, parts not directly under the surface of the plating bath will rust badly — worse than in the bluing room. The small amount of water that condenses on hanger rods and falls back into the plating bath is of no consequence. But do take precautions by keeping all easily rus-table equipment and items out of the plating room.

If you are working on a rusty gun that you want to put through a rust or bluing remover solution, you must do so before you polish the gun. Most removers contain phosphoric acid which acts as a "pacifier" to steel, and will prevent it from plating. Polishing will remove this pacified surface, so you must polish thoroughly and completely. Then the precleaning, pickling and cleaning steps in the plat-ing sequence should properly "activate" the steel surface. If you notice that the part does not "gas" in the pickling tank immediately, you may have to leave it in for a few more seconds to be sure that the surface is sufficiently activated for the nickel plating to "strike" the surface and adhere correctly.

The troubleshooting chart shown in Figure 17-6 will help you to correct problems that may arise when using Brownells Electroless Plating Method. When the chart advises to "strip and plate," it does not mean run the part through the stripper and then directly back into the plating tank. It means to take the part through the stripping sequence, then through the entire 12 steps of the plating sequence! If you skip a step and put a dirty part back into the

Figure 17-7: Millions of nickel-plated break-top revolvers were manufactured around the turn of this century. A knowledge of metal plating is necessary to restore the finish on them.

Figure 17-8: The M1 Garand rifle was the "best" there was for combat use in Wold War II and the Korean conflict. Many owners now want these fine rifles restored to their original condition; this means parkerizing the metal.

plating tank, it will not plate correctly that time either. You cannot skip any step of any sequence.

PARKERIZING

Parkerizing or phosphate coatings provide an excellent surface for holding a rust inhibiting, or lubricating compound. Oil is absorbed by the micro crystalline structure, and has the effect of a lubricant reservoir, which helps in the break-in of friction bearing surfaces. Whereas, untreated surfaces of steel are unstable and corrosion-prone, phosphate coatings are much more resistant to the elements. Phosphating solutions consist of zinc, manganese, or iron, dissolved in carefully balanced solutions of phosphoric acid. When a ferrous type, or a reactive metal, is placed in the phosphating solution, a light acid etching takes place.

Shortly thereafter, depending on the accelerators used, a micro amount of metal is removed from the surface, and a hydrogen process takes place, which in turn precipitates a phosphate coating on the steel, which is integrally bonded to the metal. Once ap-

plied, the coating can now act as a corrosion resistant to the metal, as well as improve wear resistance.

The time and temperature of immersion can be critical, depending on the amount of solution used, as well as the identity of the metal being treated. Zinc phosphate treatments will generally produce a crystalline deposit of hydrated zinc phosphate compounds on the substrate or base metal, and normally have a coating range between 0.0005 inch to 0.0015 inch in thickness, and vary in density and porosity. The variability of density and coating thickness, is not a reliable indicator of the corrosion inhibiting qualities of the finished product. The appearance of the zinc phosphate coating is a gray matte finish, with the shade varying somewhat, depending on the chemical composition of the treatment bath, and the amount of ferrous material in the metal. The zinc phosphate coating itself has an outstanding corrosion resistance, due to the fact it provides a chemically inert and insoluble barrier. It's best to follow the manufacturer's directions, and not deviate as complications can arise.

Safety

Most parkerizing solutions, such as Amer-Lene, have been professionally formulated and manufactured in compliance with all applicable safety standards. Information and recommendations concerning their use are based upon laboratory tests and field use experience. However, since conditions of actual use are beyond the control of the manufacturers, any recommendations or suggestions are made without warranty. It must be the owner's or user's responsibility to see to it that the procedures are meticulously followed, and especially that the warning and cautionary notes are heeded. Read the warning information on the container.

Make sure the shop is properly ventilated along with a window left open for fresh air intake. Do not use or store chemicals near food or in a food preparation area. Wear rubber gloves, full face shield and neoprene apron. (Train your eyes to see an accident before it happens).

Equipment

Besides the parkerizing solution, you will need a stainless steel tank large enough to accommodate the parts, a thermometer that will measure up to 180°F., a measuring cup (graduated in ounces), a pair of tongs with at least 8-inch handles, degreasing solution, applicators, sandblasting equipment, a source of heat and a means of securing the parts in the solution.

Stainless Steel Tank: For most projects, a tank 6" x 6" x 40" long will suffice. You can obtain stainless steel in sheets and do the welding yourself or have it done at a local shop. The stainless steel sheets, however, should not be less than 22 gauge. Stainless steel tanks are also available from Brownells.

An optional method is to obtain a piece of threaded stainless steel pipe about 6 inches in diameter and 4 feet long. Screw a 6-inch stainless steel cap tightly on the bottom end and rig it as

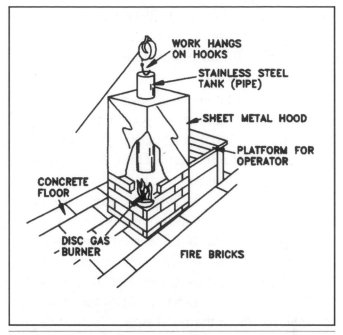

Figure 17-9: Vertical stainless steel tank system for parkerizing.

shown in Figure 17-9. The asbestos-lined sheet metal housing will help to conserve heat. Because the tank is in a vertical position, it will take up less floor space than conventional horizonal tanks, and since the solution is heated at the bottom of the vertical tank, the heat will rise and circulate to maintain an even temperature throughout. The only problem is if a small part should fall to the bottom of the tank, the entire tank will usually have to be dumped to retrieve it.

Another drawback with the vertical setup is dumping the solution once it is spent. The entire tank must be pulled out of its housing and then dumped in a safe place. You could weld a stainless steel gate valve into the bottom side of the tank, but this will add to the expense. Another way is to weld a ring or hook at the top of the tank where another hook on a cable can be attached. This cable fed through a pulley above the tank will enable you to lift the tank, filled with solution, and keep it suspended until you can dump it. If a drain is nearby, fabricate the sheet metal hood so that one side opens as well as the top. Then you can merely dump the chemicals as you gradually tip the tank over to one side. Remember, a 6-inch tank filled with parkerizing solution is not going to be light, so provide accordingly.

Heat Source: Your local gas company (natural or LP) can advise and supply you with a simple pipe burner for horizontal tanks; use a ring-type industrial gas burner for the vertical tank. For the vertical setup, mount the burner close to the floor, but above a layer of firebricks for protection and insulation. Mount the tank so that the bottom is about 4 inches above the burner, with the tank enclosed in heavy sheet metal and lined with some type of furnace insulation to conserve the heat. Firebrick should be installed all around the burner up to the bottom of the tank to where the hood stops. Of course, you need to leave an opening in the firebrick for lighting the burner.

Although not necessary, you might want to fabricate a loose fitting sheet metal cap to fit over the top of the tank to conserve heat and energy. If so, it should be perforated in the center so that it will slide freely on the suspension wires on which the work is hung for lowering into the parkerizing solution. With a 6-inch pipe, as many as four barrels and receivers can be parkerized simultaneously. It is desirable to finish as many as possible at one time due to the length of time required to complete this process.

Small parts can be grouped on small hooks of stainless steel wire or you might want to make a basket out of stainless steel screen wire. In doing so, however, the parts should be shaken frequently during the process to avoid constant contact which might leave spots on the finished work.

Sand Blasting: Rust or scale on the gun parts must be removed before putting them into the parkerizing solution. The best way to do this is by dry abrasive blasting using glass beads. Silica sand may be obtained from your local lumber yard (where it is sold for mixing white plaster), or obtain glass beads from a local auto body repair supplier. The sand blasting equipment is not cheap by any means, and it's going to take a number of parkerizing jobs to pay for the equipment. So until you have enough business to warrant such an outfit, it will probably be better to "farm out" the sandblasting operation to a local auto body shop. Most shops will be glad to do the operation for a reasonable fee. In any event, glass-bead all parts until a chrome look is obtained and no dark spots remain.

After the abrasive blasting, do not handle any of the parts with bare hands. This will leave body oil on the parts and cause spotting. Always use rubber gloves for handling the parts just as recommended

Figure 17-10: The .30-caliber M1 carbine is another rifle used during World War II and the Korean conflict that was parkerized.

for most bluing jobs. Get the parts into the parkerizing solution as quickly as possible after the abrasive treatment. Never wait more than 3 hours.

Treating: There are several suppliers of parkerizing solution and all will vary slightly, so follow instructions provided by each. One type requires that you prepare enough solution to cover all parts sufficiently at a concentration of 4 ounces of parkerizing solution per gallon of water (3 percent by volume). Mix the solution in a stainless steel tank, light the burner, and bring this solution to a temperature of between 160 and 170°F. The parts are then suspended in the solution by wires or hooks. The parts should not be touched with bare hands. Once the parts are suspended in the parkerizing solution, allow the metal to react. Turn the parts periodically to get an even treatment, but be careful not to agitate the parts where they will rub or grind against each other.

As in hot caustic bluing, temperature is of the utmost importance at this time. Be sure to maintain a temperature of between 160 to 170 degrees (for one type of solution). Nothing else will do! But remember this temperature will vary with each manufacturer.

The parts should be left in the solution for about 40 minutes and then removed and immediately rinsed in cool running water for 1 minute. Drain excess water and dry with a clean absorbent cloth. Once the parts have dried, immediately dip them in a light oil bath or spray the parts with WD-40 or some similar oil. Wipe off all excess oil and the job is completed for a gray-type finish. Repeated applications of cosmoline in place of the oil bath will usually provide a green tint to the finish.

As long as the bath is hot and the solution is clear, the bath can be used to parkerize any number of guns. A cloudy solution indicates depletion of its active ingredients. Also, once the solution has cooled, do not attempt to reheat and use. Dump the solution in a safe place once it has cooled. Check with your local health department about getting rid of any chemicals listed on the label of the container.

As with any chemicals, wear safety goggles or a face shield and avoid contact of the solution with skin.

Amer-Lene Parkerizing

Amer-Lene was developed out of a need to give the home gun enthusiast along with the professional gunsmith a way to put a military weapon's finish on firearms without expensive and costly equipment. Amer-Lene is not an epoxy paint, or bake-on process, but rather a zinc phosphating process, the same type of finish various industries in the United States are using, as well as the U.S. government uses on their weapons. The zinc phosphating process has been around for many years. The original formulas having been modified over the years. Some have worked, and some have not. Amer-Lene is one that does work.

Amer-Lene was in the research and development stage for nearly two years before it was released to the market. This was to insure that anyone could pick up and read the instructions, and do a first-class professional phosphatized finish.

Tanks

Amer-Lene is a phosphoric acid base solution and must be used in a stainless steel tank. Only one

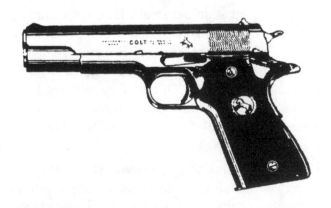

Figure 17-11: The Model 1911(A1) Colt .45 semiautomatic pistol is another candidate for parkerizing.

stainless tank is needed for this process. Brownells sells an excellent tank for this purpose, but if you wish to have one made to fit your particular needs, it is recommended that you have the tank made out of 16 or 18 GA, 302 or 316 series stainless steel. Do not use a black iron tank for this process as the zinc salts that are in the solution — which should be deposited on your parts — will now be deposited on the sides of the black iron tank, causing wasted material and thin coatings to no coatings on your parts.

Care and Cleaning of Tanks

Stainless steel is extremely durable and maintenance is simple and inexpensive. But proper care under corrosive conditions is essential. Periodic cleaning will greatly prolong the service life of your stainless steel tanks. For best results, the tanks should be cleaned as often as films or deposits become apparent. Cleanliness is of utmost importance. Deposits of dirt and grease are quickly removed with soap and water. Thoroughly rinse and dry after washing. Some zinc deposits may adhere to the bottom and sides, and in most cases, can be removed with a stainless steel putty knife. In all cases, scraping should be in the direction of polishing lines. However, some tanks that have been neglected from the start may require more vigorous means. (Warning: never use ordinary steel wool, or steel brushes on stainless steel). If rough cleaning is needed, use only stainless steel wool, or stainless brushes. When stainless steel is severely overheated it may show a discoloration or what's known as a heat tint. This can be removed by scouring with a powder such as grade FFF Italian pumice on a damp cloth or Coopers Stainless Steel Cleaner on a damp cloth.

Heavy discoloration due to overheating may be removed with Bab-O cleanser on a damp cloth or steel bright cleanser on a damp cloth. These cleaning aids will scratch stainless steel surfaces so go slow and use light pressure. When removing oil and grease coatings, trichlorethylene or acetone may be used. Do not use gasoline or mineral spirits. Upon placing your stainless steel tanks in operation, they should be degreased with the above-mentioned solvents, washed with soap and water, and dried prior to use.

Heat Source

For gunsmiths who have a small operation, a two-burner propane stove can be used along with the 20-inch stainless steel tank from Brownells. For larger operations, the 40-inch long stainless tank along with the pipe burner from Brownells will handle most jobs that your shop will take in.

Thermometer

The bluing thermometer sold by Brownells is highly recommended, but any good laboratory grade thermometer will work just as well. Do not use a kitchen grade or ambient reading thermometer for this purpose. The temperature of the solution in the tank can be run between 160-185° F. Do not exceed the 185° F temperature as the water in the tank will boil off too fast. Use the correct thermometer to bring temperature of the bath to an even range. Do not guess.

Preparing Parts for Treatment

Each gun and its related parts must be completely disassembled. Do not leave springs and plungers in such items as bolts, trigger housing, and frames, as the phosphating solution can cause these parts to freeze up. Once everything is apart, it's time to degrease and remove all traces of oil and silicons. This can be done by immersing parts in trichlorethylene or acetone, and using a small acid brush, as the above-mentioned solvents will melt them, causing a plasticized coating to form on the parts. Do not use gasoline, kerosene or mineral spirits as a degreasing agent as they will leave an oil residue on the surface. Once parts have been cleaned and degreased avoid touching them with your bare hands. Use cotton gloves or a clean dry paper towel to handle them.

Now that the parts have been degreased, the next step is to clean them of the old finish. The most efficient, economical, and fastest is the medium-size glass bead, at 90 to 100 psi. Builder's or Silica sand is not recommended for this operation as they will abrade and etch the surface too deeply. Do not use fine glass beads as they will not always leave a good, clean uniform surface for the Amer-Lene to adhere to. Once parts have been degreased and bead blasted all that is needed is for them to be placed in the Amer-Lene tank that has been previously prepared with the correct amount of water and Amer-Lene and brought to the correct temperature.

Technical Information

Amer-Lene is a concentrated solution of zinc phosphate and phosphoric acid, and must be used according to instructions.

- Pour enough water into a stainless steel tank to cover parts and allow for evaporation. When using Brownells 40-inch long tank, $2\frac{1}{2}$ to 3 gallons of water will be sufficient.

- When parts have been cleaned, degreased, and prepared by glass bead blasting, use $3\frac{1}{2}$ oz. of Amer-Lene Gray for each gallon of water used in the tank. Do not guess at the amount of water you have put in the tank. Also do not guess at what you think is $3\frac{1}{2}$ oz. of Amer-Lene Gray. Use a graduated container such as a plastic baby bottle for this purpose and do not use it for measuring oil or any other products.

- With correct amount of water in tank, heat and bring temperature up to 165 to 185° F. Once water is at correct

temperature, pour in correct amount of Amer-Lene Gray, based on instruction given above. Using a clean plastic spoon, slowly stir entire area of tank for 1 minute. Failure to do so, will cause a higher concentration of zinc in one area of the tank, causing a higher coating weight on parts that are in that location, and a thinner coating weight on parts that are in the depleted area of the tank. Do not skip this step, as the results of the finished parts will look and feel coarser than other parts that were also in the tank. It only takes a minute.

COLORING STAINLESS STEEL

Stainless steel barrels are not new. The Winchester Repeating Arms Co. introduced stainless steel barrels for their famous Model 12 slide-action shotgun many years ago. There were probably others. Cold mineral acid was sometimes used on stainless steel barrels for coloring, but the contamination of the surface with smut and the possible loss of dimensions have made the use of acid unadvisable on gun barrels. Therefore, when the blackening process wore off these barrels, most gunsmiths of the day merely used flat black paint, and forgot about oxidizing the steel.

In the past decade, however, many stainless guns have come on the market. Many of these are left in their natural "mill finish" while others have been colored by some blackening process. One such finish is known as the Du-Lite 3-0 process.

In setting up for the Du-Lite 3-0 process to blacken stainless steel, the equipment needed is very similar to that described for the conventional hot caustic process.

An alkaline cleaning bath (Du-Lite #45 or equivalent) heated to 180°F or higher is necessary together with an active running water rinsing tank.

Figure 17-12: The Winchester Model 12 slide-action shotgun was one of the first to come from the factory with stainless steel barrels.

A surface activator solution, either hot or cold, as described below, is also necessary.

In general, a Du-Lite 3-0 blackening bath is made up in an externally heated steel tank. Concentration of the bath is to be regulated to obtain an actually boiling solution at from 240° to 250° F. This will require from 4½ to five pounds of Du-Lite 3-0 salts per gallon. A convenient method of making up the bath is to fill the tank to about one-half of final capacity, the add 3-0 salts with constant stirring until the desired temperature of the boiling solution is obtained. Continue to add salt and additional water until the working level of the solution is reached. With 400 series steels, the best result is usually obtained at a boiling point of 245° F or over. With 300 series steels, a temperature of 240° to 245° F usually is most satisfactory. If the temperature is too low and the bath is boiling, add more salts.

If steels in the A.I.S.I. 400 series (no nickel) are to be processed and rigid dimensional tolerances are to be observed, activation of these steels is to be done with Du-Lite "Aldak 30," an alkaline medium. The solution is made at a strength of from 3 to 4 pounds per gallon. It is contained in an externally heated plain steel tank and the temperature must not exceed 240° F. The 400 series steel is placed in the hot "Aldak 30" solution and held

there until a gray cast appears. This should be in about fifteen minutes. At the end of this period, remove the work at once, rinse in cold running water and then place in the 3-0 boiling blackening bath for 30 minutes. When the color is satisfactory, the work is removed or dried and left unfinished, or lightly brushed on a Tampico Wheel.

Ebonol SS-52

Ebonol SS-52 is another alkaline, oxidizing type blackening compound which produces black coatings on stainless steel and high alloy steels normally difficult to blacken. Ebonol SS-52 solutions produce a mixed oxide-sulfide black coating by simple immersion.

The appearance of the black finish is dependent upon the surface of the steel being coated. Shiny black coatings are produced on buffed or polished surfaces. Uniform matte coatings are produced on brushed or etched surfaces.

The dimensional changes involved in blackening are extremely small, being less than 0.01 mil. The thickness of the black oxide coating ranges from 0.06 to 0.1 mil.

Ebonol SS-52 is supplied as a powder and is shipped in 30, 125, and 400 pound drums. The powder is dissolved in water to make the operating solution at the ratio of about 4¾ pounds of powder to 1 gallon of water. The operating temperature is from 250° to 260° F., and the metal is colored in from 5 to 15 minutes.

Make-up: Clean the tank thoroughly before making up the solution. Be sure all rust and scale is removed, since rust will dissolve in the blackening solution and will tend to redeposit on the work causing a reddish film.

Fill the tank about half full with cold water. Considerable heat will be created by the dissolution of the Ebonol SS-52 salts. Therefore, while stirring with an iron paddle, slowly add 4¾ pounds of Ebonol SS-52 for each gallon of final solution. Continue stirring until the salts are almost completely dissolved, making sure that no solid lumps of salts are on the bottom of the tank.

Add water to raise the solution level to within above 2 inches of the desired solution level; do not fill to the final level because the solution expands on heating. Apply heat, and continue to stir until the solution comes to a boil. The Ebonol SS-52 solution should start to boil at 250° F. If boiling occurs below 250° F., slowly add Ebonol SS-52 salts while heating until the desired boiling point is obtained. Then lower the heat input so that the solution just boils gently.

Temperature: The blackening solution must boil within the recommended operating temperature range, 250° to 260° F. The solution will boil at other temperatures if the concentration of the salts is not correct, but successful blackening will not occur.

As water evaporates from the bath, the solution will become more and more concentrated and the boiling point will rise. When the boiling point reaches 260° F, water must be added to dilute the solution and thereby lower the boiling point to 250° F. Do not try to adjust temperature by means of the heat input. The temperature of a liquid in an open vessel cannot exceed its boiling point. Control of the boiling point is done only by additions of water (or salts if the boiling point is too low), and the heat should be adjusted so that the solution always boils with a gentle roll. In adding water, however, remember that the solution operates above the boiling point of water and care should be taken when adding water to avoid spattering and eruption of the solution the same as when working with the conventional hot caustic bluing method.

The boiling point is controlled by the addition of water. Thus, an automatic temperature controller which regulates water input instead of heat input will maintain both the correct boiling point and the correct concentration of Ebonol salts.

Operation: Work to be blackened must be clean and free of all rust and scale. The following cleaning cycle is recommended:

- Soak and clean in hot alkaline cleaning solution.

- Rinse in running water.

- Activate in 50% muriatic acid at room temperature for 30 seconds to 5 minutes.

- Rinse in running water.

- Blacken in Ebonol SS-52 for 5 to 15 minutes at 250° to 260° F.

- Rinse in running water.

It is important that the steel be properly activated prior to blackening. The required immersion time in the 50% muriatic acid varies from 30 seconds to 5 minutes depending upon the particular alloy and any surface treatment it might have undergone.

COLORING MISCELLANEOUS METALS

As more aluminum and other non-steel parts are used in modern firearms, more and more gunsmiths are faced with the problem of getting them colored when the rest of the gun is blued. Aluminum parts absolutely cannot be put through the hot caustic bluing tanks because they'll come out looking like an ice cube on a hot summer day. Anodizing is the only way aluminum can be "blued." A brief description follows.

Anodizing is the process by which aluminum is coated with a layer of oxide by making the aluminum anodic in an appropriate solution. The process is conducted in either a chromic acid or sulfuric acid solution. The former process is seldom used in coloring gun parts because they are usually dyed black. In each method, the hardness and porosity of the coating can be controlled by the concentration, temperature, and current density. The protective value of the coatings can be improved by sealing, which consists of treatment with hot water containing chromates, or with live steam. This hydrates part of the aluminum oxide and seals the pores. Coatings made in sulfuric acid can be dyed with organic compounds to produce colors (many of which are resistant to sunlight).

Unfortunately, the expense of setting up a complete anodizing system is too great for the average gunshop. However, there are still ways to get off the hook.

The most obvious solution is to send the aluminum parts out to firms specializing in anodizing aluminum, and do the remaining work on the steel parts (bluing or browning) in your shop. When you get the parts back (in about 30 days) you can combine them with the parts you blued and reassemble the gun.

Birchwood Casey's Aluminum Black is one blackening agent on the market that is used similar to cold touch-up blue. It produces a gray to black finish immediately and requires no special equipment or skills. It is hard to get an even finish on large parts and should be used only for touch-up work.

To use Birchwood Casey's Aluminum Black, first degrease the part with some type of cleaning solvent. Remove the oxide with 00 steel wool before applying the solution. Once the surface is clean, apply the Aluminum Black solution with a

Figure 17-13: Birchwood Casey's Aluminum Black.

cotton swab. Apply it generously to all surfaces. Allow about one minute for the chemical to work and then wipe lightly with a clean cotton cloth until the surface is dry. After it is thoroughly dry, polish the surface with a clean, soft, dry cloth to remove the adhering powder.

If a darker shade is preferred than was obtained with the first coat, apply more solution, wipe dry, and polish again. These steps can be repeated as often as necessary until the desired color is obtained. Apply a wax or oil to the surface once the last coat is applied.

From time to time, the gunsmith will be called upon to color certain gun parts a color other than black or blue-black. These jobs will be infrequent, but it is good to have the knowledge at hand should the need arise. The following formulas and methods have been used over a number of years with success. Some experimentation, however, might be required to obtain the desired color, shade, etc.

Caution: Please bear in mind that many of the chemicals used in the following formulas are dangerous for home use. Whenever possible, have them mixed by a pharmacist, chemist or other qualified person.

Blackening Aluminum: Mix the following solution to blacken aluminum:

- 1 ounce of white arsenic
- 1 ounce of iron sulphate
- 12 ounces of hydrochloric acid
- 12 ounces of distilled water

Mix the dry powders first and then add the acid. Then carefully, and slowly, pour the acid solution into the distilled water.

To use, clean the aluminum part to be colored with pumice and water and then place it in a commercial cleaner such as Dicro-Clean No. 909 and rinse immediately. Immerse the part in the above solution, which should be slightly warmed, until the part turns black. Polish lightly with fine steel wool and wax or oil.

Blackening Brass: Dissolve bits of copper scraps in concentrated nitric acid diluted with an equal amount of distilled water in a glass container. Be careful with the nitric acid as it is extremely caustic and don't breathe the fumes! Immerse the brass object in the solution until the preferred shade is reached. Remove and wash well with water. This will produce a dull black. If a sheen is preferred, rub the finish with linseed oil.

Black on Brass: Dissolve 1 ounce copper nitrate in 6 ounces distilled water and apply to the brass. Then heat the brass. This changes the copper nitrate to copper oxide and produces a permanent black finish. Instead of heating, the following solution can be applied over the copper nitrate coating:

- 1 ounce of sodium sulfide

- ½ ounce of hydrochloric acid, concentrated
- 10 ounces of distilled water

Mix by first dissolving the sodium sulfide in the distilled water and then slowly add the hydrochloric acid to the mixture. When applied to the copper nitrate coating already on the metal, it changes the coating to black copper sulfide.

Golden Matte on Brass or Copper: Carefully immerse the object in a solution of 1 part concentrated nitric acid and 3 parts water in a glass container. Rock the solution gently. Wipe the object clean under a running tap. When dry, polish the surface with wax or lacquer.

Antique-Green Patina on Brass or Copper: To obtain this type of finish mix the following solution:

- 3 ounces of potassium bitartrate (cream of tartar)
- 1 ounce of ammonium chloride
- 7½ ounces of copper nitrate
- 3 ounces of sodium chloride (table salt)
- 13 ounces of boiling water

Dissolve the salts in the boiling water and apply the hot solution to the object with a piece of sponge or clean rag wrapped on a stick. When the desired effect has been reached, wash and dry.

Another method of achieving the antique-green patina finish on brass is to paint the object daily for three or four days with the following solution:

- 3 ounces of copper carbonate
- 1 ounce of ammonium chloride
- 1 ounce of copper acetate
- 1 ounce of potassium bitartrate

- 8 ounces of strong vinegar

Yellow-Orange, Blue, Red-Brown on Brass: To get colors from yellow through bluish tones, immerse the object in the following solution. Increase the concentration for the bluish tone.

- ½ ounce of sodium hydroxide (lye)

- 1 ounce of copper carbonate

- 24 ounces of hot water

If you want the red-brown shades, briefly dip the object in the following solution:

- ¼ ounce of copper carbonate

- 7½ ounces of household ammonia

- ¼ ounce of sodium carbonate (washing soda)

- 48 ounces of water, near boiling

Cold rinse the object and dip for a moment in dilute sulfuric acid (very carefully). Experiment for different shades.

Bronze on Copper: Mix the following solution to get bronze on copper.

- 1½ ounces of ferric nitrate

- ½ ounce of potassium thiocyanate

- 32 ounces of distilled water

The metal object must also be heated before immersing in the solution. This can be done by dipping the object in hot water. When the object is hot, dip in the chemical solution until the color is satisfactory. Rinse in running water and dry in the breeze of a fan.

Red-Bronze to Brown on Copper: To change copper to this color, mix the following solution:

- ½ ounce of sulfurated potassium (liver of sulfur)

- ¾ ounce of sodium hydroxide (lye)

- 32 ounces of distilled water

Heat the solution and dip the object in it. When the preferred color is attained, rinse, dry, and lacquer.

Steel-Gray on Aluminum: To change aluminum to this color, mix the following:

- 8 ounces of zinc chloride

- 1 ounce of copper sulfate

- 32 ounces of boiling water

Immerse the object in this solution until the preferred tone is obtained. Rinse in a 2 percent solution of lye (be very careful) in water and then rinse thoroughly in clear water.

Near-White and Matte Colors on Aluminum: A soft-etched, imitation anodized finish can be achieved on aluminum by dipping it in a solution of 1 tablespoon or more of lye to a pint of water. To color the aluminum, dip in a household dye solution. Rinse in hot water, dry, and coat with wax or lacquer.

Chapter 18
Stock Work

Working on gunstocks is a good place for the beginning gunsmith to start — mainly because few tools are required, and scrap pieces of wood for practice may be obtained at little or no cost.

Stock work can consist of a small repair, such as raising a dent in a stock with steam, to building a completely new stock from scratch. There are also many decorative or functional features that may be added: checkering, carving, trap buttplates, recoil pads, sling swivels, forend tips, and the like.

When working with gunstocks, never rush your work because this is when you start making mistakes. If you don't have time to do the work, wait until time is available. One slip, at the wrong time, can ruin an entire stock, wasting several hours of hard work.

The information contained in this chapter will introduce you to stocks and stockmaking. Like almost any other form of gun work, once you gain the basic knowledge, you must continually practice what you have learned to gain the most benefit and to become proficient as a stockmaker.

WOOD FOR GUNSTOCKS

Various kinds of woods have been used in the past to stock firearms of all types, but among them, black walnut was perhaps the most popular in America. This type of wood was very plentiful during early times, and also had other desirable characteristics: it was light in weight, easily worked, took a superior polish, had a rich dark color, and had good lasting qualities. In fact, black walnut was so popular that most of the other woods for gunstocks were stained and finished to look like walnut. One of the few woods that took exception to this rule was hard or sugar maple. In some parts of the country, this type of wood was used quite extensively for stocking — especially the older muzzleloading rifles. It makes a very nice stock, especially curled or tiger-stripe maple, which is really beautiful. Soft maple was also used in some of the cheaper arms, but this type of wood was usually stained and finished to look like either hard maple or black walnut.

Desirable gunstock woods share a number of common necessary characteristics:

- They must be relatively light in weight.
- They must be close-grained and dense to resist moisture absorption and warping.
- They must be straight-grained in the pistol-grip area.
- In one-piece stocks, they must be straight-grained through the forend.

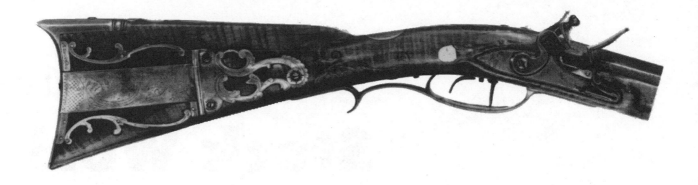

Figure 18-1: Early flintlock rifles were frequently stocked with curly maple wood.

• They should be cut from the main trunk of the tree with no sapwood.

The cheaper stocks and blanks often carry a wedge of light-colored, opened-grained sapwood which can be stained to match; or worse, a section of pith (the center of the trunk). Unless you're working with an existing stock, don't waste your time with such wood, unless you're practicing. It takes just as much effort, if not more, to finish out a lousy piece of wood as it would a stock blank or gunstock of good quality and appearance. Inferior wood always reflects its lack of quality, especially in the checkering, where the diamonds come out fuzzy rather than sharp and pointed.

Attractive, highly figured stocks, with a burl, crotch, fiddleback, etc., should always incorporate the pattern in the butt end of the stock. Such eye-catching figures, with the grain running in all directions, don't do a thing for stock strength. But they do increase the beauty and desirability (and price) of the wood.

The traditional stock wood today is still American walnut. The first American made guns — like the "Kentucky" long rifles — had stocks made of American walnut, maple, and to a lesser extent,

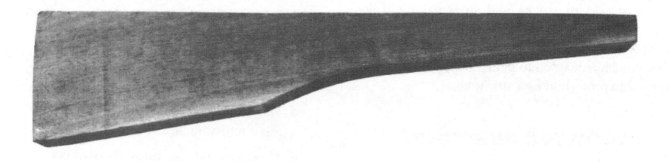

Figure 18-2: Typical plain-grained walnut stock blank.

cherry. These early flintlocks set a precedent for wood type and stock design that lasted until the early 1900s. For example, the first Winchester, Marlin, and other early lever-action rifles utilized buttstocks that were almost pure "Kentucky" in appearance.

European gunstocks were almost always made of walnut, and the comparatively trim and slim German and Austrian bolt-action rifles that came into the United States before and after World War I inspired many American stockmakers. With modifications, these European stocks evolved into the current American concept of what a rifle stock should look like.

In general, there are four basic types of walnut used by American stockmakers:

- Black walnut, which is native to North America

- English walnut, grown domestically

- Claro walnut, a California hybrid of black and English walnuts

- The various imported European walnuts; that is, French, etc.

Black Walnut: With all things being equal, black walnut is the least expensive of the four basic types. But black walnut is not cheap by any means; it becomes increasingly scarce (and costly) each year. Therefore, many firearm manufacturers are switching to such economy hardwoods as birch and beech impostors, which are stained to pose as the real thing.

The main reason for the current walnut shortage is the fact that the United States has always used black walnut for military stocks up through the now-obsolete M14 rifle. Then came the plastic-stocked M16 service rifle which helped a lot in conserving the present walnut crop for sporting guns. Furthermore, the demand for walnut veneer by domestic and foreign furniture manufacturers,

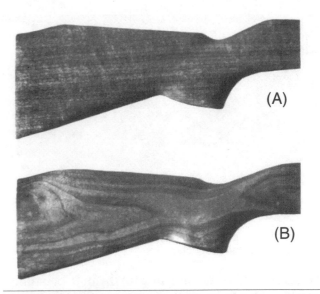

Figure 18-3: Plain-grained walnut is composed of two distinct types: (A) edge grain and (B) flat grain.

and the scrounging around in the United States for walnut by Japanese and European gun makers, have also helped deplete the supply.

Plain grain walnut is composed of two distinct types of grain, *edge* and *flat* grain as shown in Figure 18-3. There can be variations and combinations of the two in one gunstock. Both types are equal in strength and quality; the difference is made by sawing the stocks from the log at various angles to the annular rings of the tree. Choice is simply a matter of taste.

Fancy grained stocks are graded primarily on the figure and beauty of grain. Figure 18-4 shows one variation of fancy-figured walnut. Fancy-figured

Figure 18-4: A fancy fiddleback stock of American walnut.

Figure 18-5: This select American walnut blank was supplied by Johnson Wood Products.

American black walnut in crotch, butt or stump, and fiddleback grain is among the world's most beautiful wood. Figures 18-5 and 18-6 show several variations of select fancy figured American black walnut.

Environmental factors, especially water availability, greatly influence a given wood's suitability for gunstocks. Walnut trees grown in swamps, near river bottoms, or which depend on irrigation or receive a heavy annual rainfall grow fast and are softer and more open-grained than those growing in dryer climates. The best black walnut comes from the Ozark mountains of Missouri, northern Arkansas, eastern Kansas, Oklahoma, and from the hills of Pennsylvania, Tennessee, Ohio and Kentucky.

Figure 18-6: These blanks from Johnson Wood Products are select American walnut "feather crotch" wood.

Claro Walnut: This is a medium-cost gunstock wood that usually boasts a distinctive and beautiful swirl or flame pattern in dark brown and yellow shades. It is not as dense as black walnut, nor as strong or as easily checkered. However, the way stock blanks are cut and how the grain and figure are positioned within the blank have more to do with the strength of a gunstock than the type of wood used. Claro is generally darker in color than eastern black walnut.

Bastogne Walnut: This type of walnut is a cross between English and California Claro walnut. The wood is exceptionally strong and firm, equal, in this respect, to the best English, French, etc. The figure in the wood, which is predominately fiddleback, is very much like the best of Claro, but the color is more like the English walnut.

English Walnut: Although English walnut trees grow worldwide, only a small amount of wood is produced in England. Demand from British gun makers is so high that only substandard reject blanks, with few exceptions, ever find their way across the Atlantic to the United States.

English walnut trees grow in the United States and in Europe, where varying climates produce woods of different characteristics.

(Juglans Regia) commonly known as French, English, European, or Circassian walnut, depending on where it is grown, is one of the very finest woods for gunstocks. The good grade of French walnut is hard, strong and uniformly dense, with small pores. It will take a very fine checkering with sharp diamonds. It is ideal for precise inletting and fine ornamental carving. The good grades with small pores can be finished without using any special filler. The more desirable pieces have contrasting light and dark grain, and sometimes very dark watermark type irregular smoky lines and streaks that give a mellow marbled appearance.

Circassian Walnut: This wood is native to the Caucasus Mountains of southeastern Asia, where the arid heights and mineral content of the soil contribute to the finest stock wood obtainable anywhere. Today, Circassian walnut is seldom available to the Western world. A true Circassian stock is characterized by vivid rose to red to orange splotches which contrast sharply with the basic wood color. The term "Circassian" is often and incorrectly used to describe any exceptionally beautiful, highly figured wood. If you see "Circassian" gunstock wood offered or advertised, chances are they are offering high-grade French or German walnut instead.

Turkish Walnut: This wood is about as close to honest Circassian as you'll ever see, as the growing locale is close to the Caucasus Mountains. Turkish walnut is exceedingly dense, takes checkering well, and the straight grain precludes warping. There are three basic types:

- The first is characterized by a fine grain and a rather undistinguished gray color which nevertheless produces near-ultimate accuracy.

- The second type has the same close grain, but the grain stands out in deep shades of honey or gold, with stripes about $\frac{1}{8}$ inch wide.

- The third type is highly prized, with the wood so dark brown as to appear almost black, and with distinctive burls and color swirls.

Turkish walnut is expensive, hard to find, and a connoisseur's prize. Its weight ranges from 40 to 45 pounds per cubic foot.

French Walnut: This type of walnut is highly prized, and with good reason. It is highly figured and its close grain accepts checkering well. French walnut is rated at a density of about 37 to 40 pounds per cubic foot. There are two distinctive types:

- One is from inland France and has a striking and broad grain with strong brown and gold tints — similar to

Turkish walnut. It is, however, considerably lighter in color and weight.

- The second, and more common type grows near the German and Swiss borders. This wood often has a vivid cloud effect, as if a bottle of ink had been spilled on the surface of the wood.

Some types of French walnut have a bird's eye effect, resembling maple. Actually, you can find almost any grain effect, including ribbon and fiddleback. The grain color ranges from medium brown to rich chocolate.

Italian Walnut: So many shotguns are manufactured in Italy that nearly all Italian walnut is used domestically. The basic characteristics are close grain and good color — quite similar to German and French walnuts — although the color is usually darker and the grain and figure show less contrast.

Spanish Walnut: This wood has become familiar to Americans through the many Spanish shotguns imported into the United States in recent years. Due to varied climate and growing conditions, color and figure differ greatly. However, Spanish walnut is generally more open-grained and of lighter color than either the French or German woods. Little is available for export from Spain.

Czechoslovakian Walnut: The are two distinct variations:

- One type is dark and is quite similar to German walnut.

- The other is of a very light color, straight-grained, and with little figure.

Both types weigh about the same — about 35 pounds per cubic foot. While adequate for stock-making, this type of walnut does not have the inherent beauty of the other walnuts.

Yugoslavian Walnut: In recent years some fine walnut has been brought into the United States from

Yugoslavia. This is exceptionally fine quality wood, of dense grain and considerable figure, weighing over 40 pounds per cubic foot. Most of this walnut is of a rich, medium-chocolate shade with darker and contrasting streaks.

Scandinavian Walnut: The most common type of Scandinavian walnut is the very light-colored walnut used by Sako of Finland. Sometimes this wood has very wide and contrasting bands, making an extremely attractive stock. At other times it is as bland as white pine.

Mahogany: Mahogany is lighter than walnut, is usually softer, and is subject to dents except in the crotch and high figured areas. Most varieties finish well in a reddish cast and are readily checkered and carved.

Philippine mahogany is very soft, light, and porous, and should not be considered for stock wood. It is unsuitable for even cheap furniture.

Apple Wood: This makes a very attractive stock. It is close-grained and finishes and accepts checkering well. The color is pale red. Apple is much harder to work than walnut, and will quickly dull gouges and chisels. Unless a customer specifies this wood or perhaps has a blank, walnut is a better choice, considering the working time required.

Pear Wood: This wood is similar to apple, but usually finishes in an attractive yellowish color, and is normally slightly softer and a bit easier to work. Pear accepts checkering well and has adequate strength for most rifle stocks. None of the fruit woods should be used for magnum calibers.

Wild Cherry: This is a traditional stock wood dating back to the early settlers. It is quite common in the central states where it is prized as a cabinet wood. Domestic cherry trees do not produce as good quality stocks as the more hardy wild variety. The latter is an excellent and strong substitute for walnut, although its rather bland brown color provides little in the way of contrast. Close-grained, like all fruit woods, wild cherry finishes and check-

ers well, and is only a bit slower to work than walnut.

Myrtle wood: This is an exceptionally beautiful brown-toned wood which varies widely in shade and contrast. The figure is often extravagant, and the wood is easy to finish, carve and checker. Myrtle is prone to soft spots and tends to be more brittle than walnut. It should not be used for magnum-caliber rifles nor for shotguns stocks where a little wood has to provide a lot of strength — as around sidelock shotgun actions.

Maple: This is another wood used in early days on Kentucky rifles. The grain is often distinctive, including bird's eye, fiddle, and ribbon figures. Close-grained, it finishes and checkers well. The weight is close to, but a bit lighter than, black walnut. Maple is quite strong and makes a fine stock that is sometimes a bit garish, except for traditional arms. The best-quality maple comes from the eastern states.

Screwbean Mesquite: This wood, in many respects, is one of our most beautiful stock woods, due to the profusion of curls, knots, twists, and whorls. Few mesquite trees are large enough for one-piece stock blanks and the supply is limited — making this type wood quite expensive. Mesquite is much heavier than walnut and also much stronger. It is difficult to work and dull tools tend to shred the wood, similar to a draw knife or plane. Therefore, these types of tools should be avoided when working with mesquite wood. Instead, depend upon the use of rasps. Mesquite is often riffled with holes and flaws which do not weaken the wood, but do require expert inlay of matching wood. Colors can range from yellow to brown to near black, and all on one stock blank.

Do not select this wood for your first stock. Mesquite requires extra skill, time and patience, but does make one of the most exotic-looking stocks imaginable, as can be seen on the fancier Weatherby rifles. It checkers readily, but all cutting operations should be performed with care and with very sharp tools.

Figure 18-7: Screwbean mesquite, so called because of the tightly curled beanpod, has a distinct, handsome, and bold beauty that complements modern gunstock designs. It is a strong, stable wood that makes a fine gunstock.

Flat-Pod Mesquite: This variety of mesquite comes from the southwestern states and from Mexico. It has a much plainer figure and color contrast than the screwbean variety. Flat-pod mesquite is also very tough to work, but with fewer flaws, knots, etc. that require filling and inlays. The color ranges from pale red to medium brown, with little contrast in the grain.

Madrona: This tree grows along the Pacific Coast. It is a very strong, close-grained wood of a lighter reddish color than walnut, but of the same relative weight. Many blanks contain a very attractive burl figure.

Beech: Often used in Europe for military and commercial stocks, beech is an extremely sturdy wood suitable for utility-type stocks. The color is pale yellow or tan, without contrasting grain. It is now being used by some American gun manufacturers for cheaper-grade arms — notably rimfire .22 caliber rifles.

Sycamore: This is a common American wood that serves well for utility-type stocks or "working guns" which are subject to a lot of abuse and exposure. The lumber industry is pushing sycamore as a walnut substitute. The wood is light in color, accepts staining well, and takes an excellent finish. It lends itself to medium-fine checkering and is quite strong. Sycamore often shows a "lace effect" grain that is very attractive.

Miscellaneous Woods: The common dogwood makes an excellent gunstock, but works badly due to the smallness of the tree. Holly is another good wood, but presents the same objection as dogwood. Cherry and apple woods are hard to beat. Birch is used — even today — for cheap guns, stained to imitate either walnut or cherry. It has fine grain, and works very well, *but it is sometimes inclined to warp.*

Laminated Stocks: By epoxying thin layers of stock wood together and alternating grain direction, a gunstock blank can be built up that is extremely strong, virtually waterproof, and free from potential warpage. Such laminated stocks are commonly used for benchrest and varmint rifles. Contrasting woods can be used to make attractive color combinations such as walnut with maple, or cherry with maple. One striking combination is made up of $1/16$ inch maple and $1/28$ inch walnut alternate lamination. It is probably the most stable wood combination that can be used in a gunstock.

Laminated walnut is made of $5/16$ inch walnut horizontal strips. These thin, narrow pieces with very little remaining stress and tensions coordinated into one solid block result in a most stable gunstock.

Laminated blanks for sporter and varminter style stocks will incorporate a slight bend in the laminations to simulate ideal grain structure. This lends a

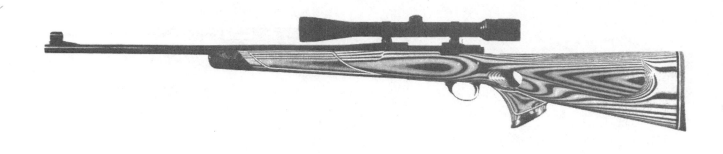

Figure 18-8: A laminated thumbhole varmint stock made from walnut and maple.

graceful appearance as well as adds strength to the toe area.

Laminated blanks constructed for competition type stocks will be straight, parallel laminations to follow the lines of this style stock parallel with the bore of the rifle.

Forend Tips

There is a wide variety of exotic and colorful woods suitable for rifle forend tips and pistol grip caps. Most woods used for these purposes are grown in tropical or semi-tropical climes. With few exceptions, these woods are too heavy and dense to serve as stock wood. Some are so close-grained that they can be polished to a high luster using only elbow grease. Some of the more common types follow:

Rosewood: Brazilian rosewood is undoubtedly the most popular wood for forend tips. It has a beautiful grain and color ranging from dark red, with lighter stripes, to a deep brown with near black stripes. Indian rosewood is not as popular and is a purplish shade with dark streaks or a cloud effect. Both provide a distinct contrast to even dark walnut, which, of course, is essential in a forend tip.

Brazilian Ironwood: This is an extremely hard wood, usually with a distinct and even reddish to orange color. It is most often paired with light or medium-brown stock wood.

Cocobolo: This wood is quite similar in color to Brazilian ironwood, but is usually a deeper red with lighter contrasting streaks. Cocobolo is very popular for pistol grips and is considerably harder than rose wood.

Lignum Vitae: This so-called "tree-of-life" is sometimes used for forend tips, as the dark greenish wood adds a distinctive contrast to light-colored stocks. It is most often combined with maple. Lignum vitae is among the hardest of woods, which probably has something to do with its use by men of some oriental countries. The wood is considered an aid to sexual prowess when ground into a powder and taken internally.

Ebony: This wood has long been the traditional forend tip on English big game rifles, especially when used with ivory spacers and a matching pistol grip cap. Ebony is seldom used now. Unfortunately, the real thing looks like plastic, which is an anathema to the purist. Consequently, black plastic is, in fact, used for many forend tips. Ebony from Africa is solid black in color. Madagascar ebony, once considered to be inferior, is making a comeback because it doesn't look like plastic. It shows a contrasting gray-streak pattern.

Domestic Woods: Some domestic woods that are extremely light or very dark and figured are often used for forend tips, pistol-grip caps, and inlays. For example, a dark, fancy-figured piece of walnut, when inlaid into a light maple or apple wood stock provides a pleasing contrast. Holly and persimmon, which are nearly white in color, are excellent for diamond inlays or for contrasting tips and grips on dark walnut stocks.

Ivory: This now rare and expensive (and illegal) material was commonly used for firearm decoration back to the time of the earliest matchlock. Even in recent times, occasional tips and caps of ivory, as well as bird and animal inlays appear on presentation-grade rifles and shotguns. Ivory is grained like wood and tends to split or show cracks, particularly if any strain occurs such as might be caused by overly tight screws.

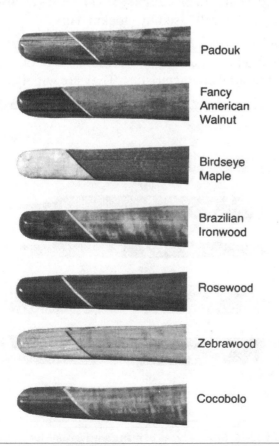

Padouk

Fancy American Walnut

Birdseye Maple

Brazilian Ironwood

Rosewood

Zebrawood

Cocobolo

Figure 18-9. Several types of forend woods installed on walnut and maple gunstocks.

Summary

The wood for gunstocks should combine strength and lightness, and at the same time be easy to work. The fibers should be very close and not inclined to split easily.

In the United States, black walnut is the type most often selected for modern firearms, followed by hard maple. However, Bastogne and French walnut seem to be the favorites of custom stockers as these types of walnut are denser in grain than black walnut and therefore will take a finer checkering pattern (more lines to the inch). Regardless of the type used, the grain of the wood should be straight at the small of the stock, which is the weakest portion. Between the grip area and the butt it makes little difference how the grain runs as the wood in this area is easily worked and there is plenty of thickness for strength.

Around the grip, due to the smallness, it is very important to make certain the grain is straight and runs in the direction of the shape given, and also continue straight until somewhat past the area where the receiver is set into the stock.

The best and most serviceable stocks are those made from parts of the tree where large branches join the trunk. In these parts, also, will be found the curled and irregular grain that is so much admired when the stock is so made that these irregularities come in the stock a little in front of the buttplate.

When large trees are cut down, it will be evident that portions of the stump have a sort of convex form which extends downward and terminates in the large roots. If these can be dug up and separated from the stump by splitting them, they are almost always of a proper shape to have the grain run nearly straight in the curves of a conventional rifle stock. Portions of some root pieces have a mottled appearance and are of a different color from the wood as cut from the trunk of the tree; this is especially true in black walnut.

Why Walnut is Best

Walnut is an acceptable and widely-used wood for gunstocks because it meets the requirements better than other woods. Gunstock wood must be workable. It has to be shaped on the outside. It must also be inletted; that is, metal has to be let into the wood so that the wood covers at least half of the exposed metal of the firearm. Gunstock wood must be hard so it will not easily dent, mar, or compress from recoil. It must also take checkering, which enables the shooter to grip the firearm securely, *and* must contribute to the appearance of the gun. Also, it must be a stable wood — not warping, expanding, or contracting to any great extent.

Walnut fills all of these requirements exceedingly well. Some other woods, however, do the same thing. Maple, for instance, is an extremely hard, very dense wood which has good wearing and inletting qualities and is rather pleasing to the eye. For those stockmakers desiring or liking a blonde gunstock, maple is a good choice. However, most stockmakers in the United States prefer the soft, mellow tones of good walnut, and this trend will remain for many years to come.

WOODWORKING TOOLS

Although many gunstocks have been built using only the minimum amount of tools, a better job can be had with the proper tools in hand.

Wood Rasps: The rasp resembles a conventional metal file at first glance, but differs from both the single and double cuts of files in the respect that the teeth are individually formed and disconnected from each other. In general, the rasp cut is a series of individual teeth produced by a sharp, narrow, punch-like cutting chisel as shown in Figure 18-10. It is an extremely rough cut and is used principally on wood, leather, lead, and similarly soft substances for fast removal of material.

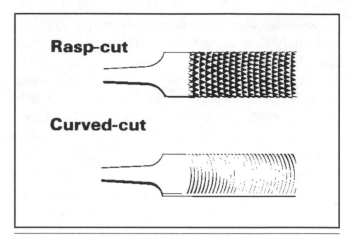

Figure 18-10: Rasps with different types of teeth.

In the half-round wood rasps, the curved side is similar to that of the half-round metal file, but in the cabinet, the pattern makers and last makers rasps, the radius is larger. Rasps are also made in flat and round shapes. Figure 18-11 shows a variety of rasps currently used by stockmakers.

Curved Tooth Files: These files cover a distinct filing field and have a considerable range of shape and structural characteristics. They are widely used

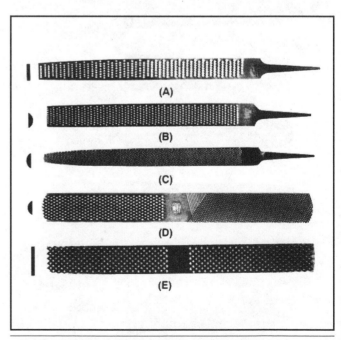

Figure 18-11: Several types of rasps are available for gunstock work. The more common rasps include the (A) wood rasp, (B) cabinet rasp, (C) patternmaker's, (D) 4-in-hand rasp, and (E) horse rasp.

in stock work for rough shaping stocks and any-thing in between to final contouring of combs, grip areas, and the like. For final finish work, the weight of the file alone will make "sawdust" cuts and leaves wood so smooth that fine sanding is usually all that will be necessary.

Cabinet Rasps: This type of rasp is used by cabinetmakers and woodworkers of all types and is available in flat, half-round, and round shapes. The cabinet rasp has a finer degree of coarseness than conventional wood rasps.

Horse Rasps: Made in two different types — plain and tanged. Plain horse rasps are double-ended and have rasp teeth on one side and file teeth on the other. They are made in regular, slim, and a pattern called the 18-inch plater's double-ended horse rasp. Tanged horse rasps are the same as plain horse rasps in tooth construction, with rasp teeth on one side and file teeth on the other and are single-cut on the edges.

Plater's special horse rasps have rasp teeth on one side with file teeth on the opposite side. Both sides are safe (no teeth) $7/8$ inch at point. The rasp cut is six teeth per row while all other horse rasps have five teeth per row.

Nicholson's Magicut plater's special horse rasp is cut deeper to last longer and work much faster than conventional horse rasps. Rasp cut is six teeth per row and single-cut on edges. The opposite side has a unique pattern of narrow chip breakers cre-ated by steep and angled serrations. This maximum cutting surface design gives rapid removal and smoother finish.

While horse rasps are designed primarily for farriers for shoeing horses at race tracks and riding stables, these thin, fine-toothed rasps are excellent for use on gunstocks also.

Pattern Maker's Rasps: Also called "last maker's cabinet rasps," this type of rasp is used where a smooth wood finish is required.

4-in-Hand Rasp File: This versatile tool is really four files in one, with a file section and a rasp

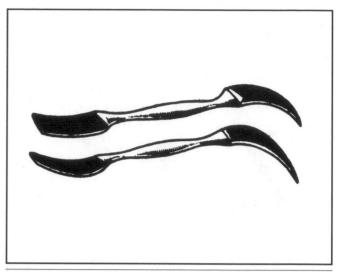

Figure 18-12: A variety of double-end rasps are available and are widely used by stockmakers.

section on the flat side and a file section and a rasp section on the half-round side. Everyone who works on gunstocks should have one.

Round Bastard Wood Rasps: This type of rasp is used for the same general purpose as regular wood rasps in places where their shapes make them par-ticularly effective.

Wood Rasps: Wood rasps in flat and half-round bastard are used by woodworkers of all types for removing wood quickly.

Double-End Rasps: Double-end rasps are excel-lent for fast cutting of wood during inletting, shap-ing, and relieving wood from the stock for sights and bolt knobs. Several shapes are available to suit practically any application.

Bull Foot Bottoming Rasps: Brownells Inc. lists several shapes of bottoming rasps especially de-signed for the stockmaker. They are for use in those hard-to-get-at bottoming cuts, where only a bull foot will ever reach.

Wood Files: Wood files are made in the same sections and size as half-round metal files except that wood files have especially coarse teeth, fitting them for use on wood. In general, they cut more smoothly than rasps.

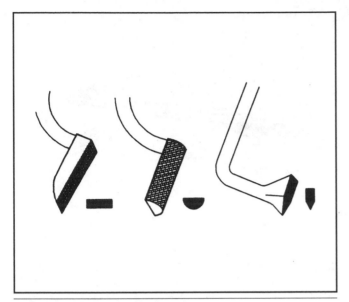

Figure 18-13: Three types of bull foot bottoming rasps.

Rotary Files and Burrs

The tremendous growth of portable electric power tools, such as the Dremel Moto-Tool, has developed a widespread use for rotating-type files and burrs. They are also operated in lathes and drill presses and through variously driven flexible shafts. This versatility in application, plus their wide range of head shapes and sizes, makes them invaluable on thousands of jobs in gunshops. They are especially suited for inletting gunstocks.

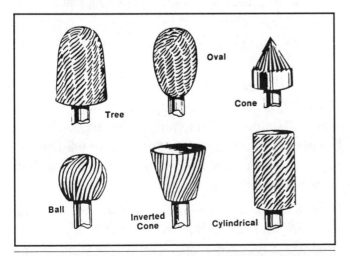

Figure 18-14: There is a style of rotary file and burr for every purpose.

Rotary files and rotary burrs are generally made from high-speed steel. Rotary burrs are also made of carbide, and though more brittle, these have up to one hundred times the serviceable cutting life of high-speed steel.

Cutting heads, in both file and burr types, are of many shapes, as can be seen in Figure 18-14. Cylindrical (with both flat and radius ends), ball, barrel, oval, tree, flame, cone, inverted cone, concave, in various angles, tapers or arcs, are the most common. Head diameters vary from $\frac{1}{8}$ inch to $1\frac{1}{4}$ inches; and shanks are usually of $\frac{1}{4}$ inch and $\frac{1}{8}$ inch diameters.

For highest efficiency and longest life, rotary files and burs should be operated at designated speeds based on their head diameters and the type of material being worked. The manufacturer's speed table and rules of usage should be closely observed.

Hand Cut Files: These are cut by an expert hand cutter, and their teeth are irregular. As a result, they work better on hard and dense metals and are recommended for use on die steel, cast iron, welds, and forgings. This type of rotary file is more often used on stock furniture than the stock itself, but it does have certain stock applications as well. When dull, hand cut rotary files may be resharpened. They are furnished in a full range of standard shapes in standard (medium), coarse, and fine cut.

Ground-from-Solid-Files: These are precision ground by a skilled operator; after hardening, this type of file has less tendency to clog. It is, therefore, more efficient for use on aluminum, brass, bronze, magnesium, and plastics as well as soft steel. When dull, this type of file can be resharpened by regrinding. They are furnished in a wide range of standard shapes in standard (medium), coarse, and fine cut.

Solid Carbide: Properly used, solid carbide burs will outperform other types by as much as 50 to 1 and generally cut twice as fast. A wide variety of shapes is available in standard and coarse. Standard cut is favored for general-purpose use on ferrous materials. Coarse cut is recommended for nonferrous and plastic materials.

Choice of cut or fluting depends on the material to be worked on, finish required, and type of equipment. Standard cut is most commonly used for general-purpose work of ferrous metals. Coarse cut is recommended for soft materials. These are available with several shank diameters. Standard $\frac{1}{8}$ inch and $\frac{1}{4}$ inch shanks are used with die grinders and straight grinders.

Miscellaneous Woodworking Tools

Spokeshave: The spokeshave is the universal tool for working down stock blanks after the heavy rasping is done and before final sanding operations are started. Scrapers are also used for this operation in stock shaping — either sharpened metal or a piece of broken glass. (With the latter, be extremely careful not to cut yourself. Always wear heavy leather gloves.)

The spokeshave is used much like a wood plane except that the spokeshave permits better control of the cut and can get in those tight corners where a plane cannot. There are several brands on the market; any made in the United States can be highly recommended, such as those manufactured by Stanley Tools. Some cheap imports have appeared on the market in recent years for sale at dime stores and discount houses; these should be avoided for any type of stock work.

Draw Knife: For quick removal of wood in rough shaping, the draw knife might find use in the stock-maker's shop. However, it takes quite a bit of practice to use these tools without removing more wood — in the wrong places — than wanted. If care is not used, it's quite possible to take a cut and find you've ripped out an inch or two of precious walnut — ruining the entire job.

There are scores of special inletting tools on the market to help the budding stockmaker do a good job the first time around. In fact, you'll probably have a hard time deciding which ones to buy. For

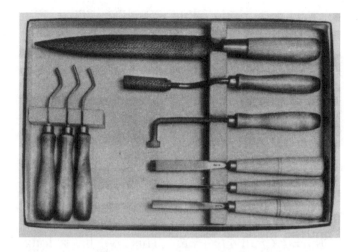

Figure 18-15: Mittermeier stockmaking kit.

openers, one complete stockmaking set is available from Frank Mittermeier, Inc. 3577 East Tremont Ave., Bronx, NY 10465. This set consists of one 8 inch smooth-cut cabinet rasp for shaping and smooth-finishing the stock, a chisel and two gouges to cut away excess wood, a bottoming file for flat bedding of the action, a barrel inletting rasp to shape the barrel channel to the exact dimensions of the barrel, sandpaper for a smooth exterior of the stock, checkering tools, diamond-shaped layout template for checkering, and full instructions on the whole procedure of inletting, shaping, finishing, and checkering of the gunstock. You will need some additional tools and supplies, but this set is a good place to start.

A Dremel Moto-Tool is also nice to have; not only for stock work, but for almost every other phase of gunsmithing. But know how to use it and be extremely careful as the project nears the completion point. The rotary rasp and burs have a tendency to "walk" and remove wood that can only be "replaced" by filling with epoxy or other wood filler. Be sure to get plenty of practice with this tool on scrap wood before using it on a good piece of walnut.

You'll also want a sharp bench knife, a scorer, a try square, a good, solid workbench, and a solid bench vise with padded jaws. Sharpening equipment is necessary, since all cutting tools must be kept sharp at all times. A little bottle of inletting black — either the commercial version or a homespun type — is essential for "seeing" the high spots in the wood.

As you progress in gunsmithing projects, there will be other helpful tools that will be added to this list to speed up the stock inletting procedure. A brief description of some of these follows:

Barrel Channel Group: This tool has a long, precision-ground parallel blade for eliminating humps and bumps in the wood barrel channel. The full-length tool-to-wood bearing surface gives plane-like finishes and its cutting edge is beveled to the inside so it will cut when held flat in the channel.

Brownells Curl Scrapers: Brownells, Inc., Route 2, Box 1, Montezuma, IA 50171 offers a set of curved and straight curl scrapers that are highly recommended for inletting work. You'll eventually find that final hand fitting is one of the real chores of inletting because you must be able to remove the tiniest possible curl of wood to get that exact fit that distinguishes a professional job from one that is so-so. You'll want the complete set of six.

Barrel Bedding Tools: There's a large array of these available to the stockmaker so you should read about each in Brownells tool catalog, and decide which ones you should purchase. In general, all are designed to shave out excess wood from the barrel channel without gouging, rasping, or final sanding. One handy tool is the Gunline barrel bedding tool which is available in four diameters: $9/16$, $5/8$, $11/16$ and $3/4$ inch.

The methods of using the tools described in this chapter are described in appropriate sections throughout the chapter to follow on stockmaking.

Wood Carving Tools

It doesn't take long to go through a small fortune when you start buying wood carving tools, so you must be selective. Wood carving tools are readily available from both Brownells and Frank Mittermeier, Inc. The chart in Figure 18-16 shows the sizes and sweeps (cutting edge) of professional carving tools in actual size. The tool's width is in mm (millimeters) and to the right of these measurements are illustrated and numbered the obtained tool forms for the sweep; that is, straight, long, bent, spoon and back bend.

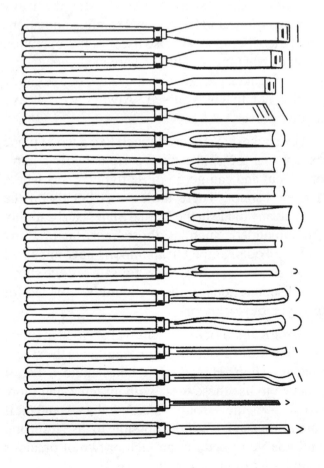

Figure 18-16: Sizing and sweeps of typical wood carving tools.

Methods of using carving tools number nearly as many as the different kinds of tools available. After some experience, however, you will learn to manipulate each tool so as to accurately remove a desired portion of wood.

Wood carving tools are used in two different ways. One is to hold the tool in one hand and then push it along with the other hand or tap it lightly with a mallet. This method is known as chase carving, which is nothing more than moving the tool along with a series of light, fast taps with a wooden mallet.

The second method is to hold the carving tools in your right hand, using the engraver's hold. To do this, grasp the tool about two inches from the cutting end with four fingers wrapped around the tool. Then lay your thumb along the side of the tool about one inch from the cutting edge. This hold gives maximum grip and lets you use the full strength of your hand and wrist for the carving motion. Your left hand can be used for a stop for your right hand, but be very careful not to let it slip and cut your hand.

SHAPING AND INLETTING GUNSTOCKS

Shaping and inletting a gunstock from a slab of walnut or other hardwood is no easy task. In fact, many beginners who attempt such a project find their half-finished blanks ending up as expensive kindling. Even professional stockmakers who have successfully completed dozens of gunstocks from wood blanks find it more convenient to purchase semifinished stocks and complete the job from that point.

As in other types of gun work, the shaping of a gunstock requires patience and attention to detail. You must also have an idea of what you are striving for; that is, the traits that distinguish a fine stock from a run-of-the-mill factory job.

In general, manufacturers of semifinished gunstocks will offer their products in two ways:

- With only the action inletted and with a standard $\frac{1}{2}$ inch barrel channel that has to be shaped and inletted to fit the barrel attached to the receiver.

- With the barrel channel and receiver completely inletted.

In either case, some inletting will be required, but even the beginner can achieve professional results if the project is approached with care and knowledge.

Tools

Constant fitting of the metal parts to the wood with slow and careful removal of the excess wood will achieve the results desired. Inletting black is applied to the action, which is fitted into the semifinished stock and then removed. This black will then indicate on the stock just what metal parts are touching, leaving a map, so to speak, of where the excess wood must be removed. If you cannot find any inletting black at a local gunshop, you can make your own by mixing lampblack oil paint with petroleum jelly.

As the job progresses you will find a need for certain special tools. The barrel inletting tool will be used to clean out the barrel channel (Figure 18-17 on the next page). High bumps can be removed with chisels and gouges. Final touch-up and cleaning can be accomplished with a bottoming file. A word of caution: remove a little wood at a time. Remember, once the wood is gone, it cannot be replaced. Once you have a few projects under your belt you can proceed with more deliberation, but at first, remember to go slow.

Yes, even the rankest beginner can turn out a reasonably good stocking job with semifinished blanks, but the work is not easy. You can figure on spending at least 40 hours of your time, and maybe even more. If you include checkering and carving,

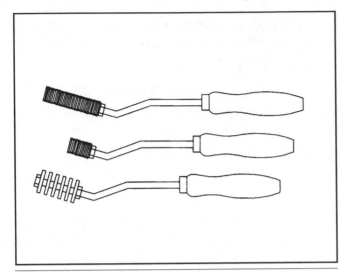

Figure 18-17: Barrel-channeling tools are necessary in inletting a semifinished stock; few channels are cut to the correct size.

add an additional 8 to 16 hours before the stock is ready to be permanently attached to your barrel and action. Once experience has been gained — say, a dozen or more such projects completed — the work will go smoother and faster, enabling you to turn out a completed project (less the time required for the wood finish to dry) in only a couple of days.

Getting Started

The starting procedure will vary depending on the type of rifle or shotgun being stocked. In the case of most bolt-action rifles with trigger guards and floorplate assemblies, the trigger guard should be inletted at the start. This must be done with extreme care, making sure to keep the guard screw holes in line with the holes drilled in the semifinished stock. Begin by trying the trigger guard unit in its appropriate place in the semifinished stock. Chances are it will start in, but will meet with wood resistance that prevents it from fitting as it should. If so, inletting black should be applied sparingly to the metal surfaces that come in contact with the wood, and the guard replaced as far as it will go and then removed again. The inletting black will indicate the areas where wood must be removed — in

small amounts — before the guard is retried for fit. Perhaps as many as 20 tries will be required before the floorplate/trigger guard assembly (and the box magazine on some rifles) fits exactly in its proper location. The fit should be *exact* (see Figure 18-18). Of course, it's easier to take out a little more wood than necessary to enable the metal parts to fit into their recesses, but this makes for poor fit and is entirely unsatisfactory.

During this initial inletting of the trigger guard assembly, you should learn the "feel" of the metal units as you remove minute amounts of wood and retry them for fit. It is important to keep the trigger guard/magazine box unit straight, level, and in exact line. Canting or tipping the unit will give the inletting black markings a false reading, which can cause you to remove wood in the wrong places.

At this stage of the game, the bottoming tool should not be used on any bottom surfaces of the trigger guard/floorplate mortise. Rather, as soon as you get a "reading" on the bottom of the semi-inletted cut via the inletting black, stop inletting work in this area for the time being.

Using Guide Screws

It is now time to turn your attention to the receiver. Although not absolutely necessary, it is best to inlet the receiver separately without the barrel attached. However, if this is impractical or inconvenient, the barrel and receiver can be inletted as a unit. In either case, you should use gunstocker's guide screws that fit the guard screw holes in the semifinished stock. These will enable you to line up the receiver and trigger guard assembly perfectly.

Guide screws can be made on a metal-turning lathe or they can be purchased from gunsmith supply houses already made for certain actions. For example, Forster Products (82 E. Lanard Ave., Lanark, IL 61046) offers stock inletting guide screws for Enfield, Japanese 6.5mm, Japanese 7.7mm, Krag, Mauser, Remington 721-722, Sako,

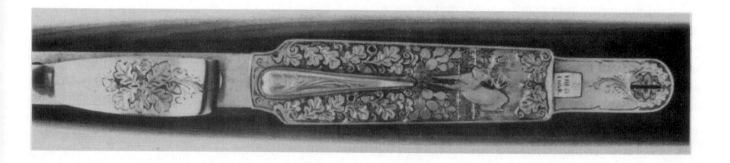

Figure 18-18: The floorplate must be inletted perfectly, with no gaps between the metal and the wood. The arcs, or curved areas, will be the most difficult to fit.

Springfield and Winchester Model 70 receivers. These screws are headless, clear of threads in the fitting area, and are absolutely necessary for fitting and inletting either semifinished or "made-from scratch" stock blanks.

Stockmakers' T-handle hand screws (Figure 18-19) are also available from Forster Products, but these should not be used during the initial inletting; they can be twisted too tightly, which might result in splitting the stock. Also, excessive tightness can give false inletting readings — resulting in too much wood being removed or wood being removed in the wrong place. Use the headless inletting guide screws at first, and make sure to bring the receiver screw holes in exact line with the ones in the trigger guard/floorplate holes.

Later, during the final accurate fitting of the stock to the receiver, you will want to use the T-handle hand screws. These are precision-made and hardened for repeated trial fittings, and will help you avoid damaging the original guard screws or ruining the stock. They will also save much time in the final fitting of a semifinished gunstock. They are available in eight different models to fit the receivers mentioned previously as well as the Savage Model 110.

In inletting the receiver do not necessarily remove wood from every place indicated by the inletting black. Inletting black is messy stuff and

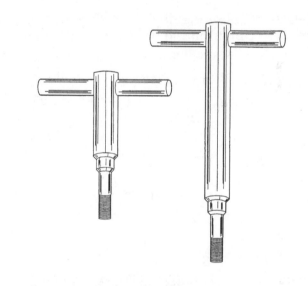

Figure 18-19: Stockmaker's T-handle hand screws are available from Forster products. These, along with inletting guide screws, are absolutely necessary for properly aligning the action to the stock blank during inletting.

has a tendency to smear on places where it shouldn't. While inserting the receiver in the semifinished stock, carefully observe it from every angle to ascertain that it is not canted or brought down out of line with the trigger guard section of the rifle. Then remove wood first only where there is a definite pressure contact made during a true alignment. Use a hard rubber (or leather) mallet to gently bump the receiver downward, at the same time making sure that the guide screws point straight down through the center of the trigger guard unit without binding. If the guard was inletted correctly, it should fit snugly and remain in place, but to make certain that it doesn't fall out, you might want to tape it with masking tape. Make sure it fits snugly against the bottom of the mortise before taking readings from the receiver above.

Inletting black is applied, and the receiver is tried and retried, removing small amounts of wood each time at pressure points. However, make certain that no wood is removed from the bottom surfaces of the mortise until the receiver ring flat and the under flat of the receiver tang have made even contact with the wood. The T-handle screws will come in handy here, as you approach bottoming, but be extremely careful not to tighten them too much. Also avoid false readings.

Now carefully observe the edges and sides of the inletted opening, looking for pressure points that should be relieved by scraping, cutting, filing, or rasping a little at a time until a perfect fit is obtained. Do not jump right in and start removing wood as soon as you notice the black contact marks. Rather, take the time to evaluate each and every one first. You might as well start striving for perfection at the outset.

You are looking for a perfect metal-to-wood fit of the receiver and trigger guard unit at this point. No visible gaps should be seen between the metal and the wood. You may not have the wood flush with the metal surfaces at this point, but this will be taken care of during the finishing of the outside surfaces of the stock. In no case, however, should the metal protrude above the wood surfaces; it should be recessed into the wood. The exact depth will vary according to the amount of excess wood left on the semifinished stock during its shaping and the type of firearm being stocked.

You must also consider the inletting of miscellaneous stock furniture such as buttplates, decorative forend tip, and the like. However, these items should be last to be inletted, after the final shaping of the gunstock.

Barrel Channel

If you removed the barrel from the receiver before inletting the receiver, the barrel must now be reinstalled and the action again inserted into the semifinished stock to open up the barrel channel. This portion of the project should give you fewer conflicting inletting black readings than were encountered during the inletting of the action. Otherwise, the procedures are the same: Apply inletting black to the underside of the barrel, set it in place, remove, notice areas of black marks, and remove them with the proper tools. The round barrel channel rasp will be most helpful at this point.

On the other hand, if the barrel was left attached to the receiver, then the barrel channel will have to be inletted at the same time that the receiver is inletted. Just be sure to keep the assembly level during this operation and you should experience little difficulty. It's just a matter of applying inletting black to both the receiver and barrel pressure points, observing the black marks, evaluating each one, and then removing small amounts of wood from the appropriate locations until a perfect fit is obtained. Again, strive for perfection.

During the final stages of fitting and inletting, you should get in the habit of being more and more careful as you remove wood. Remember, none can be replaced. However, if you do goof — say, on the bottom of the receiver mortise — glass bedding can be used to fill in some gaps. This bedding compound may also be used elsewhere, but it will be noticeable and reveal that an amateur has tackled the job. As you approach the final fitting, the top of the magazine box should either meet the bottom of the receiver or clear it by not more than .010 inch when the guard screws are cinched up firmly and there is full tension against the top of the stock's recoil lug by the receiver ring flat. The same should apply for the wood surfaces on which the guard screws pull the fore and aft ends of the trigger guard/floorplate assembly unit.

Figure 18-20: You must also inlet any flush-mounted stock furniture like this fancy combination forend tip and sling swivel.

BEDDING GUNSTOCKS

Bedding, as applied to gunstocks, refers to the methods used to mate the metal (barrel and action) to the wood. There are three basic types of bedding in common use. The barrel can bed fully or partially against the barrel channel in the stock, or in an epoxy liner known as *glass bedding*. It can also free-float with a pressure point at the forend tip. This pressure point is often adjustable in order to vary the amount of pressure applied at various points.

There has been much controversy over which method is best; it all boils down to what purpose the rifle is to serve. Alvin Linden, for example, swore by an exact metal-to-wood contact the full length of the barrel channel for use on hunting rifles; Arthur Cook liked free-floating barrels with adjustable pressure points near the forend for his match shooting. Many shooters today will not own a rifle that is not glass bedded.

The bedding of the barrel and receiver is all-important to ensure good accuracy and prevent damage to the stock under the rifle recoil. The methods used, however, vary from stockmaker to stockmaker or from shooter to shooter. Some want a free-floating barrel; others want an even pressure from receiver to end of forend, while others want pressure points only at the end of the forend. No recommendations are given here; use whichever system works best for you. In most cases, however, gunsmiths prefer a perfect metal-to-wood fit the entire length of the stock. Sure, weather conditions and moisture content in the air can change the point of bullet impact on the target, but so can these same conditions with a free-floating barrel. Again, the method is left entirely up to the shooter.

The main point of concern, regardless of which bedding method is used, is to avoid excessive tension or pressure at any point. If the receiver is pulled down into the stock in a twisted or binded tension, trouble will develop. The same is true if the barrel is pulled down into a very tight barrel channel in the stock. You want to strive for an even tension overall, as uneven tension will vary the point of bullet impact more so, during changes in humidity, than will even pressure. The point of impact can also be affected with a change in temperature or even by the natural tendency of the stock wood to shift or warp.

Of the types of bedding mentioned so far, the glass bedding method is probably the best to start with. First of all, you don't have to be as exact with the inletting procedure as with other types of bedding, and if the manufacturer's instructions are followed to the letter, even the rankest amateur should have good results.

Glass Bedding

Brownells Inc. offers two types of glass bedding kits, both of which have given good results. One type works into a mixture about the consistency of molasses while the other is a buttery smooth cream that will not drip or run as it is being applied. Acraglas (Figure 18-21) is the name of the thinner product, while Acraglas Gel is the name given to the thicker one. Both kits are very reasonably priced and should be tried by everyone who works with gunstocks of any type.

To use the kits, measure out the quantities desired according to the instructions accompanying the kits. Before doing so, make sure both the metal and wood are properly prepared to accept the bedding compound.

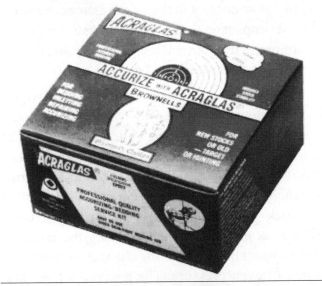

Figure 18-21: Brownells Acraglas bedding kit.

When inletting the stock, allow $\frac{1}{32}$ to $\frac{1}{16}$ inch clearance in the barrel channel and behind the recoil lug. The wood should be left in the rough rather than sanded smoothly — not to increase strength of the Acraglas Gel bond to wood, but to add strength to the wood itself by creating more exposed wood surface.

Some form of release agent must be applied to all metal parts that will come into contact with the bedding compound. If this is not done, you're going to have one solid piece of metal and wood bonded together so tightly that it will probably take a sledge hammer — with heavy blows — to separate them. The release agent that comes with the kit is ideal for this situation. To use, shake the bottle vigorously, and then apply the liquid solution to all metal parts that will come in contact with the bedding compound. When the first coat is dry, apply a second coat to ensure that it reaches all exposed metal surfaces. If any milled-out sections exist in the metal, such as dovetail slots, etc., fill these sections in with putty or modeling clay and then smooth out with a spatula. Finally, cover the clay with waterproof tape and apply the release agent over the tape. Be sure to apply the release agent to all screws. After the release agent dries, apply a thin coat of gun grease or paste wax just to be sure.

When mixing the solution, be sure to measure carefully and follow the instructions closely; a little more or less of one mixture or the other can cause the compound to set up incorrectly. The following instructions accompanies the Brownells' Acraglas Gel kit and are reprinted here with their kind permission.

Acraglas Gel need not all be mixed at one time. Mix only quantity needed. Mixing ratio is 1:1 by volume. Weighing components will give incorrect ratio. Use spoon or other measure which can be easily loaded with Acraglas Gel components. (Note: Tablespoon holds $\frac{1}{2}$ oz. volume. Teaspoon holds $\frac{1}{6}$ oz. volume. One tablespoon equals three teaspoons.) Using clean mixing stick, ladle Acraglas Gel resin into measure until full — being careful to eliminate voids and large air bubbles. Carefully strike off resin with mixing stick to give exact full measure. Wipe stick dry with paper towel, and, using the same end, work all the resin out of your measure into the mixing dish with a careful "peeling" motion. Wipe measure clean with paper towel. Use other end of mixing stick to fill and strike cleaned measure with Acraglas Gel hardener. Wipe mixing stick clean and use it to work all hardener out of measure and into mixing dish.

Thoroughly mix (do not whip) the resin and hardener with measuring stick for two minutes, by your watch. At the end of two minutes of mixing, add dye stain in quantity needed to make Acraglas Gel slightly lighter in color than wood of gunstock. If atomized aluminum or atomized steel particles are to be used, you can add up to a ratio of 1:1 at this time. (One part metal to one part Acraglas Gel by volume. For example, if you have used a tablespoon each of resin and hardener — total of two tablespoons — you can add up to two tablespoons of atomized metal.) Mix thoroughly for two more minutes, for a total of four minutes. *Always mix a total of four minutes* whether or not you are adding stain or atomized metal. Your Acraglas Gel is now ready.

Time/Temperature Note: At 72-75° F., you have approximately 20 minutes working time before your Acraglas Gel becomes too stiff to use and give a suitable bonding between epoxy and wood. At higher room temperatures the stiffening occurs much more rapidly, with proportionate decrease in working time. Working time can be lengthened by setting the mixing dish in a shallow pan of cold water and stirring occasionally.

During wintertime in cold climates, be sure your containers of Acraglas Gel resin and hardener are at least 68° F. before measuring and mixing. This same minimum temperature must be maintained during hardening as well. In warm or hot operating conditions, chill resin and hardener to approximately 76° F. before mixing to prevent too-rapid set up.

For accelerated set up of Acraglas Gel, barrel and wood should be heated until they are quite warm to the hand, which will be about 100 to 120° F.

For rapid setting, use a heat lamp 12 to 18 inches away from area where Acraglas Gel has been applied. *Note:* Remember, adding "extra" hardener *prevents* complete hardening.

To perform the actual bedding operation, first secure the stock in a bench vise with the barrel channel of the stock relatively level. With a mixing stick, spread the prepared Acraglas or Acraglas Gel in a ridge down the center of the barrel channel, which will prevent air from being trapped when the barrel is later set into place. Also fill the recoil lug recess sufficiently to completely fill the recess when the barrel and receiver are fitted. A very thin coat should also be spread around the interior of the receiver recess. When all of these steps have been completed, firmly press the barrel and receiver to the desired depth in the stock. Some stockers prefer bedding the recoil lug and other gaps between the receiver and wood first, and then when thoroughly cured, the bedding compound is applied to the barrel channel and the remaining portions of the receiver area.

When the bedding compound shows signs of taking a firm set — usually five to six hours after application — a dull knife or spatula to remove any surplus compound that is exposed. Wetting the knife or spatula with saliva will speed things up and keep the instrument much cleaner. The next day after the bedding compound has been applied, it can be trimmed with a sharp knife or woodworking chisel, but be extra careful not to scratch the gun bluing. Many stockmakers like to leave a very small bead of the bedding compound above the wood — between stock and metal — to be sanded to the contours of the stock after final curing. Small traces of the compound adhering to the barrel, receiver, cutting instruments, and hands can be removed while still tacky by rubbing with a vinegar-saturated cloth.

Under normal conditions, the metal parts can be removed from the stock in about eight hours. In cases of extremely tight fit, however, the use of a soft rubber mallet may be necessary to separate the parts. Once the parts are separated, look at the bedding very carefully to see if any voids or air bubbles exist. If so, these can be filled by applying freshly mixed bedding compound in minute quantities, after which the metal parts can be rebedded. In doing so, be certain that all voids are completely free of any release agent before filling — and you must recoat with release agent all metal parts that will come in contact with the new mixture.

For rifles with heavy recoil, many stockers prefer to first bed the recoil lug and other points of high recoil impact with Acraglas Gel containing either atomized aluminum or atomized steel particles. Then they bed the balance of the gun using pure bedding compound with perhaps a walnut stain. This method gives the strongest possible internal bedding job with the greatest exterior eye appeal to the finished gun.

Pinching

Barrels and receivers should fit perfectly in the gunstock. By *perfect,* we mean an exact fit that is not too loose or too tight. In trying to obtain this perfect fit, many stockers tend to get an ultra-tight fit — causing a squeaky, pinched fit into the bottom of the receiver and barrel channel. It takes skill, but anyone can acquire this "perfect" fit with practice — and, most of all, patience. The ultimate goal is to bottom the action and barrel into the stock so they go in easy and yet appear to be growing out of the wood! It takes only a few thousandths of an inch to clear the wood, and anything beyond this clearance will look sloppy.

Should you take off a little more wood than necessary (it happens to the best of us from time to time), there is nothing wrong with glass bedding as discussed previously; just avoid a pinch when the guard screws are tightened.

Glass Bedding Recoil Lugs

Even though you may not want to glass bed the entire barrel and receiver channel, most stockers nowadays do use fiberglass for bedding the recoil lug into the stock — especially on rifles with heavy recoil. However, merely cutting the back of the front side of the recoil lug and replacing it with glass will not do the trick. You will still have the same frontal and rearward areas for the recoil to push against.

In glassing the recoil lug area, it is important that the extra bit be taken from the left and right into each sidewall of the stock wood, and from the back with the cut-back of the front recoil lug surface by about $\frac{1}{4}$ inch. *See* Figure 18-22. When this area has been glassed in, it will be a $\frac{1}{4}$" steel-like bar of glass extending across the face of the recoil block and well into the side walls of the stock wood. This procedure, according to many experts, is far superior to the military crossbolt system found on many English and European big-bore bolt-action rifles, and it doesn't show from the outside of the gun. It also serves as added insurance against break-back of the wood recoil block, especially in heavy magnum calibers.

Figure 18-22: (A) The recoil shoulder section of stocks should be strengthened wth fiberglass compound on all magnum rifles. (B) The barrel should rest on two points, each of which is 45° off center from the bottom of the barrel channel.

In the mid-1940s when Roy Weatherby brought out his super magnums, many centerfire rifles were converted to these magnum calibers — especially the .270 Weatherby Magnum. Rifles previously chambered for the .270 Winchester were rechambered for the more powerful Weatherby cartridge, feed rails and bolt faces were then opened to accept the larger cartridge case, and this was about the extent of the conversion. Practically every one of these conversions has a damaged stock, usually involving a split from the magazine recess forward to the recoil lug bolt. If you should run across one of these conversions that does not have a split stock, it is highly recommended that the recoil lug be glass bedded.

Glassing should be done in stages — that is, the recoil lug should be done first, then the other parts of the rifle, making certain that no pinching takes place and that enough release agent is used on the metal parts.

Careful attention should also be given the barrel channel. Again, all "pinchy" fits should be eliminated, as they will seldom be uniform and can affect accuracy seriously. There is no need to float the barrel, however; the inletting should appear almost as if the wood grew around the metal. A slight clearance is more than adequate.

Some shooters prefer a twin-bar, V-block resting area for the underside of the barrel near the front end of the forend.

While such an arrangement works rather well in most cases, it does have the drawback of being sensitive to humidity — that is, whenever the weather changes and the humidity fluctuates, the forend shifts its tension, causing the point of impact to change as the barrel actually bends very slightly.

The most acceptable way to bed a rifle to ensure good accuracy is to bed the action in the stock so that it is strain-free. Then glass bed the recoil lug area as mentioned previously. Relieve all pinches.

Glass bed the chamber and the beginning main barrel taper section, leaving the remainder of the barrel full-floating.

Embedding a barreled receiver to a gunstock, the barrel rests equally on two points in the barrel groove at the forend tip, each point 45° off center from the bottom of the panel groove, and rests against these two points with a pressure of at least six pounds. The barrel should not bind, or touch with any pressure at any other point. These two points serve as a V-block would. After firing, the barrel comes to rest against the forend at exactly the same position each time. This method eliminates all side play or changed location of barrel in the stock from one shot to another.

Guns with fairly heavy barrels and rigid forends very often are glass bedded action-only, plus about two inches of the barrel ahead of action; the balance of the barrel is free-floating. The latter method is especially recommended if the gun will be subjected to extreme climatic change or very wet or humid conditions.

Barrel Tension

Barrel tension in any direction will actually bend a steel barrel enough to seriously affect accuracy, even though the bend may be only to a minute degree. For example, upper tension near the forend will cause the rifle to shoot higher. Tension against the right-hand side of the barrel will cause the rifle to shoot to the left because the barrel is actually bent in that direction. Any tension of 15 to 20 pounds will affect accuracy. This change in the stock pressure will readily change the point of impact. The effect is like a strong bow. Maintaining a firm stock pressure against the barrel will gradually weaken the wood tension, causing it to shoot elsewhere. In general, you want to achieve a relatively snug fit, with no extreme pressure points anywhere on the metal.

SHAPING

Now comes the outside surface of the stock. Most semifinished stocks are 90 percent shaped on the outside, but you will still have to remove some wood from nearly all surfaces — particularly around the trigger guard and receiver recesses. These latter areas are purposely built up to ensure a perfect fit — that is, so the wood surfaces can be made to fit exactly flush with the metal edges. Extreme care must be exercised in these areas. Many gunsmiths like to install the metal parts in the stock, use a scriber to mark around the recesses, and then remove the metal during the trimming operation to avoid damaging the bluing or other metal finishes. As the mark is approached, several tries are necessary to ensure a perfect fit. It only takes a split second to take off too much wood and ruin the whole job. In some cases gunsmiths use masking tape to protect the metal parts while they use a small end rasp and sandpaper to obtain the final results.

Once the detailed work is completed, the entire stock is sanded to shape with several sizes of sandpaper. In cases where excess wood must be removed, a belt sander can be used to remove and shape most of the surfaces and then go to either a high-speed orbital sander (or else sand the surfaces by hand, using progressively smaller grits of sandpaper down to approximately 380 grit, and finally, steel wool.

The stock is finished by any number of methods as described elsewhere in this book, but before starting this process, check over the entire stock once again to make sure that absolutely all inletting and shaping has been completed first.

The need for patience and care has been stressed in describing the procedures for inletting the semifinished gunstock. However, let's face the facts! More than likely you are going to make a few slips on your first job or two, removing a little too much wood from one spot or another. But here's a secret: It happens to the pros too! The main difference is the methods employed to cover up the mistakes. The novice often uses methods that produce an effect which appears as bad as the space or gouge would if left unfilled.

It is especially difficult to make an accurate cut on arcs and radii — an operation so frequently required in inletting a stock for receiver tangs, trigger guards, and the like. The slightest bit of deviation from the marked line, when cutting, shows up as a large cavern entrance when the metal part is seated in place. Don't be too alarmed if this happens to you. With a little practice, you will be correcting your mistakes just like the pros. The correction, however, is more time-consuming and tiring than the inletting, but this might have its advantages. . .it will make you be more careful on your next attempt so you won't have to go through the process any more often than is absolutely necessary.

Chapter 19
Gunstock Checkering

Checkering is the process of cutting diamond-like patterns on the grips and forearms of gunstocks; also on handgun grips. The diamonds are usually formed by cutting crossing lines into the wood with hand tools or electrically-powered checkering tools.

Three basic styles of checkering dominate the field, with the American style being the most popular in the United States:

- American checkering
- English checkering
- French checkering

You will find variations of these, but nearly all patterns used on firearms since the turn of the century can be identified by one of these three basic styles. *See* Figure 19-1.

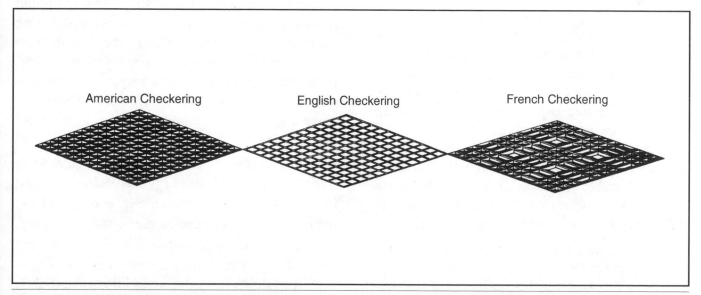

American Checkering   English Checkering   French Checkering

Figure 19-1: The most commonly found checkering styles are (from left to right) American, English, and French — the latter referred to in this country as "skip-a-line" checkering.

English Checkering: In this type of checkering, master guidelines are first laid out to the proper angle to each other, and then scored lightly with a special woodcutting tool. The tool consists of two edges, one to "ride" in the groove previously cut, while the other cuts a new groove. Perfectly-shaped diamonds are formed in this manner. The cut lines may be gone over several times to deepen them, but in English checkering, the diamonds are left flat.

American Checkering: This type of checkering is similar to English checkering, except the basic lines are gone over again with a V-tool which deepens the cuts and bevels the edges of the diamonds. It is the checkering most often used on gunstocks made in the United States.

French Checkering: This type of checkering is also known as skip-a-line checkering, since the final pattern is achieved by skipping cut lines at predetermined intervals. French checkering has traditionally been used on only high-quality guns, but this pattern has recently been used on some burnt-in patterns on Remington guns.

CHECKERING TOOLS

The beginner can save a lot of confusion and time by buying one of the checkering kits available. Many of the basic kits start out under $20 and usually have three cutters. Each of these cutters is actually a miniature rasp that will quickly cut sharp, true diamonds once you have gained some practice. Most basic kits contain a single-line cutter, a two-line cutter, and a bend cutter designed to cut on the backward stroke. The basic kit alone will allow you to get started in checkering gunstocks and usually will suffice for any job you are likely to encounter.

Before starting to checker a gunstock, the stock must be secured firmly, yet allowed to rotate as the pattern is cut, keeping the work area at the most comfortable, controlled position. A checkering cradle is the answer.

Brownells Inc. offers a reasonably priced checkering cradle, a very simple design that will handle stocks up to about 33 inches long without marring the finish, yet will permit turning the stock as the work progresses. This cradle is also handy for inletting, sanding, staining, and finishing gunstocks, allowing you to work with both hands free. While this cradle may be bolted directly to a workbench, it is recommended that it be secured in a sturdy bench vise. By doing so, you can adjust the height and angle to better suit the situation at hand.

If you are handy with tools and you have a scrap bin that contains a few odds and ends, you might want to build a cradle in your shop. Many different designs have been devised over the years, but in general, most take on the basic form of the one shown in Figure 19-2. Even if you have to buy the material, you should be able to get them for less than $30.

To build the cradle shown in Figure 19-2, note the material list alongside the drawing. Gather all the necessary components before starting, or you will more than likely end up with a half-finished project.

Start with the 48-inch-long 2 x 4 timber. Take a sheet of sandpaper and a sanding block and round the sharp corners of the timber to prevent getting splinters in your hands during the construction process, or later on when you use it for checkering. If the 2 x 4 piece of lumber is very rough, you may want to briefly sand the entire surface down to make a neater job — lumber just doesn't come off the finishing mill like it once did!

With a square and pencil, lay out the holes to be drilled in the 2 x 4. Note in Figure 19-2 that one end has 17 holes, $\frac{1}{4}$ inch in diameter, and spaced $1\frac{1}{2}$ inches on center. The opposite end has seven holes, $\frac{1}{4}$ inch in diameter, spaced 3 inches on center. Begin laying out these holes by first drawing a centerline down through the middle of the timber, centered from either side. Then measure and mark the center of each hole before laying your square

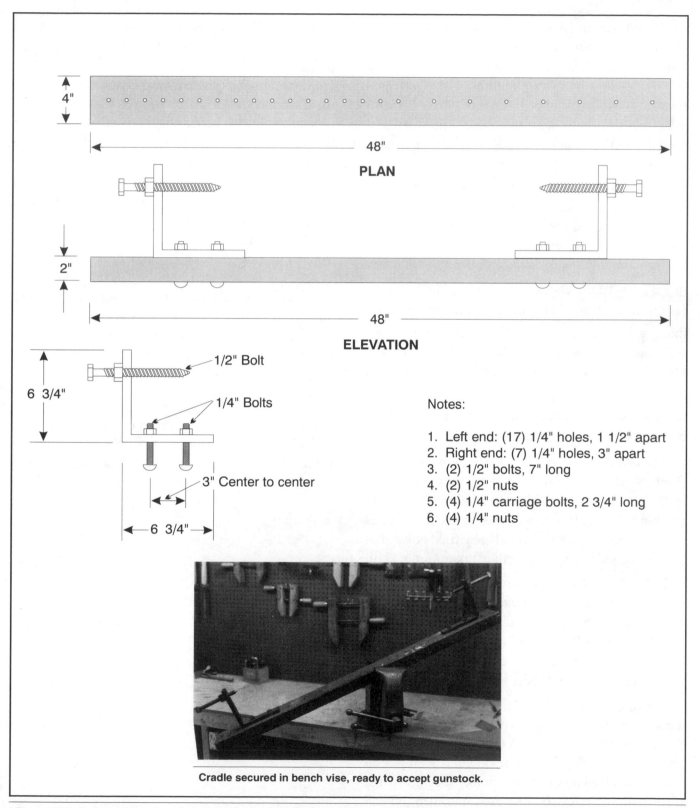

4"

48"

PLAN

2"

48"

ELEVATION

6 3/4"

1/2" Bolt

1/4" Bolts

3" Center to center

6 3/4"

Notes:

1. Left end: (17) 1/4" holes, 1 1/2" apart
2. Right end: (7) 1/4" holes, 3" apart
3. (2) 1/2" bolts, 7" long
4. (2) 1/2" nuts
5. (4) 1/4" carriage bolts, 2 3/4" long
6. (4) 1/4" nuts

Cradle secured in bench vise, ready to accept gunstock.

Figure 19-2: Construction plans for a homemade checkering cradle.

on the side of the 2 x 4 and marking the line across the long centerline at the exact location of each hole. You may want to use a centerpunch to ensure that the holes will be drilled in line. Then use a drill press or hand drill and drill the required holes with a ¼ inch drill bit. Clean out these holes well and sand around them to remove all splinters and shavings.

At this point you might as well finish the wood while you are working on the metal portions of the cradle. Use a good wood sealer and then finish with a few coats of spar varnish.

While the varnish is drying, you can start on the metal parts of the checkering cradle. The L-brackets are made from four pieces of flat iron, ½ inch thick x 1¼ inches wide x 6¾ inches long. Two such pieces are welded together to form the "L," after which the required holes can be drilled as shown in the drawing. The holes for the ½ inch bolts are also threaded; the holes for the ¼ inch carriage bolts are left unthreaded.

The ends of the ½ inch bolt should come to a sharp point so as to grip the stock when it is placed in the cradle. The simplest way is to get a local machine shop to turn 60-degree points on the ends of these two bolts. They can also be filed down, but getting a good job by this method takes a lot of skill.

The L-brackets are secured to the 2 x 4 frame with two carriage bolts for each bracket. The brackets are positioned the required distance apart to accept the stock being worked on. Each is quickly adjusted to obtain any number of varying distances between centers of the two ½ inch bolts.

For one-piece gunstocks, counterdrill a round wooden dowel (a broom handle is fine) and drill two holes through the dowel's cross-section to accept two wood screws. The dowel is then placed in the barrel channel of the stock, secured to the stock with the two wood screws, and then the end is secured in the checkering cradle by the pointed ½ inch bolt locked into the counterdrilled hole in the dowel. The opposite end (butt) of the stock is secured by merely tightening the other ½ inch pointed bolt into the base of the buttstock. This cradle can be secured to a workbench with a couple of C-clamps, but most gunsmiths like to secure it in a conventional bench vise; this allows adjusting the cradle to the desired working angle that suits each individual the best.

With the finished checkering cradle and a set of checkering tools, you are ready to start practicing. Note the word *practicing*, because you are going to need a lot of this before you are ready to start on your first good gunstock. Start off with flat pieces of hardwood, then see if you can find an old wooden baseball bat or a damaged gunstock. The curved surfaces of a baseball bat will give you good practice for the rounded portions of gunstocks that will come later.

Checkering Cutters

Checkering patterns on gunstocks require a minimum of three tools to cut the patterns. *See* Figure 19-3. First, a single-line cutting tool is used to lay out the pattern; that is, the borders and the

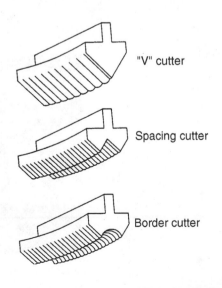

Figure 19-3: The three basic cutting tools you will need are (from top to bottom) "V" cutter, spacing cutter, and border tool.

Figure 19-4: The Full-View checkering tool has been a favorite of gunsmiths for several decades.

initial angular master cuts. This same tool is also used for deepening and cleaning the shallow cuts, once the pattern has been cut. The second tool needed is a two-line cutting tool designed to cut the two sets of intersecting parallel lines within the pattern. The third tool is a bordering tool used for cutting the border around the pattern. You will eventually want to add other helpful tools to these three, to make the work go smoother. Checkering tools are available in kits from gunsmithing supply houses.

The W. E. Brownell Full-View checkering tool as shown in Figure 19-4, is currently available from Brownells Inc. The accompanying cutters are considered to be the sharpest on the market and the combination of the Full-View handle and the cutters can be highly recommended to beginner and professional alike. The following information is furnished with the tools and is reprinted here for your information in selecting additional checkering tools and cutters.

Those who have never done any checkering before will find either the size 18 or 20 a good size to start out with. Decide what size you want and then order cutters in that size only. If you are only going to checker one gun, a good selection would be to get W. E. Brownell's special kit in the size of your choice. This kit consists of one handle (which is the same thing as a holder); one single-line

finishing cutter (any angle); one bordering cutter (small, medium, or large); one two-line spacer; one three-line spacer; and one skip-a-line spacer. The two-, three-, and skip-a-line spacers should always be ordered in the same size.

If you are going to checker only one gun, you can get by with one handle; but if you intend to checker more than one gunstock, it might be better to have more handles so that you will not waste a lot of time changing cutters. A four-line cutter and a super fine cutter might also be a good investments.

All regular Full-View cutters have nine double-edged teeth, which cut moving the tool either forwards or backwards. Thus, it is a double-action tool.

In order for Brownell's Full-View cutters to give the maximum amount of service before they become dull, chromium steel is used which has been heat-treated and tempered to such a toughness and hardness that they outwear any cutter made with ordinary steel. You may find it difficult to resharpen them because this hardness has a tendency to wear out files. However, some have resharpened the cutters by using a small four-inch knife file having a fine Number 4 cut, filing a couple of light strokes in between the teeth, crosswise of the cutter. Usually, three or four guns can be checkered with the same set of cutters before having to replace them.

The single-line finishing cutters come in three different angles: 60 degree, 75 degree, and 90 degree. These cutters are used to finish up or sharpen the diamonds after the two-, three-, or four-line spacing cutters have spaced in the diamonds to the correct size and have them about 75 to 90 percent completed. If the wood is soft or has large pores, or if you are cutting large diamonds such as size 16 or 18, or if you want the strongest and most durable diamonds, then use the 90-degree finishing cutter; it will produce the most durable diamond possible. On the other hand, if you are cutting in a small-sized diamond (size 24 or smaller), and the wood is hard and small-pored, then you can use the 60-degree finishing cutter to finish the job. These 60-degree diamonds afford a better gripping surface for the hand, but they are more easily broken off. Now, if your wood is medium-hard with medium-sized pores and you are checkering in size 20 or 22, you can finish up with a 75-degree finishing cutter and produce a nice medium diamond in size and sharpness.

The single-line super-fine finishing cutters also come in 60-, 75-, and 90-degree included angle. Instead of having nine double-edged teeth like the regular single-line cutters, they have many small teeth like a fine file; this gives a super-fine finish just as a fine, bent file would give. As far as we know, this is the first time a super-fine finishing cutter has been put on the market. It is used in place of a three-square bent file to smooth up the surfaces of the diamonds after your checkering is finished. However, it works better than a file because you can work up closer to the borders without running over. Conserve the use of this cutter for putting on a final super-smooth finish to your checkering job, unless you use it to straighten a line that has run off course when spacing in new lines. It would not be practical to resharpen this super-fine cutter as it would have to be annealed and rehardened and this would cost as much as a new cutter. The teeth on these cutters are cut in by hand and this makes them more costly.

The bordering cutters are made in small, medium, and large sizes. The large size is generally used on coarse checkering such as 16 lines per inch, although a lot of gunsmiths use the medium-size bordering cutters on everything from 16 to 22 lines per inch. The small size bordering cutter is generally used on 24, 26, 28, and 32 lines per inch checkering.

Full-View spacing cutters consist of two-line cutters, three-line cutters, four-line cutters, and skip-line cutters. All of these spacing cutters come in sizes 16, 18, 20, 22, 24, 26, 28, and 32 lines per inch. All of these cutters, with the exception of the corner tools, are interchangeable.

Power Checkering Tools

Most of the better checkering jobs have been done with hand checkering tools like the ones described so far in this chapter. However, there are several types of power checkering tools on the market that will make the work go faster and are especially helpful when a large volume of work is to be done.

Power tools are expensive — many costing from $300 upward — so they really can't be justified unless a large volume of work is encountered. An individual or a gunshop that has only a few stocks a year — or even a month — would be better off sticking to the hand tools.

The Burgess Vibro-Tool has been used for years to do many jobs around the gunshop: engraving, wood carving, filing, leather work, etc. In recent years it has been used to checker gunstocks. If you already own the tool, you can make checkering cutters by cutting the shank off on most conventional hand checkering tools — about one inch to the handle side of the bend and then chucking this into the Vibro-Tool.

A checkering cutter chucked into the Vibro-Tool is especially useful for finishing end rows and around patterns, but of course it can be used to do an entire checkering job. This tool requires no back-and-forth motion of the operator's hand; consequently, the cutter can be worked up precisely to border lines without overcutting.

For most checkering jobs, the Vibro-Tool should be used on its HI position — that is, 7200 strokes per minute. This speed gives a smooth, even hum and is best for the delicate work of stock checkering. There is also a "depth-of-stroke" adjuster that controls the length of the stroke from a minimum of zero to a maximum of over $\frac{1}{8}$ inch. To lengthen the stroke, turn the knob counterclockwise until the desired length is reached.

Maximum finger control of the Vibro-Tool can be achieved by holding it like a pencil. This is fine for engraving and wood carving, but for checkering the tool should be held more firmly to keep the lines parallel. Don't bear down too hard, as this will only shorten the stroke somewhat and tire your hand. Power tools are meant to lessen the work of the operator, so let the tool do the work for you. Also make certain that the workpiece is secured firmly in a checkering cradle or vise, and always experiment with a piece of scrap material before trying out the Vibro-Tool on a new job.

The Vibro-Tool — or any other power checkering or carving tool — will not completely replace the hand tools described earlier in this chapter; you will still need most or all of the hand tools mentioned. For example, to start a checkering job using the Vibro-Tool, first use a straightedge (or French curves where the lines curve) and a sharp knife or V-tool to cut the border lines and guide lines on the pattern as shown in Figure 19-5. Then use a single hand cutting tool to deepen the cuts made with the knife. Make certain that these initial lines are precisely cut, as they will be your "guide" for all other lines cut in the pattern. You can then insert a two-line cutter in the Vibro-Tool and proceed to cut parallel lines to the border lines previously cut with the V-tool.

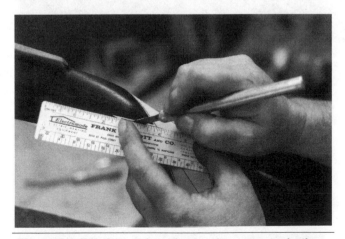

Figure 19-5: Whether you're using hand or power tools, the initial guidelines must be cut with either a V-tool or a sharp knife.

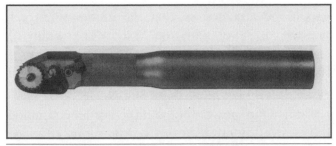

Figure 19-6: To adjust the lines per inch with the MMC power head, simply turn the adjusting knob for the desired cut.

After some experience, you should be able to checker right up to the border lines without overcutting, but if you want to be doubly sure that you won't overcut, cut the shank of a Dem-Bart S-1 tool about one inch to the handle side of the bend and mount this cutter in the Vibro-Tool. This cutter is designed to cut backwards, allowing you to place the cutter right at the border line and then work *backward* into the pattern.

Almost any hand tool cutter can be adapted for use in the Vibro-Tool as the need arises. The type of work you will be doing should suggest the types of cutters needed.

Most professionals consider the MMC power checkering outfit (Figure 19-6) developed by Bob Sconce to be the most practical power checkering outfit on the market. It is used by many top custom stockmakers and by leading U.S. and foreign firearms manufacturers on their high-grade guns. The outfit consists of a power checkering head and a Foredom industrial grade CC motor, flexible shaft, rheostat, and hand piece. The checkering head is a beautiful, precision, high-performance instrument that has proven to be a popular moneymaker for anyone who checkers guns for profit.

The checkering tool is set and tested at the factory for 18-lines-per-inch checkering, but is readily adjustable to cut any other width checkering from 16 to 24 lines per inch by turning the guide adjusting nut clockwise for coarser and counterclockwise for finer checkering. Special thin cutters are even available for cutting checkering finer than 24 lines per inch (up to 32). The depth adjusting screw should be adjusted so that the guide, when depressed, is level with the cutter. The width of checkering is set by experimenting on a piece of flat scrap walnut and measuring with either a screw-thread gauge or Brownells "CheckRchex."

To use this power tool, cut the border and guide lines to full depth as discussed previously for the Vibro-Tool. Then cut the remaining lines (parallel to the guide lines) to full depth on the first two or three passes by tilting the cutting head slightly to the left as the passes are being made. Subsequent lines, when cut to full depth, will require little if any "finishing up" with a hand tool. Be prepared to practice cutting several patterns on scrap pieces of wood before you use it on a good gunstock.

The speed of the machine is controlled by the foot pedal rheostat and is determined by conditions such as width of checkering, hardness of wood, and skill of the operator. Sufficient speed should be maintained to avoid chatter, but don't go so fast as to cause the cutter to heat up. Too low a speed can cause the load on the flexible shaft coupling to exceed the manufacturer's design specifications and cause trouble, so proceed with caution and determine the speed at which your particular tool functions best.

CHECKERING GUNSTOCKS

Before you start to lay out a checkering design on a gunstock, it might be a good idea to look over the checkering jobs on some of your guns, your friends' guns, and some down in the store window, and get a good mental picture of what a checkering design should look like. Also examine the checkering jobs done by the master stockers (Figure 19-7). Remember, a job does not have to look fancy in order to be professional-looking. Neither does this depend on the size of the diamonds. The im-

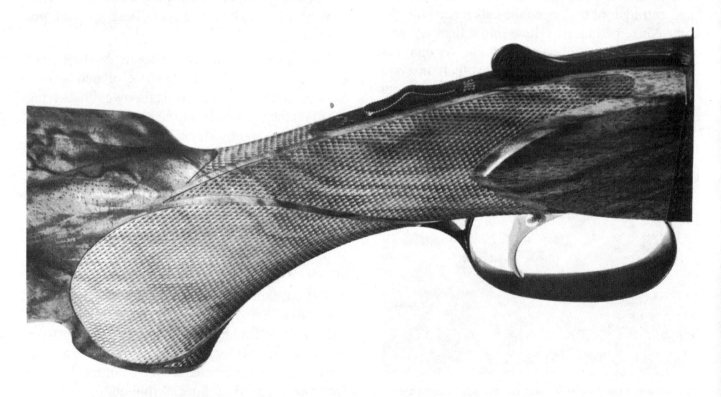

Figure 19-7: This perfectly-executed checkering was done by Shane's Gunsmithing of Micocqua, Wisconsin.

portant thing is good workmanship in neat, clean, perfectly-cut lines, and this is going to depend on teamwork between you and a set of tools that are of the best design and construction.

You may want to design your own checkering patterns, or use decal patterns (Figure 19-8) such as the ones supplied by Stan De Treville (Box 33021, San Diego, CA 92103). Stan has about two dozen different patterns from very simple to complex designs. All can be ordered directly from Stan De Treville or from most gunsmithing supply houses.

To apply the decal patterns, cut the decal pattern sheet apart as indicated by the dotted lines so that the forend pattern and both grip patterns are separate. Soak them in water just long enough for the decal to begin to loosen from the backing paper. Dampen the areas on the gunstock where the designs are to go, and apply the decals by carefully sliding them off the backing paper into the desired position. Make sure the patterns on each side of the stock are in alignment, then swab them smooth with a clean cotton cloth and wipe off excess water. Let the patterns dry thoroughly before attempting to checker over them. If you don't wait long enough, you will end up buying another set because they will wrinkle and tear apart when you start checkering. Wait about one hour before starting the checkering and you will experience no trouble at all.

If you want to design your own patterns, several methods are available. One is to place a sheet of tracing paper over an existing pattern, then rub a soft lead pencil on the paper. The exact design — including all lines — will be reproduced on the tracing paper. The tracing paper can then be secured to the stock to be checkered; proceed as usual.

Another method is to wrap a piece of drafting paper slightly larger than the proposed pattern around the fore-end of the stock in the area where the pattern is to be cut. Then crease the paper down along the barrel channel edges; release it and you have an exact pattern of the forend. This crease should be marked with a pencil before it comes out. Measure with a rule across these lines on both sides and find the centerline, which exposes just half the area you wish to put the pattern on. Then layout your checkering pattern for one side of the forend with pencil, straightedge, and perhaps a French curve. This exact pattern, in reverse, is also needed on the other half of the folded paper. To make this transfer, go to a window and place the paper pattern against the glass, pattern to the outside and the blank side towards you. If you have copied the pattern in good, bold pencil lines — or, better yet, in ink — you can see the pattern very clearly through the tracing paper and can trace it onto the blank side. Of course, you can make a light table with a piece of frosted glass with lamps installed underneath to do the same thing in a more convenient position. It depends on how much work you have.

Once the tracing is complete, you'll have a template for your pattern that can be placed back on the forend where it was originally — that is, where you creased the paper into the barrel channel. By using transparent or masking tape, secure the template in place along the edges and in the barrel channel to ensure that it will not slip.

With the template in place, use a sharp scribe or ponce wheel to prick along the pattern outlines into the wood. If a ponce wheel is used, the wheel will space the pricks for you; if not, space the prick marks about $1/16$ inch apart. Continue with these marks until they cover the pattern outline on both sides of the stock. This method is also used on designs that go completely around the forend.

The template can now be released from the stock, and in doing so, you'll find a reproduction of the pattern on the stock in the form of small punch markings. With a scribe (and a straightedge if necessary), connect these points together to outline the entire pattern.

The pattern for the grips are laid out in a similar way.

#245-100-001, Pattern #1: An attractive point pattern that looks good on most bolt action rifles. Optional curved "ribbon" design breaking through the checkering adds distinctive touch.

#245-100-002, Pattern #2: A basic point pattern that is easy to checker and easy to look at too. It is designed to fit most semi-finished sporter stocks for bolt action rifles.

#245-100-003, Pattern #3: A fleur-de-lis pattern that gives a "custom" look to almost any gun. Designed to fit most bolt action rifles, but can also be used on some shotgun stocks where the forearm is of sufficient size.

#245-100-004, Pattern #4: Combines carving with checkering, for use on the finest custom stocks. Particularly suited to Mannlicher type stocks or any stock that will permit the use of a 9½" forearm design.

#245-100-005, Pattern #5: Monty Kennedy, (Author of *Checkering and Carving of Gunstocks*) design. Divided forend design will fit a wide variety of stocks and is not too hard for the novice to checker.

#245-100-006, Pattern #6: A fleur-de-lis patten for use on the Browning Superposed shotgun but may be used on most double-barrel guns if the forend is of sufficient size.

#245-100-007, Pattern #7: An "over-the-grip" design for pump shotguns like the Winchester Model 12. Forearm pattern is designed for use on custom beavertail forearms.

#245-100-008, Pattern #8: Adapted from a design by custom stockmaker Leonard Mews, with an "over-the-top" pattern for the pistol grip. The solid diamond shapes can be inlays of ebony, ivory, plastic, or silver.

#245-100-009, Pattern #9: Resembling twin bolts of lightning, this design by Leonard Mews is very appropriate for use on rifles chambered for the high-velocity cartridges.

#245-100-010, Pattern #10: This pattern has long been one of Monty Kennedy's favorite designs for use on fine custom gun stocks. Comparatively easy to checker in spite of its distinctive look.

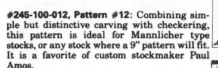

#245-100-011, Pattern #11: Another he-man pattern by Leonard Mews, the No. 11 makes even a fine stock look twice as expensive. And here's a tip! Put an engraved, silver inlay in place of the checkered diamond shape.

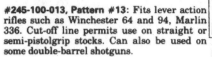

#245-100-012, Pattern #12: Combining simple but distinctive carving with checkering, this pattern is ideal for Mannlicher type stocks, or any stock where a 9" pattern will fit. It is a favorite of custom stockmaker Paul Amos.

#245-100-013, Pattern #13: Fits lever action rifles such as Winchester 64 and 94, Marlin 336. Cut-off line permits use on straight or semi-pistolgrip stocks. Can also be used on some double-barrel shotguns.

#245-100-015, Pattern #15: This easy-to-checker point pattern is similar to the standard design used on the popular Winchester Model 70 rifle.

#245-100-017, Pattern #17: Designed primarily for the Browning automatic shotgun, this pattern is a cinch to checker and looks good.

#245-100-018, Pattern #18: Ideal for the novice to learn to checker with, this small pattern fits the Ruger 10/22 and similar .22 rifles having pistol grips.

#245-100-019, Pattern #19: This oak leaf design is not only easy to carve, but is attractive and provides a good grip.

#245-100-022, Pattern #22: This pattern is the result of requests by custom stockmakers who wanted a distinctive design that was still short enough to fit the lightweight sporter stocks.

#245-200-025 Pattern #25: Deer

#245-200-026 Pattern #26: Grizzly Bear

#245-200-027 Pattern #27: Cougar

#245-200-028 Pattern #28: Bighorn Sheep

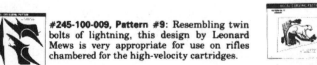

#245-200-032 Pattern #32: Canadian Goose

#245-200-034 Pattern #34: Wild Turkey

Figure 19-8: A wide variety of checkering patterns, from easy (for the beginner) to difficult (for the pro), are available from Stan de Treville. All are easy to apply and use.

Practice Pattern

Figure 19-9: Sample checkering pattern. Try checkering on a flat surface before going to curved surfaces.

Now with only single- and two-line checkering cutters in hand, let's try a sample practice design just to get familiar with the tools. Obtain a piece of flat hardwood such as maple or walnut and lay out a diamond-shaped pattern like the one in Figure 19-9. Since the shape of this pattern is a diamond, and since it is diamonds we are after, the outside borders of this particular pattern will also be the guide lines. You may make a copy of this pattern — either by tracing or else using a copy machine — and then tape the copy directly onto the piece of hardwood.

Next take a sharp knife (such as an X-acto knife) and carefully and lightly cut the borders around this diamond-shaped pattern — using a straightedge if necessary. These lines must be perfectly straight as they will be your guide lines for cutting the full pattern. The single-line checkering cutter should follow these knife cuts rather easily. Begin at the right-hand point of the diamond pattern and, using the single-line cutter, cut in the same line you cut with the knife (making sure not to cut too deeply), starting at the right-hand point and traveling upward and to the left of the pattern. Stop at the top "point" of the diamond. Now start at this top point and cut (with the single-line cutter) to the left-hand point of the diamond. These two deepened guide lines are all you need to cut the pattern.

Now take the two-line cutter and cut in a line adjacent to the first line (right-hand point to top point of diamond). One of the cutters rides in the first line cut, while the second cutter cuts a new line. Again, be sure not to cut too deeply. Never try to cut the lines to their full depth the first time over; cut them down approximately halfway. After all the lines are cut in to about half their final depth, go back over the job a couple of times, working the lines down to where they are about 85 to 90 percent complete. Then use the single-line cutter to bring all the diamonds in the pattern to a sharp point.

Getting back to our practice pattern, at this point you should have one line cut in addition to the guide or border lines around the pattern. Now skip over and place the right-hand cutter of the two-line cutting tool in the line or groove just cut; this new line will now be your guide line for the next cut. Now cut another line as you did before, stopping at the border line. Skip over and cut another, always using the line just cut as your new guide line. Continue cutting the lines in this manner until you run out of space within the diamond-shaped pattern. You now have a series of parallel lines cut within the pattern. It's now time to cut the lines in the opposite direction which will, in turn, form tiny diamonds within the pattern.

Start at the left-hand point of the large diamond pattern, placing the left-hand cutter in the guide line, and work toward the top point of the pattern, cutting a new line in this direction. Skip over and use the line just cut as your new guide line. Cut another line, stopping at the pattern's guide lines. Continue until the entire pattern has been cut.

Never work too quickly when checkering. When you cut a line, be sure that it is done correctly, regardless of how long it takes to do it. Speed will come to you as you get the feel of the tools and gain confidence in your ability to use them. Overly anxious beginners sometimes have to learn that avoidable mistakes can be made in a few seconds but may take many hours to correct. However, with patience at the start — and good tools — many beginners do a fine job on their first try.

Now examine the pattern you just checkered. Are all the lines perfectly straight? Are all of the diamonds actually diamonds or are some of them kind of taking on a rectangle shape? Try another pattern or two just to get the feel of things. When you get tired, stop; you can't do good work when you are fatigued. When you feel up to it, try another couple of these simple patterns. After doing, say, six or eight, draw the same pattern on a curved object, such as an old baseball bat, and try your skill here before attempting to checker a good gunstock. When checkering a rounded object, remember to keep your hand and checkering cutters straight, and rotate the object that is being checkered. Most beginners try to tilt the tool to follow the curvature of the wood. This is not the right way to do it. Always keep your checkering cutter straight, as if checkering on a flat surface, and rotate the object as you progress. This will ensure straight lines. If you try to tilt the cutter to follow the curvatures of the object being checkered, you will end up with crooked lines.

Cutting The Checkering

Before starting to checker, determine which size checkering (spacing of lines) to use. To be practical, the size of checkering should be coarse enough to cause and maintain definite friction between the hands gripping the stock and the stock itself. If the size is too fine, the lines will necessarily be shallow and will quickly fill with dirt, oil, and other debris. Should this occur, the original checkered surface will become smooth, causing much of the benefit of checkering to be lost. When the spacing is much greater than 18 lines per inch — 16, 14, etc. — the pattern will look somewhat crude and feel uncomfortably rough to handle. Condition and texture of the stock's grain are other considerations in selecting the size to use.

Figure 19-10: Use a single-line cutter to cut out the border and guidelines of the checkering pattern, using the groove cut with the sharp knife as a guide.

In general, checkering for hunting rifles should be between 18 and 24 lines per inch. Checkering patterns with lines spaced as close together as 32 lines per inch are sometimes encountered, but such patterns are mainly for looks and are not functional.

The shape of the small diamonds formed by the checkering varies to some extent, but most stockmakers prefer an angle of about 30 degrees between the intersecting lines. This shape gives a good looking pattern along with a good grip.

Pencil the border lines in first, and then draw in the guide lines using a flexible straightedge. Then use a single-line cutter to partially cut these lines as shown in Figure 19-10. After these lines have been cut, the two-line spacing tool is used to finish the pattern as described previously — that is, after the first set of parallel lines is cut over the entire pattern (Figure 19-11), follow by cutting the intersecting set of lines to form the diamond. The entire pattern should now be deepened and cleaned with the single-line tool, which will equalize all four sides of the small diamond-shaped designs formed by the cutting tools, causing them to become pointed and sharp.

Once the pattern is completed, the entire design must be given some sort of finish. Methods vary with different stockmakers, but a lot of gunsmiths like to use Dem-Bart finishing oil. This solution is

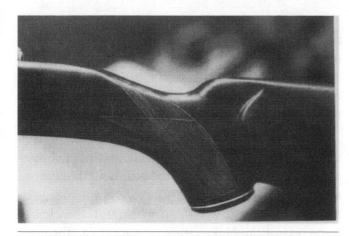

Figure 19-11: Lines of a checkering pattern cut in one direction only. Note the one guideline which will be used to cut the lines in the opposite direction to form the diamonds.

very thin and will cover the checkering without gumming. Apply a coat or two of this solution on the checkering; after it is dry, use an old toothbrush to rub briskly in both directions of the intersecting lines to polish it.

In cutting checkering patterns, a three-line spacing tool can be helpful when used with two rows guiding and one cutting. This will help avoid a wandering tendency. Experience will eventually permit cutting two rows and guide on one only, doubling the speed at which a pattern may be cut.

Don't try difficult patterns until you have mastered the simpler ones. Remember, even the simplest patterns can look very professional if checkered perfectly, while a fancy pattern poorly executed will look very sloppy.

RECUTTING EXISTING CHECKERING

When a checkered gunstock is refinished, the old checkering will have to be recut, but first remove the old finish as explained later. Any sanding that is done to the stock should not be allowed to extend over into the checkering patterns.

To remove finish in the crevices of the checkering — especially if the stock has been varnished — an old toothbrush is helpful. Merely dip it in varnish remover and start scrubbing. When doing so, however, be sure to wear some sort of eye protection as the paint and varnish remover is very caustic and can damage your eyesight if any should accidentally come into contact with your eyes.

When the old pattern is as clean as possible, use a bent three-square file or the single-line checkering tool to point up and further clean the old checkering pattern. Apply just enough pressure to keep the cutting edge of the file centered. Advance the tool in a push-pull motion, keeping your arm close to your body to maintain straight lines. Keep the grooves free of dust by blowing or brushing with a clean toothbrush.

Many stockers prefer to use a single-line cutter when recutting old checkering rather than the bent three-square file, but never use spacing tools when recutting checkering. Even the most careful worker will get variations in spacing width, and regardless of how certain you might be that your spacer is the same as the original, experience has proven that the spacer will never be exactly the same as the old pattern. On several occasions many gunsmiths have thought so, but after cutting a few rows they suddenly discovered that the new lines just didn't mesh with the old ones.

Once the old pattern is recut and cleaned, apply finish to the pattern.

English Patterns

Nearly all modern American checkering tools are designed to give the pointed-top diamond effect rather than the flat diamonds customarily found in English patterns (Figure 19-12 on the next page). If you want a true flat diamond, then you'll have to either make — or have made — special tools. However, a reasonably good compromise can be had by using standard American checkering tools. Diamonds with sloping sides and very small flat tops, can be achieved by using conventional tools (which would normally give a pointed top effect), but not working the grooves deep enough to pro-

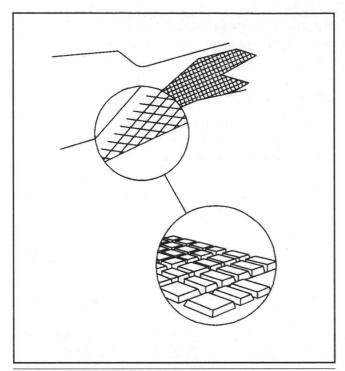

Figure 19-12: English checkering; the diamonds cut in the wood are left flat.

duce the full point. American checkering tools normally are available in both 60- and 90-degree cutter blades. Where the semi-flat top checkering style is desired, the 60-degree cutters should be used.

Border Lines

Border lines must be considered on all checkering patterns. Some, as you will note by the illustrations throughout this book, are "borderless," containing no visible border lines — but this is a very difficult style of pattern to cut, especially at the beginning.

Whenever possible, the border should be the outer sides of the diamonds, particularly on a straight-gripped shotgun or rifle. The front borders on a stock with pistol grip are usually the sides of the diamonds, but the rear borders are arbitrary curves conforming to the line of the grip. On fore-ends, the front and rear borders are again the points, but the sides are normally lines cut parallel to the

edges of the wood. Where the points form the borders, the exact position cannot be determined until the pattern has progressed. Eventually, when all the lines are in position, the exact border can be cut and the approaching lines can then be brought up to it.

If you are new at the game of checkering, as much of the border as can be predetermined should be marked out and cut with the grooving tool before starting the diamonds. This cut should be made to full depth, since it will be used through the checkering operation. Next, cut the master lines (the ones that will be used to guide the two-line spacer), and make these cuts right up to the border lines cut previously. Use the spacing tool as discussed previously to cut the pattern. Cut all lines in one direction before changing to the other angle, but don't make the first cut too deep. As these cuts approach the border, be extremely careful, working right up to the edge but not forcing the tool so that it overshoots the border line.

When the whole pattern has been cut to half depth, finish cutting any areas of the border that had been left incomplete. Then use the V-tool to work over the whole pattern again, this time cutting the grooves to their full depth. The beginner will want to make two or three final passes, cutting each one very shallow until experience is gained. Then the full depth can be cut completely on the second pass.

It would be nice to never have overruns, but these do occur — even to the best professional from time to time. These can be hidden, and the whole work given a nice "finished" appearance, by cutting another border line outside the first one. The space between the first and second border line can be left flat, but usually looks better — and hides overruns better — if it is given a concave contour. This can be achieved either by making a special tool or purchasing one of the bordering tools available on the market. Most tools made in this country produce a border that appears as a raised, rounded rib such as found on pre 1964 Model 70 Winchester rifles.

Chapter 20

Refinishing Gunstocks

Few gunstocks manage to escape a hunting season without some damage. Nicks and dents are prevalent in much-used firearm stocks — even when the owners are *extremely* careful. Most of these, however, are not serious and can be corrected, or at least alleviated somewhat. Some gunstocks, however, have seen horrible abuse, resulting in cracked or broken wood, severe dents or gouges, lack of finish, and the like. Stocks in this latter category frequently seem hopeless, making complete restocking the only apparent solution. However, there are many reasons why a firearm should not be restocked. Perhaps the gun owner lacks the experience to attempt a complete restocking project at this time, or the cost would be too high. A firearm may be a collector's item and any alteration of original parts might lower the gun's value.

Along these same lines of gunstock repair, come gunstock alterations. The alteration may consists of removing surplus wood from a thick and heavy military stock, or splicing in a high cheekpiece on a low comb stock to enable the shooter to use a telescopic sight. Perhaps the shooter wants to take a conventional factory stock and alter it to better suit his physique or shooting needs. For example,

the length of pull on most factory firearms is of a length to suit the "average" shooter. Obviously, those with shorter arms — such as women or youngsters — would need a shorter length of pull, requiring that the buttstock be shortened slightly. Perhaps the shooter is extra tall; then the stock would be too short and would have to be lengthened, usually by installing a recoil pad of the correct thickness.

Yes, there are many repairs and alterations performed each year on gunstocks. Some are functional, some are cosmetic, and some are a combination of the two. This chapter will show you exactly how to handle practically all common stock ailments as well as how to alter stocks to better suit your personal taste or needs.

GUNSTOCK REPAIRS

Removing Dents

Dents and bruises on hunting guns are probably the most common ills that you will encounter. Since neither seriously affects the normal functioning of the weapon, few shooters bother to have them removed. It is only when a serious problem occurs

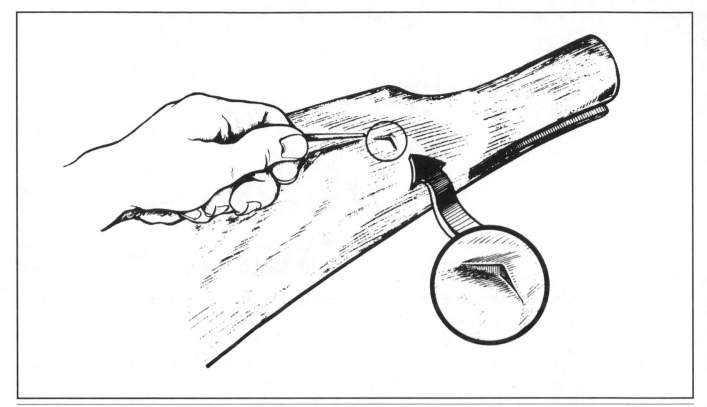

Figure 20-1: A dent as deep as this one cannot be satisfactorily sanded out. It must be either filled in or raised with steam.

— such as a split pistol grip or a break across the tang — that most shooters will consider having their stocks repaired. Others, however, take a sense of pride in their shootin' irons and want even the tiniest flaw corrected immediately.

The only tools required to raise dents in wood are a soldering iron, an old towel, and a cup of water. A dent in wood is merely a compression of wood fibers. The application of steam to the area will cause the fibers to swell and again rise to the surface of the wood.

To remove a dent from a gunstock, lay the stock on a padded surface so as not to further damage the stock's finish. Then plug in your soldering iron or soldering gun and dampen a corner of your towel. Place the damp towel over the dented area of the stock, covering only the dented area and not the wood surrounded the dent. Now place the soldering gun lightly on the damp towel right over the dent and steam will emanate from the towel almost

immediately, shooting it into the dented area. You want to make certain that you don't hold the hot soldering iron on the towel long enough to scorch the wood underneath, just long enough to convert the water to steam and that's it. As long as you can see steam pouring out from the towel, there should be no problem.

After the first application, dampen the towel again, place the hot iron on the towel over the dented area, and allow more steam to flow into the dented surface. Repeat this procedure until the dent is raised to the surface of the stock. This may take as few as three applications up to 20 or more, depending on the depth of the dent, type of wood, remaining finish on the stock, and other factors. That's all there is to it! *See* Figures 20-1 through 20-3.

The above method will handle 90 percent of the dents found in gunstocks — not gouges where wood has been *removed*; the steam method will not

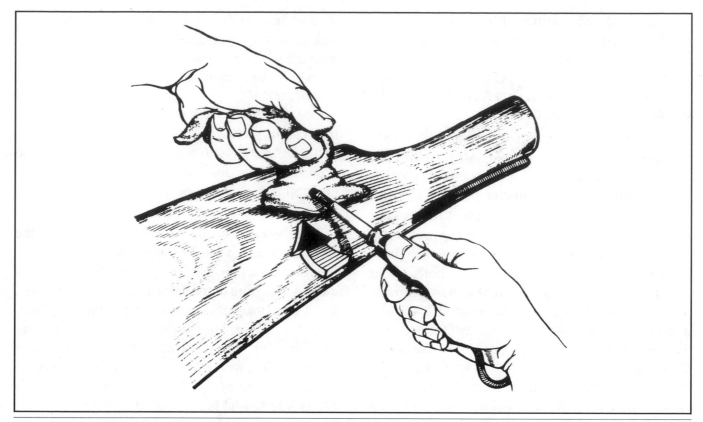

Figure 20-2: Use a damp cloth and soldering gun to raise the dent in the buttstock.

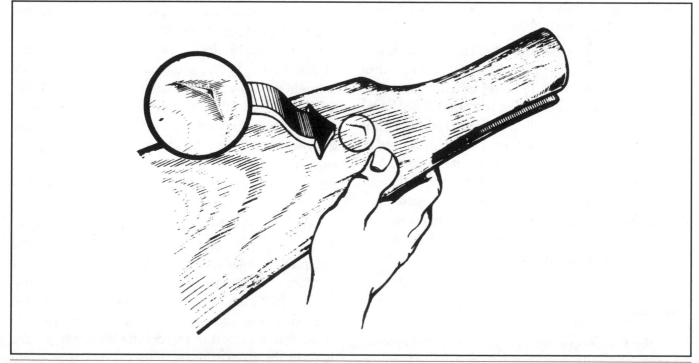

Figure 20-3: After only one application, the dent should rise considerably. However, it usually takes several more applications to raise dents flush with the adjacent surface.

replace wood, only swell the fibers and make them rise to the surface. There are, however, some dents that just won't yield to the method described above. In cases like these, apply a steady stream of steam directly to the center of the dent for a minute or two, which usually does the trick.

To make an apparatus for delivering a steady stream of steam is quite simple. All you need is a tin can with a screw-on lid, a short piece of copper tubing with an inside diameter of, say, approximately $\frac{1}{8}$", and about an 18" length of rubber hose of a diameter to fit snugly over the copper tubing. Punch a hole in the lid of the can so a 2" length of copper tubing will fit snugly into the hole; solder this in place. Then attach the rubber hose onto this piece of copper tubing. Also insert about a 4" piece of copper tubing in the opposite end of the hole. Fill the can about half full of water, screw the lid on tightly, and place it on a source of heat. In minutes the water will start to boil and very shortly thereafter you will have a steady stream of steam coming out of the copper tubing attached to the rubber hose. If more pressure is required, you can crimp the end of the tubing slightly, which will act much like the nozzle on your garden hose.

If the dent should occur in checkered areas of the stock, after raising the dent with steam, chances are the checkering itself will require touching up a bit. Usually, the entire checkering pattern will not have to be recut; only the area that came into contact with the steam. Use a conventional checkering tool or a three square bent needle file to recut the damaged area. Then take a toothbrush containing a dab of Dem-Bart Stock Finish and go over the entire pattern. This method will normally blend in the newly cut lines with the old. If it does not match, you will have to recut the entire pattern.

Repairing Gouges

Gouges or deep gashes in gunstocks that cannot be removed with steam have to be filled — either by splicing in an inlay or with a wood filler such as shellac sticks of the proper color to match the wood, walnut wood dust and glue, etc. The only trouble with the various fillers is getting an exact match to the wood being repaired. It takes a keen eye. . .plus a lot of luck. If the gash isn't too large, the raw wood can be stained to match the finished wood and then transparent shellac can be applied to form an even surface. Like most repair techniques, you should acquire a reasonable amount of experience before attempting to use this on your favorite pride-and-joy.

Deep gouges or places where the wood in the stock has been splintered away requires splicing or plugging to repair the flaw (Figure 20-4). It takes careful matching of the color and grain of the wood, but if done properly, such a splice is hardly detectable. Of course, strength of the repair is another consideration. The repaired area must be as strong as the original wood, but this should be no problem in this day and age with the many fine glues and epoxy kits available to the stocker.

To repair a small gouge in the wood, a plug is normally used. A round hole of sufficient depth is first cut out true with a Forstner bit and then the plug is turned (or obtained) to the exact size of the hole previously drilled with the bit. This plug should fit snugly, but without so much pressure that it might possibly split the wood. Walnut dowels are available, but are difficult to find all the time. Furthermore, most of these will have the end grain exposed, which makes the repair more conspicuous. A better plug is one with the side grain exposed so as to more closely match the surrounding area of the stock where the repair is to be made.

An end grain plug may be turned on the lathe by first gluing a 1 inch thick piece of walnut to some scrap stock that may be attached to the faceplate of the lathe. Set the tool rest across the bed so that it is parallel to the faceplate's surface, then turn the plug from the end — the same as when turning a disk. When turned to the correct diameter for the hole in the stock, cut the plug off to the required length. A $\frac{1}{4}$ inch plug is usually plenty for most

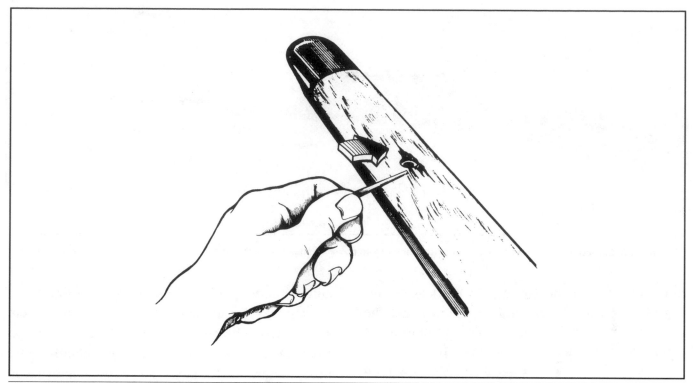

Figure 20-4: To repair a gouge like this in a gunstock, either use filler or splice a piece of wood over the gouge. This gouge would be an ideal candidate for a diamond inlay.

repairs, but on some curved surfaces, a $\frac{1}{2}$ inch plug may be necessary. As the plug is inserted into the cutout, align the grain in the plug to match that of the existing stock around the repair. Then, when stained and finished, the repair will be almost unnoticeable.

Sometimes it is almost impossible to repair a gouge without it being highly noticeable. In cases like this, it may be best to inlay an attractive piece of contrasting wood to cover the gouge much like the inlays used on Weatherby custom rifles. *See* Figure 20-5. Another technique is to carve a design in the area to camouflage the gouge, adjusting the carving to blend in with the gouge.

Split Buttstocks

One of the most common stock repairs will be repairing a split heel or toe of the buttstock. It doesn't take too much of a jolt to split off a piece

of wood a couple of inches in length when the firearm is dropped or allowed to slam to the ground. The repair entails finding a piece of matching wood — with the grain the same and running in the same direction as the original — and splicing it into the area of the broken-away wood.

The first step in this type of repair is to remove the old finish down to the bare wood, so as to clearly see the original grain and color of the wood. Now the split must be prepared to accept a new piece of wood. This is accomplished by cutting the ragged break smooth and even. Depending on the type and size of the split, you might want to first use a fine-tooth saw to cut out a square notch in the stock and then use a wood rasp and file to smooth the cut up a bit. Or, if the break is not too ragged, perhaps a rasp or plane will suffice without any sawing. To check the accuracy of the cut, lay a flat-edged ruler or other straightedge on the smoothed surface and hold it up to eye level against a strong light. Any

Figure 20-5: Sometimes it is best to use inlays in a gunstock to cover gouges rather than trying to splice a piece of matching wood.

dips or waves in the cut should be detected instantly. Additional cuts with a file will get the surface smooth and level. You now want to make certain the cut is absolutely clean — free from oil, sawdust, and the like — because a good solid joint cannot be made if dirt is present.

With the surface prepared, it is now necessary to find a piece of wood that closely matches the original in both grain and color. This might be a difficult problem, especially if the stock being repaired is rather old. This is why it would be a good idea if you saved every piece of suitable stock wood that you might come across. Often a rifle or shotgun will come in for a complete replacement of the wood. The old stock is removed and placed in the "junk" bin with the others that have accumulated over the years. Old broken stocks usually have plenty of good solid wood left on them that can be used to repair other stocks — and the age of these old broken stocks will more closely match a used stock than if new walnut or other wood is used.

Once a suitable piece of wood is found, closely examine it to see what section will be the best to use for the repair. When one is chosen, use a fine-tooth saw (like a hacksaw) to cut off a block of wood to fit into the notch in the stock being repaired. In doing so, however, be sure to allow enough wood for working the repair down to the exact shape of the original stock. During this ex-

amination, you will notice that the bottom line on most stocks (in the case of a broken toe) travels straight from the pistol grip down to the toe of the stock. On some designs, however (especially some made in Europe), the stock may curve somewhat as it approaches the buttplate. Determine which design the stock is, and proceed accordingly.

The surface of the replacement wood must be as flat and smooth as the notch cut out from the original stock. Allow about $\frac{1}{4}$ inch excess wood all around to allow for final shaping. Any excess wood can be rasped or planed off until the patch blends into the lines of the stock.

Before planing, however, the replacement wood must be tightly secured to the original stock. Mix up a batch of epoxy glue and, using a piece of clean wood (like a toothpick) as an applicator, smear a small amount of the epoxy onto the bearing surfaces of the replacement wood and also onto the existing wood where the replacement wood will make contact. These two surfaces must be completely covered with a very thin coat of epoxy for maximum strength. To ensure good coverage, press the replacement wood into the notch in the existing stock and then slide the replacement wood back and forth a few times for added insurance. Then align the replacement piece correctly, press the two

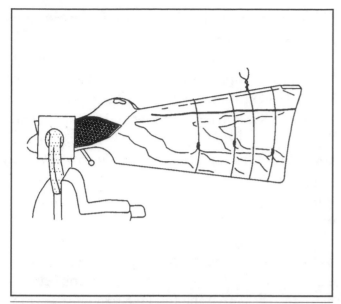

Figure 20-6: A horizontal split in this stock is first glued and allowed to dry before repairing the toe of the stock.

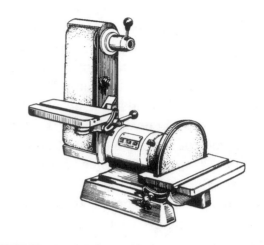

Figure 20-7: A belt/disk sander is a favorite tool in the gunshop to smooth down replacement pieces of wood for gunstocks.

pieces together firmly, and wipe away any excess epoxy that is squeezed out from the joint.

A tight fit can be obtained with this type of joint only if the pieces are held tightly together during the drying process. Conventional wood clamps can be used, but due to the angle at this point in the stock, heavy rubber bands are better. These, however, must be supplemented with either wire or tape to ensure maximum tightness. Let the joint dry overnight before continuing.

Methods of final shaping vary from shop to shop, but one preferred method is to use a sanding disk, like the one shown in Figure 20-7, to cut away the excess wood. Merely hold the stock with the glued-on replacement against the sanding disk, "eyeballing" the shape as the work progresses. As the shaping nears completion, switch to various grades of sandpaper to obtain a smooth final finish. Some stockers prefer to use wood rasps for this shaping, ending up with sandpaper and sanding blocks. Either method will work fine; use the technique that suits you best.

When the repair has been sanded to completely and accurately match the existing stock, it is ready

for finishing. Wet this portion of the stock and then dry it quickly over a heat source. Be careful not to burn the wood; hold it over the heat only long enough to evaporate the moisture. Keeping the stock moving at all times will help eliminate burning. This process will bring the whiskers in the wood to the surface, where they can be cut off with steel wool. The wood is then ready for refinishing. In doing so, match the original finish as closely as possible. If this is impractical, it is best to refinish the entire stock to ensure a better match.

In a few rare cases, it is nigh-onto-impossible to match a replacement piece of wood with the original. When these instances do crop up, remove the finish from the stock and dye the entire wood surface, adding a little here and there until a perfect shade is produced overall. The stock is then refinished by one of the methods that closely matches the original.

When restoring collector guns with a split heal or toe in the buttstock, many gunsmiths do not like to remove any of the original wood. Rather, they inlet the replacement piece with inletting black similar to the methods used for stock inletting. To do so, first obtain a piece of matching wood of approximately the correct size, with about 1/4 inch to spare. The original stock is thoroughly cleaned in the area of the break, and then inletting black is applied to the irregular wood on the original stock. The new replacement wood is then placed onto the stock and firmly pressed into place before removing. A chisel or moto-tool with a cutting burr is used to take off the black marks left by the inletting black. The process is repeated until the new replacement piece of wood looks like it grew to the original stock. This method is time consuming, but if done correctly, will give the best fit possible to the split buttstock. This technique is also useful for splits around the tangs — another area where splits are prevalent.

Many side-by-side double shotguns are in use in this country and abroad and most of them manufactured before World War II had short chambers. When firing modern high-powered 2¾-inch shotshells in these chambers, the chamber pressure increases considerably and also causes heavier recoil. After many such rounds are run through these shotguns, chances are the stocks can't take the pounding and eventually give way — usually around the grip area where the standing breech joins the stock. When such a break occurs, it is usually best to replace the entire buttstock, but if the split is only minor, a repair may be in order.

In making a repair to the forward end of a buttstock, the same technique is used as described for repairing a split in the toe — that is, the wood surface is first cleaned around the area of the repair, the surfaces are squared and planed smooth, a new replacement piece is cut and epoxied in place, and finally the replacement piece of wood is shaped to match the original. A professional refinishing job can make the repair almost unnoticeable. On some repairs of this nature, however, it may be best not to cut away any of the existing wood, especially on high-quality stocks. In cases like these, it may be best to inlet a replacement piece of wood to the existing stock. The method employed is very similar to that used to inlet barrels and receivers into stock blanks.

A replacement piece of wood that closely matches the grain and color of the original wood is obtained and cut to the approximate shape. Inletting black is then applied to the rough edges of the original stock, after which the replacement wood is firmly pressed against this area in the original wood. When lifted up, the black marks on the underside of the replacement wood indicate where wood has to be cut away. Cuts are made with a rotary rasp and again placed in position onto the original stock, lifted up again, and more wood cut away where indicated by the black marks caused by the high spots on the existing stock. This procedure is repeated several times until the replacement piece fits perfectly. The final job will be similar to splices made on Japanese furniture; that is, joints that contain no glue whatsoever but remain perfectly intact under nearly all loads and strains. A splice in the stock as just described will fit so perfectly and snugly that the stock could be turned upside down without the replacement part falling out. This type of repair obviously takes much more time than would a conventional cut-and-replace repair, but for the fine quality shotgun, the extra time is worth the investment. Of course, once a fit has been obtained, the part must be glued in place.

Cracks and repairs along the sides of stocks (not around edges) are best made with small inlays. To get the shape required, coat the stock around the defect with inletting black, press a piece of white paper over it, and trace the impression on the piece from which the inlay is to be made. Shape up the inlay carefully with a rasp and file, trying often for fit. The edges should also be tapered slightly to ensure a tighter fit. Coat the inside of the recess with epoxy and then coat the replacement inlay. Press the inlay in place and wipe away any excess glue that is squeezed from the edges of the joint. Then clamp the inlay in place and let it dry overnight. Sand down to the surface of the existing wood and finish.

Breaks At Grip

When a rifle or shotgun stock is cracked at the grip or broken completely in two, it is best to replace the entire stock. However, a temporary repair can be made by forcing the crack opens far as possible with a thin metal object (such as a hacksaw blade or chisel) and then squeezing in some epoxy. A syringe or hypodermic needle loaded with epoxy is good for this purpose. Clamp the joints together and let dry overnight, then drill through the stock from side to side and insert a $\frac{1}{8}$ inch brass wood screw. Countersink the screw head, then fill this countersink with a wood plug. Sand down and refinish.

After repairing the break in the grip, try to determine the cause — that is, why did the stock break in the first place? First disassemble the metal parts from the stock and clean them thoroughly. Coat the receiver with inletting black and fit it back into the stock; remove again. Notice where the inletting black left marks inside the bedding area of the stock and use a chisel to remove these high spots, relieving all pressure at sides, rear of receiver, etc., just as is done when inletting a barrel and receiver into a new stock blank. If the smudges indicate the recoil lug does not have a good bearing against the shoulder in the stock, use fiberglass bedding.

Many broken gunstocks can be repaired by using epoxy in combination with dowels or pins. Even broken stocks that look hopeless can often be repaired and refinished to look as good as new.

The weakest part of any gunstock is usually the pistol grip, although a lot of stocks are cracked around the toe or heel. The pistol-grip area should be repaired with epoxy as well as a dowel or pin. A birch dowel is usually considered to be best and Brownells Inc. offers a wide assortment of stock repairing pins that serve the same purpose as dowels — only they are stronger.

To repair a typical break in the pistol grip of a gunstock, select a dowel of a size that the stock will logically accept, then drill straight through the cap of the pistol grip and on through the broken surface into the other side of the break for a perfect fit. (Figure 20-8.) You will probably have to do some reshaping and sanding in the grip area after the dowel has been press-fitted. Then the opposing surfaces are liberally coated with epoxy and everything is brought together.

Now comes the problem of clamping the two pieces together. The curved surfaces always seem to resist C-clamps. A better clamping method is to use long pipe clamps, which bear against the fore-end and butt of the stock, holding the pieces in horizontal alignment. The C-clamps can be used to

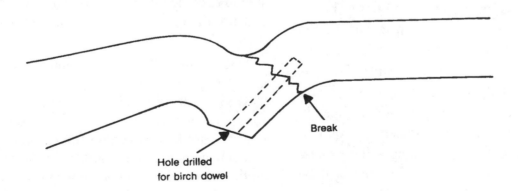

Break

Hole drilled
for birch dowel

Figure 20-8: To repair a broken pistol grip on a rifle or shotgun stock, first drill up through the grip area, then tap in a birch dowel coated with epoxy and clamp until the epoxy cures.

hold the broken pieces in vertical alignment until the epoxy has cured. You might want to supplement these clamps with heavy rubber bands.

An epoxy joint is quite strong and will probably last for years without any other reinforcement, but additional work will ensure a much better job. Drill a ⅜ inch hole in the upper tang recess, down through the pistol grip, and into the buttstock itself. A ⅜" dowel is then coated with epoxy and tapped into the hole. The excess is removed with a chisel and the tang mortise is cleaned up. If necessary, glass bed this tang area.

Once the repair has been made, remove any beads or runs of epoxy with a sharp chisel, then smooth down the epoxy until it blends into the stock contours. Any recesses or holes can be filled with dabs of epoxy, then smoothed with a damp rag after it thickens. Avoid getting glue into the checkering or marring the checkering with tools and sandpaper.

At this point, depending on how badly the area looks, a certain degree of refinishing (and perhaps recutting of the checkering) is in order.

Stocks having small lengthwise splits can sometimes be repaired by breaking them entirely apart at the splits, and then gluing them with epoxy. When the break is made, be careful not to bruise the edge and take care not to lose any of the splinters; all should be kept in position, leaving one end of any splinter attached if possible. The surfaces are then coated with the epoxy and carefully worked into place before the parts are clamped in position. Care must always be taken to acquire a perfect fit between the two sections will go a long way to ensure a tight-fitting joint that will be stronger than the original. Then, with a little care in matching dyes, stains and finishes, a job can be finished that is hardly detectable by any but the experienced eye.

REFINISHING GUNSTOCKS

There are thousands of guns in use that, either through wear or abuse, are equipped with stocks that look as though they have been dragged out of a swamp. Gunstocks get battered around in car trunks and saddle scabbards, scratched by barbed wire and briers, accidentally dropped on rock piles — some have even been used for emergency boat paddles — all of which tend to lower the cosmetic appearance greatly. Stocks that fall in this category are good candidates for a refinishing job provided the wood is generally sound and contain no severe breaks. Refinishing a gunstock is also a good way to ensure a uniform appearance when minor repairs have been made. It is also one of the most satisfying phases of gunsmithing — that is, seeing a dented, scarred, and otherwise abused hunk of wood turn into a thing of beauty.

Tools And Materials

Basic tools for refinishing gunstocks are few. All you really need are several grades of sandpaper, perhaps some sanding blocks, and a whole lot of elbow grease. The task is made easier, however, with some additional items such as power sanders, stock finish remover, and the like. The following items will be found in all professional shops. You should become familiar with each, but don't go out and buy all of them at one time; purchase them only if and when the need arises.

Disc Sander: This type of sander cuts ultra-fast and is frequently used to shape gunstocks. It is also used to cut down recoil pads on the buttstock and for many other uses around the gunshop. It should never be used, however, for final sanding of wood — even with the finest grits — because the disc cutting across the grain of the wood will invariably leave scratch marks that are extremely difficult to remove.

On badly abused stocks, the disc sander is used to cut the top finish off quickly, and also to reshape if necessary. Then most gunsmiths switch to an orbital sander to smooth out all the dents (those that cannot be raised with steam) and scratches left by the disc sander. The final sanding is done by hand with conventional abrasive paper and steel wool.

In using the disc sander for stock refinishing, just be sure not to cut too deep or too long so as not to leave scratch marks that are nearly impossible to remove.

Belt/disc Sander: If you have need for a separate belt sander, the combination belt/disc sander is a good choice. This type of sander may be used on all types of wood projects to shape, sand, polish, and clean such jobs. With the proper type belts, the belt sander is also convenient for polishing metal or for sharpening knives and other gunsmithing tools. The least expensive ones on the market start out at around $125 by the time they are set up and ready to operate. The better ones will run from $300 to $800 and are the only kind normally used in professional shops.

Orbital Sander: The palm-size orbital sanders, with 12,000 orbits per minute, are handy little tools for finishing gunstocks. Once you get the hang of their use, many stocks can be completely sanded, ready for application of finish, in about 30 minutes. Gunsmiths normally start out with 40-grit paper on badly abused stocks and progress to 280-grit before final hand sanding. The offset construction of the sanding pad allows four-way flush sanding.

Electric Paint Stripper: While an electric or gas hotplate works equally well, many gunstockers prefer to use an electric paint stripper as an aid in removing old finish (especially oil) as well as for whiskering stocks during the final sanding.

Drum Sanders: You will find some use for drum sanders during shaping and finishing gunstocks — especially when used in conjunction with one of the rotary power tools with handpieces. They are indispensable for finishing or shaping such areas on the gunstock as the forward stock comb, bolt handle recesses, bolt recesses, and the like. In a pinch, they can also be used on flat surfaces, but they are best used on corners, curves, and other round or oval shaped areas.

Metal Oil Tanks: In the days of strict oil finishing — considered by many to be the best finish available — a stock refinishing job took weeks to complete, as a certain amount of drying time had to be allotted between coats. To speed the process up slightly, many gunsmiths constructed metal containers in which the linseed oil was heated, after which the stock was lowered into the tank to absorb all the oil possible on the first application. The heat, of course, opened the pores of the wood to allow oil to seep in. Modern methods and wages permit only a few stocks to be finished this way, but every gunsmith should know how to do it.

General Refinishing

First of all, carefully remove the barrel/receiver from the wood, and then remove the buttplate, sling swivels, and any other metal parts that are present — always being careful not to split or otherwise mar the wood in the process.

Once all hardware has been removed from the wood, there are dozens of varnish and paint removers on the market to remove the existing finish. However, many gunsmiths find it best to use a proven method of scrubbing to get the old finish off. This method also automatically raises minor dents and dings in the wood during the process of removing the finish. A summary of the method is shown in Figure 20-9 on the next page. In general, get a bucket of hot water and a scrub brush. Add ½ cup of bleach and ½ cup of Mr. Clean® cleaner to the hot water. Wear rubber gloves and with the brush soaked with the solution, begin scrubbing the stock; scrub for about five minutes, wipe off any suds with a cloth and then hold the stock over a source of heat to quickly dry the wood. Don't let the stock get too hot or burn; just enough to dry the wood and to raise the grain.

When no more signs of moisture exists, take a piece of 2/0 steel wool and rub the entire wood

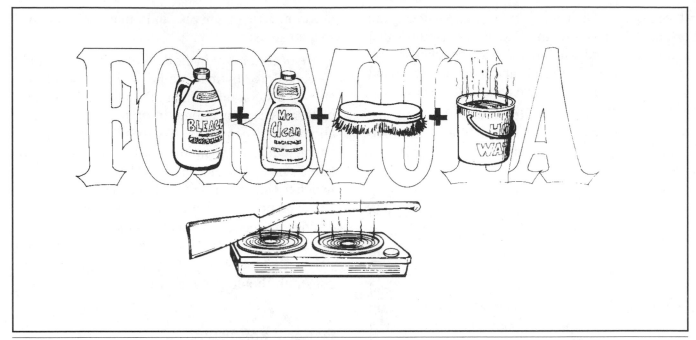

Figure 20-9: Proven formula that works well for removing any type of oil finish from gunstocks.

surface down — cutting off all whiskers and removing more of the finish. Then go back to the scrub brush — again scrubbing the stock for about five minutes. Again, hold the wood over a source of heat until it is dry and then again rub it down with steel wool. Repeat these operations until all the old finish has been removed from the stock.

With all the finish removed, carefully examine the wood for dents. Mark these with a pencil and try raising them with steam; that is, place a wet cloth over the dent, touch a soldering gun to the cloth which will immediately cause steam to "shoot" into the dent. This will raise the crushed fibers in the wood. Repeat this operation several times until the dent rises flush with the surrounding wood surface. Just be careful not to burn the wood.

Some stocks will be ready for final sanding in only two or three applications of the solution. Others may require as many as 15 passes of scrubbing, heating, and whiskering with steel wool to get the surface in good shape. . .maybe even more!

Once most of the oil is removed from the gunstock, you will almost always have a few spots that want to be stubborn. These spots will usually occur around the buttplate, the trigger guard and receiver. Rather than scrubbing the entire stock, hold these difficult spots over a heat source until the oil begins to bubble to the surface of the wood, again being careful not to get the stock too hot. Then quickly

Figure 20-10: Using the solution of bleach, Mr. Clean, and hot water, scrub the stock to be refinished for about five minutes.

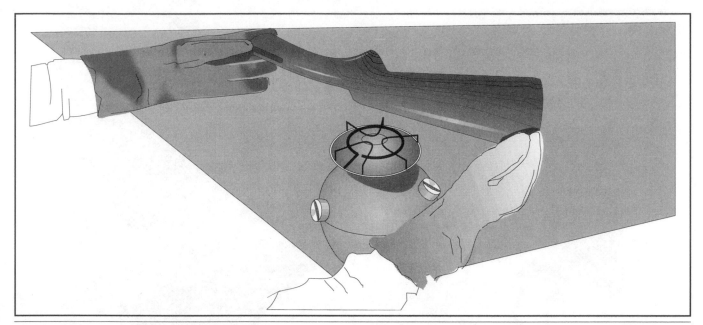

Figure 20-11: After scrubbing, heat the wet stock over a source of heat to evaporate the moisture. Use caution not to let the wood get too hot.

wipe the oil off the stock with a rag. Repeat this operation until all of the oil is raised to the surface.

To facilitate the removal of oil from the stock, you might want to purchase a small can of plain whiting at your local paint store and some type of

Figure 20-12: When all moisture has evaporated from the heating, use steel wool to cut the whiskers and smooth the wood surface.

grease solvent such as AWA 1,1,1. Put a few ounces of whiting in a small jar and stir in just enough solvent so that the mixture can be spread on the wood with a paint brush. Now heat the stubborn spots again and when the oil bubbles to the surface, coat the area with the whiting/AWA 1,1,1 mixture. If you work quickly before the solvent evaporates, it will penetrate deeply into the wood and dissolve most of the oil and grease it encounters. As it evaporates, it brings the oils and grease to the surface of the wood, which are absorbed by the whiting on the surface.

When all of the old finish is removed, use several grades of sandpaper to smooth the surface. Start with a medium grade and work down to very fine. Then use steel wool (4/0 is fine) to polish the wood even more.

For bad dents and gouges, smooth them flush with the surrounding surfaces with a piece of broken glass or wood scraper, or fill in the dents.

Before refinishing any type of gunstock, the barrel and receiver should be removed, along with all metal parts such as sling swivels, buttplates, grip

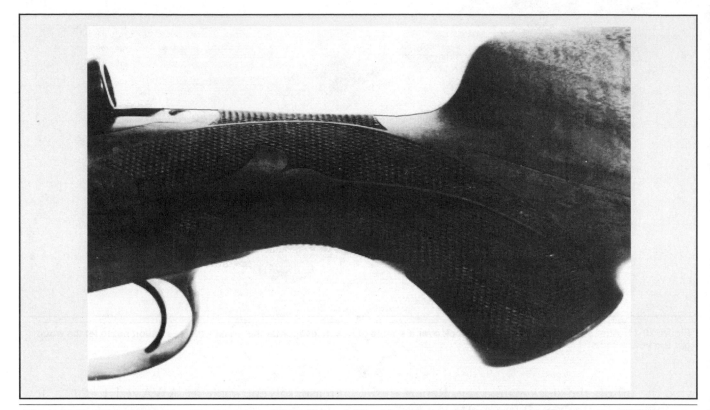

Figure 20-13: If the gunstock has checkering, a stiff bristle brush (like a toothbrush) might be required to remove the old finish.

caps, etc. This will make the entire stock readily accessible and prevent the metal parts from becoming scratched or damaged.

The old finish may be removed in many different ways, but the type of finish will dictate the best. For example, oil finishes are best removed as discussed previously. Conventional "factory" finishes are best removed with a commercial stripper.

To use the stock finish stripper, first spread newspaper or other protective material beneath the stock to protect the work area, or hang the stock in a large cardboard box so that the spray from the can will be contained therein. Spray one entire side of the stock. Immediately the old finish will begin to bubble and in three to five minutes it will be penetrated enough to remove. Then wipe the surface clean with an old rag, followed by steel wool. If the first coat of finish remover does not remove all of the finish, apply another coat as stated above until all of the old finish is removed.

If the stock being refinished has checkering (Figure 20-13) or carving, a stiff bristle brush may be required to remove the finish from the crevices. Save all of the family toothbrushes that are about to be thrown away for this purpose — they work fine!

Another precaution that should be considered while refinishing stocks and forends is possibly chipping or breaking the wood during the refinishing operation. Slim forends on two-piece gunstocks, for example, are very delicate; too much pressure applied without the magazine tube can split the forend down the middle. Consequently, many gunsmiths like to insert a hardware dowel, turned the same size as the magazine tube, during the refinishing process. See Figure 20-14.

Before applying the new finish, the entire surface of the stock must be thoroughly cleaned with turpentine and allowed to dry. Any type of paint and varnish remover may also be used to remove gun-

Figure 20-14: When refinishing thin forearms, like this one for a Winchester Model 12 shotgun, a dowel or mandrel through the forearm supports it to help prevent breakage. The dowel also provides a means of holding the work during the refinishing operation.

stock finishes, but several applications are usually required. For stubborn spots, use a piece of broken glass for scraping, but be sure not to scrape over any checkering or carving for obvious reasons.

One time-proven method to remove stock varnish is a solution of 3 level tablespoons of household lye to 1 gallon of boiling water. Rubber gloves

must be used with this solution as well as protective goggles or face shield, because any contact with the skin or eyes will cause injuries and perhaps blindness. Scrub the stock well with this solution using a stiff scrub brush, then rinse thoroughly in clear water. Once dry, the stock is ready for finishing.

Once the old finish is removed, smooth the bare wood until the surface is as smooth as glass. One way to accomplish this is to wet the stock with water and then dry it over a source of heat, such as the kitchen range or heat lamps. This procedure raises the grain of the wood; once raised, steel wool is used to cut the wood fibers and smooth the stock. Apply water again and repeat the procedure just described. Continue this operation until the grain no longer rises after wetting.

After the stock surface is as smooth as possible, some type of wood filler (and possibly stain) should be applied to the stock. One excellent brand is Birchwood Casey's Gun Stock Filler. This filler is used to prepare all types of gunstocks for final finishing. It has a warm walnut tone that helps bring out the beauty of the stock, and it dries to a clear, noncloudy finish. This, or some other filler, should be applied to the stock, wiped across the grain with a rag, and left to dry for at least four hours — preferably overnight.

When the filler has dried sufficiently on the stock, go over the entire surface with a very fine grade of steel wool (4/0) before continuing. Some stockers prefer not to use filler in the checkered areas, as gumming will probably occur. If filler is used in these areas, be certain to use a toothbrush to clean out the crevices before it dries. You can use masking tape to cover the checkering before applying the sealer. The final finish will then leave the checkered areas a little lighter than the rest of the stock.

To apply most finishes, first wipe the surface with a gunsmith's tack cloth to remove all dust or other particles that will prevent the final finish from being completely smooth and free from foreign matter. Work in a clean, dust-free area for best results. Apply the stock finishing oil directly from the container to the stock, using your fingers or a clean cloth to evenly spread the oil with the grain of the wood. Allow the first coat to dry at least two hours, or as directed by the manufacturer of the product being used. When the first coat is dry, sand the entire surface very lightly with 2/0 steel wool and then apply another coat of stock finish. Repeat these steps until the desired luster is attained; this will usually take three or four coats. This is one phase of refinishing that cannot be hurried. If coats of the finish are applied before the preceding ones have dried you will end up with a gummy mess — requiring that the entire stock be stripped of the finish and then started over.

When the final coat has dried completely — at least 24 hours — a good gunstock wax should be applied to the stock surface to protect and dress up the final finish. Another coating is Birchwood Casey's Stock Sheen, which is a good final polish for finishing gunstocks. Just apply it directly from the bottle; it requires no hand rubbing, no rotten-stone, no pumice. It also protects the finish against handling and weather.

Should a satin sheen be desired, rub the final finish with Birchwood Casey's Rubbing Compound or rottenstone to dull the glossy finish.

Gunstock finish over checkered areas is usually applied with a soft-bristle toothbrush and rubbed with the same until the finish takes hold. The same is true for carvings and other decorations on the wood.

GUNSTOCK FINISHES

The appearance of any completed gunstock often depends more on the quality of the finish — and the skill of the finisher — than on the wood itself.

Before a stock can be professionally finished, the finisher must first know what quality work is and the methods used to obtain the required finish. There are a number of different types of finishes

Figure 20-15: Once the job is complete, the refinished stock should equal or surpass the original finish.

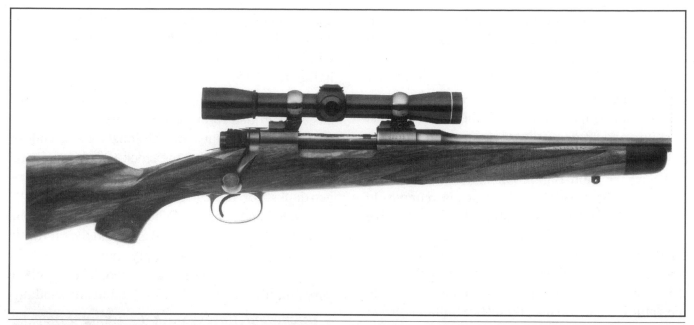

Figure 20-16: The hand-rubbed finish on this custom rifle — based on a Winchester Model 70 action — takes many hours of painstaking skill, but the final result is worth the effort.

Figure 20-17: Master craftsman at Paul Jaeger's shop applying final finish to a custom stock.

available to the stockmaker: linseed oil is the old standby, but time-consuming. Plain varnish has been used by firearm manufacturers for years, but is probably the worst finish that can be applied.

Spray-on lacquer is currently used by many manufacturers, but should be avoided by the professional stocker unless a gun is to be restored to original factory specifications. Epoxy finishes are becoming very popular, but linseed oil with fast-drying additives is probably the best all-around finish for both the beginner and professional alike. Again, the techniques employed and the care taken by the stocker are, in most cases, more important than the type of finish used.

Commercial Finishes

There are numerous stock finishes available that can produce practically any style or tone of stock finish you desire, and most are available from gunsmithing suppliers. If you want to experiment with the finishes used by the masters of yesteryear, there are several formulas listed in the latter part of this chapter.

Dem-Bart Stock Finish: This waterproof oil finish is the favorite of many stockmakers when they are trying to obtain a low-sheen, London-type finish on classic stocks. Due to the drying time required between coats, about a week is required to get a good finish. However, the fine results are well worth the extra waiting time and can be highly recommended.

You'll need the Dem-Bart Stock Sealer-Filler when using the finish on open-grain wood. This sealer-filler seals and protects the wood against moisture and prepares the stock for the final finish with minimum effort.

To use the Dem-Bart products, prepare the stock as for any other type of finish — that is, remove old finish and sand down using about 320 grit abrasive paper. . .or finer. Make sure the wood is in perfect condition before even *thinking* about applying the finish. You might even consider staining the wood if it is of a light color, but for good quality walnut, the natural color will usually suffice without further staining.

Apply the Dem-Bart Sealer-Filler with a clean brush; get a good heavy coat, but not so heavy that it runs. Allow the sealer to dry for at least 15 minutes. . .20 or 30 minutes is better. Then sand with about 220-grit abrasive paper to the bare wood — that is, the sealer should be down in the pores and not on the surface of the stock. Repeat with a second application as before, let dry, and then again sand down to the bare wood. Two coats will normally do the trick, but on some open-grain woods, a third coat may be necessary.

When applying the Dem-Bart sealer to the end grain or similar area, do not sand. Merely apply a thin coat and let dry.

Once the wood pores are filled, apply the Dem-Bart Stock Finish with the fingers — or, if you're fussy, use a clean brush. While this oil is still wet, sand the entire area with 280-grit production paper. Wipe off all excess oil to prevent running, and then set the stock in a dry area for three days. After the three-day waiting period, apply another coat and sand the stock down again with 280-grit production paper until all pores are completely filled. Wait another three days and apply another thin coat of oil; let dry for 15 minutes and wipe off all excess oil with a clean, lint-free rag. From this point on,

apply another coat every 12 to 24 hours until the desired finish has been obtained. Four more coats will usually give a satin sheen similar to the stock in Figure 20-15.

Lin-Speed Oil: This type of stock finishing oil has been around for a long time and has been used by both amateurs and professionals alike. Unless used for touch-up jobs, the stock wood is finished as usual before applying Lin-Speed oil. Apply "finger-dunks" of the oil and spread it evenly with moderate hand rubbing. When the oil is dry (about six hours), use 3/0 steel wool and sand the oil finish down to the bare wood. Apply more coats in the same way until the pores are filled. Then apply a very thin final coat and let dry without any sanding.

Birchwood Casey Stock Finishing Products: Birchwood Casey offers a wide variety of stock finishing products that are quite popular with hobbyists and professionals alike. Their famous Tru-Oil finish is a blend of linseed and natural oils; it dries relatively quickly, so most stocks can be completely finished in a day or two (depending on the weather and humidity in the air). This finish is available in liquid form to be applied with the hands, and two sizes of aerosol cans are available.

If you want to save a lot of time and confusion, you can purchase one of Birchwood Casey's Stock Refinishing Kits. If the wood is not in too bad condition, everything needed for complete refinishing of a gunstock is included in the kit. It contains Tru-Oil Stock Finish, Gun Stock Filler, Stock Sheen and Conditioner, burlap cloth, fine and coarse grit production paper, 2/0 steel cloth, fine and coarse grit production paper, 2/0 steel wool pads, polish, and service cloths. In most cases, however, you will have to purchase more abrasive than comes with the kit — especially if you have a lot of nicks and dents in the stock to be finished.

Birchwood Casey Gun Stock Wax is designed for use on guns, fine furniture, and the like. It provides a lustrous finish of exceptional beauty. It's also great for gun barrels and other metal parts.

Their rubbing compound reduces high gloss to a rich low-sheen satin without using steel wool or sandpaper. It's good for that final rubdown on a true classic stock that has been refinished with a high-gloss finish.

The Gunstock Finish Remover is an easy way to remove old varnish and lacquer finishes without raising the grain or discoloring the wood. It comes in an aerosol can; just spray it on and let the chemicals do the work.

Birchwood Casey's Perma Water Stains come in walnut, cherry and colonial red (maple). All produce a clear, rich, sunproof color which is never muddy. To use, make sure all the ingredients are well-mixed in the container. The stain is a concentration and must be diluted with equal parts of water before using. Apply the stain with a clean brush or lint-free cloth and let dry. Should the wood be too dark for your preference, the color may be lightened by sponging the wood with water until the desired shade is reached. The stain should be allowed to dry about 12 hours before an oil finish is applied.

Tuf-Sheen Polyurethane Stock Finish was specially formulated to give a clear, hard finish to protect and beautify gunstocks. It offers superior resistance to discoloration or staining by water, sunlight, heat, and bore solvents. It comes in a 12-ounce aerosol can for easy use; apply as directed on the can.

Other Birchwood Casey products can be found at most gunsmithing supply houses. Be sure to order one of their catalogs, as they are constantly coming out with new developments that can make gunstock finishing easier and better.

Epoxy Finishes

During the past decade or so many manufacturers and custom stockers have been using a synthetic resin coating on some gunstocks to provide an ultra-hard moisture-resistant finish with a high-gloss appearance. Such finishes were developed to provide maximum protection against abnormally hard use and weathering such as would be encountered on boats, workbenches, desktops, and garage floors. They are also used to seal swimming pools. Therefore, it stands to reason that such finishes would have certain advantages when used on gunstocks. In fact, epoxy finishes are claimed to be more resistant to water chemicals, and abrasion than an equivalent thickness of any organic material used singly or in combination with others. Still, epoxy will not furnish 100 percent protection at all times, under all conditions, so don't expect miracles!

The various polyurethane or epoxy finishes available to the stocker require more time and work to apply correctly than other finishes mentioned in this book. Because of the extreme hardness of these finishes when dry, checkering is almost impossible except by the use of carbide cutters on power checkering heads. It is possible to use hand tools, but conventional cutters will dull rapidly, requiring a new cutter to be installed on the tool when starting each pattern, if not sooner. The work to move the tool in a back-and-forth motion is also harder than with conventional finishes.

Minor scratches and blemishes can be covered with a spot epoxy application, which is sanded with 400 to 600 grit wet-and-dry abrasive paper, then polished to blend with the adjoining finish. However, major dents and abrasions are a different story. These latter repairs can take quite a lot of time and trouble to properly repair because when the epoxy finish hardens, it will defy all stripping agents with which most of us are familiar. Therefore, the finish over the damaged area must be sanded or scraped off. Then it takes a special touch to spot-in fresh epoxy and blend it properly into the area around the damaged spot.

When deciding whether or not to use an epoxy finish on your gunstocks, always consider the density of the wood. When the wood is close-grained and hard such as French walnut and other quality gunstock woods, the finish will be supported and resist dents and mars well. On such woods, epoxy finishes work well. Conversely, it is never a good idea to use an epoxy finish on soft and open grained wood.

To use a polyurethane or epoxy finish on a gunstock, the wood is first prepared as for other finishes — that is, the old finish should be removed and the wood sanded with various grits of abrasive paper until it is glass-smooth and shows no tool or sanding marks anywhere on the stock. Once sanded, whisker the wood and remove all dust with a tack cloth.

Filling the Pores: There are different schools of thought on sealing the wood prior to applying the epoxy finish. Some stockers use a paste filler made largely of Fuller's Earth, which is applied by rubbing the wood cross-grain with a rough rag. When dry, the stock is sanded down to the bare wood, leaving the pores filled. Commercial paste fillers are available in white and different "wood" colors. However, the possibility of a tinted or colored filler matching the wood exactly is remote. Therefore, most wood fillers used on gunstocks have a stain "built-in" to assure that the wood and filler will be blended as they should.

Another group of stockers merely use the finish material itself for sealing unless the grain is very porous. Sometimes even when an oil finish will be applied, epoxy is used to seal the pores. The compound is brushed or sprayed on, then sanded down to the wood when dry. A conventional hand-rubbed oil finish can then be applied. Such a finish combines the best of both techniques — absolute sealing and filling, plus the ease of finish and touch-up afforded by oil. Spar varnish is also used for sealing and filling, followed by an oil finish.

The only trouble with epoxy sealers is when it comes time to refinish the stock. . .then you're going to have problems!

Applying the Finish: After the pores have been sealed and filled with an approved filler, or with coats of the finish itself, the finish is then sanded down to the bare wood and inspected. Make certain that no tool marks or sanding marks are present. Many minute marks might not readily show up, so you'll want to closely examine every detail in various lights to ascertain that none are present. Should you find any, use various grits of abrasive paper — ending with 600 grit — until all are sanded out.

Epoxy finishes are applied much the same as other types of finishes. Thin coats are brushed or sprayed on, with each coat sanded and/or steel-wooled after hardening. Some epoxy finishing kits include an aerosol applicator with which to apply the finish. When using these, care must be taken not to get the nozzle of the can too close to the wood. This will cause the still-wet finish to build up on the surface and run. If this occurs, you will more than likely have to start all over again, sanding the finish down to bare wood. Remember to use only thin coats rather than heavy coats when applying the final finish.

Drying times and applications vary with different manufacturers. In most cases, use the manufacturer's specific instructions when applying the finish unless you happen to detect something that will definitely be detrimental to its use on gunstocks.

After the first coat has hardened, gently rub down any dust spots, sags, or runs with 400 grit wet-or-dry abrasive paper and water. The first coat should soak in rapidly, and if carefully applied, will not sag or run.

A thorough cleaning of the surface is necessary after the rubdown to remove any loose material. Now mix another small batch of the epoxy finish and give the entire stock another very thin coat, including the inletting. However, do not give the inletting more than one coat of the epoxy as this may adversely affect the fit of the metal parts to the stock.

This second coat should harden quickly, so you don't want to tarry any longer than necessary. Quickly flow it on, smooth out any sags or runs immediately, and then leave it alone. If you have any solution left over, store it in a cool place while the stock is drying in an area of around 80 degrees.

Another coat can be applied as soon as the surface can be lightly touched without being sticky. A hair dryer or heat lamps will speed up the curing once the finish begins to dry. However, do not apply heat while the surface is still wet; only *after* it begins to set up should any form of heat be applied.

At this point the stock should be stored in a dry area of between 70 and 80 degrees F. overnight, where it will fully harden. Then, again gently rub the hardened coat down with a fine grit of wet-or-dry abrasive paper to remove dust and sags. Repeat the number of coats until you have an even, perfectly-looking finish. Usually three coats will do the job, through more coats may be applied if necessary.

After the final coat and rubdown, you'll want to smooth the finish further by using some type of fine rubbing compound. Traditional rubbing compounds have been pumice stone and rottenstone, but some prepared commercial compounds may be better for stock work. For example, Brownells offers two types: Brownells Original Stock Rubbing Compound and Brownells Triple "F" Compound.

Once the stock has been rubbed sufficiently with a rubbing compound, it should be waxed. Birchwood Casey Gun Stock Wax can be recommended. This product protects and dresses up the epoxy gunstock finish, giving the best possible wax protection. This product contains silicones with the proper proportions of carnauba, beeswax, and special polymers.

Satin-finish epoxies have recently been introduced; these are becoming very popular because they eliminate the shiny, high-gloss finish many shooters consider objectionable and which in the past could only be toned down with rottenstone and plenty of elbow grease.

While there are several epoxy finishes available, one that is used in many gunshops is the Birchwood Casey product Tuf-Sheen Polyurethane Stock Finish, discussed previously.

Protecting Checkering

When refinishing a gunstock that has previously been checkered, you will want to keep the filler and finish out of the checkering proper, including the borders (if any) around each checkering pattern. Use regular masking tape to mask off these areas. When the finish has been completed on other parts of the stock, remove the masking tape and brush a couple of coats of Dem-Bart Stock Finish into the checkering. You want to protect the checkering against dirt and perspiration, but you don't want to gum up the lines. Although the rest of the stock surface is finished with epoxy, use this Dem-Bart Stock Finish in the checkered areas. You will probably have a different shade in these areas, but this is not undesirable.

Since the idea is to not gum up the checkering, the checkering on many new stocks is cut after the stock has been finished, after which the checkered areas are given this light coat of Dem-Bart Stock Finish or some similar light oil. Some stockers like to use a mixture of linseed oil and mineral spirits for this purpose, or Lin-speed oil and mineral spirits mixed 50-50. This latter mixture will usually dry more quickly and be ready for use sooner than if linseed oil alone is used.

Chapter 21
Gunstock Furniture

Embellishments for the gunstock are normally referred to as "gunstock furniture." Items included in this category are recoils pads, sling swivels, inlays, forend tips, and the like. Some of these items — like stock inlays and forend tips — are strictly cosmetic, but many furnishings are quite functional, enabling the shooter to have better control of his or her firearm.

Few hunters, in this day and time, would consider taking a centerfire rifle on a hunting trip without the convenience of a rifle sling. It makes carrying the gun less tiring and climbing into a tree stand without one is quite a feat. A rifle sling also increases the hunter's chances of hitting those long shots on target or game. A rifle sling is used in all match shoots to help steady the rifle. It can be used in the same way in the field.

A buttplate is another functional piece of gunstock furniture. It offers protection to this very vulnerable portion of the stock. A recoil pad will do the same thing and it will also lessen the felt recoil of the heavier "kicking" firearms.

Most gunstock furniture is easy to install, once you know the basic techniques and have a few jobs under your belt. Installing such items for yourself is another way to cash in on your gunsmithing training — saving you from $15 to $35 per hour if you had the work done by a professional shop!

This chapter is designed to show you how to correctly install all of these items on any firearm, so you can start saving money in doing the work yourself. However, it is also recommended that you engage in a little practice before attempting any of the installations on a good gun. For example, before drilling a gunstock for the installation of sling swivels, try the technique on a damaged stock or a piece of scrap wood. Before cutting the outline for a stock inlay, cut the outline on a piece of scrap wood first. Once you gain a little experience, the jobs should go rather smoothly thereafter.

SLINGS

The gun sling not only provides a means of comfortably carrying a firearm, but it also offers tremendous assistance in steadying a weapon while firing, regardless of the position — prone, sitting, kneeling, or standing. Every match shooter uses the sling in all positions, and few would attempt to shoot a match without one.

In adjusting the gun sling, the upper portion of the sling, called the *loop*, should be adjusted to such a length that it will come to within approximately 2 inches of the butt swivel. If the loop is too short, the butt cannot be fitted to the shoulder; if too loose, the sling will not be tight around the arm. The rear portion of the sling, called the *tail*, should always be loose enough so that it will never be stretched tight when the shooter is in the firing position.

To place the sling on the shooter's arm, the arm should pass through the loop from its right to its left. This twists the upper portion of the sling so that its flat rests against the shooter's wrist. Then move the left hand in a circular motion, high and to the left, over the forward part of the sling. Grasp the forend just in the rear of the front sling swivel. Then, with the right hand, pull the loop as high up on the left upper arm (for right-hand shooters) as it will go. Slip down the keeper to hold it there.

Once the sling is in place, it must never be held too tightly by brute strength alone. The muscles should be contracted only enough to hold the rifle up. Then the shooter should relax the other muscles and be calm. With experience, any one person can learn to hold a rifle steady for accurate shooting.

The sporting sling differs slightly from the target rifle sling in that its main purpose is for carrying the rifle rather than to steady shots. While hunting with a rifle, in all but rare cases, the shooter does not have time to make sling adjustments and get into a steady position before firing. Most of the time, instant snap shots are required to hit a bouncing white-tailed deer as it darts through a thicket of timber. In a second or two the animal is out of sight.

One type of sling that is recommended for sporting rifles is Brownells Latigo sling (Figure 21-1). To install this sling, first take a yardstick or ruler and measure the distance between the two sling studs on the gunstock. Deduct 2 inches from this measure to allow for sling swivel bows. To illustrate, if the measurement is 28½ inches, deduct 2 inches and use 26½ inches.

Next, remove the brass joining stud from the sling using either a screwdriver or a coin. Do not, however, disassemble the sling. On the terminal end of the strap you will find that the numbered holes are spaced more closely together. Locate hole

Figure 21-1: Brownells Latigo Sling and how to use it.

27 of these closely spaced holes and cut off the remaining end of the strap close to hole 28.

Continue by locating hole 27 again in the widely spaced hole. Match the two holes (both are number 27) and join them using the brass joining stud. Position the sling and attach the quick-detachable swivels to the mounting studs.

To attach the sling, the tip swivels should be facing each other as shown in Figure 21-2. Measure distance A-B as shown in the illustration. Using the shortest whole inch within ¾", obtain the correct measurement. That is, if the measurement is 27¾" when the tips are toward each other, 27 inches is the measurement to use.

Next to the holes punched on 2⅜" centers in the tongue end of the sling are numbers that match

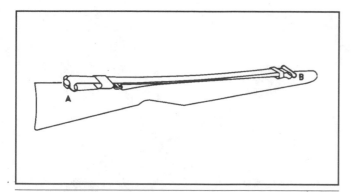

Figure 21-2: Tip of swivels must be facing each other and be located approximately 27" apart.

Figure 21-4: Feed ther sling through the forend swivel and back through the keeper.

numbers beside holes on 1" centers punched in the buckle end. Beside one of the holes in the tongue end there will be a number corresponding to the measurement between the swivels. Cut off the sling at an extra $\frac{3}{4}$" beyond this hole as shown in Figure 21-3.

Thread the sling through the swivel on the buttstock of the gun, and attach the keeper as shown in Figure 21-4. Then thread the sling through the forend swivel and back through the sliding keeper as shown in Figure 21-5. Thread the sling through the loop of the buckle and then bend it back towards the outer strap of the sling, pulling it tight in the process. The free end of the sling now becomes the center strap of the sling as shown in Figure 21-6 on the next page.

Match the measurement number on the end of the sling with the same number on the buckle end. Put the female half of the stud through the holes and screw in the other half with a coin or screwdriver to tighten (Figure 21-6 on the next page). In case these holes cannot be matched due to tightness of the sling, attach the end to the nearest convenient hole and pull the sling into shooting position. Then refasten the stud to the proper hole. The sling will automatically correct the length when pulled to a tight position.

Brownells Latigo sling is a modification of the original leather military sling and the design is sometimes known as the Whelen sling — a type designed originally by the late Col. Townsend Whelen.

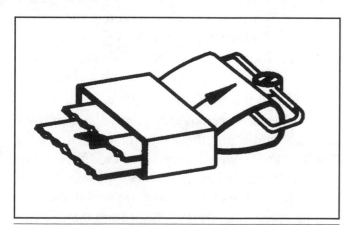

Figure 21-3: After threading the sling through the swivel, attach the keeper as shown.

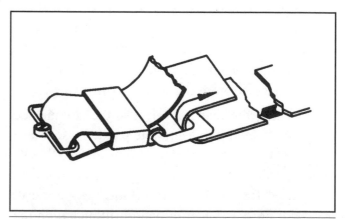

Figure 21-5: Place the free end through the buckle. This is now the center strap.

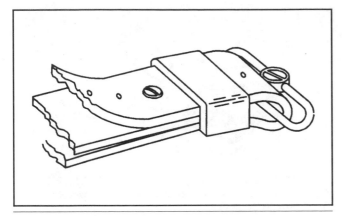

Figure 21-6: Tighten the screw stud with either a screwdriver or a coin.

Installing Rifle Slings

Sling studs are normally placed at varying distances apart, usually between 26" and 28", with the rear stud located about 3" from the toe of the stock.

If no studs have been previously fitted to the stock, two holes will have to be drilled to accept the studs and swivels. In general, the rear stud screws directly into the wood, while the front studs require a special retaining nut which presses firmly into the wood of the forend so as not to protrude against the barrel. Therefore, the front holes must be drilled completely through the stock; both holes must be countersunk.

An excellent swivel installation tool kit is available from B-Square Co. This kit enables sling swivels to be installed quickly on any stock without risk of damage. The "V" jig has a hardened drill guide bushing and will automatically locate the $\frac{5}{32}$" diameter drill (furnished with the kit) the correct distance from the forend or from the toe.

To install the rear swivel, turn the rifle upside down and clamp it in a suitable padded vise. Place the swivel jig over the edge of the stock so that its end is flush with the butt; this puts the pilot drill about 2½" from the butt. Insert the $\frac{5}{32}$" pilot drill in a drill press or electric hand drill and align the swivel jig drill stops to drill a hold approximately 1" deep. See Figure 21-7.

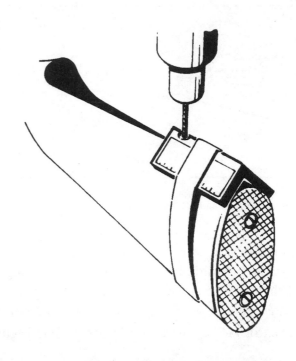

Figure 21-7: When using the "V" jig for swivel installation, simply place the jig over the edge of the stock so that it's flush with the butt. Secure the jig in place with the wide rubber band that comes with the kit.

Exchange the $\frac{5}{32}$" pilot drill for the $\frac{7}{32}$" diameter safety counter-bore and counter-bore the $\frac{5}{32}$" hole just drilled. This last operation provides for the unthreaded portion of the swivel screw.

Before inserting the swivel screw into the gunstock, it should be dipped in linseed oil to seal the wood and bind the fibers. Then, using a drift punch or a common nail as a wrench, screw the swivel screw into the gunstock until its cross hole is correctly positioned when tight down against the stock. Never use the swivel itself as a wrench.

To install the front swivel screw on most one-piece rifle stocks, remove the barreled action from the stock and clamp the stock in a padded vise so that the barrel channel is *up*. Place the swivel jig in the barrel channel with the "V" down. Its end should be flush with the forend tip so that the drill will be approximately 2½" back from the tip. The jig is designed to center the $\frac{5}{32}$" pilot drill in the barrel channel, so use this drill in the drill press or

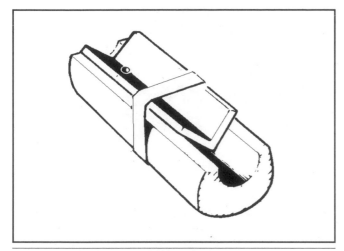

Figure 21-8: When installing the front forend swivel, place the jig directly in the barrel channel with the "V" downward. Again, use the wide rubber band to secure the jig in place.

hand-held electric drill and drill a hole completely through the forend of the gunstock. Then enlarge this hole with the No. 10 safety drill which will counterbore for the swivel nut all in one operation. Again, coat the counterbored hole with linseed oil and press the swivel screw nut into the counterbore. A small amount of Loc-Tite should be placed on the screw threads before tightening the swivel screw into the nut. Use a drift punch or a nail to tighten. Be sure that the front swivel installation is permanent; an improper installation can greatly affect accuracy not to mention the damage that could be caused to the gun if the swivel failed and the gun dropped off one's shoulder while climbing into a tree stand.

Miscellaneous Swivels

There are many different types of sling swivels. The barrel band swivel, for example, is traditional on classic big game rifles and single-shot rifles with splinter forends. Such bands are readily available in sizes from .650" to .950" to accommodate practically every barrel size. However, if the barrel varies from these dimensions, barrel band swivel bases are available with a .250" pilot hole that may be drilled out to exactly fit any barrel diameter.

This type of swivel base is installed over the barrel prior to installing any front sight or front-sight ramp. The exact placement of the barrel band is marked on the barrel before removing the bluing or other finish in this immediate area only. The band is then tinned with solder and "sweated" to the barrel.

Other types of sling swivels include those designed for mounting directly onto magazine tubes or forend caps. Most require no drilling. All that is necessary is to loosen the retaining screw on the swivel base, position the base in place on the magazine tube and tighten. Practically the same technique is required for installing sling swivels forend caps.

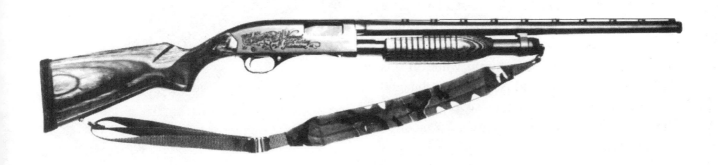

Figure 21-9: Winchester Model 1300 slide-action turkey gun. Note that the front sling swivel is an integral part of the magazine-tube cap.

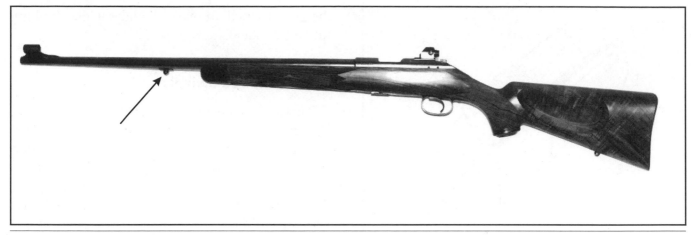

Figure 21-10: Swivel stud soldered (sweated) on the bottom of the barrel.

BUTTPLATES

Plates used to cover the wood of a rifle or shotgun vary in materials from metal to plastic to wood or rubber. The main objective of a buttplate is to offer protection to this area of the stock. The plate also provides a more comfortable feel for the shooter than plain sharp wood edges held against the shoulder. Under the same category of buttplates come recoil pads, which are also secured to the butt of a gunstock. These consist of a soft cushion of rubber or other soft material. Besides offering protection to the butt of the rifle or shotgun stock, they lessen the force of recoil, making shooting more comfortable.

Many shooters prefer a checkered steel buttplate for use on rifle stocks. Plastic or hard rubber have a tendency to become brittle with age, and can break with even the slightest bump when in this condition. On the other hand, steel can be banged around almost any way without severe damage, which in turn offers the highest degree of protection to the buttstock.

In general, there are three types of steel buttplates commonly in use: checkered steel buttplates, steel trap buttplates, and skeleton buttplates.

All three offer about the same degree of protection to the butt of the stock, but each is somewhat different from the others. The standard checkered steel buttplate is solid. Those currently available include the Neidner steel buttplate with matching steel grip cap. These are very attractive and popular, and reasonably priced.

Skeletonized buttplates and grip caps have been used on high-quality gunstocks for quite some time and are considered to be one of the more elegant and desirable refinements than can be added to a beautifully executed stock. The rifle shown in Figure 21-11 carries this feature to its fullest.

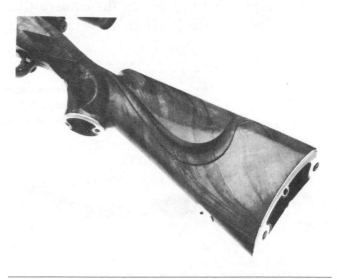

Figure 21-11: A skeleton buttplate and grip cap enhance the beauty of any gunstock.

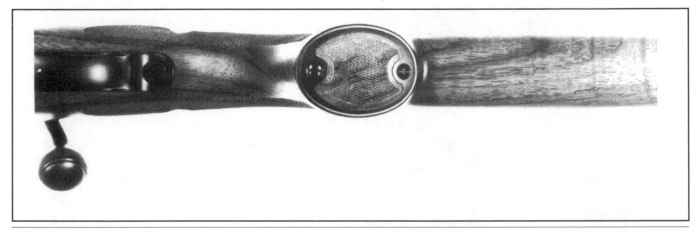

Figure 21-12: Skeletonized grip caps are a favorite of custom stockers. This standard Mauser action utilizes a Bisen skeleton grip cap. The stock work was done by Warren Heydenbeck.

When a skeletonized buttplate is installed on a rifle, usually a skeletonized grip cap is also used. The one shown in Figure 21-12 is a Bisen skeleton grip cap and installed by professional stocker, Warren Heydenbeck.

In general, the basic installation of either a skeletonized buttplate or grip cap consists of first marking the outline of the items in their appropriate places on the finished stock. Using these markings as guidelines, wood is removed from the stock to perfectly inlay the buttplate and grip cap so their edges fit flush with the adjacent wood. The two items are then removed from the stock, and the wood areas showing through the skeletonized portions of the plate and cap are checkered using conventional checkering tools and techniques. When the checkering is done, the buttplate and grip cap are once again installed to finish the job. The results appear in Figures 21-11 and 21-12.

Most steel buttplates have a slight curvature that requires precise fitting to the butt of the stock. Therefore, this curvature must first be determined and then the pattern is transferred (marked) to the stock. A coping saw or band saw is then used to cut the butt to the correct shape. A wood rasp may then be used to smooth up the cut before final finishing with various grits of abrasive paper. *See* Figures 21-13, 21-14, and 21-15.

Figure 21-13: Once the plate angle has been determined, a coping saw is used to remove the excess wood.

Figure 21-14: Saw cuts must be smoothed with wood rasps and files prior to installing the plate, especially if a skeleton-type plate is to be put on the gunstock.

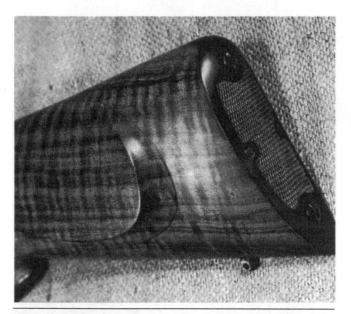

Figure 21-15: Sketeton-type buttplate by Ken Eyster of Heritage Gunsmiths, Inc.

Once a precise fit is obtained, the screw holes for the buttplate retaining screws are marked in their appropriate location on the butt of the stock and then drilled slightly undersize with a drill bit. All that is required to finalize the job is to dip the wood screw into a container of linseed oil (to seal the wood around them) and screw them into the holes to secure the buttplate in place. Make certain you use the proper size screwdriver so as not to damage the screw heads.

RECOIL PADS

The primary purpose of a recoil pad is to cushion the gun's "kick" as it is fired. Sometimes such a pad is used to extend the stock's length for a better fit. For example, one gunstock may have been fitted for a shooter with relatively short arms. Perhaps the gun was then purchased by a person with longer arms, making the stock entirely too short. Of course, the gun can be restocked, but in the case of a good walnut stock, this operation could be rather costly. It follows that a recoil pad of an inch or so in thickness could be utilized.

On the other hand, when a stock is of the correct length and fitted with a common thin buttplate, considerable wood may have to be removed when a thick recoil pad is attached.

Recoil pads for shotguns are normally manufactured in three different styles: skeet, field, and trap. The skeet style is designed for fast gun handling with a minimum degree of interference from the stock slinging to the fabric of the shooting coat. This type of pad will feature either a smooth surface or a rounded, corrugated ribbing running lengthwise with the butt's outline. Furthermore, this type of pad is not concaved like many plates and pads; rather, it is nearly straight from heel to toe.

The standard field recoil pad, found on a great number of shotguns, is slightly concave in outline and features an extended toe. The corrugation that covers much of the pad's surface runs from side to side, or opposite to that on the skeet pad. This design is intended to discourage slippage of the stock after it has been placed to the shoulder.

The trap style recoil pad is very individualistic in design, giving improved accuracy and added comfort to a trap shooter. One characteristic is that the pad is deeply concaved about midway between the heel and toe. This pronounced concave design is intended to fit snugly over the shoulder muscles to ensure holding the stock in the identical position for each shot. If this type of pad is fitted correctly, surprising results can be obtained in the way of accuracy and comfort while firing.

To correctly install a recoil pad on either a rifle or shotgun, the following preliminary steps should be taken:

- Determine the desired length of pull and substract from this dimension the thickness of the recoil pad.

- When the pad is to be installed on a rifle stock, the stock should be cut 90° to the barrel as shown in Figure 21-16.

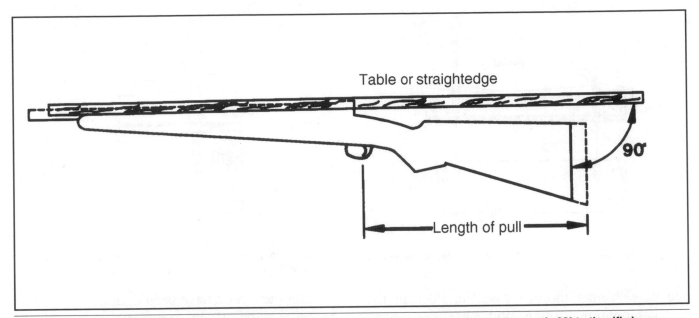

Figure 21-16: When cutting a rifle stock for the installation of a recoil pad, the cut should be made exactly 90° to the rifle bore.

- When the recoil pad is to be installed on a shotgun, cut the stock butt so as to maintain the desired pitch angle.

Once the above measurements have been obtained, use a flexible straightedge to mark a line on the buttstock from heel to toe. Then scribe it for the cuttoff line.

Having scribed the cutoff line, use a fine-toothed saw (such as a coping saw) to remove the surplus wood, being careful in doing so that the cut is square, even, and clean. To ensure a tight joint between the pad and stock, cut the stock slightly longer than necessary and work the new surface down with a disk sander or wood rasp. During this operation, test the stock often to ensure that the face of the butt is flat and even.

When selecting the pad, be certain that it is long enough to permit the existing outline along both the comb and bottom of the stock to continue straight and unbroken. See Figure 21-17.

With the preliminary work out of the way, insert a screw or dowel pin through the screw slot in the bottom face of the recoil pad as shown in Figure 21-18 on the next page. Push the screw or pin upward until the soft rubber raises slightly on the face of the pad. Mark the spot with a ballpoint pen. Do the same to the other hole.

Put some vasoline on the screws and push them through the soft rubber from the face side until the screw head rests on the washer located just above the white line spacer. Again, see Figure 21-18.

To mark the stock for drilling, push both recoil-pad screws into the pad so they barely show at the

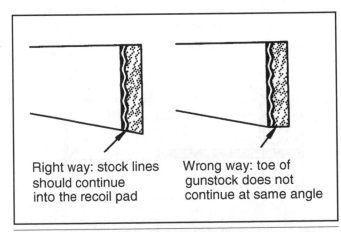

Figure 21-17: The existing lines of the stock must carry over to the recoil pad.

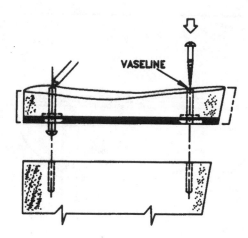

Figure 21-18: Method used to locate screw holes in the recoil pad.

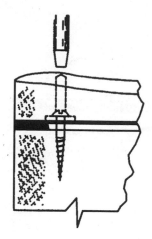

Figure 21-20: Use a narrow screwdriver with rounded corners to prevent damage to the recoil pad material.

pad base. Center the pad over the stock in the correct mounting position. With a hammer, tap the screw head lightly to mark the position of the holes to be drilled as shown in Figure 21-19. Drill the screw holes to the minor diameter of the screw's threads.

Use a narrow screwdriver with the corners rounded off (so the rubber won't be damaged) to seat the screws completely as shown in Figure 21-20. Never remove any rubber over the screw slots because if any is removed, the surface will not close over after removing the screwdriver — indicating that an amatuer has attempted the job.

After the screws have been tightened, use a belt sander to grind off any excess rubber to make the recoil pad fit exactly flush with the sides of the buttstock.

Another method used to install recoil pads requires the use of two wooden dowels, the same diameter as the screw holes in the recoil pad. Cut the dowels so that when they are inserted into the stock they will protrude about 1/4" as shown in Figure 21-21.

To mark the stock for drilling, push both screws into the pad so they barely show at the pad base. Center the pad over the gunstock butt in the correct

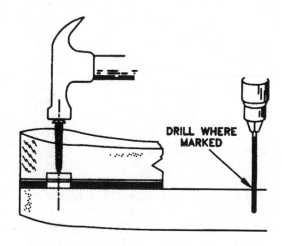

Figure 21-19: Method used to locate screw holes in a buttstock for securing recoil pad.

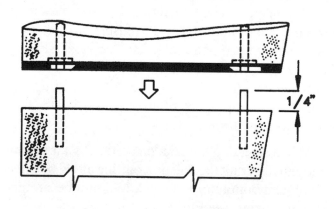

Figure 21-21: The use of wooden dowels, in place of wood screws, is another way to install recoil pads.

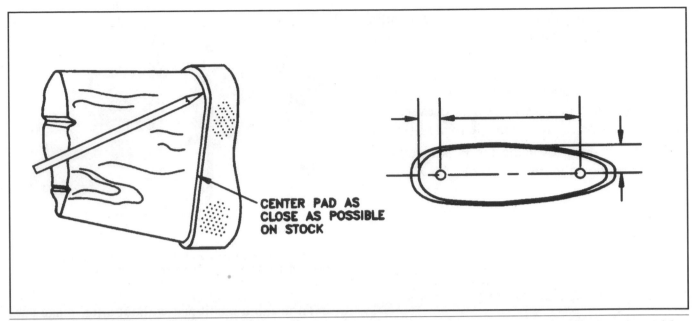

Figure 21-22: If puncturing the pad is not desirable, center the pad on the stock and trace the outline of the stock on the base of the pad. Measure the distance from the top and sides to the traced line, then transfer dimensions from edge of the stock to locate the dowel holes.

mounting position. With a hammer, tap the screw head to mark the position of the holes to be drilled. Drill these holes to $\frac{1}{4}$" diameter.

Most of the better stockers who stock high-quality shotguns prefer not to puncture the recoil pad at all. Instead, they center the recoil pad on the butt of the stock and scribe or pencil the outline of the stock on the base on the recoil pad as shown in Figure 21-22. The distance from the top and sides to the scribed line is then measured and these dimensions are tranferred to the stock itself so $\frac{1}{4}$" may be drilled in the buttstock. Again, see Figure 21-22.

Glue the dowel pins into the stock and then place some glue on both the stock and pad before joining the pad to the stock. The pad should be clamped to the buttstock until the glue has dried to obtain the tightest fit possible. One way to do this is to stretch an old inner tube over the pad and the front of the stock. This will apply pressure while the glue is drying.

After the glue dries, grind off any excess pad material as discussed previously.

Recoil Pad Jig

A handy device that can aid you in recoil-pad installations is a recoil pad jig such as the one shown in Figure 21-23. This jig enables you to shape and install any shotgun or rifle recoil pad at the correct angle. Because all shaping and sanding of the pad is done off the stock, there is no danger of damaging the stock's finish.

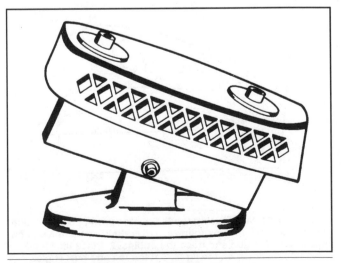

Figure 21-23: B-Square recoil-pad jig.

In general, you merely scribe the exact outline of the stock butt on the pad back and place it upside down on the pad jig. No sander alteration is required and it can be used with any disc or belt sander. B-Square guarantees that you can put on a recoil pad and your job will be perfect every time. If you can't, you can return the jig for a full refund.

The basic steps for using the B-Square Recoil Pad Jig are shown in Figure 21-24.

Figure 21-25: Masking tape helps prevent splintering or marring the stock during the final shaping of the pad.

To install a recoil pad without a jig, make sure the joint between the pad and stock are even and tight. These two parts can be drawn together with the two pad screws provided for the purpose. It is best, however, to first apply a coat of linseed oil to the raw surface of the wood before attaching the pad permanently. Locate the holes for the screws so that the heel of the pad will be drawn up as near as possible in line with the top of the heel. To do so will reduce a considerable amount of work in dressing down the oversize pad to fit the stock's outline.

After securing the pad, wrap a piece of masking tape around the stock's edge. This should be even with the base of the recoil pad to prevent marring the stock while sanding the pad down to the level of the existing stock. See Figure 21-25. Now, using a sanding disk or emery wheel, sand the newly installed recoil pad down to the correct size.

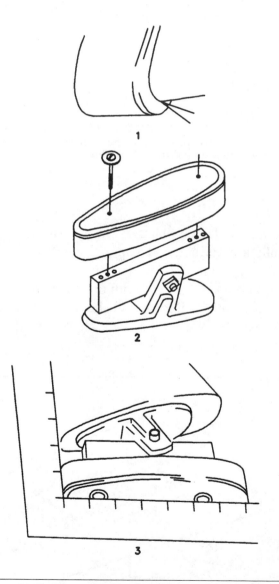

Figure 21-24: When using the B-Square recoil-pad installation jig, the procedure is as follows: 1. Carefully center the pad on the butt of the gun and trace the outline. 2. Place the recoil pad upside down on the jig. 3. Set the toe and heel angles with a square prior to final disc sanding.

MISCELLANEOUS STOCK FURNITURE

Recoil Reducers

Heavy recoil from rifles and shotguns is probably one of the chief causes of flinching, which causes the shooter frequently to miss the mark.

There are several ways to reduce the recoil felt by the shooter. One of the most important aspects of eliminating felt recoil is the design of the rifle or shotgun stock. A gunstock that fits the shooter perfectly, with good straight-line design, will do much to enable the shooter to absorb recoil even from the most powerful, hard-kicking weapons. Add to this a cushioned recoil pad and the recoil is hardly noticed.

In some cases, such as when lightweight shooters tackle a hard-kicking firearm, other steps must be taken to reduce the recoil even more. One relatively inexpensive way is to install a buffer as shown in Figure 21-26. Several types are available. One is the mercury recoil suppressor that uses mercury inertia to absorb recoil. Another uses hydraulic action to cushion recoil, while another is based on pneumatic-action. These units are easily installed in the buttstock. Some shooters are putting an extra one in the forend too.

To install a typical unit, a $^{57}/_{64}$" by 6" spur-point drill is used. The unique ability of the spur point drill to cut straight, true holes in any grain structure makes it a real lifesaver when installing these popular recoil buffers.

Another means of reducing recoil is to use a muzzle brake on the barrel. While there are several different models available, most work on a gas trap propulsion principle with an outlet for surplus gas

to escape — usually from jet-type sharp-angle ports. Such recoil reducers claim to cut recoil from 20 to 60 percent. This means that the movement of the shooter's body backward and the muzzle jump upward are reduced to a minimum. The installation of these muzzle brakes requires about $^{3}/_{8}$" of barrel extending forward of the gun sight to be threaded, using a thread of approximately 28 tpi (threads per inch); then the muzzle break is screwed on.

Some competent gunsmiths can also provide a muzzle brake on a rifle or shotgun by making it an integral part of the barrel — that is, small ports or holes are drilled around the muzzle of the barrel to allow gas to escape. This action reduces the recoil and muzzle movement of the firearm.

The Answer System

A few years ago, Sam Johnson of the Answer Products Co., 1519 Westbury Dr., Davison, MI 48423 came up with a combination recoil-reducing system consisting of three parts: A counter force recoil pad, the Answer "Quiet" muzzle brake, and a fibercomb gunstock.

The recoil pad operates on five conical springs and is designed to create progressive resistance; that is, the harder they are compressed, the harder they push back — resulting in a gentle push rather than a sudden jab on the shooter's shoulder.

The muzzle brake utilizes gas slips and a resistance diverter cone — machined internally — to lessen the muzzle report. The dozens of tiny holes further help to reduce both recoil and the ear-splitting effect so common on some earlier muzzle brakes.

The fibercomb stock is made from a regular stockmaker's blank. The trick is to keep the price down on a custom wood stock, have all the benefits of a synthetic stock, and still retain the beauty and feel of wood. In general, the stock is split end-to-end; the internal wood is then removed and this space filled with epoxy resin that is full of air pockets just like a bee hive. Titanium rods are

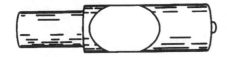

Figure 21-26: Recoil buffers that may be installed in either rifle or shotgun stocks to help reduce felt recoil. All are available from Brownells.

placed in the forend and pistol grip for added strength and the action area is liquid bedded in titanium reinforced glass. The maker claims a stock that is seven times stronger than wood and a great reduction in stock vibration.

When the firing pin hits the primer and ignites the powder to force the bullet down the barrel, the shooter is immediately hit with a portion of the rifle's recoil. The counter force recoil pad reduces this initial recoil to a push rather than a jab. The pad is also partially compressed before the bullet and hot gases reach the muzzle brake which then takes over to divert the gas and to greatly reduce muzzle jump. These two devices alone with cut felt recoil by as much as 40% or more. Then add the fiber-comb stock for an additional 15 to 20% reduction of felt recoil. The total system makes a .300 Win. Mag. feel like a .243; a .375 H&H Mag. feel like a .30-06, etc.

Contrary to popular belief, muzzle brakes do not reduce muzzle velocity. In fact, in some recent tests, the velocity was actually increased slightly when fired with a muzzle brake, but not enough to make any difference.

Forend Tips

The forend tip on a gunstock really has no practical purpose, but many shooters feel that a rifle stock without a forend tip looks kind of naked. This has been the style for several decades, and they want to continue the tradition.

There are several methods used to install a forend tip on a rifle stock: wooden dowels, metal pins, epoxy, or a combination of these. Regardless of the method used for installation, the tip should be kept clear of the barrel because this is the area where barrel whip and vibrations are great. The forend tip is exposed to the same variations of heat and moisture as the stock, and if you try to inlet the barrel to the tip, with metal-to-wood contact, rifle accuracy will normally be reduced. Consequently,

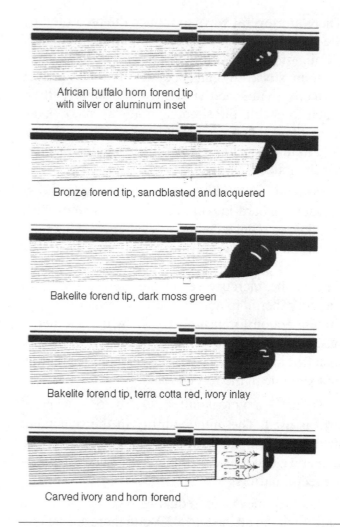

African buffalo horn forend tip with silver or aluminum inset

Bronze forend tip, sandblasted and lacquered

Bakelite forend tip, dark moss green

Bakelite forend tip, terra cotta red, ivory inlay

Carved ivory and horn forend

Figure 21-27: Sporting rifle forend tips consist of many kinds of materials. The current trend is to use some type of plastic or exotic woods, like rosewood or zebra wood.

the rifle barrel should be "free floating" in the forend tip area.

Materials for forend tips have varied considerably over the years (*see* Figure 21-27), but the current trend is to use either black plastic or a piece of exotic wood. The material used is a matter of personal taste.

To install, cut the tip material to about two inches in length and of a sufficient thickness that will allow finishing squarely on both sides and bottom of the gunstock. Drill a $^{7}/_{16}$-inch hole, $1^{1}/_{4}$ inches deep, in the center of the material where the fin-

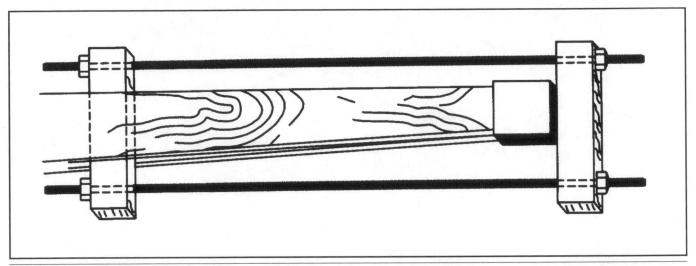

Figure 21-28: This clamp is slow action, but is quite capable of applying the required pressure onto the tip without jarring it off. The thraded rods can be cut from 3/8", or heavier, stock. The crosspiece that enters the magazine mortise can be slotted on one end to make it easier to adjust. The corners should be rounded slightly to avoid damaging the magazine mortise on the lower front edge.

ished section will be below the barrel channel. Drill a hole the same depth in the rifle stock, at the appropriate location beneath the barrel channel, after cutting the stock off square. Use a hickory or maple dowel $2\frac{1}{2}$ inches long, so it will enter the drilled holes snugly. Use inletting black to perfectly mate the forend tip material to the rifle stock. Once the forend tip matches perfectly, it is shaped flush with the original stock and the barrel channel cut so the barrel will "free-float" and not touch the forend tip at all. Some gunsmiths prefer to do this shaping of the tip off the stock, while others secure the forend tip tightly before shaping. If the former method is used, try the tip for fit often.

An epoxy cement is used to secure the tip and dowel to the rifle stock. While the adhesive is drying, use a fixture like the one shown in Figure 21-28 to draw the forend tip as tight as possible to the gunstock.

Again, the installation of a forend tip is a matter of personal taste. If you want one, install it.

Index